YOUNG CANADA

THESAURUS

Second Edition

Nelson Canada

I(T)P An International Thomson Publishing Company

Toronto • Albany • Bonn • Boston • Cincinnati • Detroit • London • Madrid • Melbourne
Mexico City • New York • Pacific Grove • Paris • San Francisco • Singapore • Tokyo • Washington

 I(T)P⁻
International Thomson Publishing
The ITP logo is a trademark under licence

© Nelson Canada
A division of Thomson Canada Limited, 1996

Published in 1996 by
Nelson Canada,
A division of Thomson Canada Limited
1120 Birchmount Road
Scarborough, Ontario M1K 5G4

Printed and bound in Canada

3 4 5 6 7 8 9 0 / TG / 4 3 2 1 0 9 8 7

Canadian Cataloguing in Publication Data

Main entry under title:
Young Canada thesaurus

2nd ed.
Includes index.
ISBN 0–17–604803–0

1. English language – Synonyms and antonyms –
Juvenile literature.   2. English language –
Dictionaries, Juvenile.

PE1591.Y68   1995   j423'.1   C95–931514–4

Adapted from the *Macquarie Junior Thesaurus*
First published in 1986 by
The Jacaranda Press
33 Park Road
Milton, Queensland 4064, Australia

© Macquarie University N.S.W., 1986

Editor: Daniel Liebman
Executive Editor: Joe Banel
Project Manager: Lana Kong
Developmental Editor: Alan Simpson
Copy Editor: Susan Wallace-Cox
Production Editors: Deborah Lonergan,
                    Sandra Manley
Manuscript Processing: Elaine Andrews
Lead Composition Analyst: Zenaida Diores
Production Coordinator: Renate McCloy
Art Director: Liz Harasymczuk
Interior Design: Katharine Lapins
Cover Design: Peggy Rhodes
Cover Illustration: Ron Job

Review Panel
The publisher wishes to thank the following educa-
tors for their valuable advice during the develop-
ment of this edition of the *Young Canada
Thesaurus*:
Lynn Archer, Consultant, School District No. 36,
    Surrey, BC
Halina Bartley, Elementary Program Consultant,
    Peterborough County Board of Education,
    Peterborough, ON
Joyce Billinkoff, Language Arts Support Teacher,
    Machray School, Winnipeg, MB
Mady Davidson, Language Arts Support Teacher,
    Machray School, Winnipeg, MB
Betty Miller, Language Arts Consultant, Calgary,
    AB
Kim Newlove, Educational Consultant, Instruction
    Elementary, Saskatoon Board of Education,
    Saskatoon, SK
William Nugent, Teacher, Andover Elementary
    School, Perth-Andover, NB
Norma Sommerville, Teacher, Alexmuir Junior
    School, Scarborough, ON
Avon Whittles, Educational Consultant,
    Instruction/Language Arts, Saskatoon
    Board of Education, Saskatoon, SK

Contents

Preface to the Second Edition

Welcome to the *Young Canada Thesaurus*. This second edition has been revised thoroughly in the following ways:

- The type has been made larger and easier to read. Other aspects of the design have also been improved and made clearer.
- Words have been more precisely defined.
- Sentence examples illustrate more clearly the meaning of the words and relate more closely to the experiences and interests of students.
- More inclusive language has been used.

We hope that you will find the *Young Canada Thesaurus* a useful and stimulating resource for expanding your vocabulary and exploring the richness of the English language in your reading and writing.

What is a Thesaurus?

thesaurus *noun* a book of words arranged in groups that have a similar meaning.

Have you ever been stuck for a word and felt very annoyed because you knew it was somewhere in the back of your mind but you couldn't think of it just then? Well, an English doctor named Peter Mark Roget (pronounced rō zhā′) dealt with this problem by writing down lists of similar words for his own use over many years. He often gave lectures to medical students, in which he needed to use just the right words to express his meaning.

In 1849, when he was 70, Roget began to put these lists in order so that they could be published. He called this treasure chest of words his "thesaurus." (In Latin, *thēsaurus* means "treasure.")

Roget put together in the same group all the words and phrases that expressed a particular idea. For example, in a word group called *force* in a thesaurus, you might find *power, strength, might, muscle,* and *vigour.* These five words refer to some aspects of the idea of *force,* but they do not have exactly the same meaning. Roget did not want his book to be like a dictionary, with definitions of every word. Rather, he wanted to gather in each group the words you might think of when a particular topic is being discussed.

Roget's thesaurus was so useful to people trying to write letters, essays, speeches, and so on, that it became very successful. Other publishers created their own versions. Gradually, the word "thesaurus" came to mean any book that lists groups of similar words, not just the book that Roget created.

What's in a Word?

Lisa and Aaron had never been away from New Brunswick before. When they arrived in Regina, they sent a postcard to their grandparents describing the journey.

"It was really *exciting,* but a bit scary to *soar* so high above the *land.* I realized that our *plane* was zooming further and further from our *home.* The flight attendants served us *terrific* meals," wrote Lisa.

"Well, I had a *great* time *flying* over here. I couldn't see the *ground* from the *aircraft* as it was too cloudy. The food was *delicious.* I knew we were travelling far from our *birthplace,*" wrote Aaron.

Lisa and Aaron managed to describe the same incident and never used the same words. There is a wealth of meaning in each word of the English language. It is very important to learn to use words so well that you know which is the right one to express exactly what you mean.

Try browsing through this thesaurus and you will certainly come to appreciate the value of words. You will meet some words that are old friends and some that are new and exciting. You will want to have a dictionary to help you as well—a dictionary and a thesaurus go hand in hand!

fine *adjective* —— ● 2. Part of
                                                                            speech

3. Keyword ●———— ▶ with the sun shining, or without rain. *I'm enjoying the **fine***
   definition   *weather that we are having at the moment.*

sunny	**Sunny** means having plenty of sunshine. *It was a lovely sunny day before the clouds came over.*
balmy	**Balmy** means fine or pleasant. *In the balmy spring weather they were often outdoors.*
5. Related word ●—— mild	**Mild** can mean not cold, severe, or extreme. *Why don't we go for a walk tonight since the temperature is so mild?*
fair	**Fair** can mean bright and free from clouds, as the sky can be. *The marine forecast was for* ———● 4. Sentence *fair weather all weekend.* example
temperate	**Temperate** can mean having a moderate temperature or climate. *My friend lives in a temperate climate zone.*

contrasting keywords: **wintry, cloudy, dreary**

---

friend *noun*

▶ someone you like and who likes you. *My **friend** Aniela and I spend our spare time together.*

playmate	A **playmate** is someone you play with. *The kids next door have been my playmates since we were little.*
pal	A **pal** is a good friend. This is more suited to ———● 7. Word use everyday language. *Good pals do things for each other.*
companion	A **companion** is someone you go out with or ———● 6. Related-travel with. *I like to go to movies with a* word companion. definition
teammate	A **teammate** is someone who is on the same team as you. *My teammates and I were excited about winning the field hockey game.*

8. Other
helpful   ●——————— similar keywords: **associate**
keywords   contrasting keywords: **enemy**

Guide to the *Young Canada Thesaurus*

Word Groups

The main section of the thesaurus consists of over 940 *word groups,* a keyword plus four or five words or phrases, all closely related to one another. On page 6, the different parts of the word groups are labelled. These parts are explained in the numbered sections below.

1. Keyword

There are two word groups on each page, each with a *keyword* at the top. The keyword gives you an idea of the overall meaning of the word group. The keywords are arranged alphabetically so that you can find them quickly and easily.

The keyword is usually a word you already know. For example, the keyword **fine** tells you that this is the group to look at if you want to find other words that express the idea "with the sun shining, or without rain."

2. Part of speech

The keyword is followed by the *part of speech.* A part of speech is a type of word that has a specific function, such as a noun or pronoun, verb, adjective, adverb, preposition, and so on.

3. Keyword definition

Only one definition of the keyword is given. You can see that this is where a thesaurus is different from a dictionary, where all meanings of a word are listed next to that word.

In the first sample on the opposite page, **fine** has been used with the group of words that mean "with the sun shining." Now look at the top half of page 185. **Fine** has been used here too, with another meaning, "good." As you can see, a word might be used several times in the thesaurus, but in a specific sense each time.

4. Sentence example

Every word in the group, whether it is the keyword or one of the related words, is followed by a sentence example that shows how it is used.

5. Related words

Four or five *related words* (or sometimes *related expressions*) are listed under each keyword. These words are related in meaning to the keyword and also to each other.

The related words are arranged so that the words most similar to the keyword come first, followed by words that may be less similar in meaning or usage. You may prefer to use one of these words because it expresses your idea more precisely, or is a more interesting or unusual word than the keyword. To help you choose the best word, each one is followed by a definition and a sentence example.

6. Related-word definition

Each related word has a definition that shows you the similarities and differences between this word and the keyword. With this information, you will be able to choose a word with precisely the meaning you want.

7. Word use

This tells you if the word is a formal word, or one you would use in everyday language.

8. Other helpful keywords

At the end of many word groups is a box showing other helpful keywords that you might wish to look up.

Similar keywords are other keywords that are like the words in this group. For example, if you look up the keyword **associate**, you will find this list of related words: *partner, colleague, collaborator, comrade.* You can see that these words have been put into their own group, separate from **friend**, because they have a different shade of meaning.

Contrasting keywords are keywords that are unlike the words in this group. For example, the keyword **dreary** shows these related words: *dismal, depressing, cheerless, bleak, grey.* All of these express an idea that contrasts with **fine**.

Appendix

At the end of the word groups, near the back of the thesaurus, is the *appendix*. An appendix is a separate section at the end of a book that gives you extra information.

In this thesaurus, the appendix contains useful lists of words related to specific topics, such as Canadian wildlife, the Canadian government, geography, computers, astronomy, music, and sports. The Table of Contents on page 3 shows all the lists included in the appendix.

Index

An *index* is an alphabetical list at the very end of a book. It lists all the topics in the book and the pages on which you can find them.

All the keywords and related words in the thesaurus are listed in the index. (The keywords are printed in heavy, bold type.) You can use the index to look up any word to find which word group it is in and which page it is on. The "Guide to the Index" on page 500 gives you more instructions on how to use the index.

A, a

---

abduct *verb*

▶ to take someone away by force. *In the adventure story, pirates* **abducted** *the sailors from the ship and took them far away.*

kidnap
To **kidnap** means to abduct and hold someone prisoner until money is paid, or some other condition is met. *The criminals kidnapped the billionaire's child, but they were arrested without getting a ransom.*

spirit away
To **spirit away** means to take someone away in secret. *The fairy tale began with the children being spirited away to a magical land.*

poach
To **poach** can mean to take animals or fish from someone's property without asking permission. *Our chickens keep disappearing, so we think someone must be poaching them.*

rustle
To **rustle** can mean to steal cattle or horses. *The outlaw rustled livestock from nearby ranches and sold them.*

> similar keywords: **capture, steal, grab**

---

abrupt *adjective*

▶ rude and sudden. *Cheung gave an* **abrupt** *answer because he was in a hurry.*

short
Short can mean rudely brief in your way of speaking. *The bus driver was very short with me when I counted out the change slowly.*

curt
Curt means rudely brief in your speech or manners. It is very similar to **short**. *His curt reply made me angry.*

brusque
Brusque means impolite and rough. *Her brusque manner upset me.*

terse
Terse means using few words, sometimes in an impolite way. *Your terse comment showed plainly what you meant.*

blunt
Blunt can mean plain and direct in your way of speaking. *Their reply was a blunt "no" when I asked them if they liked my new jacket.*

> similar keywords: **rude, sudden**
> contrasting keywords: **polite, talkative**

---

a b u n d a n t   *adjective*

▶ a great amount, or more than enough. *There was an **abundant** supply of food at the picnic.*

ample | **Ample** means large in size or amount. *There was ample space for us all to fit in the car.*

plentiful | **Plentiful** means great in amount or number. *We brought a plentiful supply of drinking water when we went hiking in the woods.*

bountiful | **Bountiful** can mean generous in number or amount. *The good weather last spring produced a bountiful harvest of corn.*

copious | **Copious** means large in quantity. *We took copious notes when we researched the topic of our report.*

prolific | **Prolific** can mean producing abundant works or results. *The prolific author wrote five new books in only four years.*

> similar keywords: **numerous, sufficient**
> contrasting keywords: **scant, insufficient**

a b u s e   *verb*

▶ to treat someone or something in a harmful way, either through actions or through words. *The criminals beat the dog, left it without food, and **abused** it in other ways.*

maltreat | To **maltreat** means to treat someone or something roughly or cruelly. *If you maltreat that cat, it may scratch you.*

victimize | To **victimize** means to cheat or harm someone. *They were victimized by the crooked art dealer who sold them a phony painting.*

torment | To **torment** means to cause someone or something a lot of pain or suffering. *Martha was tormented by a nest of angry wasps.*

torture | To **torture** means to cause severe pain, often as a cruel punishment or to get information from someone. *"You can torture me all you want," said the spy, "but I won't tell you the secret code."*

> similar keywords: **damage, hurt**

accidental *adjective*

▶ happening unexpectedly or unintentionally. *Don't be angry with me for breaking the window, because it was purely* ***accidental***.

chance	**Chance** means not due to any known cause or reason. *I found my earring purely by chance a few days after I lost it.*
coincidental	**Coincidental** means happening at the same time by accident or **chance**. *It was coincidental that we both went to the same movie yesterday.*
random	**Random** means not following a pattern or method. *The winning lottery ticket was picked out of the box at random.*
haphazard	**Haphazard** means not planned, or happening by **chance**. *They made many errors because they worked in such a haphazard way.*

contrasting keywords: **deliberate**

accompany *verb*

▶ to go or be with someone. *I am going to* ***accompany*** *my sister on her trip to the Prairies.*

escort	To **escort** means to go along with someone to guide, protect, or show honour. *The motorcycle police escorted the visiting prime minister into the city.*
chaperone	To **chaperone** means to accompany others to make sure they behave properly. *The teachers will chaperone the students at the school dance.*
associate with	To **associate with** means to spend time with someone. *They only associate with students in their own class.*
hang around with	To **hang around with** means to spend your spare time with someone. This is more suited to everyday language. *They hang around the mall with a strange bunch of people.*

accomplish *verb*

▶ to carry something out successfully. *Congratulations! You have* **accomplished** *an important task in a short time.*

achieve To **achieve** can mean to accomplish something or bring it to a successful end. *You will have to work hard to achieve your goal.*

attain To **attain** means to reach or complete something by trying hard. *Atepa attained his goal of improving his skating.*

fulfil To **fulfil** means to carry something out. *We fulfilled our promise to paint the fence.*

bring off To **bring off** is an informal way of saying to **accomplish**. *The magic trick was difficult, but they managed to bring it off.*

> similar keywords: **succeed**
> contrasting keywords: **fail**

accuse *verb*

▶ to blame someone openly for doing something wrong. *He* **accused** *me of cheating on the test.*

denounce To **denounce** means to speak out in public against something or someone. *The leader of the revolution denounced the traitors.*

frame To **frame** can mean to make someone seem to be guilty of something. *The real thief framed me by putting the stolen wallet in my drawer.*

allege To **allege** means to declare something without having proof of it. *It is alleged that they stole clothes from their own store.*

charge To **charge** means to accuse or blame someone for something. This can be a legal word. *The police charged the motorist with speeding.*

book To **book** can mean to record someone's name in order to accuse the person of doing something wrong. *If you get caught breaking the law again, the police will have to book you.*

> similar keywords: **fault**
> contrasting keywords: **forgive**

achievement *noun*

▶ something you gain by hard work. *They praised her for her **achievement** in completing the long-distance race.*

accomplishment An **accomplishment** is something you achieve through hard work. It is similar to **achievement**. *Winning the cup two years in a row was a great accomplishment.*

effort An **effort** is something done by trying hard. *The teacher thought my project was a good effort.*

success A **success** is a very good result. *Our team had great success in the chess tournament.*

feat A **feat** is something you do using great skill, strength, or courage. *It was a great feat to climb to the top of Mount Everest.*

> contrasting keywords: **failure**

actual *adjective*

▶ existing in fact. *These are the **actual** bowls made by the aboriginal people.*

real **Real** means true or actual. *This diamond is real, not fake.*

concrete **Concrete** can mean existing as an actual thing, not just an idea. *The architect prepared a concrete plan once we approved her design proposal.*

tangible **Tangible** can mean able to be treated as fact, **real**, or **concrete**. *Our class helped out at the food bank as tangible proof of our support.*

material **Material** means existing in a form you can touch. *Although she hasn't very many material possessions, she is a very happy person.*

physical **Physical** can mean having to do with **material** things in the world rather than intangible things. *We need money to buy things for our physical needs.*

> similar keywords: **true, genuine**
> contrasting keywords: **shadowy, imaginary, fake**

add   *verb*

▶ to join something on to something else in order to increase it in size or number. ***Add** more beads to the necklace to make it longer.*

supplement   To **supplement** something means to add to it. *I supplement my allowance by babysitting.*

throw in   To **throw in** means to add something as an extra. *The baker threw in an extra cookie with our purchase.*

append   To **append** means to join or add as an extra part. *I appended a list of related reading to my report.*

tack on   To **tack on** means to add something on to something else. *The sentence appears to be tacked on to the end of the paragraph.*

attach   To **attach** means to fasten or join something to something else. *We attached the trailer to the car.*

> similar keywords: **enlarge, insert, increase, count, calculate**
> contrasting keywords: **subtract, remove**

admit   *verb*

▶ to agree that something is true. *I **admitted** that I had broken the window.*

concede   To **concede** means to admit that something is true. *The politician finally conceded that she had lost the election.*

confess   To **confess** means to own up to something you have done. *The suspect was set free when someone else confessed to the robbery.*

blurt out   To **blurt out** means to tell something suddenly or without thinking. *I meant to keep it a secret, but then I blurted it out.*

acknowledge   To **acknowledge** means to say that you realize something is true. *The winning team acknowledged that the other team had played a good game.*

> similar keywords: **reveal**
> contrasting keywords: **hide**

adult *adjective*

▶ grown-up or fully developed. *The **adult** birds are quite a different colour from their young.*

mature	**Mature** means adult or fully developed. *The mature oak tree was tall and leafy.*
full-grown	**Full-grown** is so similar to **mature** you can usually use either. *When the moose is full-grown, it will have a large set of antlers.*
at your peak	**At your peak** means **mature** and at the highest level in your life. *The writer is at the peak of her career and has won several awards for her books.*
seasoned	**Seasoned** means **mature** and good at something through long experience. *The seasoned sailor knew a storm was coming when he saw the clouds and the wind.*

> contrasting keywords: **young**

advance *verb*

▶ to move or go forward. *The team **advanced** to the final round of the tournament.*

progress	To **progress** can mean to advance or move forward. *The parade progressed along Main Street.*
make headway	To **make headway** means to **progress** or move forward. *The car made little headway in the heavy rain.*
proceed	To **proceed** means to move or go forward, especially after stopping. *We drove carefully over the gravel road because the sign said "Proceed with caution."*
push on	To **push on** means to continue or go forward, usually with difficulty. *The weary travellers pushed on from one town to the next.*
forge ahead	To **forge ahead** means to move forward with great effort. *The arctic explorers forged ahead through the heavy snowstorm.*

> similar keywords: **continue, extend, persist**
> contrasting keywords: **reverse, leave**

advise   *verb*

▶ to tell someone what you think should be done. *The doctor **advised** the patient to get more exercise.*

guide	To **guide** can mean to advise, lead, or direct someone in the way you think the person should go. *My parents guided me in my decision to study art.*
suggest	To **suggest** means to put forward the idea of doing something. *My gymnastics coach suggested that I practise my front roll.*
propose	To **propose** means to put forward or **suggest** something. *Sunita proposed that we all go on a hike.*
recommend	To **recommend** means to **suggest** something as being good or worthwhile. *The librarian recommended this book to me.*
advocate	To **advocate** means to speak in favour of something. *Our dentist advocates brushing your teeth after every meal.*

similar keywords: **warn**

---

adviser   *noun*

▶ someone who gives advice, suggesting what they think you should do. *The premier's **advisers** said the time was right to call an election.*

guide	A **guide** is someone whose suggestions and advice you usually follow. *I let my conscience be my guide when I'm not sure what to do.*
mentor	A **mentor** is an adviser who is very wise and whom you trust. *When I need advice, I talk to my aunt and uncle, who have been my mentors for many years.*
counsellor	A **counsellor** is a person who is specially trained to help people solve problems or difficulties. *The school counsellor helped me to decide what I should do this summer.*
consultant	A **consultant** is a professional person who gives advice. *The consultant recommended a new menu for the restaurant.*

similar keywords: **teacher**

aggressive *adjective*

▶ likely to attack others. *That dog is **aggressive** only if you tease it.*

combative Combative means ready or wanting to fight. *Comic books are full of combative superheroes who battle villains.*

belligerent Belligerent means angry and wanting to fight. *Their belligerent behaviour toward their friends surprised us.*

pugnacious Pugnacious means likely to quarrel or fight. *She is so pugnacious that the others have stopped trying to be friends with her.*

hostile Hostile means acting like an enemy. *Their hostile reply to our invitation upset us.*

> similar keywords: **argumentative, warlike, defiant**
> contrasting keywords: **submissive, peaceful**

agile *adjective*

▶ lively and active. *The **agile** gymnast did the most difficult exercises with ease.*

athletic Athletic means physically active and strong. *Because all our players are very athletic, my wheelchair basketball team won the championship.*

lithe Lithe means bending easily. *The dancers moved their lithe bodies very gracefully.*

nimble Nimble means able to move quickly and easily. *Her nimble fingers moved smoothly and quickly over the piano keys.*

spry Spry means **nimble** or active. *Uncle Masao is just as spry now as he was when he was younger.*

light Light can mean agile or **nimble**. *The squirrel was light on its feet and avoided the car.*

> contrasting keywords: **clumsy**

agree   *verb*

▶ to say yes or to have the same opinion as someone else. *I **agreed** to the new plan.*

concur	To **concur** means to agree with something. *I concur with your decision to practise daily.*
assent	To **assent** means to agree to something. *They assented to our request for more money.*
see eye to eye	To **see eye to eye** means to have the same opinion as someone else. It is more suited to everyday language. *My sister and I see eye to eye on which TV programs we like to watch.*
go along with	To **go along with** means to agree to something. It is more suited to everyday language. *We went along with their plan just to keep them happy.*

contrasting keywords: **disagree, argue**

agreeable   *adjective*

▶ pleasing or to your liking. *Rajan is a very **agreeable** person to be with.*

good-natured	**Good-natured** means having a pleasant manner and being easy to get along with. *You are so good-natured that everyone wants to be on your team.*
likeable	**Likeable** means easy to like. *The new student was very likeable and fitted into the class easily.*
compatible	**Compatible** means able to work together or live together in harmony. *The members of our group were very compatible and our project was a success.*
amiable	**Amiable** means agreeable and friendly. *I telephoned my friend and we had an amiable conversation.*
charming	**Charming** means having the ability to please and attract people. *They are charming children and are sure to be popular.*

similar keywords: **nice, friendly**
contrasting keywords: **nasty, unfriendly**

alert *adjective*

▶ watching things carefully and being quick to react. *The lifeguards were **alert** to any danger.*

mindful **Mindful** means alert or careful to notice what is going on. *The swimmers were mindful of the strong waves.*

observant **Observant** means alert or quick to notice things. *The observant puppy noticed where the dog biscuits were kept.*

attentive **Attentive** means watching carefully. *Only the most attentive people saw how the trick was done.*

conscious **Conscious** can mean to be aware of something. *Although the TV was on, we were conscious of everything happening in the room.*

> similar keywords: **inquisitive, wary**
> contrasting keywords: **dreamy, careless**

allow *verb*

▶ to let someone do something. *Will your parents **allow** you to come?*

permit To **permit** is so similar to **allow** that you can usually use either. *My parents will permit me to go to the movie if I finish my chores.*

authorize To **authorize** means to agree or **consent** to something officially. *The principal has authorized this school trip.*

license To **license** means to give official permission to someone. *Are you licensed to drive the school bus?*

tolerate To **tolerate** means to allow something, although not very willingly. *I will tolerate the cat, but I'm not very happy about having it in the house.*

consent To **consent** means to give permission. *The coach consented to my request to miss the practice.*

> similar keywords: **approve**
> contrasting keywords: **refuse, prevent, ban**

ancestor *noun*

▶ someone related to you who lived long ago. *My **ancestors** came from Africa many years ago.*

forebear
: **Forebear** is so similar to **ancestor** that you can usually use either. *My friend's forebears lived in magnificent longhouses.*

forerunner
: A **forerunner** is someone or something that has been or gone before. *Early Greek athletes were the forerunners of Olympic competitors.*

antecedents
: **Antecedents** can mean the line of ancestors. *Horse trainers think that it is important to know the antecedents of a thoroughbred horse.*

predecessor
: A **predecessor** is someone who has gone before you, especially in a job or position. *Our new principal has just as many great ideas as her predecessor.*

> contrasting keywords: **offspring**

anger *noun*

▶ a strong feeling of annoyance caused by thinking that something wrong has been done to you. *You should learn to control your **anger** when someone insults you.*

wrath
: **Wrath** is anger or revenge. It is a rather old-fashioned word. *When I'm bad, I bring upon myself the wrath of my parents.*

ire
: **Ire** is very similar to **anger** and **wrath**. Like **wrath**, it is a rather old-fashioned word. *My ire increased as the next-door neighbour's party became noisier and noisier.*

rage
: **Rage** is violent anger. *When the bully was in a rage, everyone was frightened.*

fury
: **Fury** is a violent feeling, especially one of anger. It is very similar to **rage**. *The grizzly bear smashed the door in its fury.*

temper
: **Temper** can be an angry or resentful mood. *I'm sometimes in a temper when I've had a bad day.*

> similar keywords: **dislike**

anger *verb*

▶ to make someone or something annoyed or violent. *You will **anger** the monkeys if you tease them.*

incense	To **incense** means to make someone angry. It is a more formal word than **anger**. *The defence lawyers incensed the judge with their constant interruptions.*
enrage	To **enrage** means to make someone very angry. *The children's rude manner enraged their cousins.*
infuriate	To **infuriate** is so similar to **enrage** that you can usually use either word. *The children infuriated the bus driver when they threw snowballs at the bus.*
drive someone up the wall	To **drive someone up the wall** means to annoy someone very much. This is more suited to everyday language. *That loud music you are playing is really driving me up the wall.*

> similar keywords: **irritate, annoy**
> contrasting keywords: **pacify**

angry *adjective*

▶ very annoyed because you think that something wrong has been done to you. *I gave them an **angry** look when they were rude to me.*

irate	**Irate** means very angry. *The customer was irate when he wasn't served in his turn.*
furious	**Furious** means extremely angry. *Juan was so furious that he began to shout.*
infuriated	**Infuriated** means very angry. *My parents were infuriated when a careless driver ran into their new car.*
livid	**Livid** means almost uncontrollably angry. It is similar to **furious**. *They were livid when we told them we had broken their antique mirror.*

> similar keywords: **grumpy, annoyed**
> contrasting keywords: **glad, happy, joyful**

annoy *verb*

▶ to irritate someone or to make a person cranky. *Very loud music **annoys** me.*

aggravate
To **aggravate** can mean to annoy or provoke someone. *Don't aggravate your friend by slamming the door.*

exasperate
To **exasperate** means to annoy someone very much. *The children exasperated their parents with their stubbornness.*

hassle
To **hassle** means to worry or annoy someone. It is more suited to everyday language. *Don't hassle me when I'm doing my best.*

pester
To **pester** means to annoy or trouble someone. *Blackflies pestered us when we went camping in May.*

get on someone's nerves
To **get on someone's nerves** means to irritate or annoy someone. It is more suited to everyday language. *They get on my nerves when they complain all the time.*

> similar keywords: **irritate, upset**
> contrasting keywords: **please**

annoyed *adjective*

▶ irritated or bothered. *The **annoyed** customer complained about the store's poor service.*

indignant
Indignant means annoyed about something that you think is unfair. *I arrived on time, so I was indignant when I was accused of being late.*

cranky
Cranky means bad-tempered or cross. *The baby was really cranky when she was getting a new tooth.*

vexed
Vexed means made annoyed or irritated. It is a rather old-fashioned word. *My grandparents were vexed by the store manager's rudeness.*

fed up
Fed up means annoyed with something or tired of it. This is more suited to everyday language. *We were fed up with camping after a week of rain.*

> similar keywords: **grumpy, angry, dissatisfied**
> contrasting keywords: **glad**

annoying *adjective*

▶ likely to make you cranky or angry. *This rain is annoying; I wanted to go to the beach.*

irritating   **Irritating** means annoying or causing impatience. *You have the irritating habit of cracking your knuckles.*

exasperating   **Exasperating** means very annoying. *It is exasperating when you can't think of the exact word you want to use.*

trying   **Trying** can mean annoying or **irritating**. *The way they keep talking during the movie is very trying.*

infuriating   **Infuriating** means causing very great anger. *My computer's continual breakdowns were infuriating.*

maddening   **Maddening** is so similar to **infuriating** you can usually choose either word. *It's maddening! I put my book on my desk, but now it isn't there.*

> contrasting keywords: **nice**

---

answer *verb*

▶ to acknowledge a question, request, letter, and so on, using actions or spoken or written words. *Fatima **answered** the question with a nod of her head.*

respond   To **respond** means to answer, using actions or words. *People responded generously to the fund-raising campaign.*

reply   To **reply** means to give an answer or response. *Did you reply to the letter?*

retort   To **retort** means to give a quick or sharp answer. *When I said that they were late, they retorted by saying that I was lucky they had come at all.*

react   To **react** means to act in answer to something. *We all react to danger in different ways.*

return   To **return** can mean to answer or acknowledge. *I returned her greeting with a friendly smile.*

> contrasting keywords: **question, ask**

apathetic *adjective*

▶ having no feelings for, or interest in, things that other people find interesting or exciting. *The people passing by seemed to be **apathetic** about the demonstration.*

indifferent   **Indifferent** means showing no interest or concern. *How could you be indifferent to the problems of the homeless?*

half-hearted   **Half-hearted** means not showing much willingness or interest. *They made a half-hearted attempt to find the lost keys.*

lukewarm   **Lukewarm** means not very enthusiastic. *The new play received a lukewarm response from the opening-night audience.*

passive   **Passive** means letting things happen without taking any action yourself. *They would not be good leaders because they are too passive.*

> similar keywords: **lethargic**
> contrasting keywords: **enthusiastic**

appear *verb*

▶ to become visible. *The sun **appeared** over the horizon.*

come   To **come** can mean to appear. *There's something wrong with the TV; the picture comes and goes.*

emerge   To **emerge** means to come out into view. *Joseph emerged from behind the trees.*

loom   To **loom** means to appear, often in a large or frightening form. *From out of the shadows, the monster suddenly loomed in front of the hero.*

turn up   To **turn up** means to appear or be seen, often unexpectedly. *I didn't expect you to turn up at this party.*

materialize   To **materialize** means to appear in a physical shape. *Her figure materialized out of the mist.*

> contrasting keywords: **disappear**

appearance   *noun*

▶ the way something or someone looks or seems to look on the outside. *Don't judge people simply by their* **appearance**.

aspect

Aspect can be the way a thing appears or seems. *The lush aspect of the countryside greeted us at every turn in the road.*

image

Image can be the way someone or something looks or seems to others. *The band hoped its new image would attract a wider audience.*

complexion

Complexion can be very similar to appearance. It can usually be used in the same way. *A fresh coat of yellow paint gave the room a completely different complexion.*

presence

Presence can mean your personal appearance or your way of doing things. *The rock star had the strong presence of a great performer.*

> similar keywords: **manner**

approve   *verb*

▶ to like something and agree to it. *We* **approved** *the idea of having a holiday on the farm.*

endorse

To **endorse** means to approve of or to support something. *Do you endorse the new candidate for mayor?*

sanction

To **sanction** means to give approval or support to something. This is rather a formal word. *The principal sanctioned our plan to hold a car wash to raise money.*

okay

Okay means to approve or **endorse** something. This is more suited to everyday language. *My parents finally okayed my plans for the party.*

advocate

To **advocate** means to speak favourably about something. *In my speech I advocated restoring the historic building.*

bless

To **bless** means to approve something and to wish it every success. *They blessed our decision.*

> similar keywords: **praise, allow**
> contrasting keywords: **disapprove of, fault, block**

argue   *verb*

▶ to disagree. *We **argued** about whose turn it was to put out the garbage.*

quarrel	To **quarrel** can mean to argue angrily. *We quarrelled over who would have the first ride.*
squabble	To **squabble** means to argue angrily, but usually for a short time, about something unimportant. *Children often squabble during card games.*
clash	To **clash** can mean to disagree angrily about something you consider to be very important. *They clashed over what should be done with the vacant lot.*
conflict	To **conflict** means to disagree or be in opposition to one another. It is similar to **clash**. *Our ideas conflict about that because we are so different.*

> similar keywords: **disagree**
> contrasting keywords: **agree, cooperate**

argument   *noun*

▶ a disagreement. *We had an **argument** about who had won the race.*

quarrel	A **quarrel** is an angry argument. *You don't have to have a quarrel every time you disagree.*
dispute	A **dispute** is an argument or **quarrel**. *They had a dispute over who was the better actor.*
difference of opinion	A **difference of opinion** can mean a disagreement, especially between two people who usually get on well. *We had a difference of opinion over which comedian is funnier.*
controversy	A **controversy** is an argument or a **difference of opinion**. *There has been a public controversy over where the new airport should be built.*
altercation	An **altercation** is an angry **dispute** or disagreement. *They had an altercation over who caused the traffic accident.*

> similar keywords: **conflict, fight**

argumentative *adjective*

▶ liking to argue. *Some people are* **argumentative** *if they are criticized.*

quarrelsome **Quarrelsome** means to argue easily. *The children were quarrelsome because they were bored.*

cantankerous **Cantankerous** means bad-tempered and likely to argue. *The clerk was tired and in a cantankerous mood.*

contentious **Contentious** can mean **quarrelsome** and fond of arguing. *Contentious people like them will disagree about anything.*

contrary **Contrary** can mean always disagreeing or purposely taking the opposite view. *Your friend is sure to be contrary no matter what we suggest.*

> similar keywords: **defiant, aggressive**
> contrasting keywords: **submissive**

arrange *verb*

▶ to put something in order. *I **arranged** the books on the shelf so that I could find them easily.*

group To **group** means to gather things or people together because they are thought to be connected in some way. *The teacher grouped the students according to age for the track and field events.*

sort To **sort** means to arrange according to type or kind. *We sorted the laundry into piles according to the colour of the clothes.*

grade To **grade** means to arrange according to a stage or step on a scale of positions, quality, or value. *Eggs are graded and priced according to their size.*

classify To **classify** means to arrange according to quality or likeness. *This book classifies plants into different groups, according to where they come from.*

file To **file** can mean to put or arrange something in order. *Our family cuts out interesting travel articles and files them in folders.*

> similar keywords: **list**
> contrasting keywords: **disorganize**

ask *verb*

▶ to put a question to someone. *I'll **ask** my mother to help me with this math problem when she gets home.*

request
: To **request** means to ask for something in a formal way. *The judge requested that the public visitors be silent during the court case.*

beg
: To **beg** means to ask someone for something in a humble way. *I beg you to forgive me.*

implore
: To **implore** means to ask someone for something in an earnest or urgent way. *Don't go; I implore you!*

entreat
: To **entreat** means to **implore**. These two words are so similar you can often choose either of them. *We entreat you to help us escape.*

beseech
: To **beseech** means to ask anxiously for something. It is a rather formal word. *I beseeched them for news of the missing fishing boats.*

> similar keywords: **demand, question**
> contrasting keywords: **answer**

assemble *verb*

▶ to come together. *We **assembled** in the schoolyard before going on the field trip.*

gather
: To **gather** is so similar to **assemble** that you can usually use either. *A crowd gathered to watch the parade.*

meet
: To **meet** means to come together for discussions or a shared activity. *The club meets at nine o'clock every Friday in the community hall.*

congregate
: To **congregate** means to come together in very large numbers. *A huge crowd congregated to see the fireworks.*

turn out
: To **turn out** means to assemble for a public event or entertainment. *All her friends turned out to watch her take part in the Special Olympics.*

rally
: To **rally** means to come together for a common cause or purpose. *The people rallied behind the mayor when she announced a plan to rebuild the library.*

associate *noun*

▶ someone who is connected with you and shares your interests. *My father's accountant is a business **associate**.*

partner
A **partner** is someone who takes part in something with you. *You should always go scuba diving with a partner.*

colleague
A **colleague** is someone who does the same sort of work as you. *People can learn a lot by talking to their colleagues.*

collaborator
A **collaborator** is someone who works with you on a special task or job. *The two friends were collaborators in writing a play.*

comrade
A **comrade** is a very close friend. *My mother and his mother have been comrades since being at school together.*

---
similar keywords: **friend, helper**
---

astonished *adjective*

▶ filled with sudden and great wonder. *We were **astonished** when we saw how red the sunset was.*

surprised
Surprised means filled with a feeling of shock or wonder at something unexpected or very unusual. *I was surprised by the party my parents gave for me.*

amazed
Amazed means filled with astonishment. *I was amazed that I had managed to complete the walkathon.*

astounded
Astounded means completely overcome with astonishment. *We were astounded when we discovered gold on our land.*

flabbergasted
Flabbergasted means shocked or greatly astonished. *I was flabbergasted when I won first prize.*

stunned
Stunned means astonished and very shocked. *News of the president's death stunned the world.*

astonishing *adjective*

▶ causing great surprise or wonder. *It was **astonishing** to see the slow tortoise beat the hare in the race.*

amazing   **Amazing** means causing surprise and astonishment. *It was an amazing finish to the race.*

astounding   **Astounding** means causing complete surprise. *Those dinosaur bones are an astounding size.*

remarkable   **Remarkable** means very unusual and worthy of notice. *This is a remarkable story and should be published.*

staggering   **Staggering** means causing shock and wonder. *Soon everyone had heard the staggering news that the tortoise had beaten the hare.*

stupendous   **Stupendous** means astonishingly good. *The hero's stupendous feat would be remembered for a long, long time.*

> similar keywords: **wonderful**

attack *noun*

▶ the use of force or weapons against a person or group of people. *The soldiers loaded their rifles for the **attack**.*

assault   An **assault** is a violent attack. *An assault on another person is not acceptable.*

onslaught   An **onslaught** is a fierce rush or attack. *The sudden onslaught left many people wounded.*

ambush   An **ambush** is a sudden attack from a hidden place. *The cat's ambush caught the mouse by surprise.*

invasion   An **invasion** is the entering of something in order to attack it. *The kitchen was the scene of an invasion of ants.*

foray   A **foray** is a sudden raid or military attack. *They made a foray into the enemy's camp in the hope of capturing some hostages.*

> contrasting keywords: **defence**

attack   *verb*

▶ to set upon with violent force. *They* **attacked** *the enemy with all their strength.*

assault   To **assault** means to attack someone or something violently. *The thugs assaulted the sales clerk when he wouldn't hand over the money.*

charge   To **charge** means to attack by rushing violently at someone or something. *The bull charged us and we just managed to escape in time.*

raid   To **raid** means to attack someone or something suddenly. *We raided the other camp and stole all their sleeping bags.*

mug   To **mug** means to attack and rob someone. *Someone might mug you if you walk through that park by yourself at night.*

beat up   To **beat up** means to attack and hurt someone. This is more suited to everyday language. *Mei told the bully not to beat up her brother.*

> contrasting keywords: **protect**

attempt   *noun*

▶ a try to complete or do something. *This will be our final* **attempt** *to reach the top of the mountain.*

effort   An **effort** is a serious attempt. *Our effort to reach the top took all of our strength.*

endeavour   An **endeavour** is a try or an attempt to do something that is worthwhile. *We knew our endeavours had been worthwhile when we finally reached the peak.*

crack   A **crack** can be an attempt that may not be successful. It is more suited to everyday language. *After I tried unsuccessfully to loosen the nut on my bicycle wheel, she had a crack at it.*

stab   A **stab** is an attempt that hasn't much chance of succeeding. It is more suited to everyday language. *Solving the problem seemed impossible, but we took a stab at it.*

> similar keywords: **undertaking**

attempt *verb*

▶ to make an effort to do something. *I will **attempt** the race next year.*

try	To **try** means to make an effort or attempt to do something. *You'll never know if you can do it until you try.*
undertake	To **undertake** means to attempt or say that you will do something. *I will undertake the job tomorrow.*
tackle	To **tackle** means to take on and struggle with something or someone. *Let's tackle the problem together.*
attack	To **attack** can mean to go to work on something strongly. *We shall have to attack the next difficult task now.*
work toward	To **work toward** means to make an effort to achieve something. *We have to work toward a fair solution to the problem.*

attract *verb*

▶ to try to have someone pay attention or come near, especially by being interesting or pleasing. *The new TV show **attracted** a large audience.*

draw	To **draw** can be so similar to **attract** that you can usually use either. *The street musicians drew a large crowd.*
lure	To **lure** means to attract or tempt someone by seeming to be very pleasant or exciting. *The TV advertisement lured me to buy the product.*
magnetize	To **magnetize** can mean to attract so strongly that a person's whole attention is taken up. *The bright display of fireworks magnetized us.*
pull in	To **pull in** can mean to attract or **draw** someone, usually a large group of people. *The final hockey game pulled in the biggest crowd.*
catch your eye	To **catch your eye** means to attract attention. It is more suited to everyday language. *The display in the store window caught my eye.*

similar keywords: **charm**
contrasting keywords: **repel**

attractive   *adjective*

▶ pleasing or appealing. *Reading a good book is an* **attractive** *idea.*

magnetic	**Magnetic** can mean strongly attractive. *The new host of the TV show has a magnetic personality.*
irresistible	**Irresistible** means not able to be resisted or withstood. *The chocolate cake in the fridge was so irresistible that I had to have some.*
tempting	**Tempting** means inviting or enticing. *The clear blue water of the lake looked very tempting on such a hot day.*
seductive	**Seductive** means enticing or captivating. *I love to sit in that chair because the cushions are soft and seductive.*
charismatic	**Charismatic** means having special personal qualities that give someone influence over a large number of people. *The charismatic leader had a large following.*

avoid   *verb*

▶ to keep away from something or someone. *We went another way to* **avoid** *the traffic jam.*

miss	To **miss** can mean to avoid or fail to attend something. *I missed that movie because I thought it would be boring.*
evade	To **evade** means to avoid doing or taking notice of something. *They manage to evade the traffic laws.*
elude	To **elude** means to avoid, in a clever way, someone who is looking for you. *The crook eluded the police.*
shirk	To **shirk** means to avoid doing a job or a duty. *It is not a good idea to shirk your responsibilities.*
steer clear of	To **steer clear of** means to avoid something or someone very carefully. *We steered clear of the hornets' nest at the old cabin.*

> contrasting keywords: **seek**

B, b

bad   *adjective*

▶ nasty or unpleasant. *There's a **bad** smell coming from that factory.*

atrocious	**Atrocious** means very bad or lacking in taste. *My parents would not tolerate such atrocious behaviour.*
abominable	**Abominable** means hateful or disgusting. *Slavery is an abominable practice.*
abysmal	**Abysmal** means so bad that it could not be worse. *They found the dog living in abysmal conditions.*
monstrous	**Monstrous** means frightful or shocking. *The monstrous images in the movie frightened the young children.*
rotten	**Rotten** can mean bad or dishonest. It is more suited to everyday language. *It was a rotten trick to sell a tape player that was broken.*

> similar keywords: **nasty, pathetic, horrible**
> contrasting keywords: **nice, good**

ball   *noun*

▶ something with a round or roundish shape, such as the object that you can bounce or kick, catch, or hit in games. *Throw me the **ball**.*

sphere	A **sphere** is something completely round in shape. *The potter formed the clay into a sphere before placing it on the wheel.*
globe	A **globe** is anything shaped like a ball, particularly with a map of the world on it. *Turn the globe around so that we can see Australia.*
orb	An **orb** is a ball-shaped object. It is used in poetry to mean a planet, the sun, or the moon. *The sun is the brightest orb in the sky.*
globule	A **globule** is a very small, ball-shaped object, especially a drop of liquid. *Globules of sweat ran down her forehead.*

ban *verb*

▶ to forbid something. *The hockey league agreed to **ban** fighting from all games.*

bar
To **bar** can mean to forbid something. *Young children are barred from going to that movie because it is too violent.*

outlaw
To **outlaw** means to forbid something by law. *The government has outlawed the dumping of toxic wastes.*

censor
To **censor** means to prevent someone from seeing, hearing, or reading things that are considered objectionable for some reason. *The board censored the film because it was too violent.*

disqualify
To **disqualify** means to take away permission or to become ineligible for something. *The swimmer was disqualified for crossing into the next lane.*

boycott
To **boycott** can mean to stop buying or using something, as a means of causing change. *We boycotted the new product in an effort to convince the manufacturer to pay its workers a proper salary.*

> similar keywords: **prevent, exclude, block**
> contrasting keywords: **allow**

bandit *noun*

▶ an armed robber. *A gang of **bandits** ran into the bank and pulled out their guns.*

highwayman
A **highwayman** was someone who held up travellers on public roads and robbed them, usually on horseback. *People travelling from town to town in England were afraid of highwaymen.*

brigand
A **brigand** is a robber who lives with a gang of other robbers in hidden mountain or forest areas. *Beware of brigands when you get to that lonely mountain road.*

pirate
A **pirate** is someone who attacks and robs ships at sea. *The captain kept a lookout for pirates.*

buccaneer
A **buccaneer** is a more old-fashioned word for a **pirate**. *There are many exciting stories about buccaneers who lived long ago.*

> similar keywords: **thief, criminal, crook**

bare *adjective*

▶ having no covering. *I like the feel of cool water on my **bare** toes.*

exposed	**Exposed** can mean uncovered or bare, especially something that should be, or is, usually covered. *Exposed skin can freeze quickly during a winter storm.*
naked	**Naked** means having no clothes on. *The naked baby chuckled as he splashed in the bath.*
nude	**Nude** means **naked**, or without clothes or coverings. *A sculpture of a nude figure is in the lobby of the art gallery.*
bald	**Bald** can mean not covered with hair, or any other natural growth. *The bald desert landscape attracted me.*

bay *noun*

▶ a sheltered part of the sea or a lake formed by a curve in its shore. *The sailing boats were anchored in the **bay**.*

harbour	A **harbour** is a sheltered area of a body of water where ships may anchor. *We waited for the ferry to return to the harbour.*
gulf	A **gulf** is a part of an ocean that is partly bounded by land. *The Gulf of St. Lawrence is a large bay at the mouth of the St. Lawrence River.*
inlet	An **inlet** is a small narrow bay. *The smugglers rowed to an uncharted inlet from their ship moored in the harbour.*
cove	A **cove** is a small bay or **inlet**. *There was room for just a few cottages along the shore of the cove.*
fiord	A **fiord** is a long, narrow **inlet** bordered by steep cliffs. *The cruise ship sailed along British Columbia's fiords.*

similar keywords: **lake**

beat *verb*

▶ to hit again and again. *The drummer **beat** out a steady rhythm.*

smack
To **smack** means to hit or slap. *The whale smacked the water with its gigantic tail.*

punch
To **punch** means to strike with your fist. *The karate teacher punched a board and broke it.*

thump
To **thump** means to strike someone heavily. *They all thumped me on the back when I won the race.*

hammer
To **hammer** can mean to hit something forcefully over and over again. *She hammered on the door until someone finally opened it.*

bang
To **bang** is to hit or beat something noisily. *The children banged the pieces of wood together in time with the music.*

> similar keywords: **hit**

beautiful *adjective*

▶ pleasing and enjoyable to hear, look at, touch, smell, or taste. *The choir sang a **beautiful** song at the wedding.*

lovely
Lovely is similar to **beautiful** and you can often choose to use either. *My friend painted a lovely picture.*

exquisite
Exquisite means finely and delicately beautiful. *The antique tablecloth was made of exquisite lace.*

gorgeous
Gorgeous means richly beautiful, especially in colouring. *The peacock spread its gorgeous tail feathers.*

stunning
Stunning means beautiful in a way that surprises you or captures your attention. It is more suited to everyday language. *It was such a stunning sunset that everyone stopped to watch it.*

> similar keywords: **pretty**
> contrasting keywords: **ugly**

befriend *verb*

▶ to help or be friendly toward someone. *They **befriended** the new boy at school because he didn't know anyone.*

defend　　　To **defend** can mean to speak or act on behalf of someone or something. *Ashley defended me when they said I was just trying to show off.*

champion　　To **champion** can mean to **defend** or fight for someone. This is a rather old-fashioned way of using the word. *"I'll champion your cause," said the politician.*

stand by　　To **stand by** can mean to help or support someone loyally. *Friends should stand by each other in times of need.*

stick up for　To **stick up for** means to **defend** or support someone. *Thanks for sticking up for me when the others started disagreeing with what I'd said.*

side with　　To **side with** means to be on the side of a person or a group of people in support of an issue. *He always sided with his friend in an argument.*

> similar keywords: **help**

begin *verb*

▶ to take the first step in something. *Please **begin** your work now.*

start　　　To **start** is so similar to **begin** that you can usually use either. *I am going to start my project tonight.*

commence　　To **commence** is so similar to **begin** and **start** that you can usually use any of them. *The builders have commenced the addition to our house.*

embark on　To **embark on** means to begin something that is going to be long or important. *Zara is embarking on a new career tomorrow.*

set about　　To **set about** means to begin doing or start preparing something. *I will set about cooking dinner.*

open　　　To **open** means to begin or start something. *We opened the game with the singing of "O Canada."*

> similar keywords: **initiate**
> contrasting keywords: **finish, stop, end**

behave   *verb*

▶ to act in a particular way. *Please don't **behave** badly when the visitors are here.*

conduct yourself	To **conduct yourself** means to behave in a certain way. *He conducted himself well even though his brother teased him.*
perform	To **perform** can mean to behave. *The car performed well on our holiday.*
function	To **function** means to **perform** a certain operation or activity. *This box can also function as a cereal bowl.*
operate	To **operate** can mean to **perform** or **function**. *The computer is not operating as well as it should.*
acquit yourself	To **acquit yourself** means to show what you can do in a particular activity. This is a rather formal word. *They will acquit themselves well in the debate.*

behaviour   *noun*

▶ the way someone or something acts, especially in a particular situation. *The scientist studied how people's **behaviour** changes when they are not allowed to sleep.*

conduct	**Conduct** is someone's behaviour, especially toward other people. *The students' conduct was good, and they worked together happily.*
deportment	**Deportment** is the way someone acts. It is a rather formal word. *The government officials were expected to be polite in their deportment.*
demeanour	**Demeanour** is someone's **conduct** and appearance. It is a rather formal word. *Their cheerful demeanour made us feel welcome.*
manners	**Manners** are the ways that someone behaves toward others. *We were told to watch our manners and be courteous to our guests.*
attitude	An **attitude** is someone's manner, especially toward other people. *The rock group has an appreciative attitude toward its fans.*

believable *adjective*

▶ likely to be true or able to be believed in. *Your story is strange, but **believable**.*

credible
Credible is so similar to **believable** that you can usually use either. *I thought what happened in that film was quite credible.*

plausible
Plausible means seeming to be true or reasonable. *She had a plausible excuse.*

probable
Probable means likely to be true. *The witness gave a probable account of the accident.*

possible
Possible means maybe true, although there may be knowledge to the contrary. *It is possible that I left the door open, but normally I lock it.*

conceivable
Conceivable means able to be imagined, although maybe unlikely. *It is conceivable that the rumour is true.*

> similar keywords: **likely**
> contrasting keywords: **unbelievable, impossible**

believe *verb*

▶ to think that something is right or true. *I **believe** your story.*

accept
To **accept** can mean to believe something to be true. *I accept that what you say really happened.*

presume
To **presume** is to believe something is true because there is no evidence to think otherwise. *I presume you'll be joining us at dinner.*

trust
To **trust** means to believe or have confidence in someone or something. *I trust what you tell me.*

take for granted
To **take for granted** can mean to believe something without questioning it. *I take it for granted that she really committed the crime.*

assume
To **assume** means to believe something without proof. *I assume you're the cause of this.*

> similar keywords: **think, conclude**
> contrasting keywords: **doubt**

bend *verb*

▶ to turn something in a particular direction. *Vicky **bent** the wire into the shape of a hook and pulled her ring from the drain.*

flex To **flex** means to bend something, especially a part of your body. *You have to flex your spine when you lean over and touch your toes.*

deflect To **deflect** means to bend or turn something aside. *I tried to hit the ball straight, but the tree deflected it and it bounced into the creek.*

curl To **curl** means to bend something into a curved or twisted shape. *I like the way you have curled your hair.*

curve To **curve** means to bend something into a rounded shape. *The carpenter curved strips of wood to make the arms of the chair.*

loop To **loop** means to bend something into an oval or circular shape. *You can make a knot if you loop the rope around twice and pull the end through.*

similar keywords: **turn**

best *adjective*

▶ higher than the rest in quality or importance. *She is the **best** runner on our team.*

star **Star** means the most brilliant or well-known. *She is our star runner.*

top **Top** can mean the most outstanding or the best. *He is the top student in the class.*

leading **Leading** means the most important or chief. *Takeo is the leading dancer in the modern-dance company.*

head **Head** can mean being in the position of leadership. It is similar to **leading**. *You had better ask the head librarian.*

principal **Principal** means highest in position or importance. It is similar to both **leading** and **head**. *She is the principal actor in the film.*

similar keywords: **excellent, good, great, superior, main**

betray *verb*

▶ to be unfaithful or disloyal to someone. *The spy **betrayed** his country.*

double-cross To **double-cross** means to betray someone by promising one thing and doing another. *They said they would keep my secret, but they double-crossed me.*

sell out To **sell out** means to betray someone. This is more suited to everyday language. *Ahmed would never sell out his friends even if he thought it would get him out of trouble.*

report To **report** can mean to complain or give information about someone or something. *We reported our violent neighbours to the police.*

rat on To **rat on** means to betray someone by revealing information that should have been kept secret. This is more suited to everyday language. *They asked me to rat on her, but I wouldn't say anything.*

> similar keywords: **deceive, blab**

big *adjective*

▶ great in size or amount. *We made a **big** cake so that everyone could have a piece.*

large **Large** means of more than the usual size, amount, or extent. *An elephant is a large animal.*

bulky **Bulky** means **large** and awkward to manage because of its size and shape. *It was difficult to hide the bulky present.*

substantial **Substantial** means very great in size or amount. *The treasure hunters found a substantial fortune hidden away.*

generous **Generous** can mean big or bigger than you needed or expected. *Our neighbours gave us generous helpings of ice cream and chocolate sauce.*

ample **Ample** can mean large or well filled out. *She gets an ample allowance from her parents.*

> similar keywords: **huge, fat, tall**
> contrasting keywords: **small**

blab *verb*

▶ to tell or reveal a secret. This word is more suited to everyday language. *She was angry when I **blabbed** the name of her boyfriend to everyone.*

divulge   To **divulge** means to make a secret known. *I accidentally divulged some information about the secret experiments.*

spill   To **spill** can mean to blab or tell a secret, or something similar. It is more suited to everyday language. *Don't trust them next time, because they have just spilled everything we told them.*

let out   To **let out** can mean to tell a secret, or something similar. *Don't let out the details of our surprise party.*

give away   To **give away** can mean to let a secret be known. *Do not give away our hiding place to the others.*

similar keywords: **reveal, betray**

black *adjective*

▶ without any colour or brightness. *The moonless night sky was very **black**.*

dark   **Dark** can mean giving out very little light. *The dark woods were filled with brambles.*

pitch-black   **Pitch-black** means very black or **dark**. *The pitch-black clouds loomed on the horizon.*

inky   **Inky** means as black as ink. *The fox disappeared completely into the inky shadows.*

jet-black   **Jet-black** means of a deep, glossy black colour, like the shiny coal of the same name. *We groomed the horse until its jet-black coat shone in the sun.*

ebony   **Ebony** means black, like the valuable wood of the same name. *The cat stared at me with its large, ebony eyes.*

similar keywords: **dark**

block   *verb*

▶ to be in the way of someone or something. *The broken-down truck* **blocked** *the traffic.*

obstruct   To **obstruct** means to block or close off something. *A landslide obstructed the road.*

barricade   To **barricade** means to block or defend something with a barrier or a wall that has usually been built in a hurry. *The police barricaded the road to try to stop the escaping bank robbers.*

blockade   To **blockade** means to **close** a port, harbour, and so on, using ships or soldiers to stop supplies going in or out. *The enemy ships blockaded the main port, and food became very scarce.*

bar   To **bar** means to stop or prevent someone from doing something. *The guards barred them from entering the building.*

close   To **close** can mean to block something off. *Heavy snow closed the road.*

> similar keywords: **prevent, hinder, ban**
> contrasting keywords: **further, approve**

blue   *adjective*

▶ having the colour of a clear sky. *We searched anxiously for signs of rain clouds in the* **blue** *sky.*

azure   **Azure** means having a sky-blue colour. *The clear sky was an azure colour.*

navy   **Navy** means having a very dark blue colour. *I used a navy marker to colour the ocean in my drawing.*

aqua   **Aqua** means having a light blue-green colour. *Boats bobbed up and down on the aqua sea.*

sapphire   **Sapphire** means having a deep blue colour. *As evening approached, the lake took on a sapphire hue.*

boast *verb*

▶ to speak with too much pride about yourself. *They **boasted** about winning the volleyball tournament.*

brag
To **brag** is so similar to **boast** that you can usually use either. *A good sport doesn't brag about winning.*

crow
To **crow** can mean to boast or talk loudly of any success or victory you may have. *They wouldn't stop crowing about the way their team won the debate.*

bluster
To **bluster** can mean to boast loudly or to talk in a threatening way. *It's not wise to bluster and bully people to get your own way.*

gloat
To **gloat** means to look at or think about something with too much satisfaction. *They gloated over their opponents' bad luck.*

blow your own horn
To **blow your own horn** means to praise or say that you admire yourself. This is more suited to everyday language. *She isn't interested in what I do because she's too busy blowing her own horn.*

boil *verb*

▶ to cook something by heating it in a bubbling liquid. *We **boiled** the potatoes in the saucepan.*

poach
To **poach** means to cook something in a liquid that is just below boiling point. *Poach the eggs while I make the toast.*

steam
To **steam** means to cook something in a covered pot, using very little water. *I steamed the vegetables, so they should be crunchy.*

simmer
To **simmer** means to cook something slowly in a liquid that has only a few bubbles rising. *Put all the ingredients for the soup in a big saucepan and simmer them gently for two hours.*

stew
To **stew** means to cook something slowly in a gently boiling liquid. *I stewed the chunks of chicken with the potatoes and other vegetables.*

braise
To **braise** means to fry something quickly in a pan, then **stew** it gently in a covered pot. *I love the delicious gravy you get when you braise pork chops with lots of mushrooms and onions.*

bold *adjective*

▶ rude or not showing respect. *That was a **bold** thing to say to a police officer.*

fresh   **Fresh** can mean not showing respect, especially in the way you speak to someone. *Don't get fresh with me!*

impertinent   **Impertinent** means rude and out of place. *The children's impertinent remarks upset their grandparents.*

saucy   **Saucy** means disrespectful. It is more suited to everyday language. *That's a saucy answer to give your teacher.*

brazen   **Brazen** means shamelessly rude. *My friend's brazen behaviour embarrassed us all.*

forward   **Forward** means behaving boldly in order to make people notice you. *The children were so forward in front of the visitors that their parents sent them from the room.*

> similar keywords: **rude, unashamed, defiant**
> contrasting keywords: **shy, polite**

book *noun*

▶ a number of pages bound together inside a cover, for reading and sometimes for writing in. *We borrow **books** from the library each week.*

manual   A **manual** is a book that tells you how to do or use something. *We looked at the manual to see how to use the computer program.*

textbook   A **textbook** is a book setting out the information for a course of study in a subject. *We had two textbooks for science.*

anthology   An **anthology** is a collection of poems, plays, articles, or short stories by various authors or from various books by the same author. *We studied several of the poems in the anthology.*

volume   A **volume** is a book, especially one of a series. *There were twenty volumes of the encyclopedia.*

diary   A **diary** is a book in which you write down daily events or thoughts. *I kept a diary while we were on holidays.*

> similar keywords: **publication**

bored *adjective*

▶ feeling dull or tired because you aren't interested in what you are doing. *It rained all afternoon, and the children complained that they were **bored**.*

blasé	**Blasé** means so used to doing exciting things that they no longer interest or excite you. *I've been to the zoo so many times that I'm blasé about going again.*
tired of	**Tired of** means bored with or no longer interested in something. *We are tired of playing computer games.*
sick of	**Sick of** means very bored with or feeling that you have had enough of something. *I'm sick of people who complain.*
fed up	**Fed up** means very bored, annoyed, or frustrated with something. *I'm fed up with having nothing to do all day.*

contrasting keywords: **excited**

boring *adjective*

▶ uninteresting or wearying. *This video is so **boring** that I don't think I'll finish watching it.*

dull	**Dull** can be so similar to **boring** that you can usually use either. *The characters in the film are all very dull.*
tedious	**Tedious** means long and boring. *I changed my attitude so that the tedious task seemed more interesting.*
stale	**Stale** can mean uninteresting because it has been used so many times before. *The author has used a stale plot in his novel.*
monotonous	**Monotonous** means boring because it is always exactly the same. *The announcer had a monotonous voice.*
humdrum	**Humdrum** means boring because it is ordinary and doesn't change. It is similar to **monotonous**. *I'm going to try to change my humdrum life by finding an interesting hobby.*

contrasting keywords: **exciting**

boss *noun*

▶ someone who employs and directs people in their work. *Their **boss** is very fair and makes sure no one is overworked.*

supervisor	A **supervisor** is someone who directs or watches over people who are working. *The supervisor at the exam told the students when to stop writing.*
superior	A **superior** is someone who is higher in rank or position than you. *My superiors were pleased with the report I gave them.*
chief	A **chief** is the head person in a group. *We elected her as the chief of the committee.*
head	A **head** can mean someone who is in charge of a group or department. *The head of the department gave a speech to all the employees.*

> similar keywords: **manager**

bossy *adjective*

▶ wanting to order other people about. *They were **bossy** when they played with younger children.*

overbearing	**Overbearing** means bossy, arrogant, and expecting other people to do as you say. *I dislike their overbearing way of taking over our games.*
imperious	**Imperious** means **overbearing** or ruling over people in a severe and bossy way. *We didn't enjoy the tour because the imperious guide ordered us around.*
autocratic	**Autocratic** means ruling without caring about, or having regard for, other people. *"What an autocratic king he is,"* groaned his subjects.*
dictatorial	**Dictatorial** means **overbearing**, or tending to order other people about. *The manager's dictatorial manner made her unpopular.*
pushy	**Pushy** means getting what you want, but in an obnoxious way. It is more suited to everyday language. *Those pushy people refused to wait their turn in line.*

> similar keywords: **rude, unashamed, defiant**
> contrasting keywords: **shy, polite**

bottom *noun*

▶ the lowest or deepest part of something. *I signed the letter at the **bottom** of the page.*

floor
The **floor** is the lowest flat part of a room or other space. *The floor of the cave was quite dry.*

foot
The **foot** can be the bottom part. *We camped in the valley at the foot of the mountain.*

base
The **base** is the bottom part of anything that gives support. *We stood at the base of the huge tree and gazed upward.*

bed
The **bed** can be the bottom or ground underneath a body of water. *The shipwreck was sunk in the mud of the bed of the ocean.*

contrasting keywords: **top**

brave *adjective*

▶ ready to face danger or pain whether you are afraid or not. *Although the storm was becoming more violent, the **brave** sailors refused to give up hope.*

courageous
Courageous means able to do or face something you find frightening. It is similar to **brave**. *The courageous girl swam across the flooded river to get help.*

fearless
Fearless means not letting fear stop you, even in dangerous situations. *The fearless firefighter risked her life to save the injured child.*

bold
Bold means without fear, or ready to take risks. It is similar to **fearless**. *Their bold deeds were admired by everyone.*

heroic
Heroic means brave or acting in the daring way a hero does. *The heroic lifeguard carried the child from the ice-cold water.*

valiant
Valiant means brave or showing great courage. *His valiant efforts saved his friend's life.*

contrasting keywords: **fearful, frightened**

break   *noun*

▶ a gap or open space in something. *The cattle got out through the **break** in the fence.*

fracture
A **fracture** is a break, usually in a bone. *It was a simple fracture of the arm.*

crack
A **crack** is a slight opening. *The crack in the cup caused the tea to leak out.*

fissure
A **fissure** is a long, narrow break, usually in something hard or solid. *There was a deep fissure in the ground after the earthquake.*

rift
A **rift** is a long, narrow opening made by something breaking or dividing. *The explosion caused a rift to appear in the earth.*

crevice
A **crevice** is a **crack** or cleft that forms an opening in something. *The crevice in the rock was the home of many small insects.*

> similar keywords: **cut, hole**

brief   *adjective*

▶ using few words. *There was a **brief** report of the public meeting in the newspaper.*

short
Short can mean somewhat brief or not as long as usual. *I had a short letter from my friend.*

concise
Concise means using few words to tell a lot. *Samira gave a concise account of what had happened.*

succinct
Succinct is so similar to **concise** that you can usually use either. *James gave a succinct review of the movie.*

abridged
Abridged means made briefer by leaving out some parts. *I enjoyed the abridged version of the novel so much that I went on to read the complete edition.*

condensed
Condensed means expressed in fewer words than before. *Please give me a condensed version of what happened.*

> similar keywords: **momentary**
> contrasting keywords: **lengthy**

bright *adjective*

▶ giving out a strong light. *He drew a picture of a **bright** sun and a pale moon.*

light   **Light** means not dark. *My bedroom is always light because it has wide windows.*

brilliant   **Brilliant** can mean shining with a bright light. *They enjoyed the display of brilliant fireworks.*

dazzling   **Dazzling** can mean shining with a light that almost blinds you. *Drivers should not look at the headlights of other cars because they are too dazzling.*

glaring   **Glaring** can mean being so bright that it is uncomfortable to look at. *Naja sheltered her eyes from the glaring sunlight.*

> similar keywords: **shining, colourful**
> contrasting keywords: **dark, drab, dull**

broad-minded *adjective*

▶ able to accept other people's ideas and ways. *When you meet different sorts of people you learn to be **broad-minded** and enjoy what is different about them.*

liberal   **Liberal** means broad-minded or able to accept a wide range of ideas. *Their liberal views are a result of their desire to be fair to people with different ideas.*

tolerant   **Tolerant** means showing or having respect for, or patience with, other people's opinions or ways of doing things. *I try to be tolerant of my friends' opinions even when I totally disagree with them.*

indulgent   **Indulgent** means willing to give in to the wishes or feelings of others. *She is an indulgent teacher in most things, as long as her students are honest with her.*

permissive   **Permissive** means allowing people freedom to do as they wish, especially in moral matters. *I think his parents are too permissive, allowing him to stay out so late on school nights.*

> similar keywords: **lenient**
> contrasting keywords: **strict, narrow-minded**

broke   *adjective*

▶ out of money. This word is more suited to everyday language. *I can't pay you back until next week because I'm **broke**.*

destitute	**Destitute** means not having any money or the belongings that are necessary for everyday living. *The whole family was destitute after the fire destroyed their home.*
ruined	**Ruined** can mean having lost everything you own. *Many people were ruined by the disastrous floods.*
bankrupt	**Bankrupt** means unable to pay the money you owe to other people. *She was bankrupt after her business failed.*
insolvent	**Insolvent** means having more debts than you can pay. It is very similar to **bankrupt**. *Because he was insolvent, he could pay only half of what he owed people.*

> similar keywords: **poor**
> contrasting keywords: **wealthy**

brown   *adjective*

▶ having the colour of earth. *I want to ride that **brown** horse over there.*

beige	**Beige** means having a very light brown colour, like natural wool. *The beige drapes blended well with the woodwork.*
tan	**Tan** means having a yellowish-brown colour. *I rubbed and polished the tan leather saddle until it shone like new.*
brunette	**Brunette** means having hair that is a rich dark brown colour. *All their children have brunette hair.*
fawn	**Fawn** means having a pale yellowish-brown colour. *Gently I stroked the soft, fawn coat of the young Jersey calf.*

b u i l d *verb*

▶ to make something by putting parts together. *The little children **built** a tower with the blocks.*

construct To **construct** is so similar to **build** that you can usually use either. *Laure constructed a bookshelf with the wood.*

erect To **erect** means to build something up. *They have erected a monument to honour Confederation.*

put up To **put up** is so similar to **erect** that you can usually use either. *My mother put up a fence at the back of our house.*

shape To **shape** means to give definite form, shape, or character to something. *The potter carefully shaped the vase.*

fashion To **fashion** means to form something. *The carpenter fashioned a doll out of the piece of wood.*

> similar keywords: **make, create**

b u s y *adjective*

▶ fully occupied. *My mother was **busy** painting my bedroom.*

active **Active** means busy. *My grandparents lead active lives, even though they are both over eighty.*

hard-working **Hard-working** means always willing to work hard. *Luis does well in school because he is hard-working.*

industrious **Industrious** can mean willing to work hard. It is very similar to **hard-working**. *Elizabeth is an industrious student.*

hectic **Hectic** can mean full of activity and busyness. *We had a hectic weekend.*

flat out **Flat out** means working as hard or as quickly as possible. *I had my wheelchair going flat out during the race.*

> similar keywords: **energetic**
> contrasting keywords: **lazy, lethargic**

buy *verb*

▶ to get something by paying money. *I am saving up to* ***buy*** *a new bike.*

purchase   To **purchase** is so similar to **buy** that you can usually use either. *We purchased the CD player with our own money.*

rent   To **rent** means to pay money regularly for the use of something, often a place to live in. *We are renting a house near the school.*

lease   To **lease** means to sign a contract and pay money regularly for the use of something. *My parents decided to lease a new car for three years rather than buy one.*

redeem   To **redeem** can mean to buy something back or to get it back in exchange. *Thank goodness I managed to redeem the watch that I pawned.*

> similar keywords: **get**
> contrasting keywords: **sell**

buyer *noun*

▶ someone who pays money for something. *I am a regular* ***buyer*** *of that magazine.*

purchaser   A **purchaser** is so similar to a **buyer** that you can usually use either. *The purchaser of our old house loves it.*

customer   A **customer** is someone who buys goods from another person. *The department store is trying to attract new customers.*

shopper   A **shopper** is someone who is visiting a store with the intention of looking for and buying something. *The shoppers didn't see anything they liked, so they went to another store.*

client   A **client** is someone who hires someone or receives benefits from certain agencies. *The lawyer prepared a contract for her client.*

consumer   A **consumer** is someone who buys and uses goods or services. *Wise consumers check the prices at several stores before they make a major purchase.*

> contrasting keywords: **seller**

C, c

calculate *verb*

▶ to work out something using mathematics. *She **calculated** the area of the square.*

compute To **compute** means to calculate or work out using mathematics. *I computed the time it would take for light to reach the earth from the sun.*

figure To **figure** means to work out or calculate something. *I figure the cost to be $150, and if we save hard we can buy the bike by June.*

make To **make** can mean to add something up to a certain amount. *How much does two and four make?*

determine To **determine** can mean to get the answer to a problem by working it out. *I determined the answer by adding the numbers together.*

> similar keywords: **count, measure, add**

callous *adjective*

▶ showing no concern for someone else's feelings. *It was **callous** of them not to visit their sick friend.*

hard-hearted **Hard-hearted** means having no kind feelings toward others. *The hard-hearted landlord refused to allow the tenants any more time to pay the rent.*

unfeeling **Unfeeling** is so similar to **hard-hearted** that you can usually use either. *"No, you can't leave early," was the supervisor's unfeeling reply.*

insensitive **Insensitive** can mean lacking in feeling but not necessarily meaning to be cruel. *The insensitive coach shouted at the team.*

cold-blooded **Cold-blooded** can mean having no feelings, especially of pity. It usually describes a more callous person or action than **hard-hearted** or **unfeeling**. *They were cold-blooded murderers.*

> similar keywords: **cruel**
> contrasting keywords: **kind**

calm *adjective*

▶ not getting excited or upset. *She always stays **calm** when she does a presentation.*

cool	**Cool** means calm or not excited. *They were quite cool throughout the competition.*
poised	**Poised** means calm, confident, and self-possessed. *Some people remain poised even when they speak in front of an audience.*
relaxed	**Relaxed** means feeling at ease and unworried. *You will be able to think more clearly if you are relaxed.*
placid	**Placid** means calm and peaceful. *My cousin is a placid person who doesn't get upset by little things.*
composed	**Composed** means feeling calm in your body and mind. *I know you are upset now, but after a good sleep you may feel more composed.*

> similar keywords: **peaceful**
> contrasting keywords: **excited, upset, frightened, nervous**

cancel *verb*

▶ to put an end to the operation or effectiveness of something. *We had to **cancel** the track meet and hold it on a day when the weather was better.*

dissolve	To **dissolve** can mean to bring something to an end. *The Prime Minister asked the Governor General to dissolve Parliament.*
break off	To **break off** can mean to put a stop to something. *I decided to break off our friendship.*
abolish	To **abolish** means to put an end to something altogether. *A law was passed to abolish slavery.*
annul	To **annul** means to put an end to something, such as a law or a marriage. *Parliament annulled capital punishment.*
repeal	To **repeal** means to put an end to something legally and officially. It is similar to **abolish**. *Will the government repeal that new tax?*

> similar keywords: **finish, end**
> contrasting keywords: **initiate**

capture   *verb*

▶ to take someone or something by force. *The cat **captured** the mouse.*

arrest   To **arrest** means to take someone prisoner. *The police officer arrested the suspect.*

apprehend   To **apprehend** means to take someone or something into custody. *The police apprehended the burglar as he ran down the road.*

trap   To **trap** means to catch something or someone. *They trapped the bully who stole their toys.*

pick up   To **pick up** can mean to capture someone you are looking for, especially a criminal. *They picked up the escaped convicts at the border.*

hijack   To **hijack** means to seize something, using threats or violence. *The terrorists hijacked the plane and forced the pilot to fly to another country.*

> similar keywords: **grab, abduct, catch**
> contrasting keywords: **free**

careful   *adjective*

▶ putting time and effort into your work. *Katina is a **careful** writer.*

diligent   **Diligent** means paying careful attention to what you are doing. *The diligent worker was promoted to superintendent.*

conscientious   **Conscientious** means being particularly careful and thorough in what you have to do. *The conscientious student kept good notes.*

attentive   **Attentive** means paying careful attention to someone. *The attentive pupils learned a lot from the teacher's diagrams on the board.*

meticulous   **Meticulous** means giving attention to every detail. *The meticulous worker checks everything at least twice.*

fussy   **Fussy** means being very careful in what you are doing, sometimes in an irritating way. *He was too fussy about small details.*

> similar keywords: **thorough, wary**
> contrasting keywords: **careless**

careless *adjective*

▶ done without taking enough care or paying enough attention. *His **careless** addition resulted in an incorrect total.*

thoughtless
Thoughtless means doing or saying something without thinking carefully about it. *Her thoughtless remark hurt his feelings.*

casual
Casual can mean doing something without giving it enough thought. *Their casual attitude to their work caused a lot of errors.*

lax
Lax means careless or not strict. *The babysitter was lax in getting the children to bed at the right time.*

negligent
Negligent means not paying proper attention to what you should be doing. *They were negligent in carrying out their duties.*

irresponsible
Irresponsible means not careful or reliable, sometimes in a dangerous way. *The lifeguard's irresponsible behaviour alarmed us.*

> contrasting keywords: **careful, wary**

carry *verb*

▶ to take something from one place to another. *The ship **carried** its cargo across the ocean.*

transport
To **transport** is very similar to **carry**. *We hired a truck to transport our furniture to our new house.*

transfer
To **transfer** means to carry or move something from one place to another. *A helicopter transferred the sailors from their sinking ship to the rescue boat.*

convey
To **convey** means to carry or bring something from one place to another. *I'll convey your message to my neighbour.*

deliver
To **deliver** means to carry something and hand it over to someone else. *A courier delivers the merchandise to each store.*

run
To **run** can mean to carry or **transport** someone to a particular place. *If you're ready now, I'll run you to school.*

> similar keywords: **send**

catch *verb*

▶ to capture something, especially after a chase. *The police **caught** the thief by setting up a roadblock.*

trap	To **trap** can mean to catch an animal in a device made for this purpose. *They trapped the foxes and then decided to let them go.*
snare	To **snare** means to catch birds and small animals with a device usually consisting of a noose. *The ranger caught the poacher who had snared the pheasants.*
ambush	To **ambush** means to attack something or someone after lying in wait in a hidden place. *The cat ambushed the mouse.*
waylay	To **waylay** means to lie in wait for someone or something, especially in order to attack, rob, or capture. *They waylaid him outside his house and kidnapped him.*
take by surprise	To **take by surprise** can mean to come upon something or someone suddenly and when least expected. *Keith was walking so softly that he took me by surprise when I turned the corner.*

> similar keywords: **grab, capture**

cause *verb*

▶ to bring something about or to make it happen. *The warm weather **caused** the snow to melt.*

provoke	To **provoke** can mean to cause something or to stir it up. *Your constant teasing provoked an angry response.*
induce	To **induce** can mean to cause something or to bring it on. *A warm glass of milk can sometimes induce sleep.*
produce	To **produce** can mean to bring something into being. *The rich soil produced good crops for the farmers.*
inspire	To **inspire** can mean to **produce** or awaken a feeling or thought in someone. *His happy and kind nature inspires love in all his friends.*
evoke	To **evoke** means to **produce** something or to give rise to it. *The soft music evoked a feeling of calm.*

centre *noun*

▶ the middle and most important part of something. *There are many stores in the* ***centre*** *of the city.*

hub   A **hub** can be a busy or important centre. *The locker room was the hub of activity before the final game.*

heart   The **heart** can be the most important part, especially of an argument or situation. *We got straight to the heart of the matter and found a solution to the problem.*

core   The **core** can be the central, middle, or main part of anything. *The core of this lesson is that everyone is equal.*

nucleus   The **nucleus** can be the central and most important part or thing around which other parts are grouped. *The drummer was the nucleus of the new rock band.*

focus   The **focus** can be the main point of interest or attraction. *The new computer in the class was the focus of attention.*

> similar keywords: **inside**
> contrasting keywords: **outskirts, edge**

change *verb*

▶ to make something different. *I **changed** my story so that it would have a happy ending.*

alter   To **alter** means to make something different in some way. *Sabira altered her plans so that I could come, too.*

adapt   To **adapt** means to change something to make it better suited to a specific use or situation. *We adapted the play so that everyone could have a part in it.*

vary   To **vary** means to **alter** something a little bit. *I varied my lunch today by bringing a banana instead of an apple.*

transform To **transform** means to change the form or appearance of something. *New wheels and some bright red paint transformed the old bicycle.*

> contrasting keywords: **keep**

c h a r m   *verb*

▶ to attract, win over, or delight someone. *Chung **charmed** me with his sense of humour.*

fascinate   To **fascinate** means to attract and hold the interest of someone completely. *She fascinated us with her stories.*

entice   To **entice** means to attract or tempt someone, especially by promising money, enjoyment, or some other gain. *The luscious cakes in the window enticed us into the bakery.*

beguile   To **beguile** means to attract or enchant someone. *The kitten beguiled them by jumping into a box and peeking over the top.*

bewitch   To **bewitch** means to charm someone as if under a spell. *The audience seemed bewitched by the beautiful music.*

mesmerize   To **mesmerize** means to hold the attention of someone completely. *The beauty of the scenery mesmerized us.*

> similar keywords: **attract**
> contrasting keywords: **repel**

c h e a p   *adjective*

▶ of low price. *You can sometimes buy **cheap** fruit at roadside stands.*

inexpensive   **Inexpensive** means not costing very much money. *We want to stay at an inexpensive hotel.*

reduced   **Reduced** means being of lower price than usual. *They sold the furniture at a reduced price.*

discount   **Discount** can mean selling things at a cheaper price than usual. *We bought a washing machine at a discount store.*

no-frills   **No-frills** means paying cheaper prices because no luxuries are included. *We travelled second class and stayed at no-frills hotels.*

reasonable   **Reasonable** can mean not expensive. *This store offers high-quality shoes at reasonable prices.*

> contrasting keywords: **expensive**

cheat *verb*

▶ to take something belonging to someone else dishonestly or by tricking them. *He **cheated** me out of all this week's pocket money.*

swindle To **swindle** means to cheat someone out of something, especially money. *The dishonest business manager swindled her clients out of nearly all their savings.*

defraud To **defraud** means to cheat or deceive someone to get money, property, and so on. It is usually used in more formal language. *The employees defrauded their company of its profits.*

fleece To **fleece** means to cheat someone out of all or nearly all of something. It is usually used in less formal language. *They fleeced him of every cent he had.*

rip off To **rip off** means to cheat someone by making them pay too much for something. It is more suited to everyday language. *He ripped us off by charging us $30 for that junk.*

> similar keywords: **trick, deceive, steal**

chew *verb*

▶ to bite and crush food with your teeth. *Young babies must have their food mashed because they cannot **chew** it.*

munch To **munch** means to chew something noisily. *The horse was munching carrots.*

chomp To **chomp** means to chew noisily. It is similar to **munch**. *Don't chomp your food when you eat.*

nibble To **nibble** means to chew or bite in little bits. *The baby nibbled her cookie.*

gnaw To **gnaw** means to wear something away by biting it again and again. *The mouse gnawed through the bag and ate the bread inside.*

masticate To **masticate** means to chew in order to digest. It is a very formal word. *Charles always masticates his food thoroughly.*

> similar keywords: **eat**

c h i c   *adjective*

▶ attractive and stylish. *That's a very **chic** outfit you're wearing!*

elegant	**Elegant** means graceful or stylish. *The limousine was the most elegant car I have ever seen.*
smart	**Smart** can mean neat and keeping up with the latest fashion. *That's a smart new jacket you have.*
dapper	**Dapper** means very neat and **smart** in a slightly showy way. *Rob is very dapper in his white shirt and new bow tie.*
fashionable	**Fashionable** means in keeping with the style of clothes and appearance that most people think is attractive. *A beaver hat was once considered very fashionable.*
trendy	**Trendy** means following the latest fashion. *Those shoes are very trendy.*

> similar keywords: **modern, new**
> contrasting keywords: **old-fashioned**

c h o i c e   *noun*

▶ something or someone you have chosen or picked out from a number of things or people. *The blue one is my **choice**.*

selection	A **selection** can be a thing or things chosen carefully. *Bring your selection to the cashier.*
option	An **option** is something you have chosen or that you may choose from more than two selections or possibilities. *What are my options in this situation?*
preference	A **preference** is something that you choose or like better than another. *My preference is to travel there by plane.*
alternative	An **alternative** is one of two choices. *We had the alternative of waiting in line for an hour or going home.*
elective	An **elective** is something that is not required, but that you can choose to do. *My brother chose Spanish as his elective course of study.*

choose *verb*

▶ to settle on something or someone above all the others in a group. ***Choose** a number between one and ten.*

select
: To **select** means to choose something or someone carefully. *Have you selected a video yet?*

pick
: To **pick** means to choose or **select** something from among a number of things. *Pick your favourite colour.*

take
: To **take** can mean to choose something from more than one alternative. *We lost our way after we took the wrong road.*

decide
: To **decide** can mean to choose from various selections or possibilities. *I decided that the sensible thing to do was to just go home.*

fix
: To **fix** can mean to settle on or determine. *I've fixed the price now, and it's not too high and not too low.*

similar keywords: **prefer**

city *noun*

▶ a large or important town. *Thousands of people work in the many offices and businesses in the **city**.*

metropolis
: A **metropolis** is a large important city. *Vancouver is the biggest metropolis in British Columbia.*

capital
: A **capital** is the city of a country, province, or state where the government is situated. *Ottawa is the capital of Canada.*

suburb
: A **suburb** is a district of a city with its own shopping centre, school, and so on. *We live in a suburb of Toronto.*

town
: A **town** is a large place with many people living in it. *We go into town to buy our supplies.*

municipality
: A **municipality** is a city, town, township, or other official district. *Some municipalities collect taxes more frequently than others.*

contrasting keywords: **country, the**

civic *adjective*

▶ having to do with a city, or the people who live in it. *The municipal buildings are usually in the civic centre.*

urban	**Urban** means having to do with a city or town, or living in that city or town. *Most of the urban population work in offices and businesses.*
metropolitan	**Metropolitan** means having to do with a very large city and, often, with its suburbs. *The metropolitan area is spread over many kilometres.*
suburban	**Suburban** means having to do with or living in an area that is often quite far from the city centre. *There are many large suburban shopping malls surrounding the city.*
municipal	**Municipal** means having to do with the local government of a city, town, or township. *A new mayor was chosen in the municipal elections.*

contrasting keywords: **country**

clean *adjective*

▶ not having any dirt or stains. *We wore clean clothes to the party.*

spotless	**Spotless** means free from stains, marks, spots, or any other similar blemishes. *Everything in the home was spotless.*
immaculate	**Immaculate** means absolutely free from spots or stains. *Your uniform must be immaculate.*
hygienic	**Hygienic** means clean and free from dirt and germs. *We were taught to be hygienic and always wash our hands before meals.*
sanitary	**Sanitary** means free from dirt and germs. It is similar to **hygienic**. *The restaurant kitchen is not as sanitary as it should be.*
unpolluted	**Unpolluted** means not contaminated. *She could remember when the lakes in this area were unpolluted and safe for fishing and swimming.*

similar keywords: **tidy**
contrasting keywords: **dirty**

clean *verb*

▶ to remove the dirt from something or someone. *I **cleaned** my shoes.*

wash	To **wash** means to wet and rub someone or something, usually with soap or detergent, in order to remove the dirt. *He washed his face and hands before dinner.*
scrub	To **scrub** means to rub someone or something hard with a brush, soap, and water in order to remove the dirt. *Carol had to scrub her nails because they were covered in automotive grease.*
cleanse	To **cleanse** means to make something clean and pure. *We cleanse our skin every night.*
sterilize	To **sterilize** means to destroy the germs in something, often by boiling it. *We need to sterilize our drinking water.*
mop up	To **mop up** means to clean or wipe up dirt and so on, with a mop or something similar. *Mop up the paint you spilled!*

contrasting keywords: **dirty, spoil**

clear *adjective*

▶ easily understood. *Give us some **clear** examples.*

plain	**Plain** can mean clear to your mind. *It's plain that you don't really need to come with us.*
obvious	**Obvious** means so clear that no explanation or thought is needed. *The answer to this question is obvious.*
evident	**Evident** can mean quite clear to your understanding. *It's evident that you know more about music than I do.*
straightforward	**Straightforward** can mean not difficult or complicated. *I would rather you gave me a straightforward explanation.*
explicit	**Explicit** can mean fully set out or expressed in a clear way. *This game comes with a booklet of explicit instructions.*

similar keywords: **visible**
contrasting keywords: **confusing, vague**

clever *adjective*

▶ good at thinking or learning quickly. *It was **clever** of you to figure out that riddle.*

intelligent   **Intelligent** means having good mental ability. *They are intelligent children and understand even difficult books.*

brainy   **Brainy** means having the ability to learn and understand easily. It is a less formal word than **clever** or **intelligent**. *They are so brainy they remember everything they read.*

smart   **Smart** means clever or **intelligent**. *Our cat is smart and has learned to open doors.*

bright   **Bright** can mean good at learning and understanding. *My friend is bright and explains problems I don't understand.*

brilliant   **Brilliant** can mean very, very **smart**. *Our most brilliant pupil won a scholarship to university.*

> similar keywords: **shrewd, sensible**
> contrasting keywords: **silly**

climb *verb*

▶ to move up something. *The firefighter **climbed** the ladder.*

ascend   To **ascend** is similar to **climb**, and you can often use either. *As the plane ascended, the buildings below appeared smaller and smaller.*

mount   To **mount** means to go up something. *I could hear my friend as he softly mounted the stairs.*

scale   To **scale** means to climb up or over something, as if you were using a ladder. *Nasrin scaled the wall.*

clamber up   To **clamber up** can mean to climb something with difficulty, using both feet and hands. *As they clambered up the steep path that led to the castle, they nearly fell several times.*

shinny up   To **shinny up** means to climb something by using your hands or arms and your legs and pulling yourself up. *The boy shinnied up the apple tree.*

> contrasting keywords: **descend**

cloth   *noun*

▶ a substance formed by weaving, knitting, or pressing fibres like wool, hair, silk, or cotton together. *The weavers created many different kinds of **cloth** and sold them to buyers.*

fabric   **Fabric** is any woven, knitted, or felted cloth. *I bought some colourful fabric to make a caftan. The nursery animal mobiles were made of felt fabric.*

material   **Material** is cloth that has been or is capable of being woven. *The curtain material has a rich dark green colour.*

textile   A **textile** is any woven cloth. *Silk, wool, and cotton are natural textiles. Nylon is a synthetic textile that is used to make parachutes.*

rag   **Rag** is a scrap of cloth or cloth used in making paper. *We used old rags to clean the stove. This expensive writing paper has a high linen rag content.*

clothing   *noun*

▶ the articles or garments that you wear on your body. *I always wear old **clothing** when I work in the garden.*

apparel   **Apparel** is clothing, especially the type worn on the outside. It is a rather formal word. *This shop specializes in athletic apparel.*

attire   **Attire** is clothing for a special occasion, usually rather rich or splendid. *The guests at the opening night of the ballet wore formal attire.*

dress   **Dress** can mean a particular style of clothing. *I did a project on the dress of the Middle Ages.*

garb   **Garb** is clothing of a particular style, especially if it shows your job, hobby, or is rather eye-catching. *The doctor put on her garb before entering the operating room.*

wardrobe   Your **wardrobe** is your entire supply of clothing. *David has grown so much since last year that he needs a whole new summer wardrobe.*

cloudy *adjective*

▶ not sunny because of clouds. *The sky has been **cloudy** for days.*

overcast   **Overcast** is so similar to **cloudy** that you can usually use either. *Unfortunately, the sky was overcast the day of our picnic.*

dull   **Dull** can mean cloudy and grey. *A dull day with a lot of rain is forecast for tomorrow.*

misty   **Misty** means not clear because of fine drops of water floating in the air. *The mornings are often misty in the mountains.*

foggy   **Foggy** means dark or blurry because of fog. *The motorists drove slowly along the shore because it was foggy.*

hazy   **Hazy** means not clear because of a thin mist or cloud of dust. *You can't see much of the view today because it is too hazy.*

> similar keywords: **dreary, dark**
> contrasting keywords: **fine**

club *noun*

▶ a group of people organized together to share a particular interest, sport, or hobby. *We started a chess **club** at school.*

association   An **association** is a group of people organized for a common purpose. It is similar to **club**. *My father belongs to an association of stamp collectors.*

society   A **society** can be a group of people organized for a common purpose. It is similar to **club** and **association**. *My cousin is president of the debating society.*

assembly   An **assembly** can be a group of people gathered together for the same purpose. *The Prime Minister made a speech to the assembly of workers.*

union   A **union** is a group of workers joined together to represent their own interests. *The union bargained for safer working conditions.*

> similar keywords: **group**

clumsy   *adjective*

▶ unskillful in the way you move about or do things. *I felt **clumsy** when I knocked the glass of water over.*

awkward	**Awkward** means clumsy or not graceful. *The actor's awkward movements on stage spoiled the scene.*
gangling	**Gangling** means tall and thin and moving awkwardly. *The gangling colt had difficulty running.*
all thumbs	**All thumbs** means not being skillful with your hands. *I was all thumbs the first time I tried to knit.*
accident-prone	**Accident-prone** means likely to have a lot of accidents. *Little children can be accident-prone and should be closely watched.*
heavy-handed	**Heavy-handed** means awkward and clumsy. *Without practice, your piano playing may become heavy-handed.*

> similar keywords: **incompetent**
> contrasting keywords: **agile, competent, skillful**

coat   *verb*

▶ to cover something with a substance. *We coated the bedroom walls with fresh paint.*

spread	To **spread** can mean to cover something with a layer. *Try to spread the bread evenly with butter.*
daub	To **daub** means to coat something with a soft or sticky substance. *They daubed plaster on the cracks in the wall.*
smear	To **smear** can mean to rub or **spread** something with grease, oil, paint, or dirt. *We smeared sunscreen on our exposed skin.*
plaster	To **plaster** can mean to cover something thickly, as if with plaster. *They plastered the bread slices with peanut butter.*
pave	To **pave** means to cover a road, path, or something similar with stones, tiles, bricks, or concrete to make a flat hard surface to walk on. *We paved the area around the pool with blue tiles.*

coating *noun*

▶ a covering of some substance spread over a surface. *I put a **coating** of batter on the fish before frying it.*

veneer   A **veneer** is a thin layer of wood or other material used to cover the surface underneath. *The walnut veneer on the plywood shelf made it more attractive.*

skin   A **skin** can be a surface layer. *I peeled the skin off the potatoes before boiling them.*

crust   A **crust** can be a hard outer surface. *We could walk on the crust of the snow without sinking.*

glaze   A **glaze** is a smooth, shiny coating or surface. *The potter put a beautiful blue glaze on the vase.*

film   A **film** can be a thin layer or coating. *There was a film of grease covering the water in the sink after I washed the pots.*

coil *noun*

▶ a loop or series of loops twisting around. *We·tied the end of the rope into a **coil** and threw it to the attendant on the dock.*

loop   A **loop** is a round or oval shape twisted in a piece of ribbon, string, or something similar. *Make a loop with the string big enough to fit around the bundle of pencils.*

spiral   A **spiral** is a curve or series of curves winding around away from a centre. *The staircase went up in a spiral, twisting around and around to the very top of the tower.*

curl   A **curl** can be something that has a **spiral** or curved shape. *The waves made huge curls in the ocean.*

twist   A **twist** is something that is curved or bent around. *The bus crawled through all the twists in the road.*

swirl   A **swirl** is something that has a twisting shape or pattern. *For dessert, we had vanilla ice cream with swirls of chocolate syrup.*

cold *adjective*

▶ having or feeling a lack of warmth. *I enjoy a fresh, **cold** glass of skim milk.*

nippy
Nippy means very chilly or cold. *In the late afternoon, the breeze at the beach can be nippy.*

freezing
Freezing means extremely cold. *I'd better wear a coat in this freezing weather.*

frigid
Frigid can mean very cold in temperature. *The frigid temperature in Antarctica is perfect for penguins.*

icy
Icy means cold like ice. *The icy drink was refreshing.*

frosty
Frosty means very cold or freezing. *We wore our scarves because it was such a frosty morning.*

> similar keywords: **wintry**
> contrasting keywords: **hot**

colour *verb*

▶ to put colour onto something. *The sun at dawn **coloured** the sky with beautiful shades of pink.*

dye
To **dye** means to change the colour of something. *I dyed my old blue jeans black.*

tint
To **tint** means to colour something slightly. *The baker tinted the icing on the cake a pale pink.*

stain
To **stain** means to colour something made of wood with a liquid that soaks into it. *She stained her pine desk to show the grain of the wood.*

paint
To **paint** means to cover something with a liquid colouring substance. *We are going to paint my bedroom.*

highlight
To **highlight** means to colour something so that it stands out against the background. *The artist highlighted the cabin in the painting.*

colourful   *adjective*

▶ having many colours. *There were many* **colourful** *steel bands in the Carnival parade.*

bright **Bright** means being strong, clear, and easy to see. *The bright Hanukkah candles are a special feature of the "festival of lights."*

vivid **Vivid** means dazzling or very **bright**. *The vivid colours of the festival of Holi delighted the children.*

rich **Rich** can mean having fine, wonderful colours. *The rich velvet fabric made a wonderful graduation dress.*

garish **Garish** means being brightly coloured in an unattractive or unusual way. *The clown's garish suit made us all laugh.*

> similar keywords: **gaudy**
> contrasting keywords: **colourless, drab**

colourless   *adjective*

▶ lacking in colour. *A shower of rain brought the* **colourless** *desert to life.*

pale **Pale** means whitish or not having much colour. *His face was pale when he was ill.*

pastel **Pastel** means having soft, **pale** colours. *Pastel colours are often used in watercolour painting.*

neutral **Neutral** can mean having no particular colour that stands out. *They displayed many colourful paintings on the neutral walls.*

faded **Faded** means having lost its colour. *I love my faded jean jacket.*

bleached **Bleached** means having had the colour taken out. *I bleached my shirt to make it white.*

> contrasting keywords: **colourful**

combine *verb*

▶ to mix or put things together. *The conductor **combined** the two choirs for the concert.*

assemble   To **assemble** means to bring or put things together to make a whole. *We painted the model plane after we assembled the parts.*

blend   To **blend** means to mix things together so that they can't be separated. *You can blend flour and water to make glue.*

fuse   To **fuse** means to join two things together by melting them. *The machine fused the two metals by heating them.*

amalgamate   To **amalgamate** means to join two or more things together to make one. *The board of directors decided to amalgamate the two companies.*

> similar keywords: **mix, join**
> contrasting keywords: **separate**

come *verb*

▶ to get to a place you have been moving toward. *We will **come** to see your house in the morning.*

arrive   To **arrive** means to come to the end of a journey. *We set out early and arrived at noon.*

reach   To **reach** means to get to or **arrive** at. *We were very glad when we reached home after our long trip.*

turn up   To **turn up** means to come or **arrive**. *She turned up late for the tournament.*

show up   To **show up** can mean to **arrive**. *We all thought he wasn't coming, but he finally showed up.*

immigrate   To **immigrate** means to come to another country to settle. *Many people have immigrated to Canada from all over the world.*

> similar keywords: **land, appear**
> contrasting keywords: **leave**

comfort *noun*

▶ a lessening of sadness and worry. *I gained great **comfort** from her visits when I was in hospital.*

consolation   **Consolation** can mean comfort or cheer in your distress. *His optimism when I was sick was a great consolation.*

solace   **Solace** means comfort in a time of sorrow or trouble. *The two sisters found solace by being together when their parents were so ill.*

relief   **Relief** means freedom from pain, unhappiness, or worry. *What a relief to accomplish my goal!*

ease   **Ease** means freedom from any problem, discomfort, or pain. *He lived a life of ease after he won first prize in the lottery.*

empathy   **Empathy** means the ability to share the feelings of someone else. *They have such empathy that when I'm sad, they understand how I feel.*

> similar keywords: **pity**

comfort *verb*

▶ to cheer someone up or to make someone feel less sad or worried. *He **comforted** the baby by cuddling her.*

soothe   To **soothe** means to calm or comfort someone. *The soft music soothed me.*

ease   To **ease** means to give someone relief or comfort. *The news that the doctor was coming eased my mind.*

relieve   To **relieve** means to make someone free from pain, unhappiness, or worry. *The news that they were safe relieved us.*

alleviate   To **alleviate** means to make something easier to bear. *Talking to my parents alleviated my worry.*

lighten   To **lighten** can mean to make something less hard to bear. *Getting a new dog lightened Peter's spirits.*

> similar keywords: **pacify**
> contrasting keywords: **upset**

comment *noun*

▶ a short note or statement that gives an opinion or explanation. *The reporters asked the finance minister if she would make a comment about the budget.*

remark   A **remark** is a brief expression of your opinion. It is usually spoken. *Do you have any remarks to make about my suggestion?*

observation   An **observation** is a comment made about something you have noticed, usually not of great importance. *I said that the room looked a little messy, but it was only an observation.*

interjection   An **interjection** is a comment that interrupts a conversation or a speech. *There were several interjections from the crowd during the Mayor's speech.*

exclamation   An **exclamation** is something said or cried out suddenly in pleasure or fright. *She gave an exclamation of surprise when she opened the present.*

commotion *noun*

▶ a wild or noisy disturbance. *There was a great commotion in the playground when two dogs started fighting.*

fuss   A **fuss** can be a noise or disturbance. *Everyone made a fuss because the bus was late again.*

hullabaloo   A **hullabaloo** is a loud noisy disturbance. *She made a great hullabaloo when she won the contest.*

tumult   A **tumult** is a noisy violent disturbance or uproar, often made by a huge crowd. *A tumult of cheering burst from the hundreds of waiting fans.*

turmoil   A **turmoil** means a commotion or a condition of wild disorder. *The house was in a turmoil when we were packing to leave.*

riot   A **riot** is a disturbance of the peace by a group of people. *When the two rival gangs met, there was a riot in the street.*

similar keywords: **noise**

compete   *verb*

▶ to set yourself against one or more people to gain or win something. *The team* **competed** *at the Olympics.*

race   To **race** means to compete with someone in a contest of speed. *The cyclists raced around the track.*

run   To **run** can mean to compete or take part in a race. *We will run against three other teams in the relay race.*

vie   To **vie** means to compete against or try to beat someone. *The athletes vied for first place in the games.*

contest   To **contest** means to compete with or struggle against someone. *The rivals contested with each other at the debate.*

contrasting keywords: **cooperate**

competent   *adjective*

▶ good at doing a particular thing. *She is a* **competent** *driver.*

able   **Able** means having enough skill to do a particular job. *She is a very able pianist.*

capable   **Capable** means knowing the right way to do something and doing it well. It is very similar to **competent**. *He is a capable cook.*

expert   **Expert** means having a lot of special skill or knowledge. *She is an expert pilot.*

proficient **Proficient** means skilled or **expert**. *Hiroshi is a proficient nurse.*

efficient **Efficient** means **capable** and working in the best possible manner. *He is an efficient carpenter who rarely wastes any time or materials.*

similar keywords: **experienced, skillful**
contrasting keywords: **incompetent, inexperienced, clumsy**

complain *verb*

▶ to tell about your troubles, illnesses, pains, or anything you are not satisfied with. *I try to be cheerful instead of always **complaining**.*

grumble To **grumble** means to complain in a cranky way, usually in a low voice. *He grumbled about the way some people treat our environment.*

whine To **whine** can mean to complain in an annoying, high-pitched voice. *Those children are always whining to their mother.*

nag To **nag** can mean to keep on complaining or finding fault. *My friend nags me when I am late.*

gripe To **gripe** means to complain in a bad-tempered manner. It is more suited to everyday language. *Please do not gripe about the weather.*

protest To **protest** means to complain about or object to something. *I protested that noise pollution was hurting my ears.*

> similar keywords: **fault**

complicated *adjective*

▶ having many related or entangled parts. *This computer program is **complicated**.*

elaborate **Elaborate** means having great detail. *We worked out an elaborate plan.*

intricate **Intricate** means having fine details or puzzlingly entangled parts. *We followed an intricate maze of paths.*

complex **Complex** means difficult and complicated. *The problem was so complex it took us a long time to solve it.*

involved **Involved** means lengthy and going into great detail. *The student gave an involved reply to the teacher's simple question.*

convoluted **Convoluted** means twisted, complicated, and difficult to understand. *He gave a convoluted answer when I invited him to dinner, so I still don't know if he is coming or not.*

> similar keywords: **difficult**
> contrasting keywords: **easy**

compose   *verb*

▶ to create literature or music. *Would you please help me* **compose** *this poem?*

write
To **write** can mean to create or produce something, using words, musical notes, or other symbols. *I hope to write a novel one day.*

draft
To **draft** can mean to write or draw the outline or plan of something. *I still have a lot of work to do on my essay because I have only drafted a rough outline.*

pen
To **pen** means to **write** down something using, or as if using, a pen. This word is not often used because it can sound rather pompous. *Can you pen a few lines to go with this catchy little tune?*

dash off
To **dash off** can mean to **write** something in a hurry. *I must remember to dash off a note of thanks to my teacher.*

set down
To **set down** can mean to put something down in writing. *I must set down my memories of our trip before I forget the details.*

> similar keywords: **create, invent**

conceited   *adjective*

▶ too proud of yourself and your own importance and abilities. *They are so* **conceited** *that they think they can do everything better than anyone else.*

vain
Vain means too proud of yourself in any way. *The vain man was always boasting about his important job.*

egotistic
Egotistic means always thinking and talking about yourself. *The egotistic girl told us all about her holiday, but didn't ask about ours.*

stuck-up
Stuck-up means thinking you are better than everyone else. It is more suited to everyday language. *If you are stuck-up, you will not have many friends.*

big-headed
Big-headed means conceited or **vain**. *I hope winning this award will not make you big-headed.*

> similar keywords: **proud, pompous**
> contrasting keywords: **humble**

concentrate   *verb*

▶ to fix your mind on something. *If you* **concentrate***, you'll solve the problem.*

focus on To **focus on** means to concentrate or centre your thoughts on something. *Focus on solving this puzzle.*

consider To **consider** can mean to think carefully or direct your thoughts toward one particular thing. *Please don't rush me, because I need to consider before I reply.*

take notice of To **take notice of** means to pay attention to something or someone with interest. *You should take notice of her advice.*

attend to To **attend to** means to give something or someone your full attention. *Attend to your work!*

mind To **mind** can mean to pay close attention, especially to what you are doing or to what is happening around you. *Mind that you don't trip.*

> similar keywords: **ponder**
> contrasting keywords: **daydream**

concert   *noun*

▶ a public presentation by musicians or other performers. *The audience applauded when the band came on stage to begin the* **concert***.*

recital A **recital** is a performance given by a group of pupils. *The parents enjoyed listening to the music at the piano recital.*

show A **show** is an entertainment, such as a movie or concert. *Students wrote and directed the show that we are seeing tonight.*

production A **production** can mean a particular entertainment. *The school's production of Anne of Green Gables was the best I have ever seen.*

performance A **performance** is the giving of a play or concert. *The final performance of the play was sold out.*

jam session A **jam session** is an informal meeting of jazz or rock musicians, usually to play for their own enjoyment. *We had all brought along our instruments, so we decided to have a jam session.*

conclude   *verb*

▶ to decide something after thinking about it. *I **conclude** that the solution to this problem is impossible to find.*

deduce   To **deduce** means to work something out by reasoning. *Before finishing the book, she had already deduced who the murderer was.*

infer   To **infer** means to form an opinion after considering all the facts and information. *They inferred from the researcher's report that the competing company was planning a new advertising campaign.*

determine   To **determine** means to decide or settle something such as a question or an argument. *It's hard to determine how long it will take to do the job.*

gather   To **gather** can mean to understand something as a result of things you have heard. *I gather that you had a wonderful time at the concert.*

reason   To **reason** can mean to decide something by sensible argument. *They reasoned that the river would flood, and so they quickly began building dikes.*

> similar keywords: **think, solve, believe**

concoct   *verb*

▶ to think up something, such as a story or an excuse. *They **concocted** a humorous story to amuse the young children.*

make up   To **make up** means to invent something for a particular reason. *I can make up wonderful stories if I spend time observing nature.*

cook up   To **cook up** means to concoct something or to invent it in order to mislead or deceive someone. It is more suited to everyday language. *They cooked up an excuse for being one hour late.*

hatch   To **hatch** means to concoct or arrange something, often in secret. *They hatched a clever plan.*

contrive   To **contrive** means to invent, plan, or plot something in a clever way. *They contrived a plan to build an animal reserve.*

> similar keywords: **create**

confine *verb*

▶ to keep or shut someone or something in a place. *The puppy was **confined** to the basement until it was house trained.*

imprison	To **imprison** means to lock someone up, usually in a prison. *The kidnappers imprisoned their victim in an old farmhouse.*
jail	To **jail** means to put someone in prison. *The convicted criminal was jailed for five years.*
lock up	To **lock up** means to shut someone in a place fastened with a lock, such as a prison. *The unruly man was locked up overnight.*
restrain	To **restrain** can mean to confine or keep under control. *The mob was out of control and had to be restrained from doing further damage.*
intern	To **intern** means to keep in a guarded area, especially during wartime. *Many people were interned during the war.*

> similar keywords: **enclose, isolate**
> contrasting keywords: **free**

conflict *noun*

▶ a fight, struggle, or disagreement. *We want to avoid a **conflict** between nations so that there will be peace in the world.*

feud	A **feud** is a bitter, long-lasting quarrel, especially one between two families. *We had never met his cousin because of the family feud.*
row	A **row** is a noisy quarrel or fight. *I can't concentrate while you are having a row.*
friction	**Friction** can mean conflict between people, nations, and so on. *The friction between the bordering countries kept getting worse.*
disagreement	A **disagreement** is a failure to agree. *We are having a disagreement over whom to invite to the party.*
clash	A **clash** can mean an angry conflict. *When our ideas clashed, we shouted at each other.*

> similar keywords: **argument, fight**

confuse   *verb*

▶ to mix up your mind or your thoughts. *They both tried to show me how to play the game, but they only **confused** me.*

muddle
To **muddle** means to make someone confused or unable to think clearly. *The conflicting evidence muddled the scientist's thinking.*

fluster
To **fluster** means to make someone nervous and confused. *The boss flustered me when she asked if I had finished writing the report.*

distract
To **distract** means to make someone confused by drawing attention away from what the person is doing. *The TV will distract you while you are doing your homework.*

daze
To **daze** means to feel confused because of a fall, bright lights, and so on. *The fall from the horse dazed me for several minutes.*

> similar keywords: **puzzle**
> contrasting keywords: **explain, simplify**

confused   *adjective*

▶ feeling unsure or mixed up. *I am so **confused** that I do not know what is the right thing to do.*

puzzled
Puzzled means confused or bewildered. *She gave a puzzled frown as she read the strange letter.*

mystified
Mystified is so similar to **puzzled** that you can usually use either. *We were mystified when we couldn't find the lunch we brought.*

nonplussed
Nonplussed means completely confused and **puzzled**. *I can't think sensibly because I am nonplussed by his strange behaviour.*

undecided
Undecided means unsure or not having made up your mind. *I am undecided about which project I will choose.*

ambivalent
Ambivalent can mean uncertain or doubtful, because you can't make up your mind. *I have an ambivalent attitude to playing guitar and I don't know whether I will continue taking lessons.*

> contrasting keywords: **sure**

confusing *adjective*

▶ hard to understand. *I couldn't follow the **confusing** instructions.*

bewildering   **Bewildering** means so confusing that you don't know what to do. *It was hard to find our way out of the bewildering maze.*

perplexing   **Perplexing** means confusing and troubling, especially by being difficult to understand or answer. *This is a perplexing problem.*

mysterious   **Mysterious** means full of mystery or difficult to explain. *No one can explain the mysterious disappearance of the airplane.*

puzzling   **Puzzling** means difficult to explain or find an answer to. *We finally found a solution to the puzzling problem.*

ambiguous   **Ambiguous** means confusing or **puzzling** because it has more than one meaning. *This is an ambiguous sentence: Dimitri told him that he had won the lottery.*

> contrasting keywords: **clear, easy**

contest *noun*

▶ a race, struggle, or other event in which you try to do better than anyone else. *My story won first prize in the writing **contest**.*

competition   **Competition** is so similar to **contest** that you can usually use either. *Both friends entered the poetry competition.*

game   A **game** is a **competition** with set rules. *Let's have a game of checkers.*

match   A **match** is an official **competition**. *Some of the best players in the country are competing in the tennis match.*

race   A **race** is any kind of **competition** that is always a test of speed. *We had a race to the end of the street.*

tournament   A **tournament** is a contest with a number of players. *The golf tournament was postponed on account of the rain.*

continue *verb*

▶ to keep on. *They **continued** to walk in the rain.*

last
: To **last** means to go on or continue. *This lesson will last for half an hour.*

endure
: To **endure** can mean to **last** well. *The appeal of good music endures for years.*

hold on
: To **hold on** means to **last** or continue. *I hope you can hold on until help comes.*

survive
: To **survive** can mean to keep going or remain in existence, especially in the face of some difficulty or change. *The singer's popularity has survived through many music fads.*

persist
: To **persist** can mean to go on and on. *She persisted at the practices and did well at the track meet.*

> similar keywords: **advance, extend, persist**
> contrasting keywords: **stop, end**

continuous *adjective*

▶ going on without stopping. *A **continuous** line of people streamed into the theatre.*

constant
: **Constant** means continuing all the time. *My success is a constant source of pleasure to my family.*

steady
: **Steady** can mean continuous and regular. *Tony made steady progress in learning to play the violin.*

persistent
: **Persistent** means going on and on. *Her persistent efforts paid off when she finally won the trophy.*

endless
: **Endless** can mean seeming to have no end. *The endless ringing of the car alarm was very annoying.*

interminable
: **Interminable** means as if without an end. It is very similar to **endless**. *The long heat wave seemed interminable.*

> similar keywords: **permanent**
> contrasting keywords: **erratic, temporary**

cool *verb*

▶ to make someone or something pleasantly cold or less hot. *The gentle breeze **cooled** us when we sat down after our hot walk.*

fan   To **fan** can mean to cool or refresh someone with, or as if with, a fan. *It was so hot in the room that I fanned my face with a piece of paper.*

air-condition   To **air-condition** can mean to cool air with a machine that keeps the temperature of a room at a comfortable level. *In warm climates, many people air-condition their homes.*

chill   To **chill** means to make something cold. *I chilled the drinks quickly with ice cubes.*

freeze   To **freeze** means to turn something to ice. *We froze water to make ice cubes.*

refrigerate   To **refrigerate** means to make or keep something cold. *Refrigerate the leftover shrimp immediately.*

cooperate *verb*

▶ to work or act together. *The two village councils **cooperated** to build a new library.*

collaborate   To **collaborate** means to work together, especially on a job. *The two authors collaborated in writing the book.*

team up   To **team up** means to work together for a particular reason. This is more suited to everyday language. *The three children teamed up to make a really big sand castle.*

combine   To **combine** means to join or act together. *The two students combined their efforts to finish building the model airplane.*

unite   To **unite** means to join or work together as one. *The whole town united to save the beached whales.*

---

contrasting keywords: **argue, compete**

---

copy   *noun*

▶ something that is made the same as something else. *We need two **copies** of the report for our meeting.*

duplicate
A **duplicate** is something that is exactly the same as something else. *Is this the original key or a duplicate?*

replica
A **replica** is an exact copy. *I made a small replica of the ship.*

model
A **model** can be a small copy. *The teacher has a model of the solar system in her room.*

facsimile
A **facsimile** is an exact copy. *This picture is such a close facsimile that you would think it was the original drawing.*

likeness
A **likeness** is something that is similar to something else, but not exactly the same. *There is a definite likeness among the members of my family, so you can tell we are all related.*

copy   *verb*

▶ to do or make something the same as something else. ***Copy** this chart into your notebook.*

duplicate
To **duplicate** means to make an exact copy of something. *Can you duplicate this key while I wait?*

reproduce
To **reproduce** means to make a copy or strong likeness of something. *The artist reproduced the famous painting.*

photocopy
To **photocopy** means to make an exact copy of a page of writing or pictures on a machine using a special camera. *Nassir photocopied his birth certificate.*

trace
To **trace** means to copy something by following the lines of the original on transparent paper placed over it. *I traced the map of Canada.*

match
To **match** can mean to make something similar to or like something else. *Try to make your drawing match mine.*

similar keywords: **mimic**

correct *verb*

▶ to make something right by removing the mistakes or faults. *I **corrected** my letter carefully before I sent it.*

rectify   To **rectify** means to put something right. *Alex soon rectified the situation.*

remedy   To **remedy** can mean to correct a wrong or an evil. *You have been treated unjustly, but we will soon remedy that.*

revise   To **revise** means to check or correct something in order to make it better. *I decided to revise my story after reading it through.*

amend   To **amend** means to correct or change something for the better. *You need to amend the rules of this game.*

reform   To **reform** means to improve something by correcting and changing the mistakes or bad parts. It is similar to **amend**. *We decided to reform the student council policies.*

> similar keywords: **improve, repair**
> contrasting keywords: **damage, hurt**

council *noun*

▶ the governing body of a town, city, or municipality. *The town **council** approved the plan for the new shopping mall.*

parliament   A **parliament** is a group of people elected to make the laws for a country or province. *Our Member of Parliament flew to Ottawa in September.*

senate   A **senate** is one of the decision-making bodies in the government of a country. *She was honoured to be appointed to the Canadian Senate.*

caucus   A **caucus** is the meeting of the members of parliament who belong to a particular party. *The political party held a caucus to decide on its strategy for the election.*

congress   A **congress** is a meeting of people to discuss ideas of interest to them all. *A congress of health workers was held here last week.*

board   A **board** is a group of people in charge of a business or organization. *The board of the daycare centre is holding a meeting next week.*

count *verb*

▶ to use numbers to find the sum of a collection of things. *She **counted** the apples to see if there would be enough for everyone.*

add up To **add up** means to find the sum of a number of things. *Who can add up these three numbers?*

total To **total** means to find the sum or whole amount of something. *Please total the money to see if I gave you enough.*

tally To **tally** means to count up or calculate something. *Will you tally my bill and tell me how much I owe you?*

number To **number** means to give a number to each of a series of things. *Please number the pages of your story at the top.*

> similar keywords: **calculate, add**

countless *adjective*

▶ too many to count. *I'm surprised that they haven't broken that window, because their baseball has hit the wall around it **countless** times.*

untold Untold can mean more, or almost more, than can be counted or measured. *It was a nation of untold wealth.*

myriad Myriad means of a very great but unknown number. *There are myriad stars in the night sky.*

infinite Infinite can mean **endless** or never seeming to run out. *There are an infinite number of grains of sand on the beach.*

endless Endless means having or seeming to have no end. *There seemed to be an endless number of cookies in the box.*

umpteen Umpteen means having to do with something that is unknown, especially a number that can't be counted. It is more suited to everyday language. *I have told you umpteen times not to put your feet on the table.*

> similar keywords: **numerous**

country *adjective*

▶ coming from or having to do with the land outside the towns and cities. *It's fun visiting our* **country** *friends on their farm.*

rural **Rural** means having to do with the country or with farming. *I prefer a quiet rural road to the crowded city streets.*

agrarian **Agrarian** means having to do with farming. *Do you think agrarian work is healthier than office work?*

pastoral **Pastoral** can mean having to do with farming, particularly the grazing of animals. *This is rich pastoral land.*

rustic **Rustic** means having to do with or living in the country, especially living a quieter and more peaceful life as opposed to a hectic city existence. *I spend my days in rustic pastimes such as milking cows.*

contrasting keywords: **civic**

country *noun*

▶ an area of land separated in some way from other areas. *China and India are two* **countries** *in Asia.*

nation A **nation** is a large group of people living in one country and under one government. *Canada became a nation in 1867.*

Confederation **Confederation** is the name given to the ten provinces of Canada. *Newfoundland was the last province to join Confederation.*

kingdom A **kingdom** is a country ruled over by a king or queen. *When the king died, the young princess became the new ruler of the kingdom.*

realm A **realm** is the same as a **kingdom**. *He ruled his realm wisely and fairly.*

republic A **republic** is a **nation** that has an elected president, not a king or queen. *They elected a new president to be the leader of the republic.*

country, the *noun*

▶ the less-developed land outside the towns and cities. *Many people who live in* **the country** *are farmers.*

countryside   The **countryside** is the rural part of a country, often the scenery of a particular country area. *The countryside was so pretty that we stopped and took some photos.*

land   The **land** means the rural areas outside the city. *Many city dwellers yearn to return to the land.*

bush   The **bush** can mean uncleared forest regions far away from the towns. *We are going to the bush for a hike.*

outdoors   The **outdoors** means the world of nature that lies outside the world of human dwellings. *I became a logger because I wanted to work in the outdoors.*

> contrasting keywords: **city**

courage *noun*

▶ the ability to act calmly when threatened by danger or difficulty. *It took* **courage** *to speak in front of the class for the first time.*

bravery   **Bravery** is so similar to **courage** that you can usually use either. *The mountain climber showed her bravery by going up the cliff first.*

valour   **Valour** is similar to **courage** and **bravery**. It is a rather formal word. *The doctors and nurses were given an award for their valour during the crisis.*

nerve   **Nerve** is the ability to face danger or pressure with a strong mind. *He must have a lot of nerve to dive off the high board.*

spunk   **Spunk** is the ability to face danger or difficulty in a brave, lively way. It is more suited to everyday language. *Even though it started to rain, they showed their spunk and continued their hike.*

course *noun*

▶ the way along which anything moves. *The map showed the **course** the St. Roch took during its historic Arctic voyage.*

path
Path can mean a way from one place to another. *The small boat hurried out of the path of the ship.*

route
A **route** is a regular line of travel. *The bus takes the long route around town.*

track
A **track** is a rough **path** or trail. *The swimming hole is at the end of the track.*

beeline
A **beeline** is a direct line, like the course bees take when returning to the hive. *The children made a beeline for the playground at recess.*

orbit
An **orbit** is the curved **path** or line of flight followed by a planet or satellite around another heavenly body, such as the earth or sun. *The astronomers carefully studied the satellite's orbit around the earth.*

cover *verb*

▶ to lie over or be spread over something. *A fine layer of dust **covered** all the furniture.*

blanket
To **blanket** can mean to cover something with a layer or covering. *Crisp, white snow blanketed the ground.*

envelop
To **envelop** can mean to surround something completely. *The heavy fog soon enveloped the whole town.*

wrap
To **wrap** can mean to surround someone or something, often as if with folds. It is similar to **envelop**. *The night wrapped us in its cloak of darkness.*

wreathe
To **wreathe** can mean to surround or cover something in curving or curling masses. *Mist wreathed the mountains and valley.*

shroud
To **shroud** can mean to cover something completely, causing a feeling of mystery. *Darkness shrouded the old gold mine.*

similar keywords: **enclose**

cower *verb*

▶ to shrink away in fear. *They **cowered** among the trees as the snarling lion came into the clearing.*

quail
To **quail** means to shrink with fear or lose courage when in a difficult or dangerous position. *We quailed at the thought of the lion catching sight of us.*

flinch
To **flinch** means to draw back suddenly from something dangerous or unpleasant. *A twig snapped under my foot, and we all flinched at the sound.*

waver
To **waver** can mean to act uncertainly, sometimes because of fear. *The brave guides did not waver as they watched the lion calmly.*

cringe
To **cringe** means to crouch or bend from fear. *They cringed at the idea of what might happen.*

chicken out
To **chicken out** means to back out or go away because you are scared. This is more suited to everyday language. *We chickened out, though, and went back to the truck.*

create *verb*

▶ to make, using your own ideas or imagination. *Lee **created** a new computer program.*

design
To **design** can mean to invent and then draw up plans for something. *An architect designed our house.*

develop
To **develop** can mean to bring something into being. *The gardener developed a new kind of rose.*

devise
To **devise** means to invest or plan something. *We devised a new system for arranging our books.*

improvise
To **improvise** means to create or compose something on the spot. *Anthony improvised a tune for the song.*

similar keywords: **invent, concoct, compose, make, build**

criminal *noun*

▶ someone who is guilty of a crime. *The police were sure he was the **criminal**, but they could not prove it.*

offender   An **offender** is someone who has broken the law in some way. This is a rather formal word. *Don't vandalize the railway cars—offenders will be prosecuted.*

felon   A **felon** is someone who has been convicted of a serious offence. *The judge sentenced the felon to life imprisonment.*

outlaw   An **outlaw** is someone who has broken the law and is wanted by the police. *There were pictures of outlaws on posters at the police station.*

gangster   A **gangster** is a member of a gang of criminals. *I saw three of the four gangsters get out of the car and go into the bank.*

thug   A **thug** is a robber or murderer. It is more suited to everyday language. *The thugs robbed the bank and attacked the customers.*

> similar keywords: **crook, bandit, prisoner**

crook *noun*

▶ a dishonest person. This is more suited to everyday language. *I hope that **crook** learns to change his behaviour.*

cheat   A **cheat** is a dishonest person who tries to get things by deceit or trickery. *He is a cheat, and I will not play games with him anymore.*

fraud   A **fraud** is someone who is not what he or she claims to be. *She said she was an expert, but she was a fraud.*

swindler   A **swindler** is a person who cheats someone, usually of their money. *He said he would repay me, but he turned out to be a swindler.*

shark   A **shark** can be a person who makes money dishonestly from other people, usually through false or unfair deals. *When you want to borrow large sums of money, be careful of loan sharks.*

> similar keywords: **criminal, bandit**

crooked *adjective*

▶ curved or not straight. *We turned left and right along the **crooked** street.*

bent	**Bent** means curved or made into an angled shape. *There was a bent spoke in the wheel of my bike.*
warped	**Warped** means **bent** out of its usual shape. It is most often used about something straight and flat like timber. *The builder could not use the warped plank.*
buckled	**Buckled** means **bent**, or pushed out of shape. *My bike had a buckled wheel after the accident.*
twisted	**Twisted** means pulled into curves and bends. *I used a piece of twisted wire to hold the chain together.*
distorted	**Distorted** means crooked or pulled out of shape. *Her distorted face showed her extreme pain.*

cross *verb*

▶ to go from one side of something to another. *The bridge **crossed** the river just near its mouth.*

traverse	To **traverse** means to pass across or over something. *The hikers traversed the mountain pass as soon as the mist lifted.*
ford	To **ford** means to cross a river where it is shallow enough to walk or ride across. *They had to wait for the flood waters to go down before they could ford the river.*
bridge	To **bridge** means to make a bridge over something so that it can be crossed. *It was easier for the explorers to bridge the deep, narrow gorge than to travel around it.*
span	To **span** means to extend or stretch across something. *The bridge spanned the river at its narrowest point.*
portage	To **portage** means to carry a canoe, boat, goods, and so on from one stretch of water to another. *On the company trip, we hiked, canoed, and portaged.*

> similar keywords: **extend**

crowd *noun*

▶ a large number of people or things gathered closely together. *Ann pushed her way through the crowd of children.*

throng	**Throng** is so similar to **crowd** that you can usually use either. *A throng of people gathered to watch the parade.*
mob	A **mob** is a large crowd that is sometimes rowdy or violent. *An angry mob gathered outside Parliament Hill.*
flock	A **flock** is a number of animals of the same kind, especially sheep, goats, or birds, feeding or kept together. It can also be used to mean a crowd of people. *A shepherd looks after a flock of sheep.*
herd	**Herd** is similar to **flock**, but is usually used about cattle. *Max drove the herd to a new pasture.*
pack	A **pack** is a group of certain animals living and hunting together. Like **flock** and **herd**, it can also be used to mean a group of people, especially criminals. *A pack of wolves lives in this forest.*

> similar keywords: **group**

cruel *adjective*

▶ likely or liking to cause pain or unhappiness. *The cruel remark made me cry.*

savage	**Savage** can mean cruel or fierce. *The savage dog growled and barked, but couldn't leap over the fence.*
brutal	**Brutal** means fiercely or extremely cruel. *It was a brutal blow when the flood destroyed all our crops.*
barbaric	**Barbaric** means extremely **savage** or cruel. *Everyone condemned the army's barbaric treatment of the poor villagers.*
vicious	**Vicious** means very **savage**, cruel, or harmful. *The vicious dog settled down after obedience lessons.*

> similar keywords: **callous, violent, mean**
> contrasting keywords: **lenient, kind**

cry   *verb*

▶ to shed tears. *We all **cried** when our pet dog died.*

weep
To **weep** is so similar to **cry** that you can usually use either one. *I was so disappointed that I wanted to weep.*

bawl
To **bawl** means to cry loudly. *The child bawled when he fell off his tricycle.*

wail
To **wail** means to give a long sad cry. *The crowd wailed when the home team lost the game.*

sob
To **sob** means to cry, making a gulping noise as you breathe. *The little children were sobbing when their father found them.*

whimper
To **whimper** means to cry weakly. *The puppies whimpered when they were hungry.*

> contrasting keywords: **laugh, smile**

cunning   *adjective*

▶ able or likely to trick someone. *Here's a **cunning** plan to make them think we've gone away.*

crafty
Crafty means cunning or clever in deceiving someone. *The hare was amazed that the crafty tortoise beat him.*

wily
Wily is very similar to **crafty**. *The wily fox escaped the hunters by swimming downstream.*

sly
Sly means cunning in a clever or deceitful way. *His sly answer made us think he was innocent.*

devious
Devious means tricky, usually not in a completely honest way. *Her devious behaviour caused her to lose nearly all her friends.*

artful
Artful means clever and cunning in getting what you want. *The artful speaker convinced us of her theory.*

> similar keywords: **dishonest, shrewd**
> contrasting keywords: **honest**

cut *noun*

▶ an opening in something made with a sharp object. *I have a **cut** on my finger.*

gash	A **gash** is a long, deep cut. *The doctor had to stitch the gash in my leg.*
slit	A **slit** is a long, straight cut or opening. *The nail has torn a slit in my skirt.*
incision	An **incision** is a deep cut, usually made for a particular reason. *The doctor started the operation by making a deep incision.*
wound	A **wound** is a cut in the flesh, made by an injury. *I cleaned the wound on my leg and then put on a bandage.*
notch	A **notch** is a small, sharp cut. *There was a notch on the edge of the table.*

> similar keywords: **break, opening**

cut *verb*

▶ to separate or make something shorter using a sharp instrument. *I **cut** a piece of string.*

snip	To **snip** means to cut something using short, quick strokes. *Dad snipped the roses off the bush.*
trim	To **trim** means to shorten something by cutting it. *The barber trimmed my hair.*
clip	To **clip** means to cut off or shorten something using scissors or shears. *She clipped the hedge.*
mow	To **mow** means to cut something off or down with a scythe or machine. *I mowed the lawn.*
prune	**Prune** means to cut off branches. *We pruned the fruit trees in March.*

> similar keywords: **scratch, tear**

D, d

damage *verb*

▶ to harm, injure, or break a part of something. *Yana **damaged** the car when he backed into the tree.*

mar
To **mar** means to damage or **ruin** something. *The young child marred the book by scribbling on it.*

sabotage
To **sabotage** means to damage something on purpose or in order to cause problems for the owner. *The spy sabotaged the enemy planes.*

vandalize
To **vandalize** means to damage or destroy something deliberately for no good reason. *It is such a waste when people vandalize buildings.*

ruin
To **ruin** means to damage something so badly that you can't use it. *The hailstorm ruined the harvest.*

wreck
To **wreck** is so similar to **ruin** that you can usually use either one. *She wrecked the tape player when she dropped it on the hard floor.*

> similar keywords: **destroy, hurt, spoil, abuse**
> contrasting keywords: **repair, correct**

dangerous *adjective*

▶ likely to cause harm or injury. *Plastic bags are **dangerous** toys for children.*

unsafe
Unsafe is so similar to **dangerous** that you can usually use either. *The diving board is unsafe because it has a crack in it.*

perilous
Perilous means dangerous because you are exposed to harm or injury. *We breathed a sigh of relief when we finished our perilous climb up the steep slope.*

hazardous
Hazardous means dangerous because there is a possibility of harm or injury. *Smoking is hazardous to your health.*

precarious
Precarious means dangerous or not safe. *Lin pulled her brother away from his precarious position at the edge of the cliff.*

> contrasting keywords: **safe**

dare *verb*

▶ to face a risk boldly. *You should never **dare** someone to do something foolishly dangerous.*

brave	To **brave** means to approach something in a fearless way. *We braved the storm and set out for home.*
risk	To **risk** means to take a chance and face possible harm. *Our family risked a lot of money when we opened a new business.*
venture	To **venture** means to **risk** something or to dare to do something. *I ventured an opinion, even though I knew it was an unpopular one.*
confront	To **confront** means to face someone or something bravely. *The small army confronted the enemy troops, knowing it would be a difficult battle.*

dark *adjective*

▶ with little or no light. *The **dark** room filled with light when I opened the window.*

dim	**Dim** means without bright light, but not completely dark. *I could just see her shape moving in the dim passageway.*
shadowy	**Shadowy** means slightly dark or having light and shade. *We walked through the shadowy forest.*
murky	**Murky** means unpleasantly and gloomily dark. *We avoided entering the murky cave.*
obscure	**Obscure** can mean dark and out of the way. *He put his books in an obscure corner of the room.*
pitch-dark	**Pitch-dark** means completely dark. *The night was pitch-dark, and we couldn't see where we were going.*

> similar keywords: **cloudy, black**
> contrasting keywords: **bright**

darken *verb*

▶ to make something have very little or no light. *Thick clouds **darkened** the sky.*

shade   To **shade** means to darken something by shutting out light. *Heavy curtains shaded the room.*

dim   To **dim** means to make something less bright. *Tamara dimmed the lights in the sick child's bedroom.*

obscure   To **obscure** means to make something hard to see because of darkness. *A sudden thunderstorm obscured our view of the mountains.*

eclipse   To **eclipse** can mean to block the light of a heavenly body from the earth, thus causing darkness. *Sometimes the moon eclipses the sun and causes the earth to become dark in the middle of the day.*

fog   To **fog** means to make something blurry or hard to see through. *Mist fogged the windshield of our car.*

dart *verb*

▶ to move suddenly and quickly. *I lost sight of her as she **darted** through the crowd.*

scurry   To **scurry** means to move quickly and lightly. *The rabbit was too fast for us as it scurried around the corner.*

scamper   To **scamper** means to run or hurry away quickly and lightly. *The groundhog scampered across the road and into its burrow.*

dive   To **dive** can mean to move very quickly into something. *I dived into the subway car just before the door closed.*

scramble   To **scramble** means to climb or move quickly and awkwardly. *Our feet slipped as we scrambled over the rocks to escape the huge wave.*

scoot   To **scoot** means to dart or move along very quickly. It is more suited to everyday language. *I scooted down the stairs and along the path to see what came in the mail.*

---

similar keywords: **speed, hurry**
contrasting keywords: **dawdle, walk, trudge**

---

dawdle   *verb*

▶ to waste time by being slow. *You'll never get there if you **dawdle** so much!*

dally	To **dally** means to waste time or be very slow. *Stop dallying and do your work!*
delay	To **delay** means to move or do something slowly. *If you delay, we'll be late again.*
linger	To **linger** means to stay on in a place because you don't want to leave. *We lingered at the monkeys' cage because they made us laugh.*
procrastinate	To **procrastinate** means to put something off until later. *It's better to do your homework on Saturday morning instead of procrastinating all weekend.*
tarry	To **tarry** means to wait or be slow in starting to do something or go somewhere. This is a rather formal word. *We tarried until it was almost too late to catch the train.*

contrasting keywords: **hurry, speed, dart**

daydream   *verb*

▶ to imagine pleasant things in a dreamy way. *I often **daydream** about reaching my goals.*

muse	To **muse** means to think about something so deeply that you become dreamy. *I mused happily on what I would do over the weekend.*
be lost in thought	To **be lost in thought** means to think about something so deeply that you do not pay attention to anything else. *I did not hear what she said because I was lost in thought.*
fantasize	To **fantasize** means to daydream, usually about something that is unrealistic. *We fantasized about winning a million dollars.*
let your thoughts wander	To **let your thoughts wander** means to stop concentrating on a particular thing. *I was supposed to be doing homework, but I let my thoughts wander to more pleasant things.*

similar keywords: **imagine**
contrasting keywords: **concentrate, ponder**

dead   *adjective*

▶ no longer alive or useful. *In the autumn, **dead** leaves fall off deciduous trees.*

lifeless	**Lifeless** can mean no longer having life. *They lifted the lifeless body into the ambulance.*
deceased	**Deceased** means dead. It is usually used to refer to people. *Both my grandparents are deceased.*
departed	**Departed** is very similar to **deceased**. It is a less common word. *My recently departed uncle was a very kind and humorous person.*
late	**Late** can mean having recently died. *The late Ms. Rasheed was well respected in our community.*
extinct	**Extinct** means no longer existing. *The dodo is an extinct bird.*

deceive   *verb*

▶ to trick someone by not telling the truth. *You **deceived** us by saying you'd found the money when you'd really stolen it.*

dupe	To **dupe** means to trick or deceive someone. *She duped them into believing she would pay them for doing the work.*
hoodwink	To **hoodwink** is very similar to **dupe**. It is usually used in less formal language. *They hoodwinked us with promises they knew they couldn't keep.*
mislead	To **mislead** can mean to lead or guide someone wrongly, often on purpose. *You misled us when you said that the paint would match our carpet exactly.*
delude	To **delude** means to trick or **mislead** someone. *He deluded them into thinking he was an honest person.*
take for a ride	To **take for a ride** means to trick or deceive someone. This is more suited to everyday language. *They certainly took you for a ride when they promised to come back with the money they borrowed.*

similar keywords: **trick, cheat, outwit, betray**

decent   *adjective*

▶ acting in a way that is approved by most people. ***Decent** people never beat their pets.*

proper	**Proper** can mean correct in behaviour. *Is it proper for children to sit in a bus while older people stand?*
right	**Right** means fair and good. *It was right for you to refuse to help them cheat during the exam.*
moral	**Moral** means acting according to the rules of what is thought to be right. *Matthew took a moral stand against animal testing.*
respectable	**Respectable** means good or worthy of respect, especially in the sense of being socially acceptable. *They are a respectable family, well known for their volunteer work.*
ethical	**Ethical** means in agreement with the rules for **right** and **proper** conduct. *Our school expects high ethical standards from us.*

> similar keywords: **honest**
> contrasting keywords: **indecent, evil, mean**

decrease   *verb*

▶ to become less. *The time I take to swim the length of the pool **decreases** the more I practise.*

diminish	To **diminish** is so similar to **decrease** that you can usually use either. *The number of dancers diminished as the competition became more fierce.*
fall	To **fall** can mean to become lower in value or amount. *The price of gold fell last year.*
abate	To **abate** means to become less in strength. *At last the storm abated.*
wane	To **wane** can mean to gradually become less, especially in strength of feeling, power, and so on. *Our enthusiasm waned when we realized how long it would take to row across the lake.*

> similar keywords: **shrink, minimize**
> contrasting keywords: **increase, expand**

decrepit *adjective*

▶ broken down or made weak by old age, illness, or hard use. *The **decrepit** house was almost beyond repair.*

infirm **Infirm** means weak in body or health. *He's infirm since the accident, so you'll have to help him.*

timeworn **Timeworn** means worn with age or showing signs of disrepair because of long use. *I got my grandparents' timeworn family photo album out of the drawer and looked at the faded pictures.*

threadbare **Threadbare** can mean worn and thin, usually with age. *My favourite sweater has become threadbare over the years.*

dilapidated **Dilapidated** means old and falling apart. *Be careful walking down the dilapidated staircase.*

crumbling **Crumbling** can mean decaying or disappearing bit by bit. *We looked sadly at the crumbling walls of the house we once lived in.*

> similar keywords: **defective, weak, fragile**
> contrasting keywords: **strong, hardy, powerful**

deed *noun*

▶ something someone does. This is a rather formal word. *Going into the burning house to save the owner was a brave **deed**.*

act An **act** is something someone does. It can often be used instead of **deed**. *It was the act of a hero.*

action An **action** is so similar to **deed** or **act** that you can often choose any of these words. *The newspaper printed a report of her brave action.*

exploit An **exploit** is a notable and daring deed. *They told fascinating tales of their exploits in the jungle.*

move A **move** can mean something you do for a particular reason. *Saving his energy for the end of the race was a clever move.*

> similar keywords: **achievement**

defeat *verb*

▶ to overcome someone in a battle or contest or as if in a battle or contest. *They* ***defeated*** *the other team after a hard-fought basketball game.*

beat To **beat** means to defeat someone, especially in a contest. *The winning team beat us by two runs.*

conquer To **conquer** means to overcome someone or something by force or as if by force. *The new vaccine conquered the deadly disease, polio.*

vanquish To **vanquish** means to defeat someone, especially in battle. It is a more formal word than defeat or conquer. *The Huns vanquished the Roman army.*

thrash To **thrash** can mean to defeat someone completely or thoroughly. *Our soccer team trained very hard and thrashed the other team.*

trounce To **trounce** can mean to **thrash** someone. *We're going to trounce them at volleyball because our team is better.*

> similar keywords: **subdue**

defective *adjective*

▶ having a weakness, mistake, or blemish. *The mechanic replaced the* ***defective*** *car battery with a new one.*

faulty **Faulty** means having weaknesses or mistakes. *A light in the ceiling wasn't working because of faulty wiring.*

unsound **Unsound** means having defects or weaknesses. *The engine was unsound and had to be repaired.*

substandard **Substandard** means below the normal grade or level, or not as good as it should be. *Mom was annoyed because the lawyer's work on the contract was substandard.*

shoddy **Shoddy** means of poor quality or badly made. *The manufacturer has produced shoddy clothing.*

> similar keywords: **inferior**
> contrasting keywords: **perfect**

defence   *noun*

▶ something that keeps you safe from harm or acts as a protection against attack.
*The moat was an important part of the castle's **defence**.*

protection	**Protection** is a form of defence from injury, danger, or annoyance. *We keep a watchdog for protection against burglars.*
security	**Security** is something that keeps you safe. *Staying together when we got lost in the bush was our greatest security.*
safeguard	A **safeguard** is something that helps protect or defend you. *A goalie's mask is a safeguard against a head injury.*
shield	A **shield** can be anything you use to protect yourself from harm. *Indihar held her hands to her eyes as a shield against the sun.*

contrasting keywords: **attack**

defer   *verb*

▶ to put off something until later. *We'll have to **defer** making a decision about buying a new computer until we find out how much money we have.*

delay	To **delay** means to put off something until later, often because of an inconvenient situation. *We can't delay the meeting just because they haven't arrived.*
postpone	To **postpone** means to put off something until a future time. It is very similar to **defer**. *They postponed the game because of rain.*
adjourn	To **adjourn** means to put off something. It is often used about court cases, debates in parliament, and other formal proceedings. *The judge adjourned the trial until the following week.*
suspend	To **suspend** can mean to stop something for a time. *The magistrate suspended the reckless driver's licence for twelve months.*
shelve	To **shelve** can mean to put off considering or thinking about something for a while. *That's such a tricky problem, I'll have to shelve it until I find out more about it.*

defiant *adjective*

▶ boldly going against authority. *The **defiant** child marched out of the room.*

rebellious   Rebellious means openly or actively defiant. *The rebellious citizens refused to pay taxes until the government heard their complaints.*

antagonistic   Antagonistic means disagreeing with and acting against something or someone. *They were antagonistic toward any new ideas.*

recalcitrant   Recalcitrant means resisting authority or control. *The recalcitrant children complained about their parents' household rules.*

dissident   Dissident means disagreeing or differing, especially with a particular political system. *The dissident groups held a rally to protest against the harsh new laws.*

militant   Militant means fighting or ready to fight, especially for a cause. *If the dictator won't resign, the citizens may become militant.*

> similar keywords: **argumentative, disobedient, aggressive, bold**
> contrasting keywords: **submissive**

deliberate *adjective*

▶ carefully considered and done on purpose. *Someone had made a **deliberate** attempt to keep the land in its natural state.*

intentional   Intentional means done with a purpose or reason. *To mislead the other team, they made an intentional mistake.*

purposeful   Purposeful means having a set reason for doing something. *Rose set about her work in a purposeful way and soon finished it.*

conscious   Conscious can mean fully aware of what you are doing. *Amardip made a conscious effort to help others.*

premeditated   Premeditated means planned beforehand. *The judge said it was a premeditated crime and sentenced the accused to life in prison.*

planned   Planned means done according to a plan. *Our planned fishing trip had to be postponed because of bad weather.*

> contrasting keywords: **accidental**

delicious   *adjective*

▶ very pleasant to smell or taste. *That was a **delicious** dinner you cooked.*

luscious   **Luscious** means very pleasant or delicious to taste or smell. *What a luscious peach!*

scrumptious   **Scrumptious** means very tasty or delicious. It is usually used in less formal language than **luscious**. *We had a scrumptious ice cream cone while we were shopping.*

appetizing   **Appetizing** means so delicious that it makes you feel hungry. *The appetizing smell of roast chicken wafted through the house.*

mouth-watering   **Mouth-watering** means looking or smelling so delicious that you want to eat it at once. *I stared at the mouth-watering cakes and pastries in the shop window.*

yummy   **Yummy** has the same meaning as **scrumptious**. It is usually used in less formal language. *We had a yummy snack of fruit and cheese.*

> contrasting keywords: **inedible**

demand   *noun*

▶ an urgent or forceful request or need. *Our **demand** for information must be met.*

claim   A **claim** is a demand placed on someone or something that is expected to be met, even if it is difficult or unfair. *Zonta had an active social life, even though her job made many claims on her time.*

ultimatum   An **ultimatum** is a final statement of terms or conditions that must be accepted. *The ultimatum was that the work must be handed in by Monday or it would not be marked.*

requisition   A **requisition** can be a formal or official request for something you need. *Our school put in a requisition for new computers.*

levy   A **levy** is something, often a fee or tax, demanded from you by an official body. *The council imposed an extra levy on people using the parking lot at night.*

> similar keywords: **order**

demand   *verb*

▶ to ask for something forcefully, as if it's your right. *They **demanded** equality for both men and women.*

order
: To **order** can mean to ask for or request something. *I'm going to order a milkshake.*

insist
: To **insist** means to demand something very strongly. *I insist that you come with me to see the doctor.*

require
: To **require** can mean to demand or **insist** on something. *The committee requires the finished report by this afternoon.*

stipulate
: To **stipulate** can mean to demand something as an essential part of an agreement. *He stipulated that if we ate out, we would have pizza.*

---

similar keywords: **ask**

---

dependant   *noun*

▶ someone who relies on or needs the support of another person. *Children are the **dependants** of their parents.*

protégé
: A **protégé** is someone who is protected or supported by someone else. This is a French word that has been adapted into the English language. *The musician's protégé was a young pianist who had a lot of potential.*

ward
: A **ward** is a young person who has been legally placed under the care or control of a guardian. *She was made a Crown ward because her parents were not able to look after her.*

satellite
: A **satellite** can be something that depends on or is dominated by something else. *The new town will be a satellite of the capital city.*

hanger-on
: A **hanger-on** is someone who stays around or depends on someone whom they admire. *Rock stars have lots of hangers-on who follow them from one performance to another.*

parasite
: A **parasite** can be someone who lives on the money earned by other people without doing anything in return. You use this word to describe someone whose behaviour you don't approve of. *He was such a parasite that he always lived on his parents' money.*

descend *verb*

▶ to go or come down. *The plane has started to* ***descend***.

drop

To **drop** can mean to descend very suddenly. *The plane dropped when it entered an air pocket.*

sink

To **sink** can mean to descend gradually to a lower level. *The sun is sinking in the west.*

coast

To **coast** means to go down a hill without using any power. *The hill was so steep that they could coast all the way to the bottom.*

plunge

To **plunge** means to fall quickly into a liquid or a steep place. *The diver plunged into the pool.*

climb down

To **climb down** means to go down, usually using both hands and feet. *The painter climbed down the ladder when the job was finished.*

> similar keywords: **fall**
> contrasting keywords: **climb**

describe *verb*

▶ to give a picture of something or someone by using words. *Laurie* ***described*** *the painting in a detailed way.*

represent

To **represent** can mean to describe or state something in words. *Does his novel really represent the life of an Albertan rancher?*

portray

To **portray** can mean to describe or explain something in words. *Her story portrayed the excitement she felt when she won the prize.*

depict

To **depict** can mean to describe or show something in words. *My grandmother tells me stories depicting life when she was a girl.*

illustrate

To **illustrate** can mean to make something clear by giving examples to help people picture or imagine it. *Atepa illustrated his talk on bravery with stories about First Nations warriors.*

express

To **express** means to put thoughts into words. *Try to express your ideas clearly so we all know what you mean.*

> similar keywords: **explain, tell**

destroy *verb*

▶ to wreck or damage something completely. *The tornado **destroyed** many houses.*

demolish	To **demolish** means to knock down or destroy something. *The workers demolished the old house.*
wipe out	To **wipe out** means to defeat someone or destroy something completely. *The new vaccine wiped out that terrible disease.*
annihilate	To **annihilate** means to destroy or defeat something completely. *The vaccine annihilated the virus that caused the disease.*
exterminate	To **exterminate** means to destroy something in order to get rid of it. *We exterminated the cockroaches in the kitchen.*
eradicate	To **eradicate** means to root out or destroy something. *We want to eradicate crime in large cities.*

> similar keywords: **damage**
> contrasting keywords: **make, create**

deteriorate *verb*

▶ to become less good in condition or quality. *The house **deteriorated** while it was not lived in.*

worsen	To **worsen** means to become not even as good as it was before. *The condition of the house worsened after being empty for many years.*
degenerate	To **degenerate** means to become bad or worse than before. *Your health will degenerate if you don't get enough food, sleep, and exercise.*
fall apart	To **fall apart** means to break down or crumble. *Rust caused the old car to fall apart.*
decline	To **decline** can mean to deteriorate or become worse. *His health has declined since he came here.*
waste away	To **waste away** can mean to lose your strength or health, usually from an illness or disease. *Their bodies wasted away during the famine.*

> similar keywords: **rot**
> contrasting keywords: **recover, improve**

die *verb*

▶ to stop living. *My pet dog **died** last week.*

expire	To **expire** can mean to die or give out your last breath. It is a rather formal word. *She had been ill for weeks before she expired.*
breathe your last	To **breathe your last** means to die. It is similar to **expire**. *The king breathed his last at half past two today.*
perish	To **perish** means to die in an unnatural way, sometimes from violence or lack of food. *The explorers perished in the desert.*
pass away	To **pass away** means to die naturally. People usually use it because they think it is less upsetting than the word **die**. *I am calling to tell you that your uncle passed away peacefully in his sleep.*

> contrasting keywords: **live**

difficult *adjective*

▶ not easy to do or understand. *This **difficult** puzzle has taken me hours to complete.*

hard	**Hard** can mean difficult to do or explain. *It was a hard exam.*
complex	**Complex** means difficult to understand or explain because it is complicated. *The problem is so complex that several of us will try to work it out together.*
tough	**Tough** can mean very difficult to deal with. *Aaron has a tough job to do.*
arduous	**Arduous** means needing a lot of hard work. *Reiko was tired after the arduous canoe trip.*
demanding	**Demanding** means needing a lot of time, hard work, and energy. *Nursing is a demanding profession.*

> similar keywords: **complicated**
> contrasting keywords: **easy**

dig *verb*

▶ to break up, turn over, or remove something, such as earth, using your hands or an implement. *My dog often **digs** up the soil in the garden to bury her bones.*

scoop	To **scoop** means to take something up or out, as with a spoon or your cupped hands. *Tracy scooped sand out to make a moat around her sand castle.*
hollow out	To **hollow out** means to make a hole in something by digging out the inside. *We hollowed out the pumpkin to make a jack-o'-lantern.*
excavate	To **excavate** means to make a hole or tunnel by digging something. *The archaeologists excavated the ancient village, hoping to find pottery and other artifacts.*
gouge	To **gouge** means to dig out something roughly or crudely. *Heavy machines gouged earth and rocks out of the side of the mountain.*
mine	To **mine** means to dig something, such as earth, to get minerals, precious stones, and so on. *At Dawson, in the Yukon, they mine the earth for gold.*

dirty *adjective*

▶ covered with dirt or stains. *We had **dirty** hands by the time we had finished cleaning our bikes.*

grubby	**Grubby** means dirty, messy, or untidy. *Wash your grubby hands before you eat!*
grimy	**Grimy** means very dirty, especially on the surface. *Underneath the grimy surface, the walls were painted bright blue.*
grungy	**Grungy** means dirty or unattractive. This is more suited to everyday language. *The grungy carpet was dusty and full of holes.*
filthy	**Filthy** means very dirty or unpleasant. *The beach was filthy where the sewage emptied onto it.*
polluted	**Polluted** means made dangerously dirty or unfit to use. *The water was too polluted to swim in.*

> similar keywords: **untidy**
> contrasting keywords: **clean**

dirty   *verb*

▶ to make something unclean, or cover it with marks and stains. *Who **dirtied** the clean floor?*

soil
To **soil** means to make something dirty or stained. *We soiled the new carpets with our muddy feet.*

smear
To **smear** means to rub or spread dirty marks over something. *I didn't mean to smear paint on the walls.*

smudge
To **smudge** means to mark something with dirty streaks. *Jack smudged the white door with his greasy hands.*

spot
To **spot** can mean to mark or stain something. *You have spotted your jacket with ink.*

> similar keywords: **spoil**
> contrasting keywords: **clean**

disagree   *verb*

▶ to fail to agree about something. *The two reviews of the book **disagree** over the meaning of the ending.*

differ
To **differ** means to disagree or have different ideas or feelings about something. *The brothers differed over which was the quickest way home.*

dissent
To **dissent** means to disagree or have a different opinion. *Ten members of the club agreed to change the rules, and two members dissented.*

dispute
To **dispute** means to argue about or debate, sometimes angrily. *They hotly disputed the need to work longer hours.*

bicker
To **bicker** means to squabble or argue about little things. *The children have been bickering all day.*

wrangle
To **wrangle** means to argue or quarrel noisily. *The children wrangled over who would be captain.*

> similar keywords: **argue**
> contrasting keywords: **agree**

disappear   *verb*

▶ to go out of sight. *Petra **disappeared** around the corner.*

vanish To **vanish** means to disappear quickly. *With a wave of the magician's wand, the rabbit vanished before our very eyes.*

dematerialize To **dematerialize** means to disappear without a trace. *In the movie, the hero dematerialized to avoid his enemies.*

fade To **fade** means to disappear slowly. *Her smile faded as her ice cream fell to the ground.*

dissolve To **dissolve** means to disappear gradually. *The ghostly shape dissolved into the mist.*

evaporate To **evaporate** means to **fade** gradually and is similar to **dissolve**. *His attention evaporated during the boring movie.*

> contrasting keywords: **appear**

disappointment   *noun*

▶ failure to have your hopes satisfied. *It was a great **disappointment** to me when it rained on my birthday.*

letdown A **letdown** is so similar to **disappointment** that you can usually choose either word. *After all our hopes, it was a letdown when we couldn't go to the zoo.*

anticlimax An **anticlimax** is an event that is much less interesting or important than expected. *We were excited about the party, but it was so dull that it proved an anticlimax.*

blow A **blow** is a sudden shock or disappointment. *It was a blow when the clouds drifted away and the farmers didn't get the rain they needed.*

setback A **setback** is something that stops or slows down your progress. *The drought was a setback that would be hard to overcome.*

frustration A **frustration** is something that stops you from getting or achieving what you want. *After many frustrations, they closed down their new business.*

disapprove of *verb*

▶ to have a bad opinion of something or someone. *I **disapprove of** people who throw litter on the sidewalk.*

frown on	To **frown on** means to disapprove or have a bad opinion of something. *My friends frowned on my plan for a picnic in the rain.*
take a dim view of	To **take a dim view of** means to have a bad or unfavourable opinion of something. *The neighbours take a dim view of your dog's barking.*
take exception to	To **take exception to** means to object to something strongly. *I take exception to what you just called me.*
look down on	To **look down on** means to have no respect for or to regard someone with scorn. *You shouldn't look down on him just because his ideas are different from yours.*

> similar keywords: **fault**
> contrasting keywords: **approve, praise**

disaster *noun*

▶ any sudden terrible happening that causes great suffering and damage. *The earthquake was one of the worst **disasters** we've had in years.*

catastrophe	A **catastrophe** is a sudden disaster. *The explosion was a catastrophe that we had not expected.*
calamity	A **calamity** is a terrible happening. *The newspaper said that building a highway through the national park would be a calamity.*
tragedy	A **tragedy** is any very sad or dreadful happening. *It was a tragedy when the family died in the accident.*
debacle	A **debacle** is a dreadful disaster. *Their business venture proved to be a debacle in which they lost all their money.*
fiasco	A **fiasco** is the kind of disaster in which everything seems to go wrong. *The show proved to be an utter fiasco. The star forgot his lines, the curtain got stuck, and very few people showed up.*

> similar keywords: **misfortune**

discard   *verb*

▶ to throw away or reject something. *We **discarded** all the unnecessary papers.*

shed	To **shed** means to cast off something. *The snake shed its skin by rubbing against a rock.*
jettison	To **jettison** means to throw something off because you don't want it or need it. *The pilot jettisoned most of the spare fuel before making the crash landing.*
scrap	To **scrap** means to throw something away because it is useless. *We scrapped any broken toys that couldn't be mended.*
dump	To **dump** can mean to throw something down or get rid of it. *They dumped the garbage into a hole in the ground.*
ditch	To **ditch** means to get rid of something. It is more suited to everyday language. *You should ditch that old bicycle before you hurt yourself.*

> contrasting keywords: **use, keep, store**

discourage   *verb*

▶ to try to prevent someone from doing something. *You should **discourage** children from playing with matches.*

dissuade	To **dissuade** means to persuade someone not to do something. *We dissuaded her from leaving home.*
deter	To **deter** means to prevent someone from doing something. *The fact that you don't want me to learn to hang-glide won't deter me.*
talk out of	To **talk out of** means to argue with someone in order to stop the person from doing something. It is more suited to everyday language. *My parents talked me out of spending all my money.*
advise against	To **advise against** means to suggest strongly that someone shouldn't do something. *The sign advised us against taking a truck on the dirt road.*

> contrasting keywords: **encourage, persuade**

disgust *verb*

▶ to cause you to dislike something totally. *Cruelty **disgusts** me.*

horrify   To **horrify** means to cause someone to feel great disgust and fear. *Hearing about that accident on the news horrified me.*

offend   To **offend** can mean to displease someone or to affect someone disagreeably. *Your rudeness offends me.*

sicken   To **sicken** means to make you feel sick. *Violence on TV sickens me.*

nauseate   To **nauseate** means to make you feel you want to vomit. *I was nauseated by the long roller-coaster ride.*

revolt   To **revolt** can mean to make you feel sick and disgusted. *When I saw what the vandals had done, it revolted me.*

> contrasting keywords: **please**

dishonest *adjective*

▶ likely to lie, cheat, or steal. *The **dishonest** employees lost their jobs.*

deceitful   **Deceitful** means likely to lie or try to trick or mislead people. *His deceitful plans were discovered, and he was asked to resign from the club.*

shifty   **Shifty** means **deceitful** and looking as if you have something to hide. *She was questioned about the crime because of her shifty behaviour.*

hypocritical **Hypocritical** means pretending to be what you are not. *I don't want a hypocritical friend who talks about me behind my back.*

crooked   **Crooked** can mean dishonest or likely to swindle people. It is more suited to everyday language. *The crooked banker was arrested for fraud.*

shady   **Shady** can mean of doubtful honesty or lawfulness. It is more suited to everyday language. *He has been mixed up in some shady deals.*

> similar keywords: **cunning, illegal, indecent**
> contrasting keywords: **honest, frank**

dislike *noun*

▶ a feeling of not liking, or a distaste for, someone or something. *I could not hide my **dislike** of them.*

hatred
Hatred means very strong dislike. *They looked at their enemies with hatred.*

aversion
Aversion means strong dislike, usually with a feeling of disgust. *I have an aversion to large insects.*

antipathy
Antipathy means a longstanding dislike or feeling of disgust. It is very similar to **aversion**. *He has an antipathy to spiders.*

hostility
Hostility means unfriendliness or the treating of someone as an enemy. *There was hostility between the two opposing teams.*

animosity
Animosity means a feeling of dislike or unfriendliness. It is very similar to **hostility**. *The party was spoiled by the animosity between the two families.*

> similar keywords: **anger**

disobedient *adjective*

▶ refusing to obey. *The **disobedient** children were told to apologize.*

unruly
Unruly means disobedient and uncontrollable. *More police had to be called to control the unruly crowd.*

willful
Willful means stubborn and determined to have your own way. *The willful children wouldn't pay any attention to the warning.*

delinquent
Delinquent means having broken the law. *The delinquent teenagers were helped by a guidance counsellor.*

headstrong
Headstrong means hard to control and determined to have your own way. *My headstrong cousin is always telling us what to do.*

insubordinate
Insubordinate means not obeying your superiors. *The sailor was sent to the brig for insubordinate behaviour.*

> similar keywords: **naughty, defiant**
> contrasting keywords: **obedient, well-behaved, submissive**

disobey *verb*

▶ to refuse to obey someone or something. *They were punished when they **disobeyed** the instructions.*

defy
To **defy** means to challenge or to refuse boldly to obey someone. *The soldiers defied their orders and refused to attack the innocent civilians.*

flout
To **flout** means to show no respect for authority by being disobedient. *They flouted the referee's instructions by cheating throughout the game.*

violate
To **violate** means to break a rule or law deliberately. *The United Nations censured the nation that violated the international treaty.*

infringe
To **infringe** can mean to disobey rules or laws. *You'll put yourself in danger if you infringe the rules of the swimming pool.*

> similar keywords: **rebel**
> contrasting keywords: **obey**

disrupt *verb*

▶ to interrupt something and throw it into disorder. *The sound of the fire engine going by **disrupted** the singing lesson and we had to start again.*

disturb
To **disturb** means to unsettle someone or something. *The unexpected news disturbed us and we didn't know what to do next.*

upset
To **upset** can mean to put something into disorder or confusion. *The rain upset our plans for a picnic.*

interfere with
To **interfere with** means to get in the way of something. *His long visit interfered with our plans to repaint the apartment.*

mess up
To **mess up** can mean to make something confused. *The train strike messed up our holiday plans.*

mix up
To **mix up** means to get something confused. *Douglas and Judith mixed up the time they were to meet, and they missed the bus.*

> similar keywords: **interrupt**
> contrasting keywords: **arrange**

dissatisfied *adjective*

▶ annoyed because your wishes or needs haven't been fulfilled. *From her **dissatisfied** look I could tell that her holiday had gone badly.*

displeased **Displeased** means annoyed or offended. It is very similar to **dissatisfied**. *I am displeased with your behaviour.*

discontented **Discontented** means not feeling happy, pleased, or satisfied. *He is discontented with his allowance.*

disgruntled **Disgruntled** means annoyed and sulky. *She is disgruntled because she has to leave for work so early.*

disappointed **Disappointed** means unhappy because your hopes or expectations were not satisfied. *We were disappointed that our team did not make the playoffs.*

querulous **Querulous** means dissatisfied and complaining. *"Why is this train always late?" he asked in a querulous voice.*

> similar keywords: **angry, annoyed**
> contrasting keywords: **satisfied, glad**

distant *adjective*

▶ far off. *The space probe travelled from earth to a **distant** planet.*

faraway **Faraway** is so similar to **distant** that you can usually use either. *I dream of visiting faraway lands.*

remote **Remote** means very far off and out of the way. *We visited a remote village in the mountains.*

outlying **Outlying** means far from the centre of things. *The cows had wandered into an outlying field.*

isolated **Isolated** means separated or apart from other people. *Their isolated cabin was a two-day hike from the nearest town.*

> contrasting keywords: **near**

distinguished *adjective*

▶ having an air or quality that impresses people. *They gathered to honour her career as a **distinguished** politician.*

noble
: **Noble** means of a high quality that you admire. *Giving up a comfortable life to help the sick and the poor was a noble gesture.*

refined
: **Refined** can mean without any coarseness or roughness. *Our dinner guest had very refined manners.*

classy
: **Classy** can mean **refined** or elegant. It is more suited to everyday language. *We enjoyed going to the classy restaurant, even though it was expensive.*

aristocratic
: **Aristocratic** can mean proud or distinguished. *The black stallion looked aristocratic.*

similar keywords: **superior, grand, famous**
contrasting keywords: **ordinary, inferior**

distribute *verb*

▶ to give something out. *The teacher **distributed** the books to the class.*

issue
: To **issue** means to give or send out. *Each worker was issued a shovel and work gloves.*

allot
: To **allot** means to hand out and distribute in shares or parts. *Their parents' wills allot equal shares of the farm to the two children.*

dispense
: To **dispense** means to deal something out. *The courts attempt to dispense justice.*

allocate
: To **allocate** means to set something apart for a special purpose. *The children allocated some of their money to buy a chess game.*

ration
: To **ration** means to give out the fixed amount of something that is allowed to one person or group. *During the emergency, the authorities rationed food because it was in short supply.*

similar keywords: **share**

double *adjective*

▶ having two parts. *Only half of the **double** door was open.*

dual	**Dual** means having to do with two or having two parts. *That book has a dual purpose: to teach you and to entertain you.*
two-piece	**Two-piece** means having two parts that go together. This is usually used about clothing. *Her two-piece suit had a jacket and skirt.*
duplicate	**Duplicate** can mean double or having two parts that are similar or go together. *The twins wanted to look different, and refused to wear duplicate sweaters.*
two-fold	**Two-fold** means having two parts. This is usually used about reasons, purposes, and so on. *My decision to go to the concert was two-fold: first, my brother was performing in it; second, it featured one of my favourite singers.*

contrasting keywords: **single**

doubt *verb*

▶ to be uncertain or unsure. *I have reason to **doubt** their excuse for being late.*

distrust	To **distrust** means to doubt or have no confidence in someone or something. *I distrust weather forecasts because they are often wrong.*
disbelieve	To **disbelieve** means to **distrust** or have no faith in something or someone. *I disbelieve anything you tell me.*
question	To **question** can mean to doubt something and want to know more about it before you believe it. *I question the truth of that story.*
query	To **query** means to ask questions about or to doubt something. *You should query the manager if you think the price is too high.*
take with a grain of salt	To **take with a grain of salt** means to doubt all or part of something that someone tells you. This is more suited to everyday language. *I take the things they say with a grain of salt.*

contrasting keywords: **believe**

drab *adjective*

▶ looking dull and uninteresting. *Those **drab** curtains spoil the look of the room.*

sombre **Sombre** can mean dull in colour. *His sombre clothes gave no sign of his happiness.*

dingy **Dingy** means not bright or new-looking. *The abandoned house had a room filled with dingy furniture.*

gloomy **Gloomy** can mean dull and dark. *They were locked in the gloomy dungeon.*

mousy **Mousy** can mean having a grey-brown or drab colour. It is often used with regard to the colour of hair. *A red hat would brighten up your mousy hair.*

> similar keywords: **dull**
> contrasting keywords: **bright, gaudy, colourful, spectacular**

dreamy *adjective*

▶ vague or lost in a dream; thinking about something else. *Yoshio had a **dreamy** look on his face as he thought about his holidays.*

preoccupied **Preoccupied** means completely taken up with your own thoughts. *I was so preoccupied I didn't hear a word you said.*

bemused **Bemused** means lost in thought. *While our teacher read the story, my friend had a bemused look on her face.*

half-asleep **Half-asleep** means vague and **preoccupied**. *Because you were half-asleep, you missed the joke.*

inattentive **Inattentive** means not paying attention to what is going on around you. *You were certainly inattentive when I gave out the instructions.*

absent-minded **Absent-minded** means being so vague that you forget things. *What an absent-minded person you are to put on different coloured socks!*

> contrasting keywords: **alert, inquisitive**

dreary *adjective*

▶ dull or gloomy. *It was a **dreary** afternoon with no sunshine.*

dismal   **Dismal** means causing a feeling of sadness or gloom. *The weather has been dismal for days.*

depressing   **Depressing** means causing a feeling of great sadness or lack of energy. *It is depressing when it rains all day.*

cheerless   **Cheerless** means without brightness or warmth. *They spent the cheerless day trying to get warm.*

bleak   **Bleak** means cold and harsh. *It was a bleak winter's day.*

grey   **Grey** can mean dark and overcast. *Don't hurry to get up, because it's a grey morning outside.*

> similar keywords: **cloudy, dull**
> contrasting keywords: **fine, bright**

drink *verb*

▶ to take liquid through your mouth. *I **drink** eight glasses of water a day.*

sip   To **sip** means to drink something in small mouthfuls. *The children sipped their lemonade to make it last longer.*

imbibe   To **imbibe** means to drink. It is a rather formal word. *The premier's guests imbibed excellent wine with their dinner.*

quaff   To **quaff** means to drink thirstily and with enjoyment. It is a rather formal word. *We quaffed our fruit juice with gusto after winning the wheelchair basketball game.*

guzzle   To **guzzle** means to drink or eat greedily and noisily. *They were so thirsty that they guzzled the juice straight from the bottle.*

swallow   To **swallow** means to take liquid or food into your stomach through your throat. *The child swallowed the medicine quickly and then had a jellybean.*

d r i p *verb*

▶ to let drops fall. *The tap **drips** all the time.*

dribble	To **dribble** means to flow in small drops. *Soapy water dribbled from the wet cloth.*
leak	To **leak** means to let liquid or gas escape out of a small hole or crack. *Air slowly leaked from the front tire of my bike.*
trickle	To **trickle** means to flow in a very small or slow stream. *Milk trickled out of the hole in the carton.*
seep	To **seep** means to **leak** slowly or flow through something gradually. *Water seeped through the crack in the ceiling.*
ooze	To **ooze** means to flow slowly, as if through small openings. It is very similar to **seep**. *Mud oozed through our toes as we walked barefoot in the wet yard.*

> similar keywords: **flow**

d r o p *verb*

▶ to allow something to fall or go to a lower position. *Careful! Don't **drop** the bowl of soup on the floor.*

lower	To **lower** means to put something in a lower position. *We lowered a rope over the side of the cliff.*
let down	To **let down** is similar to **lower**, and you can often use either. *I had to let down the hem of my pants because I had grown taller.*
dip	To **dip** means to **lower** something briefly before lifting it again. *Dip the ladle into the soup.*
sink	To **sink** means to make something go down to the bottom. *The boat filled with water and sank.*
submerge	To **submerge** means to put something under the surface of the water. *The captain submerged the submarine before attacking.*

> similar keywords: **fall, sag**
> contrasting keywords: **lift**

dry *adjective*

▶ not wet or damp. *The crops were very **dry**, so we watered them.*

arid   **Arid** means dry and hot. *We carried plenty of water in our car when we drove across the arid badlands.*

parched   **Parched** means having become very dry. *The flowers died in the parched garden while we were away on holidays.*

dehydrated   **Dehydrated** means having lost all its water or moisture, or having had it removed. *The dehydrated sailors were in desperate need of clean drinking water. Raisins are dehydrated grapes.*

withered   **Withered** means dried up and shrunk or decayed. *The grapes had a withered look after the heat wave caused them to dry up.*

> contrasting keywords: **wet**

dull *adjective*

▶ not bright, shiny, or clear. *The top of this table was very **dull** before I polished it.*

flat   **Flat** can mean not shiny. It is mainly used about paint. *We used flat paint so that the room wouldn't look too bright.*

matte   **Matte** means having a dull surface. *I prefer matte snapshots to glossy ones.*

lacklustre   **Lacklustre** means without brightness or lustre. *The cat's lacklustre coat was a sign of its poor health.*

lifeless   **Lifeless** can mean dull and lacking vitality. *If you used brighter colours, your picture wouldn't look so lifeless.*

tarnished   **Tarnished** means without brightness or a shine. It is usually used to describe metallic surfaces. *The tarnished silver pot gleamed after I polished it.*

> similar keywords: **drab, dreary**
> contrasting keywords: **shiny, bright**

E, e

earth *noun*

▶ the softer part of the dry land, rather than rocks or sand. *The children made mud pies out of **earth** and water.*

clay
Clay is a dense earth that holds water and is used in making pottery and bricks. *I need to wet the clay before I make a vase.*

soil
Soil is earth, especially the kind in which you can grow plants. *The soil in our garden needs plenty of fertilizer.*

ground
Ground is earth or **soil**. *We dug a hole in the ground for the posts.*

dirt
Dirt is loose earth or **soil**. You usually think of dirt as being very dry. *The strong wind blew dirt in my drink.*

loam
Loam is a loose **soil** made up of **clay**, sand, and natural fertilizers. *Good crops grow in the loam at the edges of the river.*

easy *adjective*

▶ not difficult or hard to do or understand. *Swimming is **easy** once you have been taught.*

simple
Simple means easy to understand, do, or use. *It was a simple explanation.*

uncomplicated
Uncomplicated means not hard to use or understand. *She gave me uncomplicated instructions.*

effortless
Effortless means done easily or without much effort. *Making that giant leap seemed effortless to the talented dancer.*

foolproof
Foolproof means designed not to fail and to be easy to use even if you are inexperienced. *There is a foolproof recipe for making cookies in this cookbook.*

painless
Painless means causing no pain and requiring little effort. *I thought it would be hard to get in shape, but the exercises were painless.*

---

contrasting keywords: **difficult, complicated, confusing**

---

eat *verb*

▶ to take food into your mouth and swallow it. ***Eat*** *your ice cream cone before you get into the car.*

taste
: To **taste** means to eat just a small amount of something to see if you like it. *Karl tasted the soup to see if it needed more pepper.*

consume
: To **consume** means to eat or drink something. It is a more formal word. *The chocolates were so delicious, we consumed every one.*

devour
: To **devour** means to eat something very hungrily. *I was so hungry that I devoured nearly a whole loaf of bread.*

gobble
: To **gobble** means to eat something very quickly without chewing it well. *We gobbled our dinner so we could go out to play.*

gulp
: To **gulp** means to swallow something quickly, often a large amount at a time. *The large dog gulped his meat down quickly.*

---
similar keywords: **chew, drink**
---

edge *noun*

▶ a line, side, or boundary where two parts or surfaces meet. *The **edge** of the cardboard box was dented.*

border
: A **border** is the edge or side of anything. *I painted a design around the border of my drawing.*

margin
: A **margin** is the edge of something. *I wrote my comments in the margin of the page.*

rim
: A **rim** is an outer edge, especially of a circular or round object. *The rim of the wheel is bent.*

brim
: A **brim** is the top edge of a hollow container or a hat. *Varuna filled the glass to the brim.*

brink
: A **brink** is the edge of a steep or dangerous place. *They put up a fence on the brink of the cliff.*

---
similar keywords: **outskirts, outside**
contrasting keywords: **inside, centre**
---

educated *adjective*

▶ having had a good education. *My grandfather was a very smart person although he was poorly **educated**.*

learned
Learned means having a lot of knowledge from study. *My aunt is a learned woman who knows a lot about science.*

knowledgeable
Knowledgeable means having knowledge or understanding, especially about a particular subject. *Sam is very knowledgeable about the wildflowers of British Columbia.*

well-informed
Well-informed means having a wide general knowledge or knowledge of a variety of subjects. *My uncle helped me with my current affairs project, as he is a very well-informed person.*

literate
Literate means able to read and write. It also means educated. *Nema is highly literate, and can speak several languages.*

> similar keywords: **clever, shrewd**
> contrasting keywords: **ignorant**

elastic *adjective*

▶ able to be pulled out or extended and then go back to its original shape again. *The **elastic** sides of the boots help them go on easily and fit snugly around my ankles.*

stretchy
Stretchy means elastic or able to be extended. *This stretchy belt will fit almost anyone.*

springy
Springy means elastic or able to regain its shape after being stretched. *We jumped up and down on the springy mattress.*

bouncy
Bouncy means able to spring back into shape, or rebound as a ball does. *The trampoline has a very bouncy surface.*

rubbery
Rubbery means like rubber, and often tough. *We complained to the server about the rubbery chicken dinner.*

resilient
Resilient means able to resume its original shape. *Rubber is such a resilient material that many small children's toys are made of it.*

> similar keywords: **flexible**

emphasize *verb*

▶ to point out the importance of something. *The group leader **emphasized** the need for everyone to respect each other's ideas.*

stress	To **stress** is so similar to **emphasize** that you can usually use either. *The group leader stressed the need for cooperation.*
accentuate	To **accentuate** means to make something seem important or noticeable. *Ari accentuated the main parts of his speech by pointing his finger in the air.*
highlight	To **highlight** means to make something stand out. It is very similar to **accentuate**. *I highlighted my lines in the script by underlining them.*
labour	To **labour** can mean to develop something in detail, usually because you consider it very important. *The camp counsellor really laboured the point about how educational the trip would be.*

contrasting keywords: **minimize**

empty *adjective*

▶ containing nothing. *The children were disappointed when they discovered that the large box was **empty**.*

void	**Void** means completely empty or without contents. This is a very formal word. *In outer space, there are huge distances that are void of stars or planets.*
blank	**Blank** means without any writing, images, or marks. *I couldn't think what to write, so I left that page blank on the test.*
hollow	**Hollow** means having a space inside. *We thought the candy had a liquid centre, but it was hollow.*
vacant	**Vacant** can mean not occupied by anyone. *The house has been vacant since the last owner moved out.*
deserted	**Deserted** means left empty or alone. *The town was deserted for many years after the earthquake.*

contrasting keywords: **full**

enclose *verb*

▶ to shut in or close in on all sides. *A high fence **enclosed** the kindergarten playground.*

box in	To **box in** means to confine or enclose someone, as if in a box. *The crowd of people boxed me in and I couldn't get out.*
coop up	To **coop up** means to keep someone or something in a small place. *The rabbits were all cooped up in one cage.*
contain	To **contain** can mean to hold or include something in an area. *The people piled up sandbags to contain the flood waters.*
surround	To **surround** means to go around something or someone completely. *The police surrounded the criminals so that they could not escape.*
encircle	To **encircle** means to enclose something by making a circle around it. *A deep moat encircled the castle.*

similar keywords: **cover, confine, isolate**

encourage *verb*

▶ to spur on or cheer someone on. *We **encouraged** the team with shouts and banner waving.*

urge	To **urge** means to push or drive someone or something on. *I urged my brother to try again.*
inspire	To **inspire** means to have an encouraging effect and influence on someone. *We were inspired by her bravery.*
motivate	To **motivate** means to give someone a strong reason for doing something. *My high class marks motivated me to study hard for the exams.*
set an example to	To **set an example to** means to encourage someone by being a good model to follow. *Their physical fitness set an example to everyone in the camp.*

similar keywords: **persuade, further**
contrasting keywords: **discourage**

end   *noun*

▶ the last or final point of something. *I fell asleep before the **end** of the movie.*

finish
: **Finish** is so similar to **end** that you can usually use either. *Judy ran the marathon race and was third at the finish.*

conclusion
: The **conclusion** is the point at which something comes to an end. *At the conclusion of the concert the curtain fell.*

close
: **Close** is similar to **end** or **conclusion**, and you can often use any of these words. *We all shook hands at the close of the volleyball championship.*

finale
: A **finale** is the special last part of a performance that comes just before the end. *The band saved its latest hit for the finale of the concert.*

termination
: **Termination** means the bringing of something to an end. *The termination of their friendship was a great disappointment to them.*

> contrasting keywords: **start**

end   *verb*

▶ to come to the finishing point. *The storm **ended** almost as suddenly as it had begun.*

terminate
: To **terminate** can mean to end or finish. It is usually used in more formal language. *They terminated the meeting with the club pledge.*

stop
: To **stop** means to finish or to come to a halt. *We stopped when the whistle blew.*

cease
: To **cease** is very similar to **stop**. It may be used in more formal language. *The court order gave the company a final warning to cease polluting the river.*

expire
: To **expire** can mean to come to an end. *Please lend me 25¢, because the time limit on the parking meter has expired.*

> similar keywords: **stop, finish, cancel**
> contrasting keywords: **start, continue, persist**

endanger *verb*

▶ to put someone or something in danger. *They **endangered** their lives by going fishing during the electrical storm.*

jeopardize
: To **jeopardize** means to put something in danger, or to chance its loss or harm. *Don't jeopardize all your good work by being careless now!*

expose
: To **expose** can mean to leave something open to danger or harm. *The football team exposed the quarterback to attack when they made that daring play.*

threaten
: To **threaten** can mean to be likely to cause damage or harm to something or someone. *The drought threatened our crops.*

put at risk
: To **put at risk** means to put something in a position or situation where it may be damaged or harmed. *Smoking definitely puts your health at risk.*

contrasting keywords: **protect, save**

endure *verb*

▶ to bear something patiently or without making a fuss, usually for a long time. *The Inuit hunters **endured** harsh conditions to bring home food for their people.*

put up with
: To **put up with** means to endure something that you don't like or that is hard to do. It is more suited to everyday language. *I put up with their bad behaviour as long as I could before saying something.*

tolerate
: To **tolerate** can mean to endure or **put up with** something. *I tolerated their loud music because they hadn't had a noisy party for a long time.*

abide
: To **abide** means to **tolerate** or **put up with** something. It is usually used with the word "not." *I simply cannot abide your bad manners.*

stick out
: To **stick out** can mean to endure or **tolerate** something, even though you may be tempted not to. *If we can only stick out the bad weather for the next few days, I'm sure our holiday won't be ruined.*

suffer
: To **suffer** can mean to endure or **put up with** something that may hurt you very much. *She suffered their insults with quiet dignity.*

enemy   *noun*

▶ someone who hates or wishes to harm someone else. *They were good people and had* no **enemies**.

foe
Foe is a rather old-fashioned word for an **enemy**. *The soldiers went into battle against their foes.*

antagonist
An **antagonist** is an enemy or someone you are striving against, often in an unfriendly way. *The antagonists fought to the bitter end, each one wanting to win the trophy.*

adversary
An **adversary** is someone you compete against or fight with. *The ninjas' adversaries in the movie were much larger in number than they were.*

opponent
An **opponent** is someone who is on the opposite side to you in a contest or argument. *Her opponent fought hard to win the last point in the tennis match.*

rival
A **rival** is someone who is aiming at the same thing as another person, or who tries to equal or outdo someone else. *Teresa is my main rival for the championship.*

contrasting keywords: **friend**

---

energetic   *adjective*

▶ strong and active. *Puppies are very* **energetic**.

vigorous
Vigorous means strong, energetic, and full of life. *We were hot after our vigorous workout.*

dynamic
Dynamic means energetic and forceful. *The coach of the hockey team was a dynamic person.*

animated
Animated can mean lively. *The birthday party was quite animated, with lots of talking and laughing.*

spirited
Spirited means showing lively courage. *The spirited horse wouldn't let anyone ride it.*

similar keywords: **busy, lively**
contrasting keywords: **lazy, lethargic, tired, weak**

enlarge *verb*

▶ to make something bigger. *I am going to **enlarge** this photo and frame it.*

expand
To **expand** can mean to make something bigger or wider in scope. *She expanded her knowledge by reading lots of books.*

augment
To **augment** means to increase the amount of something by adding to it. *We augmented our allowance by doing jobs for our neighbours.*

amplify
To **amplify** can mean to enlarge something or make it greater. It is usually used about sound. *Her drums were amplified for the rock concert.*

boost
To **boost** means to raise something or make it bigger or stronger. *My win in the first heat of the race boosted my confidence.*

> similar keywords: **add, increase, extend**
> contrasting keywords: **shrink, decrease**

entertainer *noun*

▶ someone who sings, plays for, or amuses people in a public place, usually for payment. *Aaron earns his living as an **entertainer** in clubs.*

performer
A **performer** is someone who performs any skill or displays an ability in front of an audience. *You will have to be a good performer to be picked for the musical.*

jester
A **jester** was a clown who entertained royalty in medieval courts. *"Ask my jester to come and sing to us," shouted the king.*

comedian
A **comedian** is a professional entertainer who tells jokes or does other things that make you laugh. *The comedian was so popular that she got her own TV show.*

actor
An **actor** is someone who performs in plays, films, on TV, or in other entertainments. *The actor signed a contract for a part in a new musical comedy on Broadway.*

player
A **player** is a rather old-fashioned word for **actor**. It is also used for someone who plays a musical instrument or performs in sports. *The villagers were excited when they heard about the visiting band of strolling players.*

enthusiastic *adjective*

▶ having a lively interest in something. *They are **enthusiastic** about their new job.*

keen
Keen means full of enthusiasm. *Jason has a keen interest in music and is learning to play the guitar.*

eager
Eager means really wanting to do something. *Aida is eager to help us build the cabin.*

anxious
Anxious can mean sincerely and earnestly **eager**. *They were anxious to make a good impression on the guests.*

avid
Avid means wanting to do something as often as possible. *Leonor is an avid baseball fan.*

willing
Willing means agreeing happily to do something. *Peter was a willing helper.*

> contrasting keywords: **apathetic, unwilling**

equal *adjective*

▶ being of the same number, value, or other quality as something or someone else. *Everyone's share is **equal**.*

equivalent
Equivalent means of equal or matching value or rank. *An admiral in the navy is the equivalent rank to a general in the army.*

identical
Identical means being exactly the same as something or someone else. *The twins were identical, and I found it hard to tell them apart.*

even
Even can mean equal. *The teams' scores remained even at the end of regulation time.*

symmetrical
Symmetrical means having the parts arranged so that they balance each other exactly. *The pattern on the wallpaper is symmetrical.*

uniform
Uniform means having the same appearance. *The packages were of uniform size.*

> similar keywords: **similar**
> contrasting keywords: **uneven, unlike**

err *verb*

▶ to make an error or be incorrect. *I know this answer isn't right, but I can't see where I have **erred**.*

miscalculate	To **miscalculate** means to make a mistake in working out the amount of something. *I thought I bought enough flour for the cake, but I miscalculated.*
blunder	To **blunder** means to make a foolish mistake because of carelessness or ignorance. *I blundered when I served my vegetarian friend beef for lunch.*
make a slip	To **make a slip** means to make a mistake. *We don't want to make a slip at the last moment.*
mistake	To **mistake** means to err, or understand something wrongly. *I have mistaken you for someone else.*

escapee *noun*

▶ someone who has broken out of prison. *The newspaper said that the **escapee** might be dangerous.*

fugitive	A **fugitive** is someone who is running away, usually from the police. *The fugitive hid in the old shed so that she wouldn't be sent back to jail.*
absconder	An **absconder** is someone who runs away secretly, usually to avoid the law. This is a rather formal word. *The police caught the absconder with a briefcase full of money.*
runaway	A **runaway** is someone who has escaped or run away, often a child who has left home. *The runaways wouldn't tell where they lived.*
truant	A **truant** is someone who stays away from school without permission. *They suspected that the child in the park was a truant.*
refugee	A **refugee** is someone who escapes to another country for safety, often during war. *The refugees crossed the border and then travelled by sea to their new country.*

contrasting keywords: **prisoner**

evil *adjective*

▶ breaking the laws of right or moral behaviour. *Many people have tried to understand why some people do **evil** things.*

wicked

Wicked means evil and causing great harm. *In the children's storybook, the wicked sorcerer cast a spell on the prince and princess.*

sinful

Sinful means **wicked**, and often refers to the breaking of religious laws. *They were told to give up their sinful habits and to live happy and healthy lives.*

villainous

Villainous can mean very **wicked**. *The villainous robber threatened the passengers until they gave him their wallets and jewellery.*

heinous

Heinous means extremely wicked and hateful. *Kidnapping is a heinous crime.*

> similar keywords: **indecent, dishonest, illegal**
> contrasting keywords: **decent**

examine *verb*

▶ to inspect or look at someone or something carefully. *The doctor **examined** me to make sure I was not hurt in the accident.*

analyze

To **analyze** means to examine something in detail in order to find out or show its meaning or importance. *The jury members analyzed all the facts before they came to a decision.*

study

To **study** means to examine or look at something closely. *We studied the computer brochures before making our purchase.*

assess

To **assess** means to work out the value of something by examining it in detail. *The mechanic assessed the amount of damage to the car.*

vet

To **vet** means to examine or check carefully. *The human resources manager vets all the people who apply for a job.*

review

To **review** can mean to examine something, especially in a formal or official way. *The major reviewed the troops to see that all was in order.*

> similar keywords: **investigate, test, inspect**

example *noun*

▶ one of several things, or a part of something, that shows what the whole thing is like. *Sikander gave us an **example** of what he wanted us to do.*

sample	A **sample** is a small part or piece of anything that is meant to show what the whole is like. *I have seen a sample of her artwork and will be very happy to sell her paintings in my gallery.*
model	A **model** can be an example used for copying or comparing. *The teacher handed out a model of a well-written book report.*
specimen	A **specimen** is a sample, a person, or a thing regarded as typical of a larger amount or of a whole group. *The nurse took a specimen of my blood for tests.*
guide	A **guide** can be anything that shows you the way to do something. *The gardening book served as a reliable guide when we planted the vegetables.*
pattern	A **pattern** can be a **model** that shows how something can be made. *I bought some material and a paper pattern to make a new dress.*

excellent *adjective*

▶ remarkably good or of the highest quality. *Your schoolwork is **excellent**.*

outstanding	**Outstanding** means so good that it stands out from all others. *Katherine is an outstanding hockey player.*
fantastic	**Fantastic** means extremely good or wonderful. *We saw a fantastic movie last week.*
terrific	**Terrific** means very good or excellent. *The team spirit before the game was terrific.*
sensational	**Sensational** can mean extraordinarily good. It is more suited to everyday language. *We found some sensational bargains at the garage sale.*
exceptional	**Exceptional** means of unusually high quality or ability. *Only exceptional people are made members of the Order of Canada.*

> similar keywords: **good, great, perfect, superior, wonderful, best**
> contrasting keywords: **bad, ordinary**

excess *noun*

▶ an extreme amount. *We had an **excess** of food at the party, and ate leftovers for a week.*

surplus
: A **surplus** is an amount that is more than is needed or used. *We stored the surplus grain in a warehouse, in case we need it next year.*

glut
: A **glut** is a very big **surplus**. *There was such a glut of coffee beans on the market that they were very cheap.*

oversupply
: An **oversupply** is too large an amount of something that has been supplied to you. *The team received an oversupply of hockey sweaters.*

backlog
: A **backlog** is a piling up of things that need to be done. *I have a backlog of letters to answer.*

overabundance
: An **overabundance** is an excessive amount of something. *The weary parents felt the twins had an overabundance of energy.*

> contrasting keywords: **lack**

exchange *verb*

▶ to give one thing in return for another. *I think I'll take this shirt back to the store and **exchange** it for a smaller one.*

swap
: To **swap** means to exchange. They are so similar you can usually choose either word. *I swapped my duplicate baseball card for one of my friend's cards.*

replace
: To **replace** means to put one thing or person in the place of another. *I have to replace the cup I broke with a new one.*

substitute
: To **substitute** means to put something in the place of something else. *The coach substituted another player for the injured forward.*

stand in for
: To **stand in for** means to act in place of someone. *I will stand in for you while you have lunch.*

transpose
: To **transpose** means to make two or more things change places. *If you transpose the letters in the word "on" you get "no."*

excited   *adjective*

▶ having the strong feelings you get when you are looking forward to something or enjoying something very much. *The children were **excited** about going to the beach.*

thrilled   **Thrilled** means very excited. *Carmen was thrilled to see you.*

exhilarated **Exhilarated** means filled with energy and excitement. *They felt exhilarated after the ride on the roller coaster.*

restless   **Restless** means unable to remain quiet and still. *Everyone in the class was restless because it was almost time for the play to begin.*

delirious   **Delirious** can mean highly excited. *Marc was practically delirious when he won the race.*

frenzied   **Frenzied** means wildly or furiously excited. *The dog began a frenzied barking when it saw its owner.*

> similar keywords: **glad, joyful**
> contrasting keywords: **calm, bored**

exciting   *adjective*

▶ arousing feelings of eagerness or interest. *This book is so **exciting** that I can't put it down.*

exhilarating **Exhilarating** means filling you with energy and excitement. *I love the exhilarating feeling of zooming across the water in a speedboat.*

stimulating   **Stimulating** means stirring up interest and enthusiasm for something. *That stimulating story about skating made me feel like going to the arena right away.*

rousing   **Rousing** means stirring into action and interest. *The speaker made many rousing remarks at the start of the environmental conference.*

thrilling   **Thrilling** means causing a tingling feeling of strong excitement. *I couldn't get to sleep after that thrilling movie.*

breathtaking **Breathtaking** means causing excitement and awe. *We had a breathtaking view of the mountains from the cable car.*

> contrasting keywords: **boring**

exclude   *verb*

▶ to shut or keep something or someone out. *Your name was accidentally* **excluded** *from the list of candidates.*

leave out | To **leave out** means to exclude or fail to include someone or something. *Don't leave me out when you make up the list of volunteers for the clean-up crew.*

drop | To **drop** can mean to exclude someone from a group. *The manager dropped them from the team after they missed several practices.*

skip | To **skip** means to pass over something without reading or noticing it. *He often skips sentences when he's reading out loud.*

delete | To **delete** means to take out or wipe out something written. *I suggest you delete that comma from your sentence.*

> similar keywords: **ban, isolate, prevent**
> contrasting keywords: **include**

expand   *verb*

▶ to express something in greater detail so as to make it longer, usually by adding more words. *Bik* **expanded** *her short story into a novel.*

develop | To **develop** can mean to expand or enlarge upon the detail of something. *Paul is trying to develop his ideas about noncompetitive games before he gives his talk to the class.*

amplify | To **amplify** can mean to expand something by adding more details. *Amplify your suggestion so that I can understand what you mean.*

embroider | To **embroider** can mean to improve or make a story more interesting with untruthful additions. *My friends embroidered the tale so much that I could hardly believe what they said.*

pad | To **pad** can mean to fill out a speech or piece of writing with unnecessary words or information. *You padded your news report with too many unimportant details.*

> similar keywords: **enlarge, increase**
> contrasting keywords: **shorten, decrease**

expect *verb*

▶ to think that something is likely to come or happen. *I **expect** the storm will arrive in the next hour.*

anticipate
To **anticipate** can mean to expect something will come to pass. *We anticipate the release of the new CD tomorrow.*

foresee
To **foresee** means to expect or see something in advance. *We have planned well, and I can foresee success.*

count on
To **count on** means to depend upon or expect something. *Our teammates are counting on us to be on time.*

bargain for
To **bargain for** means to expect or be prepared for something. *We didn't bargain for the crowd at the picnic ground.*

look forward to
To **look forward to** means to expect something with pleasure. *We are looking forward to your visit.*

expel *verb*

▶ to drive or force out or away. *The student was finally **expelled** because of violent behaviour during recess.*

eject
To **eject** means to dismiss or expel. *If you break the rules, you'll be ejected from the club.*

evict
To **evict** means to turn someone out of a place or remove them. *The tenants were evicted when they refused to pay the rent.*

banish
To **banish** means to send someone away as a punishment. *The rebels were banished from the kingdom.*

exile
To **exile** means to **banish** someone from their country. *The Acadians were exiled from their homeland.*

throw out
To **throw out** is an informal way of saying **expel**. *The usher finally threw out the rude, noisy moviegoers.*

> similar keywords: **isolate**

expensive *adjective*

▶ costing a lot of money. *The CD player they wanted was too **expensive**, so they chose one with fewer features.*

exorbitant	**Exorbitant** means being far more in amount than you think is reasonable. *Their prices are really exorbitant so we don't shop there.*
pricey	**Pricey** means costing more money than you think is necessary. *That is a pricey hotel.*
dear	**Dear** means costing too much money. *Those jeans are too dear and I'm not going to buy them.*
costly	**Costly** means expensive or costing a great deal, usually because it is very precious or fine. *Emeralds are beautiful but costly.*

> contrasting keywords: **cheap**

experienced *adjective*

▶ skillful as a result of having done something many times. *The **experienced** sailboarder gave some useful tips to the beginner.*

professional	**Professional** means following an activity to earn a living from it. *Mr. Lee is a professional golfer.*
qualified	**Qualified** means having passed examinations or other requirements to enable you to do a job. *He is a qualified nurse.*
practised	**Practised** means being skillful at something because you have done it a lot. It is similar to **experienced**. *Neelam is a practised photographer who has had many exhibits.*
veteran	**Veteran** means having had many years of experience in doing something. *Tina is a veteran bush pilot.*

> similar keywords: **competent**
> contrasting keywords: **incompetent, inexperienced**

expert *noun*

▶ someone who has a lot of skill or knowledge about something. *Marie is a skating* **expert**.

authority   An **authority** is someone who is a reliable source of information about something. *Antonio is an authority on snakes.*

consultant   A **consultant** is an expert who charges you for advice. *The engineering firm called in a consultant to help plan the new bridge.*

specialist   A **specialist** is someone who has concentrated on a special area of study or work. *The heart specialist explained the operation to her patient.*

ace   An **ace** is an expert who is usually quite famous. *Billy Bishop, the pilot, was an ace of World War I.*

prodigy   A **prodigy** is someone, usually a child, who has an extraordinary talent for something. *Mozart was a musical prodigy.*

similar keywords: **star**

explain *verb*

▶ to make something clear, plain, or easy to understand. *Can you* **explain** *what that word means?*

clarify   To **clarify** can mean to make an idea or explanation clear or able to be understood. *Can you clarify your answer?*

spell out   To **spell out** can mean to explain something in a very simple way to make sure that nothing has been missed. *Mike is only five, so you had better spell out the rules of the game.*

illustrate   To **illustrate** can mean to explain something by giving examples of it. *Zaira used a simple comparison to illustrate her theory.*

interpret   To **interpret** can mean to explain the meaning of something. *I seldom know what that group's songs are about, but my friend helps me interpret them.*

similar keywords: **describe, tell**
contrasting keywords: **confuse, puzzle**

extend *verb*

▶ to continue or be drawn out over some distance. *The mountain range* **extends** *the entire length of the island.*

reach	To **reach** means to extend over a distance. *The fence reaches from the cottage to the beach.*
spread	To **spread** means to extend or stretch out, especially over an area. *The flood waters spread over the entire farmland area.*
stretch	To **stretch** means to extend for a long distance. *The prairies stretched all the way to the horizon.*
run	To **run** can mean to extend or continue. *The expressway runs between the two cities.*
traverse	To **traverse** means to extend across or over something. *The railway bridge traverses the river.*

similar keywords: **continue, cross, persist, advance**

extra *adjective*

▶ more than usual or necessary. *There is always* **extra** *work to do in the garden when we come back from vacation.*

additional	**Additional** is so similar to **extra** that you can usually use either. *Marie has additional money because her salary was raised.*
spare	**Spare** can mean extra, or ready as a replacement. *The spare tire was in the trunk of the car.*
superfluous	**Superfluous** means more than is needed. *There was a superfluous number of players on the field.*
excessive	**Excessive** means more than usual or proper. *The excessive snowfall this week caused the roof to sag.*
redundant	**Redundant** means more than is necessary. *The factory manager can't hire new workers because they would be redundant.*

contrasting keywords: **scant, necessary, insufficient**

F, f

fail *verb*

▶ to be unsuccessful or fall short in something. *He **failed** his math test because he could answer only a couple of questions.*

fall through	To **fall through** means to be unsuccessful or to fail. *Their plan fell through because they hadn't prepared well enough.*
collapse	To **collapse** means to fail suddenly. *The plans for the peace talks collapsed when one of the leaders said that she would not attend.*
fizzle out	To **fizzle out** means to fail after a good start. *The idea fizzled out even though everyone was enthusiastic at first.*
flunk	To **flunk** means to fail in schoolwork. It is more suited to everyday language. *You could flunk the exam if you don't study.*
flop	To **flop** can mean to fail. This is more suited to everyday language. *The play flopped as a result of some terrible reviews.*

contrasting keywords: **succeed, thrive, accomplish**

failure *noun*

▶ something or someone that doesn't succeed. *The artist felt that his exhibition was a **failure** because only a few people came to see it.*

disaster	A **disaster** can mean a total failure. *The school play was a complete disaster because nearly all the actors forgot their lines.*
fiasco	A **fiasco** is an embarrassing or ridiculous failure. *The party was a fiasco because only half the guests turned up.*
flop	A **flop** is something that is a failure. This is more suited to everyday language. *The critics said the play would be a flop because the acting wasn't very good.*
loser	A **loser** is someone or something that lacks the ability to succeed. *You can tell that the skinny horse is a real loser.*

contrasting keywords: **achievement**

fair *adjective*

▶ treating everyone equally and not showing favouritism. *The judge's decision was a* ***fair*** *one.*

impartial　　**Impartial** means not taking one side against the other. *The judge was impartial.*

just　　**Just** means fair or rightly judged. *Most people agreed that her decision was a just one.*

right　　**Right** means fair and good. *Rajan was right not to judge you too harshly.*

objective　　**Objective** means being fair and not allowing your own opinions to influence you. *You need an objective mind to make good decisions.*

> similar keywords: **neutral**
> contrasting keywords: **unfair**

faithful *adjective*

▶ always staying true to someone, or to what you believe in. *I will be **faithful** to you until I die.*

loyal　　**Loyal** means faithful and true. *Martin stayed loyal to the same political party for 30 years.*

devoted　　**Devoted** means loving and **loyal**. *He is my devoted friend.*

trustworthy　　**Trustworthy** means deserving trust or confidence by showing that you are faithful. *They were our trustworthy supporters during the conflict.*

constant　　**Constant** can mean unceasingly faithful. *Their constant love kept their marriage happy for 50 years.*

trusty　　**Trusty** means faithful and able to be trusted. *My dog has been my trusty friend for 15 years.*

> similar keywords: **reliable, steadfast**
> contrasting keywords: **unfaithful, fickle**

fake   *adjective*

▶ made or done in such a way as to trick other people. *We were all fooled by the fake jewels.*

phony	**Phony** means not real or genuine. It is more suited to everyday language. *The phony $20 bills were not accepted by the bank.*
false	**False** can be so similar to **phony** that you can usually use either. *He wore a false nose to the costume party.*
imitation	**Imitation** means designed to resemble a genuine object. *The imitation whipped cream tastes like the real thing.*
counterfeit	**Counterfeit** means made to look exactly like something else in order to deceive people. It is usually used to describe something that is illegal. *Not even the police could identify the counterfeit money at first.*
bogus	**Bogus** means **counterfeit** or not real. It is more suited to everyday language. *She was caught when she tried to use the bogus passport.*

> contrasting keywords: **genuine, actual**

fall   *verb*

▶ to come down suddenly from a higher to a lower position because of loss of balance or support. *The ripe apples fell from the tree during the high winds.*

slip	To **slip** means to lose your footing and fall. *Be careful not to slip on the icy sidewalk.*
topple	To **topple** means to fall forward because of lack of balance. *The tightrope walker accidentally toppled into the safety net.*
trip	To **trip** means to fall over, or nearly fall, because you struck your foot against something. *I tripped over that wire.*
stumble	To **stumble** means to fall, or nearly fall, when walking or running. It is very similar to **trip**. *The horse stumbled on the uneven ground.*
plunge	To **plunge** means to fall quickly into a liquid or steep place. *Alma plunged into the cold lake.*

> similar keywords: **descend, drop**

family *noun*

▶ a parent or parents and their children. *The whole family went on a picnic.*

relatives   **Relatives** are people who belong to your wider, or extended, family, such as uncles, aunts, cousins, and grandparents. *All our relatives came to celebrate our parents' wedding anniversary.*

kin   **Kin** means all your relatives. This word is not used as often as **relatives** or **relations**. *Her mother's kin are Jamaican.*

relations   **Relations** are your **kin** or **relatives**. These words are all so similar you can usually choose any one of them. *Most of Joshua's relations live in Israel.*

flesh and blood   **Flesh and blood** means someone's children or other close **relatives**. This is often used by people who are feeling very emotional about the person they are talking about. *I didn't think my own flesh and blood would do such a thing.*

famous *adjective*

▶ widely known. *The famous pianist played a concert in our town.*

renowned   **Renowned** means very widely known and well thought of. *The renowned scientist has just won another award.*

celebrated   **Celebrated** means so famous that you are publicly recognized and praised. *The celebrated author was surprised and pleased when we gave a dinner in her honour.*

noted   **Noted** means famous or honoured for a particular achievement. *Terry Fox was noted for his courage and determination.*

notable   **Notable** means important or worthy of being noticed. *Norman Jewison is a notable filmmaker who has had a lot of success.*

notorious   **Notorious** means famous or well-known for something bad. *The hockey player was notorious for always getting penalties.*

> similar keywords: **important, distinguished**
> contrasting keywords: **insignificant**

fashion   *noun*

▶ a custom or way of doing things. *Platform shoes were in **fashion** during the 1970s.*

style   A **style** is a fashion. You can usually use either word. *The new store carries many styles of clothing.*

vogue   A **vogue** is a fashion at a particular time. *I want to buy shoes that are in vogue to replace the ones I've worn out.*

fad   A **fad** is something that is popular for a short time. *Mini-skirts are a fad that comes and goes.*

craze   A **craze** is very similar to a **fad**. You can usually choose either word. *Where I live, the latest craze is wearing Australian miners' boots.*

trend   A **trend** is a tendency or movement that leads to a fashion. *There is a trend toward making your own clothes these days.*

fast   *adjective*

▶ able to move at a great pace. *Elena is a very **fast** wheelchair racer.*

quick   **Quick** means fast or without any delay. *The rabbit was so quick it got away before we could catch it.*

rapid   **Rapid** means very fast or **quick**. *The subway in our city provides rapid transit.*

speedy   **Speedy** is so similar to **rapid** that you can usually use either word. *Even though Salim's work was speedy, he didn't make one mistake.*

swift   **Swift** means able to move very quickly and smoothly. *With one swift dive, the bird grabbed my sandwich in its beak and flew off again.*

express   **Express** means very fast, without stopping or delaying. *She took the express train because she had no time to spare.*

contrasting keywords: **slow**

fat *adjective*

▶ weighing more than average. *The vet said that the dog was too **fat** and should get more exercise.*

plump	**Plump** means rather fat and well-rounded. *The new puppies were plump and cuddly.*
chubby	**Chubby** means short and fat. *Chubby babies often become tall and slender in their teens.*
overweight	**Overweight** means fat, but it is less likely to be taken as an insult. *His clothes were tight, so he knew he was a bit overweight.*
stout	**Stout** means rather **overweight** and often looking thick and heavy. *Sir Winston Churchill was a stout man with a big, booming voice.*
obese	**Obese** means extremely fat. *Most people who are obese try to lose some weight.*

similar keywords: **stocky, heavy, big**
contrasting keywords: **thin, slight**

fatal *adjective*

▶ causing death. *The cat suffered **fatal** injuries when it fell from the apartment balcony.*

deadly	**Deadly** means likely to cause death. *A rattlesnake's bite can be deadly.*
lethal	**Lethal** is so similar to **deadly** that you can usually use either. *Some household cleaners can be lethal if children swallow them.*
malignant	**Malignant** can mean very harmful or tending to produce death, as a disease does. *My dog, Sandy, died from a malignant tumour.*
terminal	**Terminal** can mean causing or happening at the end of your life. *The vet told us that Sandy had a terminal illness and had only a few months to live.*

fate   *noun*

▶ a fixed and inescapable plan for the whole of your life, supposedly designed by some unknown power. *The psychic said that we met because of **fate**.*

destiny	**Destiny** is something that had to happen, especially related to the events in someone's life. *It was Nelson Mandela's destiny to be a great leader.*
providence	**Providence** is the care and protection of a divine being, nature, or some unknown power. *It must have been by providence that the children survived overnight in the bush without warm clothing.*
luck	**Luck** is something, either good or bad, that happens to a person without any apparent reason. *As luck would have it, the bus came just as it started to rain heavily.*
fortune	**Fortune** is so similar to **luck** that you can usually use either. *It was by good fortune that a doctor was close by when I broke my leg.*
chance	**Chance** can be fate or an accidental or unforeseen happening. *If by chance we meet again, I will ask how your career plans worked out.*

fault   *verb*

▶ to find an error or mistake in something. *They couldn't **fault** his wonderful singing.*

criticize	To **criticize** means to find fault with something or someone. *Please don't criticize my table manners in front of my friends.*
condemn	To **condemn** means to express strong disapproval of something or someone. *The team captain condemned the violence during the hockey game.*
damn	To **damn** can mean to declare something to be bad, wrong, or illegal. *The destructive activities of the vandals were damned by everyone in our town.*
pick apart	To **pick apart** means to **criticize** something, especially in small details. *They picked apart my work and pointed out every little thing that was wrong with it.*

> similar keywords: **scold, disapprove of, accuse**
> contrasting keywords: **approve, praise**

fear   *verb*

▶ to feel concern or worry for something. *I always **fear** for your safety while you are rock climbing.*

tremble To **tremble** can mean to feel so afraid that you can't help shaking. *The dog trembled when it heard the thunder.*

shudder To **shudder** can mean to feel so worried and afraid that you suddenly start to shake. *The children shuddered at the thought of walking past the spooky old house.*

lose your nerve To **lose your nerve** means to be afraid to do what you set out to do. *The diver lost his nerve when he looked down at the pool far below.*

panic To **panic** means to feel sudden great terror, sometimes without obvious reason. *The horses panicked when the fire spread to the fence.*

dread To **dread** means to fear something greatly. *They dreaded the thought of performing before the huge audience.*

> similar keywords: **worry**

fearful   *adjective*

▶ feeling or showing fear. *When I first sang in front of an audience, I was **fearful** of hitting a wrong note.*

timid **Timid** can mean easily frightened. *The timid kitten hid underneath the furniture.*

cowardly **Cowardly** means lacking courage in a way that disgraces you. *The cowardly lion in* The Wizard of Oz *showed that he was really brave after all.*

spineless **Spineless** can mean having no strength of character or courage. *It is foolish to call someone spineless who is simply cautious.*

fainthearted **Fainthearted** means lacking courage or being easily shocked. *This horror movie is not for the fainthearted.*

> similar keywords: **frightened, nervous**
> contrasting keywords: **brave, calm**

feeling *noun*

▶ a particular physical experience or mental state experienced through one of your senses, such as touch or hearing. *There was a **feeling** of excitement in the schoolyard as spring approached.*

sensation A **sensation** is a particular way you feel because of the working of one or more of your senses. *Wading in a cool stream during a hot summer day is a very pleasant sensation.*

awareness An **awareness** is a feeling or knowledge coming to you through your senses. *As Halima watched the waves beat against the rocks, she felt an awareness of the power of the ocean.*

perception **Perception** is **awareness** or the gaining of knowledge through your senses. *Arthur's perception of a movement in the bushes told him that a moose was nearby.*

impression An **impression** can be a vague feeling or indication of something. *I had the impression that the whole class was enchanted by my story.*

sense A **sense** can be any physical or mental feeling. *A sense of joy came over us as we heard the news on the radio.*

female *noun*

▶ a woman or a girl. This is a formal word that is sometimes used in discussions about medicine and biology. *"**Females** tend to live longer than males," said the professor to her students.*

woman A **woman** is a mature or adult female. *The two women had been business partners for many years.*

girl A **girl** is a female who has not reached adulthood. *All of those girls are in grade two.*

young woman A **young woman** is a female who is almost an adult, or a **girl** who behaves in a mature way. *The mayor called Keiko a brave young woman for her role in last week's rescue.*

lady **Lady** is another term for a **woman**. It is used mainly on formal occasions. *Good morning, ladies and gentlemen.*

similar keywords: **male**

fickle *adjective*

▶ likely to change your mind or behaviour. *They are such **fickle** people, I never know whether they are going to show up or not.*

changeable **Changeable** means likely to change or behave differently from one occasion to another. *He's so changeable that one day he'll smile at you and the next day he'll ignore you.*

flighty **Flighty** means often changing your mind or feelings. *I'm so flighty today I can't make a decision.*

capricious **Capricious** means likely to change your mind without any apparent good reason. *You are so capricious I can never be sure if you're serious or joking.*

mercurial **Mercurial** means rapidly changing in mood. *Tim has a mercurial nature. He can be happy one moment, then suddenly become very sad.*

temperamental **Temperamental** means moody or **changeable** in your behaviour. *We had to wait while the temperamental star decided what to wear.*

> similar keywords: **unfaithful**
> contrasting keywords: **reliable, faithful**

fidget *verb*

▶ to move about restlessly and not be able to keep still. *I **fidgeted** nervously as I waited for my turn.*

squirm To **squirm** means to move around uncomfortably or uneasily. *The performer squirmed with embarrassment when the audience laughed at the mistake.*

wriggle To **wriggle** means to move or twist about because you are feeling uneasy. *The children wriggled in their chairs until they heard their names called.*

writhe To **writhe** means to twist the body as if in pain or embarrassment. *The listeners writhed at the constant shouting of the speaker.*

twitch To **twitch** can mean to move in a jerky manner. *The children twitched in their seats during the movie's romantic scenes.*

fight *noun*

▶ a violent struggle or contest. *Robin's arm was bruised in the **fight**.*

brawl
A **brawl** is a noisy struggle or fight. *What was meant to be just a confrontation, quickly developed into a brawl.*

fray
A **fray** is a noisy fight or quarrel. *By the time the cowpokes joined the fray, the whole place was in an uproar.*

battle
A **battle** is a large-scale or serious fight. *A battle was fought between the two armies.*

combat
A **combat** is a fight or struggle. *Soldiers are trained for combat.*

skirmish
A **skirmish** is a small **battle**. *The armies met, but it was only a skirmish.*

---

similar keywords: **conflict, argument**

---

fight *verb*

▶ to take part in a violent contest. *The children **fought** over who owned the ball.*

struggle
To **struggle** means to fight with an enemy, usually without weapons. *The owner struggled with the thief.*

grapple
To **grapple** means to **struggle** or fight with someone while gripping the person firmly. *The angry cowpokes grappled with each other.*

tussle
To **tussle** means to fight roughly or with vigour. *The children tussled on the grass.*

scuffle
To **scuffle** means to **struggle** or fight in a confused way. *A few players began to scuffle until the team captain broke it up.*

come to blows
To **come to blows** means to start fighting with someone. *They almost came to blows over the referee's decision.*

find *verb*

▶ to come upon something by chance or after a search. *Teresa **found** her glasses under a chair.*

discover   To **discover** means to find, especially for the first time. *Alex discovered a new way to cook noodles.*

locate   To **locate** means to find the place where something is. *At last I located the fault in the engine.*

unearth   To **unearth** can mean to find or uncover something by chance or after a search. *The archaeologists unearthed the site of the Aztec city.*

detect   To **detect** means to notice or find, especially after looking carefully. *The sailor detected storm clouds on the horizon.*

trace   To **trace** can mean to find by looking in an orderly way. *Daphna traced her family's history by writing to relatives in different countries.*

fine *adjective*

▶ with the sun shining, or without rain. *I'm enjoying the **fine** weather that we are having at the moment.*

sunny   **Sunny** means having plenty of sunshine. *It was a lovely sunny day before the clouds came over.*

balmy   **Balmy** means fine or pleasant. *In the balmy spring weather they were often outdoors.*

mild   **Mild** can mean not cold, severe, or extreme. *Why don't we go for a walk tonight since the temperature is so mild?*

fair   **Fair** can mean bright and free from clouds, as the sky can be. *The marine forecast was for fair weather all weekend.*

temperate   **Temperate** can mean having a moderate temperature or climate. *My friend lives in a temperate climate zone.*

contrasting keywords: **wintry, cloudy, dreary**

finish *verb*

▶ to bring something to a satisfactory final point. *I am trying to think of an interesting way to **finish** my story.*

close
: To **close** can mean to finish something or to shut something down completely or only for a short time. *The chairperson closed the meeting by thanking everyone who came.*

conclude
: To **conclude** can mean to finish something or bring it to an end. *We will conclude the lesson by reading a poem.*

complete
: To **complete** can mean to bring something to an end after having done everything necessary. *We completed our plans for the surprise party just in time.*

terminate
: To **terminate** means to bring something to an end, often something that could have gone on further. *The severe injury to his leg terminated the dancer's career.*

quit
: To **quit** can mean to leave your computer work when you are finished. *Remember to save your document when you quit that program.*

> similar keywords: **end, cancel, stop**
> contrasting keywords: **begin, initiate**

flat *adjective*

▶ having a fairly level and even surface, as a prairie or a desktop has. *The long, **flat** road stretched out in front of us.*

level
: **Level** means having no part higher than any other part. *We found a level area of ground where we could pitch our tents.*

smooth
: **Smooth** means having no bumps or lumps. *The road had only recently been built and was smooth compared with the rough track we had just left.*

even
: **Even** can mean flat, **smooth**, or **level**. *A tennis court should have an even surface.*

horizontal
: **Horizontal** means parallel or in line with the horizon. *The waves left hundreds of horizontal lines on the sandy beach.*

flatter *verb*

▶ to try to please by complimenting or praising someone, even if you don't mean it. *He flattered me so I would invite him to the party.*

fawn To **fawn** means to flatter someone in an overly obvious and even grovelling manner. *The television host fawned over the movie star, forever praising her and laughing at even her silliest jokes.*

sweet-talk To **sweet-talk** means to persuade someone to do what you want by saying very nice things. It is more suited to everyday language. *If we sweet-talk them enough, they might take us to the theatre.*

cajole To **cajole** means to persuade someone to do something by using flattery. *I cajoled him into running the errand by telling him how fast he is.*

butter up To **butter up** means to flatter someone in an open and obvious way. It is more suited to everyday language. *Let's butter Mom up so she'll give us money for ice cream.*

similar keywords: **praise**

flee *verb*

▶ to run away, especially from danger. *They fled from the angry hornets.*

escape To **escape** means to get away, especially from somewhere unpleasant or dangerous. *He escaped from the prison camp.*

abscond To **abscond** means to run away secretly. This is a rather formal word. *The treasurer absconded with the club's funds.*

elope To **elope** means to run away secretly to be married. *They didn't want a big wedding, so they eloped.*

take to your heels To **take to your heels** means to run away quickly. It is more suited to everyday language. *They took to their heels when the rain started.*

take off To **take off** can mean to run away, especially to avoid being caught. It is more suited to everyday language. *I've got to take off before they find out I'm here.*

similar keywords: **leave**

flexible   *adjective*

▶ easily bent into a different shape. *I need some **flexible** wire to tie around this gate.*

pliable
: **Pliable** means easily bent. It is similar to **flexible**. *Bamboo is a kind of pliable grass used for making baskets and furniture.*

supple
: **Supple** means able to bend easily without breaking or being harmed. *A dancer needs a strong, supple body.*

limber
: **Limber** means having a flexible body. *The limber gymnast worked hard to strengthen her muscles.*

malleable
: **Malleable** means easily worked or moulded into a different shape. *Clay is a malleable material used by potters and sculptors.*

floppy
: **Floppy** means bending in a droopy way, often out of its usual shape. *My beach hat has a big, floppy brim.*

> similar keywords: **elastic**
> contrasting keywords: **hard**

flood   *verb*

▶ to supply someone with a great amount of anything. *Our neighbours **flooded** us with gifts after our house burned down.*

swamp
: To **swamp** can be so similar to **flood** that you can usually choose either word. *Everyone swamped us with kindness and offers of help.*

inundate
: To **inundate** can mean to load or heap someone with a very large amount of something. *Orders for the new novel inundated the publisher because it had received so many good reviews.*

smother
: To **smother** can mean to surround someone with too much of something. *They smothered us with games, books, and all kinds of presents.*

engulf
: To **engulf** means to surround or swallow up someone with something. *Sorrow engulfed them after their tragedy.*

overwhelm
: To **overwhelm** can mean to affect you deeply in mind or emotion. *Our feeling of gratitude almost overwhelmed us.*

flourish *verb*

▶ to grow strongly. *The apple tree we planted began to **flourish** after we gave it some fertilizer.*

bloom
To **bloom** can mean to flourish and produce flowers. *Our rose bush blooms in summer.*

flower
To **flower** means to produce flowers. It is usually used about plants, often those whose flowers form and develop into fruit or vegetables. *Our tomato plant flowered early this year.*

blossom
To **blossom** can mean to produce flowers. It is usually used about trees. *Many trees blossom in the spring.*

sprout
To **sprout** means to send up shoots as a seed does. *I planted some bean seeds last week and they have already sprouted.*

germinate
To **germinate** means to begin to grow and send up shoots. *The seeds germinated and now we can see the little green shoots above the ground.*

> similar keywords: **thrive**

flow *verb*

▶ to move along in an easy manner, as a stream does. *The river **flows** out to the sea.*

stream
To **stream** means to flow steadily or continuously. *Tears streamed from his eyes.*

surge
To **surge** means to rush forward or upward, as waves do. *The heavy rain caused the river to rise and surge over its banks.*

spurt
To **spurt** means to flow suddenly. *Hot water spurted out of the tap when we turned it on.*

wash
To **wash** can mean to flow against or over something. *The waves washed against the sides of the boat.*

gush
To **gush** means to flow suddenly in large amounts. *The water gushed through the hole in the pipe.*

> similar keywords: **drip**

fluctuate   *verb*

▶ to change all the time. *They **fluctuated** between yes and no until they finally made up their minds.*

waver
To **waver** means to be unsure or show doubt. *Even after they said yes they began to waver.*

vacillate
To **vacillate** means to be unsure or to put off making a decision. *He vacillated right up to the moment we got on the train.*

oscillate
To **oscillate** can mean to change your mind back and forth between two different opinions or ideas. *I oscillated between buying the video game and saving my money.*

hedge
To **hedge** means to hesitate about giving a direct answer. *After several minutes of hedging, Denise said she would complain to the store manager.*

blow hot and cold
To **blow hot and cold** means to keep on changing your mind. This is more suited to everyday language. *Michael blew hot and cold on the idea of going winter camping.*

fluent   *adjective*

▶ able to speak easily. *My cousin is **fluent** in Hindi.*

articulate
Articulate means able to say what you mean clearly. *Shashi was chosen to explain the situation because she is so articulate.*

eloquent
Eloquent means able to speak in a flowing, expressive manner. *She was so eloquent that I was nearly crying by the time she finished.*

silver-tongued
Silver-tongued means able to speak so expressively that you can persuade people easily. *That auctioneer is successful because he is silver-tongued.*

smooth
Smooth can mean having a pleasant speaking manner, especially when insincere. *Your smooth talk was flattering, but I wasn't fooled.*

slick
Slick can mean having a pleasant and clever way of talking, although insincere. It is similar to **smooth**. *She is a slick salesperson.*

contrasting keywords: **inarticulate**

fly *verb*

▶ to move through the air with the help of wings, wind, or some other force. *Amy watched the hawk* **fly** *high above the trees.*

flap	To **flap** can mean to fly by moving the wings up and down. *The colony of bats suddenly took off and flapped across the darkening sky.*
flutter	To **flutter** can mean to fly by moving the wings quickly up and down. *Brightly coloured butterflies fluttered among the flowers.*
flit	To **flit** means to move lightly and quickly. *Dragonflies flitted through the long grass.*
soar	To **soar** means to fly upward. *The airplane soared through the clouds into the blue sky above.*
hover	To **hover** means to stay in one spot in the air, as if hanging. *Bees hovered just above the blossoms, collecting nectar.*

follow *verb*

▶ to come or go after someone or something. *You go ahead, and I'll* **follow** *you.*

pursue	To **pursue** means to follow in order to catch someone or something. *Frankenstein's monster pursued its maker persistently.*
chase	To **chase** means to follow quickly in order to catch or overtake someone or something. *The cat chased the mouse across the field.*
shadow	To **shadow** can mean to follow someone secretly. *The detective shadowed the suspect to find out where she was going.*
tag along	To **tag along** can mean to follow someone closely, especially without being invited. *My little brother tries to tag along wherever I go.*
track	To **track** can mean to follow, or hunt by following the footprints or tracks of someone or something. *The photographer tracked the elephants across the grassland.*

similar keywords: **seek**

food *noun*

▶ anything that can be eaten to keep your body alive and help it grow. *My favourite Jamaican **food** is chicken roti.*

cuisine   **Cuisine** is food or a certain style of preparing food. This is a French word that has been adapted into the English language. *That restaurant serves Thai cuisine.*

fare   **Fare** can mean the food provided by someone. *At home we have simple fare, like rice and beans.*

nourishment   **Nourishment** is food, especially the goodness of food. *Babies need lots of nourishment to help them grow.*

provisions   **Provisions** are supplies of food. *They took enough provisions for ten days on their camping trip.*

staples   **Staples** are basic food items. *We packed up bread, milk, juice, flour, and other staples.*

> similar keywords: **meal**

force *noun*

▶ the ability to have a strong effect or influence on something, especially a physical one. *The **force** of the wind caused the tent to fall down.*

power   **Power** can be so similar to **force** that you can usually use either. *Anne's easy leap over the fence showed the power of her legs.*

strength   **Strength** means the quality of being strong or having great **power** or effect. *The strength of the weight lifter was amazing.*

might   **Might** means force or **power**. *We felt the might of the tornado as it tore great trees out of the ground.*

muscle   **Muscle** can mean **strength** or force. It is usually used about people. *You need to put some muscle into chopping that wood.*

vigour   **Vigour** means **strength** and energy, usually of a kind that helps you do something easily or happily. *Jaad attacked the difficult job with vigour.*

force *verb*

▶ to make someone do something, often by using threats or violence. *The thief **forced** them to hand over the money.*

compel	To **compel** means to make others do something, usually because you are more powerful, and they cannot disobey you. *The armed robbers compelled the bank customers to hand over all their money.*
coerce	To **coerce** means to force someone to do something, usually with arguments or threats. *The children were coerced into accepting the decision as final.*
drive	To **drive** can mean to use a lot of effort to make yourself or someone else do something. *I always drive myself hard to finish my work on time.*
bully	To **bully** means to hurt, frighten, or order about someone who is smaller or weaker than you. *Don't try to bully us into agreeing with you.*
bulldoze	To **bulldoze** can mean to force others to do something without caring whether they want to or not. It is more suited to everyday language. *You can't bulldoze us into going if we don't want to.*

> similar keywords: **threaten**

forecast *noun*

▶ an opinion about or warning of what is going to happen in the future. *The financial **forecast** for next year is economic growth.*

prediction	A **prediction** is similar to a **forecast** and can often be used in the same way. *She made a prediction that the school team would win this year.*
prophecy	A **prophecy** is similar to a **prediction** or a **forecast**. *My prophecy is that you will win the election!*
prognosis	A **prognosis** is a doctor's opinion of how an illness will affect a patient. *Dr. Shankar's prognosis was that I would recover in a day or so.*
omen	An **omen** is a sign of something that might happen in the future. *I don't think that breaking a mirror is an omen of bad luck.*
tip	A **tip** can be a piece of useful information about something that might happen. *The caller gave the police a tip that a robbery would take place at the bank.*

foreign *adjective*

▶ from a country other than your own. *We learned a **foreign** language to help us when we travelled.*

immigrant **Immigrant** means moving to another country to live after leaving your own. *The immigrant family came from Hong Kong to live in Canada.*

alien **Alien** means living in a country without being a citizen of it. *The alien residents decided to become citizens.*

ethnic **Ethnic** means having to do with the customs, history, or language of a particular group of people. *We saw colourful costumes from all over the world during the display of ethnic dancing.*

imported **Imported** means brought in from another country. *Some people buy imported cars from Japan, Korea, and Germany.*

exotic **Exotic** means foreign or not belonging naturally to your own country. *Many exotic plants can be seen at the botanical gardens.*

forgive *verb*

▶ to no longer have bad feelings against someone who did something wrong. *I will **forgive** you if you say you are sorry.*

excuse To **excuse** can mean to overlook a wrongdoing or fault. *I'll excuse your thoughtless remarks this time, but please try to be more polite in future.*

let off To **let off** can mean to **excuse** and not punish someone. *I'll let you off this time, but next time you may not be so lucky.*

pardon To **pardon** can mean to forgive and not punish someone. This can be a legal word. *The prisoner was pardoned after spending many years in prison.*

spare To **spare** means to forgive and not harm someone you have power over. *The queen spared her treacherous cousin.*

clear To **clear** can mean to free someone from blame. *The witness's statement at the trial cleared the prisoner.*

---

contrasting keywords: **accuse**

---

formal *adjective*

▶ following the proper and usual procedure. *A **formal** statement was issued by the court.*

established **Established** means done in the customary or usual way. *This is the established method of applying for a passport.*

official **Official** means properly approved or arranged. *We made an official request for a crosswalk outside our school.*

ceremonial **Ceremonial** means following the proper procedure used on an important occasion. *They wore their best clothes to the ceremonial opening of the new museum.*

ritual **Ritual** means following the set procedure used on religious or other special occasions. *The ritual dance was performed to celebrate the harvest season.*

> similar keywords: **legal**
> contrasting keywords: **informal**

fragile *adjective*

▶ very easily broken or damaged. *I held the **fragile** china cup very carefully and admired its fineness.*

delicate **Delicate** means easily damaged or weakened. *I dusted everything on the shelf except the delicate glass animals.*

frail **Frail** can mean easily destroyed or broken. *The frail lace curtain tore as we pulled it.*

brittle **Brittle** means likely to break very easily. *We packed the brittle seashells in newspapers to keep them safe.*

breakable **Breakable** means easily fractured or broken into pieces. *I put away the pans while Dad dried all the breakable plates and glasses.*

> similar keywords: **slight, decrepit, weak**
> contrasting keywords: **strong, hardy, powerful**

frank *adjective*

▶ very honest, saying exactly what you think. *We had a **frank** discussion about our differences of opinion.*

direct **Direct** can mean going straight to the point. *His direct question about the financial affairs of the committee embarrassed the treasurer.*

straightforward **Straightforward** is so similar to **direct** that you can usually use either. *The straightforward directions you gave made it easy to find your house.*

candid **Candid** means honest and sincere. *She gave a candid answer to the reporter's question.*

forthright **Forthright** means speaking your mind openly. *John is a very forthright person and sometimes hurts people's feelings without meaning to.*

genuine **Genuine** can mean showing real feelings, not pretend ones. *Carla was genuine in her praise of the painting.*

> similar keywords: **honest**
> contrasting keywords: **dishonest**

free *adjective*

▶ not confined, restricted, or limited. *In a democracy, people are **free** to express their opinions.*

uninhibited **Uninhibited** means behaving just as you like without worrying about what people think. *They were quite uninhibited about doing somersaults across the classroom floor.*

unconventional **Unconventional** means not doing things according to the usual or accepted ways. *People were curious about his unconventional way of dressing.*

spontaneous **Spontaneous** means doing things in a natural and sometimes unexpected way. *Kim's spontaneous smile pleased me because I didn't think she liked my poem.*

open **Open** can mean doing things in a way that shows you are not hiding anything. *He was quite open about trying to take my place on the team.*

wild **Wild** can mean not restrained or controlled. *Their parents had to stop the wild party.*

free *verb*

▶ to set someone or something at liberty. *I want to **free** my pet starling, but it may not survive in the wild.*

release
> To **release** means to set someone or something free, especially after being locked up. *The government decided to release the convict when new evidence was brought forward.*

liberate
> To **liberate** means to set someone or something free, especially from some kind of oppression. *The army liberated the enemy-occupied town.*

emancipate
> To **emancipate** means to set someone free from any kind of restraint. *William Wilberforce was an 18th century politician who worked to emancipate the slaves in the British Empire.*

rescue
> To **rescue** means to free someone or something from a dangerous or harmful situation. *The cat was rescued from the burning house.*

deliver
> To **deliver** can mean to save or set someone free. *The rescuers delivered me from certain death as my raft neared the waterfall.*

•

> contrasting keywords: **subdue, confine, capture**

friend *noun*

▶ someone you like and who likes you. *My **friend** Aniela and I spend our spare time together.*

playmate
> A **playmate** is someone you play with. *The kids next door have been my playmates since we were little.*

pal
> A **pal** is a good friend. This is more suited to everyday language. *Good pals do things for each other.*

companion
> A **companion** is someone you go out with or travel with. *I like to go to movies with a companion.*

teammate
> A **teammate** is someone who is on the same team as you. *My teammates and I were excited about winning the field hockey game.*

> similar keywords: **associate**
> contrasting keywords: **enemy**

friendly *adjective*

▶ showing friendship or acting like a friend. *Everyone at the party was* **friendly**.

warm
Warm can mean kind and affectionate. *They gave us a warm welcome.*

neighbourly
Neighbourly means kind and friendly. *The Goh family gave us some neighbourly help when we moved next door.*

outgoing
Outgoing means able to mix with people easily. *Outgoing people usually make friends quickly.*

sociable
Sociable means wanting to be with other people. *Sociable people are easy to talk to.*

genial
Genial means having a warm and friendly manner. *Salim's genial manner made us all feel relaxed.*

> similar keywords: **agreeable, kind, loving**
> contrasting keywords: **unfriendly**

frighten *verb*

▶ to fill someone with fear. *The barking dog* **frightened** *the baby.*

scare
To **scare** means to fill someone with sudden fear. *The loud clap of thunder scared the little children.*

alarm
To **alarm** means to cause someone to feel fear. *The smell of smoke in the house alarmed me.*

petrify
To **petrify** can mean to make someone stiff with fear and unable to move. *The growling bear petrified me.*

terrify
To **terrify** means to frighten someone very, very much. *The sound of rattling chains terrified the hero in the ghost story.*

terrorize
To **terrorize** can mean to frighten or cause someone to feel very great fear or terror. *The outlaws terrorized the local shopkeepers and then demanded money from them.*

> similar keywords: **shock, threaten**
> contrasting keywords: **pacify**

frightened   *adjective*

▶ showing or feeling fear. *The **frightened** children huddled together during the storm.*

scared   **Scared** means feeling sudden fear. *The scared rabbits ran away from the angry farmer.*

afraid   **Afraid** means frightened or feeling great fear. It is never used before the noun it is describing. *They were afraid of being caught stealing carrots.*

panicky   **Panicky** means feeling so frightened that you can't think clearly or act sensibly. *The camp counsellor calmed the panicky children who had seen the snake.*

alarmed   **Alarmed** means frightened suddenly. *They were alarmed when the tree branch crashed against the window.*

petrified   **Petrified** can mean feeling so frightened that you can hardly move or do anything sensible. *The petrified children wished they hadn't gone into the haunted house at the fair.*

> similar keywords: **nervous, fearful**
> contrasting keywords: **calm, brave**

frightening   *adjective*

▶ causing you to feel afraid. *The skateboard accident was a **frightening** experience.*

scary   **Scary** means causing fear or fright. *Walking along the road at night can be scary.*

creepy   **Creepy** means frightening or unpleasant. *We got a creepy feeling as we entered the deserted old warehouse.*

grim   **Grim** can mean having such a fierce or angry appearance that it makes you feel afraid. *When the outlaw saw the marshal's grim face, he knew he could expect no mercy.*

forbidding **Forbidding** means dangerous and frightening. *The forbidding appearance of the cliff made us decide not to climb to the top.*

> similar keywords: **horrible**

frolic *verb*

▶ to leap around playfully, as a lamb or kitten does. *They **frolicked** joyfully in the warm, spring sunshine.*

dance   To **dance** can mean to move about quickly and lightly, usually because you are excited or happy. *We danced for joy when we heard the good news.*

caper   To **caper** means to jump or **dance** about. *The children capered along the trail in search of the hidden treasure.*

gambol   To **gambol** means to jump around in play. *The bunnies gambolled in the garden.*

skip   To **skip** means to jump lightly from one foot to the other. *He skipped up the path and through the open door.*

prance   To **prance** means to leap about gracefully. *The crowd cheered as the horses pranced into the ring.*

> similar keywords: **jump**
> contrasting keywords: **walk, limp, trudge**

frown *verb*

▶ to wrinkle your forehead to show you are annoyed or puzzled. *They stopped talking when I **frowned** at them and shook my head.*

glare   To **glare** means to give a long, fierce look to show that you are angry. *We glared at them when they rudely laughed at us.*

glower   To **glower** means to look or stare in a bad-tempered way. *Paul just sat and glowered when he didn't get his own way.*

scowl   To **scowl** means to have an angry look on your face. *The children scowled when their dad said they couldn't go.*

pout   To **pout** means to push out your lips in a sulky way. *My little brother pouted until we gave in and let him play with us.*

grimace   To **grimace** means to twist your face in a way that shows unhappiness. *I grimaced when the doctor said I needed a booster shot.*

> contrasting keywords: **smile**

full *adjective*

▶ filled up. *The milk carton was **full**.*

crowded **Crowded** means filled with people or objects. *We couldn't see our friends in the crowded arena.*

packed **Packed** means so full that no more people or things can fit in. *The pianist played to a packed concert hall.*

bursting **Bursting** means very full, as if ready to break open. *The bag of apples was filled to the bursting point.*

laden **Laden** means having a full load or holding a lot. *The peach tree was laden with fruit.*

crammed **Crammed** means stuffed tight. *Nothing else would fit into my crammed suitcase.*

> similar keywords: **whole**
> contrasting keywords: **empty**

funny *adjective*

▶ causing you to laugh. *We all enjoyed his **funny** stories.*

amusing **Amusing** means causing laughter or smiles. *The children watched the clown's dogs perform many amusing tricks.*

comical **Comical** means funny, often because it is odd or unusual. *The clown's dogs looked comical walking on their hind legs and wearing clothes.*

humorous **Humorous** means funny or full of humour. *Her humorous comment about being able to run as fast as a snail made the children laugh.*

hilarious **Hilarious** means very, very funny. *They thought the clown's performance was hilarious.*

droll **Droll** means amusingly odd. *Johann's droll sense of humour made us realize how funny the situation was.*

further *verb*

▶ to help, improve, or develop something. *Regular training will **further** your chances of becoming a top swimmer.*

advance   To **advance** means to develop something and make it better. *Earth Day events advance the cause of environmental awareness.*

promote   To **promote** means to further something so that it has a better rank or position. *They promoted the new fruit drink by running ads on TV.*

facilitate   To **facilitate** means to help or further something by making things easier. *The librarian facilitated our group research project by showing us how to do a computer search for resource books.*

ease   To **ease** means to help something by taking away any problems or difficulties. *Talks between the two presidents eased the tension between their countries.*

> similar keywords: **help, encourage**
> contrasting keywords: **hinder, block**

future *adjective*

▶ happening in the time that has not yet come. *Our **future** plans include visiting our relatives in Winnipeg during the summer holidays.*

prospective   **Prospective** means expected to happen in the future. *My mom's prospective pay increase will help us afford the trip out west.*

next   **Next** can mean immediately following in time. *At last we could say that the holidays would begin the next day.*

imminent   **Imminent** means likely to happen at any moment. *We said goodbye and boarded the plane when we knew its departure was imminent.*

impending   **Impending** means near at hand or **imminent**. *Our departure was delayed by the impending arrival of another plane.*

upcoming   **Upcoming** means about to take place. *Tell us more about your upcoming visit to our town.*

> contrasting keywords: **past**

G, g

gasp   *verb*

▶ to struggle for breath with your mouth open. *The people in the smoke-filled room were **gasping** for air when the firefighters rescued them.*

pant   To **pant** means to breathe hard and quickly because of effort or emotion. *All the runners were panting after the relay.*

wheeze   To **wheeze** means to breathe with difficulty, making a whistling sound. *My asthma makes me wheeze if I run too fast.*

puff   To **puff** means to breathe quickly, especially after vigorous exercise. *We were puffing after the workout.*

heave   To **heave** can mean to breathe heavily and noisily, with a great effort. *The exhausted swimmer heaved and gasped for air after the long race.*

gather   *verb*

▶ to bring together. *I **gathered** my belongings and put them in a bag.*

collect   To **collect** means to gather things together, usually for a particular reason. *Katrina collects baseball cards.*

accumulate   To **accumulate** means to gather a large quantity of something. *She has accumulated over 100 cards.*

amass   To **amass** means to gather things together for yourself. *By the end of his life, my uncle had amassed a large fortune.*

pile up   To **pile up** means to bring things together into a pile. *We piled up the newspapers for the recycling collection.*

rake in   To **rake in** means to gather or **collect** a lot of something. This is more suited to everyday language. *They raked in thousands of dollars in donations during the telethon for the hospital.*

> similar keywords: **store**
> contrasting keywords: **scatter**

gaudy *adjective*

▶ very bright or ornate in order to attract attention. *My **gaudy** towel is very easy to find on the crowded beach.*

showy   **Showy** means attracting attention in a very obvious way. *The peacock's brightly coloured tail is very showy.*

flashy   **Flashy** means bright and **showy**. *We went for a ride in the flashy red sports car.*

loud   **Loud** can mean very brightly coloured, usually in an unpleasant way. *I thought his new purple and pink tie was too loud.*

tawdry   **Tawdry** means cheap and gaudy. *She said the glass beads I bought at the fair were too tawdry to wear.*

> similar keywords: **colourful, spectacular**
> contrasting keywords: **drab, simple**

generous *adjective*

▶ unselfish or ready to give money or gifts. *A **generous** woman has given a lot of new books to our library.*

extravagant   **Extravagant** means giving or spending more than is necessary. *Your extravagant present embarrassed him at his birthday party.*

lavish   **Lavish** means very generous in giving. *You are too lavish with your gifts.*

hospitable   **Hospitable** means being very welcoming and generous to strangers or guests. *Our hospitable neighbours invited us to dinner the day we moved to our new house.*

charitable   **Charitable** means giving money or help to people who need it. *Our school collects money for charitable organizations.*

magnanimous   **Magnanimous** means unselfish and generous in a noble way. *Martha is too magnanimous to hold a grudge.*

> similar keywords: **kind**
> contrasting keywords: **mean, selfish**

genuine   *adjective*

▶ true or real. *She has a **genuine** antique Ming vase.*

authentic	**Authentic** means genuine or known to be what it claims to be. *We saw an authentic ancient Chinese tomb at the museum.*
legitimate	**Legitimate** can mean true or reasonable. *He had a legitimate excuse for being late.*
factual	**Factual** means based on facts. *This book gives a factual account of life in China.*
proven	**Proven** means shown to be true or right. *Speeding is a proven cause of car accidents.*

> similar keywords: **actual, true**
> contrasting keywords: **fake**

get   *verb*

▶ to obtain. *My sister **got** a new computer screen as a graduation present.*

gain	To **gain** means to get or obtain, usually something you desire. *You will gain more confidence if you practise making the speech.*
acquire	To **acquire** can mean to get as your own, usually through your own actions or effort. It is a more formal word. *She acquired leadership skills by working as a camp counsellor each summer.*
win	To **win** can mean to get something by making a special effort. *My friend Alex won an award for his work with needy children.*
receive	To **receive** can mean to get something or have it given to you. *Tadashi received some new tapes for his birthday.*
procure	To **procure** means to get or obtain, especially using a lot of care or effort. *The detective procured all the evidence she needed to arrest the suspect.*

> similar keywords: **grab, buy**
> contrasting keywords: **give**

ghost *noun*

▶ the spirit of someone who has died, imagined as visiting living people. *The children screamed because they thought the white shape in the corner was a **ghost**.*

spectre
Spectre is so similar to **ghost** that you can usually use either. *In Shakespeare's play* Hamlet, *a young man is visited by the spectre of his father.*

phantom
A **phantom** is a ghost or a ghostly appearance. *I went to see the musical play* The Phantom of the Opera.

vision
A **vision** can be someone or something that appears only in the mind. *In Michelle's story, the fortuneteller sees a vision in his crystal ball.*

apparition
An **apparition** is something, such as a ghost, that appears in an out-of-the-ordinary way. *He said he fainted because he saw the apparition of a very old man in the mirror.*

wraith
A **wraith** is the ghostlike appearance of a living person, supposed to be seen just before that person's death. *Some people thought they saw the wraith of the dying queen in the palace grounds.*

gift *noun*

▶ something that is given to someone. *The computer game was my favourite birthday **gift**.*

present
Present is so similar to **gift** that you can usually use either. *I always give birthday presents to my brothers and sisters.*

inheritance
An **inheritance** is a gift of money or property made through someone's will. *She left her children an inheritance of $10 000 each.*

donation
A **donation** is a gift, usually to charity. *We made a donation to the food drive.*

contribution
A **contribution** is something given for a specific purpose. *Our family made a contribution to help purchase new equipment for the hospital.*

allowance
An **allowance** is a certain amount of money given to someone regularly, usually by parents to their children. *I saved my allowance for a new baseball glove.*

give *verb*

▶ to hand something over freely. *They will **give** Josh a present before he moves away.*

donate   To **donate** means to give something as a gift. *We donated some money to the flood-relief fund.*

present   To **present** means to give, especially in a formal way. *The mayor presented the prizes.*

award   To **award** means to give somebody something for merit or achievement. *The school awards prizes for students who do very well in a subject.*

confer   To **confer** means to give something to somebody as a gift, a favour, or an honour. *The fire chief conferred a medal for bravery on my sister.*

grant   To **grant** means to give something to somebody, usually when the person has asked for it. *The farmer granted them permission to hike through the fields.*

> contrasting keywords: **take, get**

give in *verb*

▶ to admit that you are defeated. *Do you **give in** now that you know you can't win?*

yield   To **yield** can mean to give in because you are powerless to go on. *The country yielded to the invading army.*

surrender   To **surrender** means to give yourself up into someone else's power. *They surrendered to the authorities after hiding for days.*

capitulate   To **capitulate** means to give in under specified conditions. *The government capitulated to the hijackers' demands in order to save the lives of the innocent passengers.*

submit   To **submit** can mean to **yield** to the power of others. *He finally submitted to the orders of his boss.*

succumb   To **succumb** means to give in to a stronger force. *In the end, I succumbed to temptation and bought a milkshake.*

> contrasting keywords: **resist**

glad *adjective*

▶ happy about something. *I am **glad** that Helena arrived safely.*

pleased	**Pleased** means happy or satisfied with something. *We are pleased that you are enjoying your classes.*
delighted	**Delighted** means very glad. *We are delighted that you'll be visiting us soon.*
thrilled	**Thrilled** means so glad that you feel excited. *Liam said he was thrilled to be going to the theatre.*
tickled pink	**Tickled pink** means greatly **pleased** or amused. This is more suited to everyday language. *They were tickled pink by your compliments.*

> similar keywords: **happy, joyful, excited, satisfied**
> contrasting keywords: **sad, miserable, glum, angry, annoyed**

glue *noun*

▶ a substance used to stick things together. *I used white **glue** to stick the pieces of my balsa-wood plane together.*

paste	**Paste** can be a mixture of starch or flour and water used for sticking paper onto another surface. *Make up some paste so we can put up that new wallpaper.*
adhesive	An **adhesive** is any substance used for sticking things together. *What's the best adhesive for mending this torn vinyl chair?*
cement	**Cement** is a soft substance that hardens or sets to join or bind things together very strongly. *I'll need some special cement to stick these broken tiles back together.*
mortar	**Mortar** is the special mixture used for joining bricks. *If you don't use enough mortar, the bricks won't stick firmly and the wall may fall down.*

g l u e y *adjective*

▶ sticky like glue. *He scraped the **gluey** cake batter off his hands with a spoon.*

gelatinous	**Gelatinous** means jelly-like. *The gelatinous mass on the beach was the body of a dead jellyfish.*
viscous	**Viscous** means sticky and **thick**. *I took the honey from the refrigerator and tried to spread the viscous substance on my bread.*
gummy	**Gummy** means sticky, like chewed gum. *The adhesive label left a gummy mark on the lamp.*
slimy	**Slimy** means unpleasantly wet and slippery. *There was slimy, green scum on top of the pond.*

> contrasting keywords: **liquid**

g l u m *adjective*

▶ unhappy or depressed. *After trying so hard, they were really **glum** when they failed to make the team.*

moody	**Moody** means having a change in your mood, often being **gloomy**. *He's a very moody person; sometimes he is happy and sometimes he can be quite angry and unhappy.*
sullen	**Sullen** means angry, silent, and sometimes ill-mannered. *She is sullen because she was wrongly accused of cheating.*
surly	**Surly** means unfriendly and bad-tempered. *I don't like shopping there because the salesperson has a surly manner.*
morose	**Morose** means bad-tempered or unfriendly because you are unhappy. *It was hard for Lee not to be morose when everything was going wrong.*
gloomy	**Gloomy** can mean feeling unhappy or depressed. *I don't know why I feel so gloomy today. Maybe it's the weather.*

> similar keywords: **sad, miserable**
> contrasting keywords: **happy, joyful, glad**

good *adjective*

▶ of a high standard or worthy of praise. *This is a **good** piece of work.*

satisfactory **Satisfactory** means good enough to meet your requirements. *Erik gave a satisfactory answer.*

fine **Fine** can mean very good or of a high quality. *Alan is a fine musician.*

commendable **Commendable** means worthy of praise. *They held a party for Yoko to thank her for her commendable work on the committee.*

all right **All right** means **satisfactory**. *She did an all right job for us in very demanding circumstances.*

admirable **Admirable** means highly worthy of approval. *Going shopping for your sick neighbour was an admirable thing to do.*

> similar keywords: **great, excellent, nice, best**
> contrasting keywords: **bad, nasty**

gossip *noun*

▶ silly or unkind chatter about another person's business. *I don't listen to **gossip** because it is often harmful or untrue.*

talk **Talk** can be so similar to **gossip** that you can usually use either word. *Have you heard the talk about Christine's argument with Greg?*

rumour A **rumour** is a story that is widely spread, without any proof about the facts. *Are the rumours true about your band breaking up?*

hearsay **Hearsay** is so similar to **rumour** that you can usually use either word. *It's just hearsay that they are going to sell their farm.*

whisper A **whisper** can mean a secretly expressed belief, **rumour**, or hint. *I heard a whisper that you are planning a surprise party for Jacques.*

slander **Slander** is a false spoken statement intended to hurt a person's reputation. *The singer sued the TV entertainment show host for slander after she made false statements about him.*

> similar keywords: **information**

grab   *verb*

▶ to take something suddenly. *Don't **grab** the ball before it's your turn.*

seize	To **seize** means to take hold of someone or something suddenly or by force. *Efra seized her little brother to keep him from running across the busy street.*
snatch	To **snatch** means to take hold of something suddenly or rudely. *The thief snatched my bag as I walked down the crowded street.*
snap up	To **snap up** means to grab something quickly. *The shoppers snapped up the bargains at the department store sales.*
nab	To **nab** means to catch or **seize** someone suddenly. It is more suited to everyday language. *My father nabbed me as I was trying to sneak off.*
nail	To **nail** can mean to catch or **seize** someone, usually a suspected criminal. It is more suited to everyday language. *"We've nailed you,"* said the posse as they burst into the outlaws' hide-out.*

> similar keywords: **take, capture, abduct, hold, catch**

grade   *noun*

▶ a particular position on a scale of standing, status, quality, or value. *This fruit is of the highest **grade**.*

step	A **step** can be a particular position or degree on a scale. *We must all understand the first step before we can complete the rest of the instructions.*
stage	A **stage** can be a single **step** on a scale or in a particular process. *Now we are ready to go on to the next stage.*
level	A **level** is one person's position on a scale compared with other people's positions. *Fernando was promoted to a higher level of the company because of his good work.*
rank	A **rank** can be an official position or grade. *My aunt reached the rank of colonel in the armed forces.*
class	**Class** can be how others judge someone's place in society, based on work, possessions, or family. *During the Depression, factories closed down and many members of the working class were unemployed.*

grand *adjective*

▶ fine, splendid, or important. *The Mardi Gras parade was a **grand** spectacle.*

lofty   **Lofty** means very noble or high in character. *I wish everyone had her lofty ideals.*

dignified   **Dignified** means showing nobleness of mind or character. *His dignified conduct when he lost the race inspired us.*

magnificent   **Magnificent** means very fine or impressive. *There is a magnificent view of the mountains from this park.*

majestic   **Majestic** can mean great or impressive in appearance. *The majestic view left them speechless.*

stately   **Stately** means looking formal, grand, or **majestic**. *The stately tree was tall and beautiful and very old.*

> similar keywords: **important, distinguished**
> contrasting keywords: **humble**

grateful *adjective*

▶ feeling or showing gratitude or thanks. *Dad said he was **grateful** that I cooked dinner when he was sick.*

thankful   **Thankful** means feeling or showing thanks to someone who has been kind. It is very similar to **grateful**. *I was thankful when Lisa offered to drive me home in the storm.*

appreciative   **Appreciative** means showing or feeling appreciation or gratitude. *Amrik was most appreciative of Ian's offer to help him paint the house.*

obliged   **Obliged** means feeling under an obligation because of a kindness that has been shown. *I am obliged to you for lending me your camera while mine is being repaired.*

indebted   **Indebted** means feeling that you owe a debt of gratitude for help, a favour, or the like. *I am indebted to you for looking after the baby when I had to go to the drugstore.*

> contrasting keywords: **ungrateful**

great *adjective*

▶ very good or fine. When great is used this way, it is more suited to everyday language. *We had a **great** time at the party.*

splendid   **Splendid** means extremely good. *The orchestra gave a splendid performance.*

superb   **Superb** is so similar to **splendid** that you can usually use either. *The meal was superb.*

super   **Super** can mean extremely good or pleasing. It is more suited to everyday language. *We had a super holiday at the beach.*

first-rate   **First-rate** means very good or outstanding. *She got a high mark for her first-rate work.*

> similar keywords: **good, excellent, best, superior, wonderful**
> contrasting keywords: **bad, nasty, horrible**

greedy *adjective*

▶ wanting an unreasonable amount of something, especially food or money. *Those **greedy** children ate all my cookies.*

avaricious   **Avaricious** means greedy for money. *The avaricious factory owners underpaid their workers.*

grasping   **Grasping** means wanting much more than you are entitled to. *In the Western movie, the grasping cattle owner tried to drive the settlers from their land.*

rapacious   **Rapacious** means taking things from other people in a greedy and violent way. This is a rather formal word. *The rapacious outlaw robbed the villagers and burned their houses.*

insatiable   **Insatiable** means never being satisfied with what you have. *The politician had an insatiable desire for power.*

voracious   **Voracious** means eager or greedy for something, especially food. *I have a voracious appetite when I come home from school.*

> contrasting keywords: **satisfied**

green *adjective*

▶ of the colour of growing leaves and grass. *Sheep and cattle grazed along the lush* **green** *banks of the river.*

emerald	**Emerald** means having a clear, bright green colour. *In the book, the Emerald City only looked green because the Wizard of Oz made everyone wear green sunglasses.*
lime	**Lime** means having a greenish-yellow colour. *We mixed some yellow and green together to make a lime paint for the kitchen.*
hazel	**Hazel** means having a greenish-brown colour. *He stared at me through his large, hazel eyes.*
olive	**Olive** means having a dull brownish-green colour. *We recognized the army trucks by their olive colour.*
turquoise	**Turquoise** means having a bright greenish-blue colour. *The Navajo artist makes beautiful turquoise and silver jewellery.*

grey *adjective*

▶ having a colour between black and white. *We looked at the* **grey** *sky and knew there would be a storm.*

charcoal	**Charcoal** means having a very dark grey colour that is almost black. *After the forest fire, the tree trunks had turned a charcoal colour.*
slate	**Slate** means having a dull, dark, bluish-grey colour. *The paint we chose was a slate colour to match the tiles on the roof.*
silver	**Silver** means having a shiny whitish-grey colour. *The wedding gift had a beautiful silver ribbon and matching bow.*
steel grey	**Steel grey** means having a dark bluish-grey colour with a metallic look. *My new mountain bike is a shiny steel grey colour.*

grieve *verb*

▶ to feel very sad because you have suffered some sorrow. *I **grieved** for our broken friendship.*

mourn
: To **mourn** can mean to grieve or express sorrow because someone you love has died. *Mr. Lambert mourned for a long time after his wife died.*

lament
: To **lament** means to feel or express deep sorrow or grief. *The townspeople lamented over the disappearance of the fishing boats.*

pine
: To **pine** means to become sick from grief and longing. *In the romantic novel, the main character pines for his lost love.*

brood
: To **brood** can mean to worry or think moodily about something. *The child brooded all day after his friends said he couldn't go to the movie with them.*

mope
: To **mope** means to be sunk in an unhappy mood. *She has moped ever since she was dropped from the team.*

> contrasting keywords: **rejoice**

groove *noun*

▶ a long narrow cut or hollow, especially one made by a tool. *Joana used a narrow chisel to make decorative **grooves** in the table legs she was making.*

rut
: A **rut** is a groove made in the ground. *The whirling wheels of the stagecoach made deep ruts in the dirt road.*

furrow
: A **furrow** is a groove, especially one made in the earth by a plough. *The farmer planted corn in the furrows.*

ditch
: A **ditch** is a long, narrow hollow dug in the earth. *I fell off my bike into the muddy ditch by the side of the road.*

channel
: A **channel** can be a **ditch** dug for water to flow through. *The farmers pumped water from irrigation channels to water their crops.*

trench
: A **trench** is a deep **ditch**, especially one dug by soldiers to protect themselves from the enemy. *The soldiers in the trenches fired at the approaching enemy.*

group   *noun*

▶ a number of people connected in some way and sometimes gathered together. *Bhagat has a large **group** of friends.*

bunch   A **bunch** can be a group of people. It is more suited to everyday language. *She is one of our bunch.*

gang   A **gang** is a group of people acting together. *They were robbed by a gang of thieves.*

band   A **band** can be an official group of First Nations people. *My grandparents are members of the Cowichan band.*

circle   A **circle** can be a small group of people connected in some way. *Rita and her circle of friends enjoy camping.*

huddle   A **huddle** is a small group of people crowded together to discuss something in private. *The huddle of friends whispered together in a corner.*

> similar keywords: **crowd, club, organization**

grumpy   *adjective*

▶ bad-tempered. *I'm always **grumpy** when I don't get enough sleep.*

irritable   **Irritable** means easily annoyed. *I'm irritable when I am ill.*

snappy   **Snappy** can mean speaking angrily or sharply. *The salesperson was snappy with the customer who was complaining.*

grouchy   **Grouchy** means grumpy and unpleasant. *Justin was in a grouchy mood because our friends were late and he was hungry.*

crotchety   **Crotchety** means bad-tempered or **irritable**. *My crotchety neighbour wouldn't let me get my ball when it went over the fence.*

petulant   **Petulant** means showing impatient annoyance, especially over something unimportant. *The petulant student threw the pen on the floor when it wouldn't write.*

> similar keywords: **annoyed, touchy, angry, miserable**
> contrasting keywords: **happy**

H, h

halt *noun*

▶ a stop, especially a temporary one. *The umpire called a **halt** to the baseball game because of the pouring rain.*

stalemate   A **stalemate** is a situation where no progress can be made. *The management and the baseball players' union reached a stalemate in the dispute.*

deadlock   A **deadlock** is the point in an argument when neither side will give way. *Brian and Jenny have reached a deadlock over who is going to use the car tonight.*

standstill   A **standstill** is a halt, especially of work or movement. *Work came to a standstill in the classroom when the lights went off.*

> similar keywords: **end**

happen *verb*

▶ to take place. *The surprise **happened** just as we were opening the door.*

occur   To **occur** is so similar to **happen** that you can usually use either word. *The parade occurred yesterday.*

arise   To **arise** means to happen or to come into being. *No confusion arose, because we had decided where to eat before we went out.*

transpire   To **transpire** can mean to happen or to pass. It is a more formal word than happen. *Three years transpired before Tim and Rohana saw each other again.*

come about   To **come about** means to **occur** or to happen over time. *It came about that after five years the family quarrel was forgotten.*

fall   To **fall** can mean to happen or take place. *My birthday falls on a Monday this year.*

happiness *noun*

▶ pleasure, contentment, or gladness. *The children's **happiness** was complete when they were given a puppy.*

merriment **Merriment** is happiness mixed with laughter. *The house was filled with sounds of merriment.*

satisfaction **Satisfaction** can be the fulfilment of a need or want. *Completing the long race gave us a sense of satisfaction.*

mirth **Mirth** is amusement and laughter, such as is caused by something silly. *The audience rocked with mirth at the comedian's jokes.*

high spirits **High spirits** is a very happy mood. *Nicholas was in high spirits after doing so well in the game.*

joy **Joy** is a strong feeling of pleasure or happiness. *The good news filled us with joy.*

> contrasting keywords: **misery**

happy *adjective*

▶ delighted, or glad about something. *I was very **happy** when Karen invited me to the concert.*

cheerful **Cheerful** means happy and in a good mood. *Cheung is usually in a cheerful mood on Friday night.*

merry **Merry** means happy and laughing. *We were a merry group as we hiked happily along to the beach.*

jolly **Jolly** means good-humoured and full of fun. *The bus driver was jolly and made us laugh a lot.*

> similar keywords: **joyful, glad, satisfied**
> contrasting keywords: **sad, miserable, glum, solemn**

hard *adjective*

▶ solid and not able to be pushed out of shape. *That old wooden chair is really **hard**.*

stiff   **Stiff** means not easily bent or moved. *My new fishing rod is a lot better than the old, stiff one.*

firm   **Firm** means solid, hard, or **stiff**. *I like to sleep on a firm mattress.*

rigid   **Rigid** means not able to be bent or moved. *The tent pole was rigid and withstood the strong winds of the storm.*

inflexible   **Inflexible** means **stiff** or **rigid**. *This wire is so inflexible that even the pliers won't bend it.*

tough   **Tough** means strong or **firm** but flexible. *These sports sunglasses seem tough enough to withstand lots of activity.*

> contrasting keywords: **soft, flexible, elastic**

harden *verb*

▶ to make or become solid or firm to the touch. *The yogurt mixture will **harden** in the freezer.*

stiffen   To **stiffen** means to become so hard and firm that it is not easily bent. *It's so cold out that my damp gloves have stiffened.*

solidify   To **solidify** means to become firm or solid right through. *The molten metal solidified as it cooled.*

set   To **set** means to become harder or more solid. *The vanilla pudding set as it cooled in the fridge.*

petrify   To **petrify** can mean to become changed into stone or something like stone. *It took millions of years for that tree trunk to petrify.*

freeze   To **freeze** can mean to become hard by being exposed to very low temperatures. *I hope the river freezes well enough to skate on.*

> contrasting keywords: **soften**

hardy *adjective*

▶ able to stand up to rough treatment or conditions. *Only a **hardy** cyclist would be able to ride up that hill.*

durable	**Durable** means lasting for a long time. *Winter boots should be made of durable material.*
sturdy	**Sturdy** means strong and able to stand up to rough use. *The sturdy tree survived the heavy storm.*
tough	**Tough** can mean not easily broken or damaged by bad conditions. *They tied up the boat with a tough rope.*
heavy-duty	**Heavy-duty** means strong and designed for heavy use. *A heavy-duty battery will last you much longer than an ordinary one.*
rugged	**Rugged** can mean having a strong appearance. *The rugged mountain guides came from Nepal and Bhutan.*

> similar keywords: **strong, powerful**
> contrasting keywords: **weak, fragile, decrepit**

hate *verb*

▶ to regard something or someone with strong dislike. *I **hate** seeing litter in the park.*

detest	To **detest** means to dislike something or someone intensely. *I detest it when people cheat.*
loathe	To **loathe** means to feel strong opposition, hatred, or distaste for something or someone. *I loathe horror movies.*
despise	To **despise** means to look down on someone or something, especially with hate or scorn. *They despised her for not helping her friend.*
abhor	To **abhor** means to think of something or someone with disgust and hatred. It is a somewhat formal word. *I abhor all cruelty.*
abominate	To **abominate** means to regard something or someone with great hate or disgust. It is very similar to **abhor**, but is more formal. *I abominate the garbage floating in our rivers and lakes.*

> contrasting keywords: **love, worship**

healthy *adjective*

▶ free from disease or sickness. ***Healthy*** *children have lots of energy.*

well   **Well** means in good health. *Now that I've had a few days to rest, I'm well again.*

fine   **Fine** is so similar to **well** that you can usually use either. *My uncle was in hospital last week but is fine now.*

sound   **Sound** means healthy or in good condition. *Even though the canoe is very old, it is still sound.*

fit   **Fit** can mean strong and healthy. *Rita is very fit after attending the summer training camp.*

robust   **Robust** means strong, healthy, and hardy. *You must be a robust swimmer to swim across that lake.*

> contrasting keywords: **sick**

heap *noun*

▶ a group of things lying one on top of another. *My favourite shirt was somewhere in the* ***heap*** *of laundry.*

pile   A **pile** can be a group of things lying one on top of another in a fairly orderly way. *Dalia carried the pile of logs into the living room.*

stack   A **stack** is an orderly **pile** of things. *Then she took a large log off the stack of firewood.*

mound   A **mound** is a heap of earth, sand, or stones. *We planted the potatoes in a mound of soil.*

cluster   A **cluster** is a bunch or a group of things. *Mark took a cluster of grapes from the bowl.*

rampart   A **rampart** is a wide **mound** of earth built around a fort to protect it. *The children sledded down the ramparts around the old fort.*

heavy *adjective*

▶ difficult to lift or carry. *The piano was so **heavy** that three people had to move it for us.*

massive   **Massive** means large and extremely heavy. *They blasted the massive boulder with dynamite and took away the pieces in trucks.*

hefty   **Hefty** means heavy. It is more suited to everyday language. *Those books are a hefty load for anyone to carry.*

solid   **Solid** can mean heavy or not flimsy, slight, or light. *That's a pretty solid picnic table you've built.*

leaden   **Leaden** means heavy like the metal, lead. *After weightlifting, Nicole's arms felt so leaden she could hardly lift them.*

> similar keywords: **stocky**
> contrasting keywords: **light**

help *noun*

▶ support, or something that makes what you have to do easier. *Don't worry, because **help** is on its way.*

assistance   **Assistance** is support or help. *Sometimes I ask for my older sister's assistance when I do my homework.*

aid   **Aid** is so similar to **help** and **assistance** that you can usually use any one of these. *The government provided food and other aid after the hurricane.*

relief   **Relief** can be freedom or release from pain, unhappiness, or worry. *During the crisis, volunteers provided some relief for the overworked nurses.*

charity   **Charity** can be help or aid given to people who need it. *We give money and food to charity in order to help those less fortunate than we are.*

backing   **Backing** means support of any kind, such as money made available to help a project. *Will the sportswear company give the team its backing?*

help *verb*

▶ to do something with someone so that it is done more easily. *Will you **help** me with my homework please?*

assist   To **assist** means to help someone do something, often in a time of trouble. *She assisted me by helping me to find another job.*

aid   To **aid** means to give what is useful or necessary in achieving an end. *The physiotherapist aided in the athlete's recovery.*

oblige   To **oblige** means agreeing to help by doing someone a favour. *They obliged by giving me a lift home.*

support   To **support** means to give help, strength, or courage to someone. *We showed our support by applauding the candidate's speech.*

nurse   To **nurse** can mean to help something or someone by looking after it carefully. *Alex nursed the seedlings until they were big enough to plant in the garden.*

> similar keywords: **befriend, further**
> contrasting keywords: **hinder**

helper *noun*

▶ someone who does something with you so that it is done more easily. *I need three **helpers** to set out the paints.*

assistant   An **assistant** is someone who helps another person, especially one in a more important position or job. *The scientist hired an assistant to do some of the experiments.*

aide   An **aide** is a personal helper or **assistant**. *The diplomat's aide helped write the speech.*

supporter   A **supporter** is someone who pledges aid to another person. *During her victory speech, the politician thanked her loyal supporters.*

deputy   A **deputy** is a person chosen to assist or act for another person. *We elected a deputy to take over when our club president is away.*

> similar keywords: **associate, friend**

helpful *adjective*

▶ willing to help or support someone. *Thanks for being so* **helpful** *and clearing the table.*

useful	**Useful** means of use or service to someone or something. *Putting the leaves in the compost pile would be a useful thing to do.*
cooperative	**Cooperative** means showing a desire to be helpful. *He was cooperative and helped with the chores without having to be asked.*
obliging	**Obliging** means willing to do someone a favour or be of service. *The salesperson was most obliging and showed us lots of shoes to choose from.*
accommodating	**Accommodating** means helpful and easy to deal with. *The bank teller was most accommodating when I opened my account.*
supportive	**Supportive** means giving help, strength, and encouragement to someone else. *My friends were very supportive when I was unhappy.*

hermit *noun*

▶ someone who lives alone in an out-of-the-way place and keeps away from other people. *The* **hermit** *came out of the forest once a month to shop for supplies.*

recluse	A **recluse** is someone who lives alone and doesn't often mix with other people. *The artist became a recluse so that she could concentrate on her work.*
loner	A **loner** is someone who doesn't like being with other people. *In the Western movie, the hero was a loner who decided to ride off rather than stay and become town sheriff.*
introvert	An **introvert** is someone who is mainly interested in his or her own thoughts and feelings. *He had only a few close friends because he was an introvert.*
monk	A **monk** is a member of a religious group of men living apart from the rest of the world. *The monks lived in the monastery and spent their days meditating and working in the grounds.*

hide   *verb*

▶ to keep something from being seen or discovered. *Pirates used to* **hide** *their treasure by burying it.*

conceal	To **conceal** means to hide something or keep it out of sight. *I concealed the present at the top of the cupboard.*
cover	To **cover** can mean to put something on or over a thing in order to hide it. *He covered his mouth with his hand when he yawned.*
disguise	To **disguise** means to try to hide your true identity or the way something really is by changing your appearance, or making it seem different. *I disguised myself by wearing a wig. They tried to disguise their sadness by smiling.*
mask	To **mask** means to hide or **disguise** something. *We laughed and joked to mask our disappointment at not being chosen for the team.*
camouflage	To **camouflage** can mean to do something that you hope will hide or **disguise** the way things really are. *The soldiers camouflaged the trucks with leaves and branches.*

> contrasting keywords: **show, reveal**

high-pitched   *adjective*

▶ played, sung, or spoken at a high, shrill level of sound. *It annoys me when my brother's watch makes a* **high-pitched** *beep every hour.*

shrill	**Shrill** means loud and high-pitched. *We could hear the shrill yapping of the playful puppy.*
high	**High** can mean sharp in sound. *I can't sing the very high notes in that song.*
treble	**Treble** means of the highest pitch or range when referring to a voice part, singer, or instrument. *If you turn up the treble on the CD player, you can hear the words in the song better.*
soprano	**Soprano** means of the range of notes that can be sung by a woman or boy with a high voice. *She sang in the soprano section of the choir.*
falsetto	**Falsetto** means very high-pitched. *The man used a falsetto voice when he pretended to make the puppet speak.*

hinder *verb*

▶ to slow down something or make it difficult. *My sore leg **hindered** my efforts to run.*

hamper

To **hamper** means to hold back or interfere with something or someone. *The loose wheel hampered her progress in the wheelchair race.*

frustrate

To **frustrate** means to hinder or stop someone or something by putting difficulties in the way. *I was frustrated because I couldn't get past the traffic jam.*

retard

To **retard** means to hinder something or someone, slowing it down. *If you wrap the fish carefully, it will retard spoilage.*

impede

To **impede** means to slow down or block the way of something or someone. *The new treatment impeded the spread of the disease.*

inhibit

To **inhibit** means to hold back or control something or someone. *Wood chips spread over your vegetable garden will inhibit the growth of weeds.*

> similar keywords: **prevent, block, interrupt**
> contrasting keywords: **further, help**

hint *verb*

▶ to make an indirect suggestion. *They **hinted** they'd like to come to the party.*

suggest

To **suggest** can mean to hint, or give the idea of something indirectly. *I think his pale appearance suggests too much hard work and not enough recreation.*

insinuate

To **insinuate** can mean to **suggest** something unpleasant without saying so outright. *I was angry when you insinuated I had cheated.*

imply

To **imply** means to **suggest** something without actually stating it. *Nasima's silence implied that she agreed with us.*

allude to

To **allude to** means to mention something casually. *In his speech, Ben alluded briefly to the book he had just written.*

hit *verb*

▶ to give a hard blow. *Marie **hit** the ball right out of the park.*

strike	To **strike** means to hit or give a blow to something. *I'm going to strike that log with my axe and split it in two.*
knock	To **knock** can mean to bump or **strike** something. *The tennis ball knocked the hat off his head.*
bat	To **bat** means to hit something with, or as if with, a bat. *I batted in a run to win the ball game.*
tap	To **tap** means to hit lightly. *We tapped the wall to find out where the wooden boards were.*

> similar keywords: **beat**

hold *verb*

▶ to have or keep something in your hands or arms. *I **held** the ladder while Marinna changed the battery in the smoke detector.*

grasp	To **grasp** means to hold something very firmly or strongly. *I grasped the railing to make sure I wouldn't fall.*
grip	To **grip** means to seize something or hold it firmly in your hands. *Jake gripped the bat tightly and hit a home run.*
clutch	To **clutch** means to hold or **grip** something tightly in your hands. *I clutched my hat so it wouldn't blow away.*
clasp	To **clasp** means to take a firm hold of something. *The child clasped his teddy bear tightly and finally went to sleep.*
cling to	To **cling to** means to hold tightly to something. *The little kitten clung to its mother's fur.*

> similar keywords: **hug, grab**

hole   *noun*

▶ an opening in or through something. *Do you think this **hole** in the cliff is an entrance to a cave?*

gap	A **gap** is a break or opening in something. *There's a gap in the fence that a puppy could crawl through.*
slot	A **slot** can be a straight, narrow opening. *Rema put her coins into the slot in the soft drink machine.*
perforation	A **perforation** is a hole punched or pierced through something. *The perforations on the coupon made it easy to tear out of the brochure.*
chink	A **chink** can be a narrow opening in something. *I could just slip my fingers through the chink in the log-cabin wall.*
aperture	An **aperture** can be any hole or opening. It is often used about the opening in a camera that controls the amount of light entering the lens. *Be sure to open up your camera's aperture setting when it gets darker outside.*

similar keywords: **break, cut**

holy   *adjective*

▶ set apart for a religious purpose, or having religious significance. *We visited the ruins of the **holy** temple in the ancient city.*

sacred	**Sacred** means holy or worthy of religious respect. *Many religions have sacred books and sacred music.*
hallowed	**Hallowed** means regarded or honoured as holy. *In some religions, you take off your shoes as a sign of respect before you walk upon hallowed ground.*
blessed	**Blessed** means set apart as holy. *In many cultures, the birth of a child is considered to be a blessed event.*
saintly	**Saintly** means like or suited to a saint. *The woman was honoured for her saintly acts of compassion.*

similar keywords: **religious**

home *noun*

▶ the place where someone lives. *I'd like you to come to my **home** and have dinner with us.*

abode	An **abode** is someone's home. It is a rather old-fashioned word. *"Come to our humble abode and rest," said the kind farmer to the weary traveller.*
residence	A **residence** is the place where someone lives. It is a more formal word than **home**. *The prime minister of Canada has a residence in Ottawa.*
dwelling	A **dwelling** is a place for someone to live in. It is a formal word like **residence**. *Several small stone dwellings were all that remained of the ancient village.*
household	A **household** is a home, including the people who live there and the things they do. *Our household is a busy place on Monday morning.*

honest *adjective*

▶ fair, not lying, cheating, or stealing. *If you are always **honest**, people will know they can trust you.*

truthful	**Truthful** means showing you can be relied on to tell the truth. *Why should we doubt his story? He has always been truthful.*
honourable	**Honourable** means acting with high principles and honesty. *I believe what you say because you are an honourable person.*
upright	**Upright** means honest and just. *The school custodian is an upright person whom we all respect.*
sincere	**Sincere** means expressing true and honest feelings. *Their sincere compliments pleased me.*
scrupulous	**Scrupulous** can mean being very exact about doing what is right. *The store owner is scrupulous in her dealings with her customers, and she guarantees whatever she sells.*

> similar keywords: **frank, decent, fair**
> contrasting keywords: **dishonest, cunning**

horrible *adjective*

▶ causing a strong feeling of fear or disgust. *I couldn't bear to watch the **horrible** earthquake scene in the movie.*

dreadful **Dreadful** can mean causing great fear or terror. *They spent a dreadful night worrying about the damage the tornado might cause as it passed by the town.*

horrendous **Horrendous** means horrible and **dreadful**. *It took the farmer a long time to recover from the horrendous sight of the hail destroying all the crops.*

terrible **Terrible** means causing great fear. *In my nightmare, a terrible beast was chasing me.*

frightful **Frightful** means alarming and unpleasant. *They had a frightful time trying to cross the flooded river.*

> similar keywords: **nasty, frightening, bad**
> contrasting keywords: **nice**

hot *adjective*

▶ having a high temperature or giving out heat. *Don't eat the soup yet, because it's still very **hot**.*

blazing **Blazing** means very hot or burning fiercely. *The blazing fire soon warmed the whole room.*

sweltering **Sweltering** means very, very hot and somewhat damp. *We were glad of the fan on that sweltering day.*

fiery **Fiery** can mean like fire. *A blast of fiery heat hit me as I opened the door.*

flaming **Flaming** can mean like flames. *The flaming hot barbecue coals cooked our dinner quickly.*

scorching **Scorching** means intensely hot. *The scorching sidewalk burned her bare feet.*

> similar keywords: **humid**
> contrasting keywords: **cold, wintry**

hug *verb*

▶ to put your arms tightly around someone in order to show your affection for them. *I **hugged** my parents when I arrived home.*

cuddle   To **cuddle** means to hug gently. *We cuddled the kitten until it stopped trembling.*

embrace   To **embrace** means to hug or hold in your arms. This is a more formal word. *The two sisters embraced after their long time apart.*

cradle   To **cradle** means to hold and rock gently, especially a baby. *The father cradled the sick baby in his arms.*

press   To **press** can mean to hug tightly or hold close to you. *In the movie, she pressed him to her and kissed him goodbye.*

> similar keywords: **hold**

huge *adjective*

▶ very, very large or immense. *We had to lean way back to see the top of the **huge** building.*

gigantic   **Gigantic** means extremely large or huge. *The gigantic mountain towered over the village.*

colossal   **Colossal** means huge or of extremely great size. *There was a colossal statue in the harbour in ancient Rhodes.*

enormous   **Enormous** means very large. *The enormous arena holds thousands of people.*

tremendous   **Tremendous** means very large or **enormous**. It is more suited to everyday language. *Even the smallest elephants appeared to be a tremendous size.*

vast   **Vast** means huge or of very great area, bulk, or size. *Vast forests cover much of British Columbia.*

> similar keywords: **big, heavy**
> contrasting keywords: **small**

humble *adjective*

▶ not full of pride; being aware of your weaknesses and sometimes seeming to have a low opinion of your own importance or abilities. *Dale remained **humble** even after winning the award.*

modest
: **Modest** means having a moderate opinion of yourself and your abilities. *We were surprised at the modest behaviour of such a famous writer.*

meek
: **Meek** means being obedient and patient in a humble way, even though you are treated badly. *The little boy was so meek that he didn't complain about being bullied.*

self-effacing
: **Self-effacing** means keeping yourself in the background because you feel humble. *My self-effacing partners are too modest about the good work they did.*

lowly
: **Lowly** means being meekly obedient and not having a high opinion of your abilities. *You can be humble without having to behave in a lowly manner.*

> contrasting keywords: **proud, pompous, conceited, grand**

humid *adjective*

▶ moist and damp, especially when it's also warm. *We perspired a lot in the **humid** weather.*

muggy
: **Muggy** means unpleasantly warm and humid. *The air became very muggy as we approached the marsh.*

sultry
: **Sultry** means unpleasantly hot and humid. *The air was sultry just before the thunderstorm arrived.*

close
: **Close** can mean lacking fresh air. *The air in the room was too close until we opened the window to let some fresh air in.*

oppressive
: **Oppressive** can mean hard to bear or causing discomfort. *The heat was so oppressive, we couldn't do any work outside.*

> similar keywords: **hot**

hurry *verb*

▶ to act quickly to save time. ***Hurry** or you'll miss the bus.*

dash	To **dash** means to move very quickly and suddenly. *I dashed into the elevator just before the doors closed.*
rush	To **rush** means to move very quickly or to do something in a great hurry. *Milana rushed to finish her dinner so she wouldn't miss the bus.*
hasten	To **hasten** means to move or act quickly. *Daniel hastened to catch the glass before it fell.*
shake a leg	To **shake a leg** means to hurry as fast as you can. This is more suited to everyday language. *If I don't shake a leg, the train will leave without me.*
get a move on	To **get a move on** means to hurry up. This is more suited to everyday language. *We had better get a move on or we won't finish in time!*

> similar keywords: **speed, dart**
> contrasting keywords: **dawdle, walk**

hurt *verb*

▶ to cause pain or damage. *He **hurt** his leg when he slipped on the ice.*

harm	To **harm** means to hurt or damage. It is sometimes used when there has been a danger of some hurt or damage that never actually happens. *The hijackers did not harm the hostages.*
injure	To **injure** means to hurt a living thing, especially a person or an animal. *Kim injured her knee when she fell off her bike.*
wound	To **wound** means to make a cut in the flesh. *Many of the soldiers were either killed or wounded in the War of 1812.*
maim	To **maim** means to cause an injury to someone, especially to an arm or leg. *The accident maimed him for life.*

> similar keywords: **damage, abuse**

I, i

ignorant *adjective*

▶ knowing little or nothing. *He could speak three languages but was completely* ***ignorant*** *in mathematics.*

uneducated   **Uneducated** means not having been formally taught or instructed. *Although my great-grandfather was uneducated, he was very knowledgeable about many subjects.*

illiterate   **Illiterate** means unable to read or write. *Our school offers night classes for illiterate adults.*

uninformed   **Uninformed** can mean **uneducated** about a particular subject. *This simple explanation of nuclear physics is especially for the uninformed people in the audience.*

> contrasting keywords: **educated**

illegal *adjective*

▶ not allowed by law. *Smoking in public places is* ***illegal*** *in many cities.*

illicit   **Illicit** means unlawful or not having permission to operate. *The police raided the illicit gambling house.*

criminal   **Criminal** means having to do with crime. *Their criminal activities soon became known to the police.*

felonious   **Felonious** means having to do with a serious crime, such as murder or burglary. *She was arrested for her felonious activities.*

fraudulent   **Fraudulent** means having to do with deliberate trickery or cheating. *The manager saw the clerk's fraudulent attempt to fake the accounts.*

contraband   **Contraband** means having to do with goods that have been imported or exported illegally. *The smuggler was fined for trying to bring contraband computers into Canada.*

> similar keywords: **dishonest, evil**
> contrasting keywords: **legal**

imaginary *adjective*

▶ existing only in the mind. *Little children often play with **imaginary** friends.*

made-up	**Made-up** means invented or worked out in your mind. *It was only a made-up story about a unicorn.*
fanciful	**Fanciful** means unreal or imaginary. *I read a fanciful story about a flying carpet.*
fictitious	**Fictitious** means not real or genuine, coming instead from your own imagination. *No one believed their fictitious story about meeting a goblin at the bottom of the garden.*
fantastic	**Fantastic** can mean imaginary or without basis or reason. *Don't let such fantastic fears worry you!*
mythical	**Mythical** can mean imaginary or invented. *The unicorn is a mythical creature.*

> contrasting keywords: **actual**

imagine *verb*

▶ to form a picture of something in your mind. ***Imagine** you are exploring underwater as you listen to the music.*

dream	To **dream** can mean to imagine something that is usually pleasant or enjoyable. *I dreamed about becoming a famous medical researcher.*
pretend	To **pretend** means to imagine something to be true, usually as a game. *The children pretended they were on a trip to Mars.*
make believe	To **make believe** is so similar to **pretend** that you can usually use either. *The children made believe they were astronauts.*
feign	To **feign** means to **pretend** or to appear to have something, sometimes in order to deceive someone. *He feigned illness in order to stay home, but his parents convinced him that going to kindergarten would be fun.*

> similar keywords: **think, daydream**

important *adjective*

▶ having great influence or power. *We planned a special welcome for the **important** visitor.*

great
: **Great** can mean notable or important. *The great occasion was celebrated with fireworks and parades.*

eminent
: **Eminent** means well-known or high in rank. *The eminent scientist talked to us about her experiments.*

prominent
: **Prominent** means very important or standing out ahead of others. *Because he was a prominent cabinet minister, we listened to him.*

pre-eminent
: **Pre-eminent** means most important or much better than others. *She is the pre-eminent scientist in her field.*

prestigious
: **Prestigious** means having a high reputation or standing. *Thanks to years of outstanding work, he now holds a prestigious government position.*

> similar keywords: **grand, famous, significant**
> contrasting keywords: **insignificant**

impossible *adjective*

▶ not able to be done or used. *It seems **impossible** that he solved that problem all by himself.*

unattainable
: **Unattainable** means not able to be achieved, even with great effort. *Most goals are not unattainable if you work hard at reaching them.*

unthinkable
: **Unthinkable** can mean not able to be imagined or thought about as a real possibility. *Thirty years ago it was unthinkable that people would have home computers.*

hopeless
: **Hopeless** means impossible or highly unlikely to be carried out. *Difficult situations are not always hopeless.*

insurmountable
: **Insurmountable** means not being able, or being extremely difficult, to be overcome. *Despite nearly insurmountable difficulties, the team made the playoffs.*

> contrasting keywords: **possible, likely**

improve   *verb*

▶ to make something of higher quality or bring it into a better condition. *I want to* ***improve*** *my public speaking skills.*

better	To **better** means to improve something or to increase its good qualities. *They are working to better the living conditions in their country.*
enrich	To **enrich** means to improve the quality of something. *The farmer enriched the soil with organic fertilizer.*
upgrade	To **upgrade** can mean to improve the quality of something. *They upgraded the plumbing in their old house by putting in new pipes.*
enhance	To **enhance** means to increase or improve something. *Upgrading the plumbing will enhance the value of the house.*
perfect	To **perfect** can mean to improve something or to remove any faults. *The manufacturer perfected the new product before selling it.*

> similar keywords: **correct, repair**
> contrasting keywords: **deteriorate**

inarticulate   *adjective*

▶ not able to use clear speech that everyone can understand. *His shyness made him* ***inarticulate****, and it was hard to understand what he was trying to say.*

hesitant	**Hesitant** can mean pausing while or before speaking, usually because you are unsure of what you are saying. *We could tell from her hesitant answer that she didn't understand the question.*
faltering	**Faltering** can mean **hesitant** or often stopping and starting again when speaking. *His faltering speech showed us how nervous he was.*
tongue-tied	**Tongue-tied** means not able to speak, usually because you are too shy or nervous. *Don't be surprised if you are tongue-tied for a minute the first time you give a speech in public.*
disjointed	**Disjointed** means not fitting together properly. *His story was so disjointed that we couldn't work out who had really hidden the money.*

> contrasting keywords: **fluent**

include *verb*

▶ to consist of or contain as a part. *Education **includes** what we learn both at home and at school.*

comprise
To **comprise** means to include or be composed of something. *This school comprises kindergarten through grade six.*

involve
To **involve** means to include as a necessary part of something. *The job of an art gallery guide involves giving talks about the major works on display.*

incorporate
To **incorporate** means to include something and make it part of something else. *We incorporated several of your ideas into the format of the report.*

embrace
To **embrace** can mean to include or contain something. *The committee's decision embraced all the main points raised in the public meeting.*

cover
To **cover** can mean to include or provide for something. *This computer book covers all the basics.*

contrasting keywords: **exclude**

incompetent *adjective*

▶ lacking the skill or ability you should have. *The **incompetent** clerk sent me the wrong forms.*

unskillful
Unskillful means showing or having very little skill. *He made an unskillful attempt to fix it.*

amateurish
Amateurish means having very little skill or not up to a professional standard. *Dad did an amateurish job of painting the house.*

fumbling
Fumbling means handling something clumsily. *Her fumbling fingers finally tore open the parcel.*

inept
Inept means awkward or lacking in skill. *He made an inept attempt to sew on the button.*

similar keywords: **inexperienced, clumsy**
contrasting keywords: **competent, skillful**

incomplete *adjective*

▶ not being whole, or having some parts missing. *This model kit is **incomplete**.*

partial	**Partial** can mean not total or complete. *Here are partial instructions, and I'll give you the rest tomorrow.*
fragmentary	**Fragmentary** means broken or not whole. *The news was fragmentary because the radio picked up so much static.*
unfinished	**Unfinished** means incomplete or not brought to an end. *I have some unfinished business I must take care of today.*
piecemeal	**Piecemeal** means done piece by piece. *They were very disorganized and had a piecemeal approach to their work.*
rough	**Rough** can mean incomplete or not exact. *She has completed a rough version of the script.*

> similar keywords: **insufficient**
> contrasting keywords: **whole, thorough**

incorrect *adjective*

▶ wrong or having mistakes. *Your answer is **incorrect**.*

inaccurate	**Inaccurate** means not right or exact. *Your inaccurate description of the house gave us the wrong idea about its size.*
untrue	**Untrue** means not true or right. *I knew the statement was untrue because I saw what really happened.*
false	**False** means incorrect or not true. *They made some false accusations just to cause trouble.*
erroneous	**Erroneous** means incorrect or containing a mistake. *The old theory about the position of the earth and the sun was erroneous.*
off base	**Off base** means wrong or incorrect. This is more suited to everyday language. *That answer is so far off base, it's not even close to the truth.*

> contrasting keywords: **true**

increase *verb*

▶ to become more or bigger. *The population of the world **increases** every year.*

expand To **expand** can mean to increase in size, especially by spreading out. *The more air Kate blew into the balloon, the more it expanded.*

grow To **grow** means to become bigger. *The town began to grow when gold was discovered nearby.*

multiply To **multiply** can mean to increase in amount or number. *Nasrin's achievements have multiplied so much over the past year that he has nowhere to put all of his awards.*

mount To **mount** can mean to increase in amount. *Our savings are mounting every month.*

accumulate To **accumulate** can mean to increase by growing into a heap. *I don't want to let too much junk accumulate on my desk.*

> similar keywords: **add, extend**
> contrasting keywords: **decrease, shrink**

indecent *adjective*

▶ not proper or in good taste. *We were shocked by the movie's **indecent** language.*

improper **Improper** can mean indecent or not suitable. *Their disgusting behaviour is improper and embarrassing.*

immoral **Immoral** means wicked or wrong. *I think that cheating is immoral.*

corrupt **Corrupt** means dishonest or able to be bribed. *The corrupt judge had been in the pay of criminals for years before being found out.*

depraved **Depraved** means evil or morally bad. *The mad scientist was as depraved as the wicked monsters he created.*

perverted **Perverted** means turned away from what is right or proper in your behaviour or beliefs. *We don't find your perverted sense of humour funny at all.*

> similar keywords: **evil, dishonest**
> contrasting keywords: **decent**

independent *adjective*

▶ not needing or relying on the help of others. *As children get older, they are more independent and want to do more things for themselves.*

self-sufficient   **Self-sufficient** means able to supply your own needs. *They were able to be self-sufficient because they grew their own food.*

separate   **Separate** means not connected to anything or anyone else. *Although they lived in the same apartment building, they led completely separate lives.*

unaffiliated   **Unaffiliated** can mean not connected with any particular person or group. *The new student enjoyed sports, but was unaffiliated, for a while, with any school teams.*

sovereign   **Sovereign** means self-governing or able to govern or rule on your own. *Canada has been a sovereign nation since 1867.*

freelance   **Freelance** means not working for a wage, but selling work to more than one employer, especially as a writer does. *The freelance writer sold her stories to several magazines and newspapers.*

indicator *noun*

▶ something that points to or shows something. *The indicator showed that the boat had a full tank of gas.*

sign   A **sign** can be anything that shows something exists or is likely to happen. *A rainbow can be a sign that it has stopped raining.*

marker   A **marker** is something used to mark or indicate something. *We used a pile of stones as a marker to show the way we had gone.*

pointer   A **pointer** is anything that draws your attention to something of interest. *The pointer of the barometer showed that fair weather was coming.*

guide   A **guide** is something or someone who shows you the way. *The reflectors on the posts by the side of the road are a guide to drivers at night.*

cursor   A **cursor** is a symbol on a computer screen, often a flashing bar or line, that shows where you are currently working. *Meghan moved the cursor to the beginning of the paragraph.*

inedible *adjective*

▶ not able or fit to be eaten. *That cheese is so hard that it's **inedible**.*

unpalatable   **Unpalatable** means tasting so unpleasant it is difficult to eat. *The fast food was so unpalatable that even the dog wouldn't eat it.*

stale   **Stale** means so old it is no longer pleasant to eat. *Give the stale bread to the birds, and we will eat the fresh loaf.*

rotten   **Rotten** can mean unfit for eating because it is old and decaying. *The rotten apples were soft and brown.*

off   **Off** can mean not fit for eating, usually because it is too old or overripe. It is more suited to everyday language. *The milk was off and made my cereal taste terrible.*

> contrasting keywords: **delicious**

inexperienced *adjective*

▶ lacking the knowledge or skill you gain from doing, seeing, or living through something yourself. *An **inexperienced** driver has to be particularly careful in wet weather.*

raw   **Raw** can mean inexperienced or not trained. *Training and daily drills turned the raw recruits into fine firefighters.*

amateur   **Amateur** can mean not skilled, or having only slight knowledge of a job. *He is an amateur plasterer, and his wall is very uneven.*

untrained   **Untrained** means having had no training for a particular activity. *She is an untrained singer, but she has a lovely voice.*

green   **Green** can mean **untrained** or inexperienced. It is usually used after a verb. *You could see he was green by the way he tried to start a fire with wet wood.*

> similar keywords: **incompetent, naive**
> contrasting keywords: **experienced, competent**

inferior   *adjective*

▶ of low quality or value. *Although you are inexperienced, your work is never* ***inferior***.

poor	**Poor** can be so similar to **inferior** that you can usually use either word. *The shopper was surprised by the poor quality of the stereo speakers.*
shoddy	**Shoddy** means badly made. *This cupboard is so shoddy that the door won't close properly.*
worthless	**Worthless** means of such low quality as to have little or no value. *That worthless toy broke two days after the child's parents bought it.*
crummy	**Crummy** means of low quality or little value. It is more suited to everyday language. *The concert was great even though our seats were crummy.*

> similar keywords: **defective, mediocre**
> contrasting keywords: **superior, distinguished**

influence   *noun*

▶ some force that affects or produces a change in someone or something else. *He is a good* ***influence*** *on his friends.*

power	**Power** can mean strength or force. *The new government will have the power to change many things.*
hold	**Hold** can mean a controlling force or influence. *The actor's hold on the audience was so great that the theatre was completely silent.*
clout	**Clout** can mean influence or effectiveness. *You need some clout to get a good table in that fancy restaurant.*
sway	**Sway** can mean control or rule. *The dictator held sway for many years until the people overthrew him.*
charisma	**Charisma** is a special quality that some people have to attract and influence others. *A popular leader usually has charisma.*

influence *verb*

▶ to have an effect on someone or something. *Try to make up your own mind without letting your friends **influence** you too much.*

manipulate   To **manipulate** can mean to influence someone cleverly or unfairly. *I don't like it when people try to manipulate others in order to get their own way.*

prejudice   To **prejudice** means to influence someone without sensible reason. *They were prejudiced against her because she came from another town.*

bias   To **bias** means to influence someone, usually unfairly. *They tried to bias my opinion about the film by telling me what they didn't like about it.*

condition   To **condition** means to influence or affect someone by training the person in a certain way. *What we are taught by our parents and teachers helps to condition the way we live.*

> similar keywords: **persuade**

inform *verb*

▶ to give news or knowledge to someone. *I **informed** him of your success.*

instruct   To **instruct** can mean to inform or give information to someone. *They instructed me to go straight ahead and then turn left.*

notify   To **notify** means to inform or tell someone of something, especially in an official way. *The coach notified us that the day of the game had changed.*

advise   To **advise** can mean to give someone information about something important. *We advised the magazine of our new address before we moved.*

announce   To **announce** means to tell something to someone or make it known in public. *The date of the track meet was announced during the assembly.*

> similar keywords: **tell, reveal, publish**

informal *adjective*

▶ without ceremony or formality. *The prime minister had an **informal** chat with the visiting athletes.*

unofficial   **Unofficial** can mean not done with official approval. *According to an unofficial report, there will be 300 new jobs when the company moves to our town.*

casual   **Casual** can mean informal or not having to do with special occasions. *We wore casual clothes to the movie.*

relaxed   **Relaxed** can mean informal and at ease. *Once the ceremony was over, the guests were more relaxed.*

easygoing   **Easygoing** means not being strict about the way things are done. *Our relatives are easygoing people who don't mind if we arrive a little late for dinner.*

contrasting keywords: **formal**

information *noun*

▶ knowledge given or received about some fact or happening. *It is always a good idea to get some **information** about a country if you plan to visit it.*

news   **News** can be information considered suitable for reporting or not known before. *Have you heard any news about the elections in India?*

data   **Data** are facts or information, especially a group of facts from which a conclusion will be drawn. This is a plural noun. *If you give me the data, I'll figure out what can be done to improve the situation.*

intelligence   **Intelligence** can be information or knowledge of an event or happening given to or received from someone. *Have you received the latest intelligence about the robbery from the police in Winnipeg?*

propaganda   **Propaganda** is information that is used to try to convince you of a certain point of view. *The booklet was full of political propaganda designed to influence the way we would vote.*

similar keywords: **gossip**

inhabit   *verb*

▶ to live or dwell in a place, as people or animals do. *Polar bears **inhabit** the arctic regions of Canada.*

populate   To **populate** can mean to inhabit or live in a place, as a group of people do. *The rocky land around our town is sparsely populated.*

occupy   To **occupy** can mean to **settle** or take possession of a place. *The aboriginal people allowed the European settlers to occupy land on both sides of the river.*

settle   To **settle** means to make your home in a certain place. *Our friends have decided to settle in Saskatchewan.*

colonize   To **colonize** means to establish a colony or settlement ruled by the parent country. *Many of the treaties with the First Nations were broken when France and England colonized North America.*

> similar keywords: **reside**

initiate   *verb*

▶ to begin something or to set it going. *I'm going to **initiate** a discussion about the news item I saw last night.*

establish   To **establish** means to set something up. *There were so many children in the area that the district had to establish a new school.*

found   To **found** means to set something up or **establish** it. *The city of Dawson was founded when gold was discovered at Bonanza Creek.*

institute   To **institute** means to set something up or get it going. *Our sports club instituted a new karate course.*

launch   To **launch** means to start or to get something going. *We launched the food drive last night.*

pioneer   To **pioneer** means to begin something or to be one of the first to do it. *Banting, Best, and their associates pioneered the research into diabetes.*

> similar keywords: **begin, invent, start**
> contrasting keywords: **finish, cancel, stop**

inquiry   *noun*

▶ a search or probe into a matter. *The **inquiry** into the need for a new crosswalk took several weeks.*

investigation   An **investigation** is a close look at something. *The investigation into the cause of the fire showed that there had been an electrical fault.*

examination   An **examination** means the act of careful looking and testing. *The dentist's examination of Lynn's teeth revealed no broken fillings.*

survey   A **survey** is a study of the views of people in order to write a report about what they think or do. *They did a survey to see what people thought about the new juice container.*

poll   A **poll** means a counting of people, votes, or opinions. *The TV station did a telephone poll to see what people thought of the government's plans to change the tax system.*

inquisitive   *adjective*

▶ wanting to find out all about something. *Our new cat was very **inquisitive** and looked all around our house.*

questioning   **Questioning** can mean so inquisitive about the world around you that you can't help asking questions. *Jacques has such a questioning mind that he spends a lot of time looking things up in the library.*

inquiring   **Inquiring** means seeking information or knowledge. *The child had an inquiring mind and was eager to learn.*

curious   **Curious** can mean wanting to learn, especially about things that are strange or new. *We were curious about the new person in our class.*

nosy   **Nosy** means interested in things that aren't your business. *We thought our next-door neighbours were nosy when we saw them peeking through their curtains at us.*

snooping   **Snooping** means prying into things in a sneaky or sly way. It is more suited to everyday language. *My snooping brother was always trying to discover where I hid my diary.*

---

similar keywords: **alert**

insert *verb*

▶ to put or set in something. *She moved the cursor with the mouse and **inserted** a comma into the sentence.*

enclose   To **enclose** can mean to put something inside something else. *I enclose a photograph with this letter.*

slip   To **slip** can mean to put or pass something into anything else with a smooth, sliding movement. *I slipped the money into my wallet.*

introduce   To **introduce** can mean to bring or put something new into a place, surroundings, and so on. *The biologist introduced a new species of fish into the aquarium.*

ease   To **ease** can mean to move something or someone slowly and carefully into anything. *I carefully eased the pie into the oven.*

> similar keywords: **add**
> contrasting keywords: **remove**

inside *noun*

▶ the inner part or side of something. *The **inside** of their apartment is always bright.*

interior   The **interior** is the internal or inside part of something. *The interior of the store was decorated with striped wallpaper.*

contents   The **contents** are whatever is inside or contained in something. This is a plural noun. *We were keen to discover the contents of the old box we found in the storeroom.*

innards   **Innards** can be the essential or inner parts of something. This is a plural noun. *Teresa looked at the innards of the broken engine to find the problem.*

belly   A **belly** can be the inside of something. *The sailor crawled right into the belly of the ship to look for the leak.*

> similar keywords: **centre**
> contrasting keywords: **outside, edge**

insignificant *adjective*

▶ unimportant, without much power, or not worth consideration. *I'm more interested in the point of the story than in **insignificant** details.*

unimportant   **Unimportant** means not powerful or worthy of notice. *The colour of your boots is unimportant, so long as your feet are warm.*

dispensable   **Dispensable** means of little importance; something that may be done without. *Our new house is much smaller, and we had to decide which furniture was dispensable.*

expendable   **Expendable** can mean not necessary or not worth keeping. *Those old typewriters became expendable when we bought the new computers.*

peripheral   **Peripheral** can mean not essential or important. *The work of the social committee was peripheral to the club's main purpose of raising money for the hospital.*

small-time   **Small-time** means of little importance. This is more suited to everyday language. *The police kept a watch on the small-time criminal and hoped he would lead them to the mastermind of the bank robberies.*

> similar keywords: **minor, subordinate**
> contrasting keywords: **significant, main, important**

inspect *verb*

▶ to look carefully at something. *The doctor **inspected** her patient's ears and nose.*

look over   To **look over** means to view or examine something carefully. *Tracy looked over several used bikes before deciding which one to buy.*

search   To **search** means to look at or through something very carefully, hoping to find something. *I searched the ground for my lost bracelet.*

survey   To **survey** can mean to take a general look at something. *We surveyed the beautiful valley from the top of a hill.*

scan   To **scan** can mean to look at something closely. *The doctor scanned the blood sample for any evidence of disease.*

> similar keywords: **examine, see, investigate**

insufficient *adjective*

▶ not enough or not having as much as is wanted or needed. *There is **insufficient** paint to give the room a second coat.*

inadequate   **Inadequate** means not enough to fill a need. *The crops were small because of inadequate rain.*

lacking   **Lacking** means showing the lack or absence of some important part. *This soup is lacking in flavour.*

deficient   **Deficient** means incomplete or **lacking**. *If you eat plenty of fresh fruit and vegetables, you will seldom be deficient in vitamins.*

short   **Short** can mean not having or being enough. *Please lend me two dollars; I'm a little short of money right now.*

> similar keywords: **scant, incomplete**
> contrasting keywords: **abundant, extra**

insult *verb*

▶ to act or speak rudely to someone. *I was hurt when you **insulted** me in front of everyone.*

slight   To **slight** means to treat rudely by ignoring someone. *You slighted me by not replying to my invitation.*

snub   To **snub** is similar to **slight**, and you can often use either word. *He snubbed me by looking the other way when we met on the street.*

humiliate   To **humiliate** means to make someone feel ashamed or foolish. *Their rude remarks about my mistake humiliated me.*

belittle   To **belittle** means to make someone or something feel or seem unimportant. *The supervisor belittled their efforts even though they had done their best.*

affront   To **affront** means to hurt someone's feelings or pride. *She affronted his visitors by making rude comments about their manners.*

> similar keywords: **tease**
> contrasting keywords: **worship**

intend *verb*

▶ to mean, or to have an idea, to carry out something. *I **intend** to make a model airplane this weekend.*

aim
: To **aim** is to intend or to have as a goal. *We are aiming to have the work done by Wednesday.*

plan
: To **plan** is to form a purpose or scheme. *We plan to build a new set of shelves next week.*

vow
: To **vow** is to declare your intention solemnly. *He vowed to be very careful and never go hiking by himself again.*

have in mind
: To **have in mind** is to be thinking about or to intend. This is suited to everyday language. *What do you have in mind for us to do today?*

choose
: To **choose** can mean to decide or prefer to do something. *Justine chose to go to the movie instead of the museum.*

intense *adjective*

▶ very great or strong. *I had to stop for a drink of water often during the hike because of the **intense** heat.*

severe
: **Severe** can mean harsh or extreme. *The severe cold of a winter wind can lead to frostbite.*

profound
: **Profound** means very deeply felt. *We thought for a long time about the wise woman's profound words.*

vivid
: **Vivid** means intense and clear. *He is a good writer because he has a vivid imagination.*

passionate
: **Passionate** means showing a strong feeling or emotion. *She is very passionate about her objection to the plan to build a superstore in the historic neighbourhood.*

violent
: **Violent** can mean forceful or intense in a rough way. *The violent wind made driving difficult.*

contrasting keywords: **moderate**

interrupt *verb*

▶ to break into what someone is saying or doing. *They **interrupted** me many times with their questions.*

disturb   To **disturb** means to interrupt someone or something in a way that hinders or interferes. *Your constant chatting is disturbing the speaker.*

punctuate   To **punctuate** can mean to interrupt quite often. *They punctuated her speech with cheers.*

cut off   To **cut off** means to break in in the middle of something. This is more suited to everyday language. *I cut him off before he finished giving his answer.*

disconnect   To **disconnect** means to break a connection or link between two things. *We were disconnected in the middle of our telephone conversation.*

> similar keywords: **hinder, disrupt, intrude**

intrude *verb*

▶ to enter or force yourself in where you are not wanted or invited. *We were having fun playing together until she **intruded**.*

interfere   To **interfere** means to take part in someone else's affairs without being asked. *She always interferes by trying to tell us what to do.*

meddle   To **meddle** means to **interfere** with something that doesn't concern you. *He finished his own work early and then started to meddle in ours.*

butt in   To **butt in** means to interrupt or **interfere**. This is more suited to everyday language. *We were having a private talk when Wilf butted in.*

barge in   To **barge in** means to intrude in a forceful and obvious way. This is more suited to everyday language. *I'm going to barge in on their meeting and tell them what I think.*

interject   To **interject** means to make a remark that interrupts a conversation or speech. *I interjected loudly because I didn't agree with what he said.*

> similar keywords: **interrupt**

invent *verb*

▶ to think up something new. *Did you know that it was a Canadian who **invented** basketball?*

devise	To **devise** means to think out, plan, or invent something. *I have devised a way for us all to earn some extra money for our holiday.*
conceive	To **conceive** means to think of or form something. *We conceived the plan while we were walking to school.*
innovate	To **innovate** means to introduce something new. *They innovated an effective new way of separating coins.*
coin	To **coin** means to make or invent something, especially a new word or phrase. *Shakespeare coined many new words that no one had heard before.*

> similar keywords: **create**

investigate *verb*

▶ to look into or examine something closely. *The police are **investigating** the bank robbery.*

probe	To **probe** means to examine or search something thoroughly. *The police have to probe the whole area in order to find evidence.*
scrutinize	To **scrutinize** means to examine something closely and carefully. *The art dealer scrutinized the painting to see whether it was genuine.*
explore	To **explore** means to examine or go over something very carefully. *They explored the whole cave to see if there was another way out.*
research	To **research** means to study closely or scientifically in order to understand or learn more about a subject. *The students researched the topic thoroughly before completing their geography assignment.*
delve into	To **delve into** means to search or look into something thoroughly or in great depth. *Mario delved into all the encyclopedias he could find for information for his project.*

> similar keywords: **examine, test, inspect**

invisible *adjective*

▶ unable to be seen. *We could all hear the airplane even though it was **invisible**.*

unseen   **Unseen** means invisible or not seen. *The unseen animals could be heard moving through the woods.*

hidden   **Hidden** means kept from sight. *The hidden entrance to the rabbit's warren was in the long grass.*

concealed   **Concealed** means placed out of sight. *My parents had a concealed safe installed in the den in case our home gets burglarized.*

imperceptible   **Imperceptible** means not easily seen or noticed. *The slope in the ground was so imperceptible that I did not notice I was climbing a small hill.*

> contrasting keywords: **visible**

irrational *adjective*

▶ absurd or not based on sound judgment. *Filipe had an **irrational** fear of water.*

illogical   **Illogical** means not based on sensible or correct thinking. *Wearing an overcoat on a hot day is illogical.*

unreasonable   **Unreasonable** means not based on good sense. *It's unreasonable to insist on going out when the roads are icy.*

groundless   **Groundless** means without any reason or basis. *I know the children are frightened that there is a mouse in the cellar, but their fears are groundless.*

inconsistent   **Inconsistent** means having no order or agreement between the parts of something. *Your use of quotation marks in that story is inconsistent and confusing.*

arbitrary   **Arbitrary** means based on your own feelings and ideas rather than on rules or reasons. *The director made an arbitrary decision about who would be first on the stage.*

> similar keywords: **silly, fickle**
> contrasting keywords: **sensible, sane**

irritate *verb*

▶ to annoy or to make someone angry. *The audience's chatter **irritated** the speaker.*

vex To **vex** means to annoy or worry someone. This is a rather formal word. *The king was vexed by all the talk of reform.*

irk To **irk** means to annoy and upset someone. *Mary's refusal to help Craig irked him.*

provoke To **provoke** can mean to stir up and make someone angry or annoyed. *They provoked me by telling me my opinions were silly.*

goad To **goad** can mean to tease. *They goaded me, but I didn't lose my temper.*

peeve To **peeve** means to annoy or irritate someone. *His basic questions did not peeve the instructor.*

> similar keywords: **annoy**
> contrasting keywords: **please**

isolate *verb*

▶ to keep someone or something apart from others. *The scientists **isolated** the new virus.*

ostracize To **ostracize** means to keep someone away from others, or send them away from everyone. *The other children ostracized the boy who told on his friends.*

quarantine To **quarantine** means to isolate people or animals for a certain period of time to make sure they don't spread a disease to others. *The officials quarantined the animals that had been in contact with the sick cow.*

segregate To **segregate** means to set someone or something apart from other people or things. *We should segregate all the damaged supplies so that no one uses them by mistake.*

seclude To **seclude** means to keep yourself apart from others. *The hermit secluded herself in a cabin in the woods.*

> similar keywords: **expel, exclude, separate, confine, enclose**

J, j

jealous *adjective*

▶ wanting very much to have what other people have. *Paolo is **jealous** of his sister's guitar-playing ability.*

envious
Envious means feeling or showing discontent and ill will at seeing what someone else has. It is very similar to **jealous**. *I am envious of your good luck in winning the prize.*

covetous
Covetous means wanting very much what someone else has. It is a rather formal word. *He was so covetous of her new book that he took it without asking.*

possessive
Possessive means wanting to control or possess someone or something all by yourself. *My little brother is very possessive of his new bike.*

green
Green can mean extremely jealous. It is more suited to everyday language. *I was green with envy when I saw his new CD player.*

> similar keywords: **resentful**

job *noun*

▶ employment for which you are paid. *I have a **job** delivering the weekend newspaper.*

work
Your **work** can be the job by which you earn money. *His work is teaching.*

occupation
Your **occupation** is your usual type of job or employment. *What is your mother's occupation?*

business
A **business** is the job or trade you have in order to earn a living. *We have a business building decks and patios.*

career
A **career** is the job or profession you hope to have for the rest of your life. *She wants to make medicine her career.*

vocation
A **vocation** is a particular job or profession that you believe to be very important. *I want to make teaching my vocation.*

> similar keywords: **profession, position**

join   *verb*

▶ to put two or more things together. *Sunita **joined** the broken pieces with glue.*

connect   To **connect** means to join or **unite** something. *Carl connected both ends of the model railway track together.*

link   To **link** is so similar to **join** and **connect** that you can usually use any of these words. *You can link these rings together to make a chain.*

couple   To **couple** means to join one thing to another. *The workers had to couple the cars together before the train could leave.*

unite   To **unite** means to join two or more people or things together as one. *The three of us are united in our efforts to organize a school play.*

consolidate   To **consolidate** means to **unite** or combine things. *All the groups consolidated their efforts to produce a class project.*

> similar keywords: **combine**
> contrasting keywords: **separate**

joke   *noun*

▶ something that is said or done to make people laugh. *She told us a **joke** about a man who took a refrigerator to the South Pole.*

jest   A **jest** is a joke that is sometimes a mocking one. *He made a jest about his clumsiness to hide his embarrassment.*

laugh   A **laugh** is something that suggests amusement, happiness, or lively joy. It can also be used to mean the opposite of what is being said. *Walking through the Hall of Mirrors was a laugh. "That's a laugh," he said, when I asked if he had any money.*

gag   A **gag** is a joke or funny trick. *The comedian's gag kept the audience laughing.*

crack   A **crack** can be a joke, often an unkind one. It is more suited to everyday language. *He made a crack about my purple hair.*

> similar keywords: **wisecrack**

journey *noun*

▶ a trip or course you take when travelling from one place to another, especially by land. *Our journey took us across the Prairies and into the Foothills of the Rockies.*

trip	A **trip** is a journey, usually a short one. *We'll plan a trip to the city on the holiday weekend.*
tour	A **tour** is an organized journey through a place or from one place to another. *We went on a bus tour to see the major historical sites.*
expedition	An **expedition** is a journey made for a special reason. *Many explorers made expeditions to try and find the Northwest Passage.*
excursion	An **excursion** is a short journey or **trip**, usually taken for a special reason. *Our class is going on an excursion to the science museum.*
jaunt	A **jaunt** is a short **trip** made for fun. *Let's take a jaunt to the beach this afternoon.*

joyful *adjective*

▶ full of great happiness and delight. *The family had a joyful reunion when their grandparents came from Vietnam.*

jubilant	**Jubilant** means joyful because you have been successful. *We were jubilant when we got permission to make an outdoor skating rink.*
elated	**Elated** means in very high spirits. *We were elated to hear how well you recovered.*
ecstatic	**Ecstatic** means having a sudden feeling of great joy. *They were ecstatic when they met each other at the airport.*
rapturous	**Rapturous** means filled with great joy and happiness. *We spent a rapturous hour watching the sun set over the lake.*
blissful	**Blissful** means extraordinarily happy. *They had a blissful time together after so many years apart.*

similar keywords: **happy, glad, optimistic, excited**
contrasting keywords: **glum, miserable, sad, pessimistic**

judge   *verb*

▶ to form an opinion about something. *I didn't **judge** the width of the car properly, so I scratched the car door on the wall of the garage.*

evaluate To **evaluate** means to test and find the value or quality of something. *Our essay topic was to evaluate the statement "Nuclear energy is not dangerous."*

appraise To **appraise** means to judge the value of something. *The jeweller appraised the gold bracelet.*

value To **value** means to form an opinion about how much something is worth. *She valued Arun's friendship.*

size up To **size up** something means to form an idea about it. *The team's manager thought about the pitcher's performance and then sized up the situation.*

adjudicate To **adjudicate** means to make a judgment about something. *The older students adjudicated the speeches in our debate.*

> similar keywords: **measure, examine**

jump   *verb*

▶ to move suddenly from the ground or some other support, using the leg muscles. *I was so happy that I **jumped** up and down.*

leap To **leap** means to jump lightly and quickly. *I leaped over the puddle in the middle of the road.*

spring To **spring** means to **leap** or move upward with sudden energy. *She sprang out of her seat when the bell went.*

bound To **bound** can mean to move with jumps or **leaps**. *The dog bounded right over the fence and ran up the path.*

hop To **hop** means to move by springing, often using only one leg. *He hopped over to the tree when he sprained his ankle.*

vault To **vault** means to jump, often with your hands on something to support you. *When she couldn't open the gate, she vaulted over it.*

justify *verb*

▶ to show an act, or something similar, to be right or reasonable. *You can sometimes justify what you have done by explaining why you did it.*

warrant
To **warrant** can mean to show there is a good reason or need for something. *The urgency of the situation warranted quick action.*

explain
To **explain** can mean to account for something or make the reason for it clear. *Please explain your unusual answer.*

excuse
To **excuse** can mean to justify or serve as a reason for a fault or wrongdoing. *Your tiredness does not excuse your silliness.*

vindicate
To **vindicate** means to show someone to be innocent or right; to clear from suspicion. This is rather a formal word. *The new evidence vindicated the people who had always claimed they were innocent.*

rationalize
To **rationalize** something means to find reasons for it. *I don't like it when people try to rationalize their thoughtless behaviour.*

similar keywords: **prove**

K, k

keep *verb*

▶ to make something continue in the same way or state. *We must **keep** our lakes and forests as clean as we can.*

maintain	To **maintain** means to keep something up or keep it in good condition. *You maintain a bike by oiling it and keeping the tires filled.*
preserve	To **preserve** means to keep something from going bad. *We picked so much fruit from our tree that we had to preserve some of it.*
retain	To **retain** means to keep, or keep on, using something. *The painters retained our house key until they finished the job.*
prolong	To **prolong** means to make something last longer. *I wish we could prolong our holiday because we're having such a good time.*

> similar keywords: **store**
> contrasting keywords: **change, discard**

kill *verb*

▶ to cause the death of something or someone. *We **killed** the rats with poison.*

murder	To **murder** means to kill someone deliberately. *The detective overheard the plan to murder the security guard.*
assassinate	To **assassinate** means to **murder** a well-known person, such as a politician. *The man who assassinated the leader was arrested with the gun still in his hand.*
execute	To **execute** can mean to put someone to death in a way allowed by the law. *Criminals are no longer executed in Canada.*
put down	To **put down** can mean to kill an animal humanely in order to end its suffering. *The dog was so badly injured that the vet had to put it down.*
slay	To **slay** means to kill someone or something using violence. It is an old-fashioned word. *The knight grabbed the sword to slay the dragon.*

k i n d   *adjective*

▶ warm-hearted, friendly, and wishing good things for other people. *It was **kind** of him to show the new student around the school.*

nice   **Nice** can mean kind or pleasant. *They were nice people to associate with.*

thoughtful   **Thoughtful** means thinking of other people and considering their needs. *It was thoughtful of you to send me some magazines when I was home sick.*

considerate   **Considerate** means kind or thinking of other people's needs and feelings. *Although he could hardly keep his eyes open, the considerate boy read his sister her favourite story.*

unselfish   **Unselfish** means thinking about other people and not just yourself. *It was very unselfish of you to share your last piece of cake.*

well-meaning   **Well-meaning** means having good intentions in the way you act or treat people. *She was very well-meaning, but when she attempted to help she nearly flooded the kitchen.*

similar keywords: **friendly, polite, loving**
contrasting keywords: **selfish, mean**

L, l

label *noun*

▶ a piece of paper put on something to show what it is, who owns it, or where it is going. *The **label** on my suitcase gives my name and address.*

tag

A **tag** is a piece of cardboard or strong paper attached to something as a label. *I took the price tag off the gift before I wrapped it.*

tab

A **tab** is a small label. *A tab with the manufacturer's name was sewn to the inside of the shirt collar.*

ticket

A **ticket** is a label or **tag**, showing the price of something and other information about it. *The hockey tickets included the time and date of the game, the team names, and the location of our seats.*

sticker

A **sticker** is an adhesive or gummed label, usually with an advertisement or other information printed on it. *The bag of fruit had a sticker with the price on it.*

label *verb*

▶ to describe something with a label. *We always **label** our suitcases when we travel on trains or airplanes.*

mark

To **mark** means to put a sign or label on something to give information about it. *I marked my in-line skates so I could tell they were mine.*

tag

To **tag** can mean to put a tag or label on something, giving information about it. *The store tags every item of new stock when it arrives.*

identify

To **identify** means to recognize a particular thing or person, sometimes as one's own. *As soon as she comes on the air, the disc jockey plays this song to identify her program.*

stamp

To **stamp** can mean to print a mark on something. *When I went to Mexico, the customs official stamped my passport.*

lack *noun*

▶ absence of something you want or need. *I felt tired because of a **lack** of fresh air.*

shortage A **shortage** is a lack in the supply of something. *There was a shortage of water during the long dry spell.*

deficiency A **deficiency** can be an inadequate amount of something. *We made up for the temporary deficiency in our diet by taking vitamins.*

dearth A **dearth** is a lack or very small supply of something. *There was a dearth of recent videos at the rental store when we finally got there on Saturday.*

deficit A **deficit** is a shortage in the amount of something, especially money. *Dad promised that if I saved up half the money for new skis, he would make up the deficit.*

> contrasting keywords: **excess**

lake *noun*

▶ a large area of water surrounded by land. *We canoed around the shoreline of the small **lake**.*

lagoon A **lagoon** is a pond of shallow water that is often separated from the sea by low banks of sand. *The children played safely in the lagoon only a hundred metres from the crashing surf.*

basin A **basin** can be a low area of land, sometimes with water in it, surrounded by higher land. *The river basin lies between the two mountain ranges.*

pond A **pond** is a body of still water smaller than a lake. *The pond was filled with lily pads and weeds.*

dam A **dam** is a wall used to hold back water or the body of water held back by this wall. *The farmers dug ditches from the dam to water their crops.*

reservoir A **reservoir** is a place where water is stored. *Pipes carry water from the dam to the town reservoir.*

> similar keywords: **bay**

land *verb*

▶ to come to rest on the ground or by the shore. *The airplane **landed** so smoothly that the passengers hardly felt a thing.*

touch down To **touch down** is similar to **land**, but is only used about aircraft. *The space shuttle touched down after a successful four-day mission.*

alight To **alight** means to get down out of a vehicle after a journey. *The passengers alighted from the bus.*

dismount To **dismount** means to get off a horse or a bike after a ride. *Angeline pulled up outside the gate and dismounted hurriedly.*

dock To **dock** means to enter a dock for loading or unloading. *The boat docked alongside the pier.*

disembark To **disembark** means to get off a ship or out of a plane after a journey. *Passengers should watch their step as they disembark.*

similar keywords: **come, descend**

language *noun*

▶ the arrangement of words we use when we speak or write. *English is the most widely spoken **language** in the world.*

dialect A **dialect** is a form of speech or language spoken in a particular area or by a particular group of people. *In one Newfoundland dialect, the word "fudline" means coarse fishing line.*

tongue **Tongue** can be another word for a language or a dialect. *The visitor spoke in a foreign tongue.*

jargon **Jargon** is the language made up of special words and phrases used only by people in a particular occupation. *Many people find it hard to understand the jargon of legal documents.*

colloquialism A **colloquialism** is an expression that is suitable only for everyday language. *To "break up," meaning to laugh, is an example of a colloquialism.*

slang **Slang** is everyday language that is not suitable for formal speech or writing. *Avoid using slang in your science reports.*

laugh *verb*

▶ to make sounds that show amusement, happiness, or scorn. *The children **laughed** as the clowns played tricks on one another.*

chuckle To **chuckle** is to laugh softly with amusement. *I chuckled as I read Justine's funny letter.*

howl To **howl** means to laugh loudly. *We howled when she told us that joke.*

guffaw To **guffaw** means to laugh loudly and noisily. *The audience guffawed at the comedian's hilarious routine.*

break up To **break up** can mean to explode into or collapse with laughter. This is more suited to everyday language. *We broke up when Jacques came in wearing a funny mask.*

> similar keywords: **smile**
> contrasting keywords: **cry**

lawyer *noun*

▶ someone whose work is to give advice about the law and to argue on behalf of people in law courts. ***Lawyers** have to know all about new laws so that they can advise their clients.*

counsel A **counsel** is a lawyer who represents a client in a court case. *The counsel convinced the judge that the defendant had been wrongly charged, and the case was dropped.*

barrister A **barrister** is a **counsel** who is authorized to plead cases in Canadian or British superior courts. *That Vancouver lawyer is a well-known barrister.*

solicitor A **solicitor** is a lawyer who advises clients, represents them in lower courts, and prepares cases for **barristers** to plead in higher courts. *The law firm's business card stated that they were barristers and solicitors.*

paralegal A **paralegal** is someone who can perform some legal services, but is not qualified as a lawyer. *We went to a paralegal who was an ex-police officer when we decided to take our traffic tickets to court.*

layer *noun*

▶ a single thickness. *The lasagna had at least six* **layers** *of pasta covered in tomato sauce, vegetables, and cheese.*

stratum A **stratum** is a horizontal layer of any material. *We could see a stratum of granite running across the face of the cliff.*

seam A **seam** can be a thin layer of a different kind of rock or mineral in the ground. *The new seam of coal discovered yesterday will keep the miners working for another year.*

vein A **vein** can be a layer of metal or ore in the middle of rock. *The miners were excited when they found the rich vein of gold.*

deposit A **deposit** can be a layer that collects on a surface. *As the flooded river went down, it left a rich deposit of loam on the farmlands.*

> similar keywords: **coating**

laze *verb*

▶ to be lazy or spend your time doing very little. *It was so hot last Saturday that I just* **lazed** *around all day.*

idle To **idle** can mean to spend your time doing nothing. *My friend doesn't understand that I am not simply idling when I am drawing, reading, thinking, or meditating.*

loaf To **loaf** means to do nothing. It is similar to **laze** and to **idle**. *When you've been working too hard, take a break and just loaf.*

lounge To **lounge** can mean to spend your time relaxing. *They lounged around the pool instead of cleaning the yard.*

not pull your weight To **not pull your weight** means to avoid doing your fair share of something. *You won't be a productive member of the group if you don't pull your weight.*

loll To **loll** means to lean or lie around in a lazy way. *He said he just wanted to loll in bed all day.*

> similar keywords: **rest**
> contrasting keywords: **work**

lazy *adjective*

▶ not liking work or effort. *I thought he was being **lazy** when he didn't help with the housework, but he was actually feeling quite ill.*

idle   **Idle** means not doing or wanting to do anything. *We were idle until the blizzard stopped.*

indolent   **Indolent** means lazy or tending to avoid work. *He was so indolent that all he seemed to do was spend the weekends lying in front of the TV.*

slack   **Slack** can mean lazy, careless, and neglectful. *She is sometimes slack about going to basketball practice.*

slothful   **Slothful** means extremely lazy. It is often used in an insulting way. *Thanks to your slothful ways, our project won't be finished in time.*

> similar keywords: **lethargic, apathetic**
> contrasting keywords: **busy, lively, energetic**

learn *verb*

▶ to come to have knowledge about something or to develop a skill in it. *He wants to **learn** to speak Filipino before he visits his cousins in the Philippines.*

memorize   To **memorize** means to put something into your memory or learn it by heart. *The singer memorized the words to several songs.*

absorb   To **absorb** can mean to take something into your mind. *The student absorbed all the facts.*

assimilate   To **assimilate** means to learn or **absorb** something so completely that it becomes part of you. *In order to give an interesting and informed talk, I assimilated all I could find out about life in Sri Lanka.*

take in   To **take in** can mean to understand and remember something. *Did you take in what she was telling you?*

digest   To **digest** can mean to think something over and take it into your mind. *Make sure you have time to digest all the information before the test.*

> similar keywords: **understand**
> contrasting keywords: **teach**

leave *verb*

▶ to go away from somewhere. *We have to **leave** when our taxi comes.*

depart	To **depart** means to leave. It is a more formal word. *The train departs at 10:00 a.m.*
withdraw	To **withdraw** means to take yourself away from a place, especially a room. It is a rather formal word. *She withdrew to her study.*
retreat	To **retreat** means to go back. *The nature photographer retreated to a more hidden position.*
emigrate	To **emigrate** means to leave your own country to go to live in another one. *Many people have emigrated from the Caribbean to Canada.*

> similar keywords: **flee, quit**
> contrasting keywords: **come, advance**

legal *adjective*

▶ allowed or decided by law. *The contract had a lot of **legal** terms that were difficult to understand at first.*

lawful	**Lawful** means allowed by law. *It is now lawful for bookstores in our community to remain open seven days a week.*
legitimate	**Legitimate** means according to the law or established rules. *Being sick is a legitimate reason for being unable to do jury duty.*
permissible	**Permissible** means allowed. *Talking quietly is permissible behaviour in the library.*
authorized	**Authorized** means having been given permission to do something. *Elisabeth was authorized to speak on behalf of all the members of the club.*
proper	**Proper** means right or approved. *If you have been treated well in a restaurant, the proper thing to do is to tip your server 15–20%.*

> similar keywords: **formal**
> contrasting keywords: **illegal, dishonest**

lengthy *adjective*

▶ long or using many words. *She gave us such a **lengthy** explanation that we were able to finish the task with few problems.*

rambling **Rambling** can mean lengthy and not keeping to one train of thought. *Their rambling account of what happened puzzled us.*

wordy **Wordy** means using more words than are needed. *Sometimes showing an example is more effective than giving a wordy explanation.*

tedious **Tedious** means tiresomely long and boring. *People fidgeted and coughed throughout the award-winner's tedious speech.*

long-winded **Long-winded** means talking for too long. *He seems long-winded at times, but he just wants to make sure you understand.*

> similar keywords: **continuous**
> contrasting keywords: **brief**

lenient *adjective*

▶ not harsh or severe in treatment. *The judge gave a **lenient** sentence because it was the defendant's first offence.*

merciful **Merciful** means showing kindness by not punishing someone, or not being cruel. *The newly elected government was merciful to the former dictator and his supporters by allowing them to stay in the country.*

compassionate **Compassionate** means showing pity and kindness to someone. *The compassionate children took care of the injured bird until it was well enough to look after itself.*

humane **Humane** means showing feelings of pity or tenderness in the way that kind and decent human beings should. *The guards in the prison were well-known for their humane treatment of inmates.*

mild **Mild** can mean not severe or harsh. *Her mild manner made the children feel less worried about getting a scolding.*

> similar keywords: **broad-minded, polite**
> contrasting keywords: **strict**

lesson   *noun*

▶ an amount or unit of teaching given at one time. *Kim has a one-hour drum* **lesson** *this afternoon.*

lecture	A **lecture** is a long speech made in front of an audience or class and meant to teach or inform. *The professor gave a very interesting lecture on African-American music.*
seminar	A **seminar** is a meeting of students to discuss a particular subject. *I enjoyed the discussion in our history seminar, and I asked lots of questions.*
class	A **class** can be the information taught to a student or students at one time. It is similar to **lesson**. *We had a class on aboriginal literature.*
course	A **course** is a series of lessons. *I'm taking an art course once a week for the next ten weeks.*

lethargic   *adjective*

▶ being in a state of sleepy laziness. *I feel so* **lethargic** *today that I don't want to do anything energetic.*

listless	**Listless** means having no energy or interest in anything. *It was such a hot day that we were all very listless.*
sluggish	**Sluggish** means moving slowly with no energy. *The car was very sluggish going up the hill.*
enervated	**Enervated** means drained of strength and energy. *The intense humidity enervated the hikers.*
languid	**Languid** means weak, tired, or slow-moving. *Don't be surprised if the flu makes you languid.*
inert	**Inert** means motionless or **sluggish**. *In science we learned that an inert object will remain motionless unless it is acted upon by a force.*

> similar keywords: **apathetic, lazy, tired, slow**
> contrasting keywords: **energetic, lively, busy**

lift *verb*

▶ to move or bring something upward or to a higher position. *Please help me **lift** this heavy trunk.*

raise
To **raise** is so similar to **lift** that you can usually use either. *He was so tired that he could barely raise his head from the pillow.*

elevate
To **elevate** can mean to lift or **raise** something. This meaning is usually used in more formal language. *They elevated the speaker's platform so that everyone could see.*

hoist
To **hoist** means to **raise** or haul up with or as if with a mechanical device. *The workers hoisted the bronze sculpture onto its concrete base.*

lever
To **lever** means to lift and move something by putting a bar under it and pushing down on the other end of the bar. *The railway workers levered the huge boulder out of the way.*

jack up
To **jack up** means to lift something very heavy with a special tool called a jack. *Mom had to jack up the car so that she could change the tire.*

> contrasting keywords: **drop**

light *adjective*

▶ of little or less than usual weight. *I'm glad to be wearing **light** clothing again after such a long, cold winter.*

feathery
Feathery means light and airy like feathers. *The ballet dress was soft and feathery.*

thin
Thin means having opposite surfaces close together or having small thickness. *The birthday present was covered in thin wrapping paper that you could almost see through.*

fine
Fine can mean very **thin** or slender. *I don't think this thread will be strong enough, because it's too fine.*

flimsy
Flimsy means not strongly made. *This flimsy fence will probably blow down in the wind.*

> contrasting keywords: **heavy, thick**

like   *verb*

▶ to find someone or something pleasant. *I **like** everyone in my class.*

enjoy
To **enjoy** means to take pleasure in something. *I enjoy working in groups on an interesting project.*

appreciate
To **appreciate** means to value or be aware of the good things about something or someone. *We appreciate all the little things you have done to make us feel at home in our new neighbourhood.*

welcome
To **welcome** means to receive or regard something or someone with pleasure. *I welcome the cooler weather after all this heat.*

fancy
To **fancy** can mean to take a liking to someone or something. *Some days I just fancy a bowl of soup and a small salad for lunch.*

> similar keywords: **love**
> contrasting keywords: **hate**

likely   *adjective*

▶ reasonably or apparently going to happen. *Looking at the sky tonight, I'd say it will **likely** be a fine day tomorrow.*

probable
Probable is so similar to **likely** that you can usually use either. *Do you think it is probable that they will arrive by this afternoon?*

expected
Expected can mean likely to happen or come about. *The expected result in the election is for the government to be returned with an increased majority.*

liable
Liable can mean likely. It is often used in regard to a negative outcome. *Problems are liable to come up.*

apt
Apt means likely or inclined to do something. *He is apt to arrive at any moment.*

plausible
Plausible means reasonable or apparently true. *It is plausible that she could have done it by herself.*

> similar keywords: **possible, believable**
> contrasting keywords: **unbelievable, impossible**

limit   *verb*

▶ to keep something within a certain amount or space or time. *I **limit** my TV watching to two hours a week.*

restrict	To **restrict** is so similar to **limit** that you can usually use either. *We restricted the time we spent working out so that we would have time for other activities.*
control	To **control** can mean to keep something in check. *We had to control our spending so that our pocket money would last all week.*
curb	To **curb** means to **control** or hold back something. *I tried to curb my appetite by eating small, nutritious snacks throughout the day.*
inhibit	To **inhibit** means to hold back or hinder something. *You can use wood chips to inhibit the growth of weeds in your flower garden.*
stifle	To **stifle** can mean to keep back or stop. *She stifled a yawn during the early-morning practice.*

> similar keywords: **confine**

limp   *verb*

▶ to walk unevenly and with difficulty because one leg or foot is injured or weak. *My sprained ankle ached as I **limped** along the path home.*

hobble	To **hobble** means to walk unevenly and with difficulty. *I hobbled around after stubbing my toe.*
shuffle	To **shuffle** means to walk slowly, dragging your feet along the ground. *Michael was so tired after the long walk that he shuffled straight off to bed.*
totter	To **totter** means to sway or to walk unsteadily. *The newborn colt tottered across the floor of the barn.*
toddle	To **toddle** means to walk with short, unsteady steps. *My baby brother toddled along on his chubby little legs.*

> similar keywords: **walk, trudge**
> contrasting keywords: **frolic, march**

line *noun*

▶ something arranged like a long, narrow mark or stroke made on a surface. *A **line** of trees grew on each side of the street.*

row	A **row** is a line of people or things. *We saw the movie from the last row of the theatre.*
lineup	A **lineup** can be a single line of people or cars or animals waiting in turn for something. *We had waited in the lineup to buy tickets for nearly an hour.*
string	A **string** is a **row** or line of things. *The West Indies is a string of islands in the Caribbean Sea.*
file	A **file** is a line of people or things, one behind the other. *The lane was so narrow that we had to walk in single file.*
rank	A **rank** is a **row**, line, series, or range. *The workers stood in ranks, waiting for the new plant to open.*

liquid *adjective*

▶ flowing like water. *Oil is sometimes referred to as **liquid** gold because it is so valuable.*

fluid	**Fluid** means liquid or able to flow. *Mercury is a metal that is fluid at room temperature.*
runny	**Runny** means pouring out liquid, or flowing. *The runny apple pie spread all over the plate.*
watery	**Watery** means watered down or resembling water. *The salad was good, but the soup was watery.*
sloppy	**Sloppy** means wet and slushy. *The sloppy snow left salt stains on our boots.*
molten	**Molten** means made liquid by heat. *Lava is the hot, molten rock that comes out of a volcano.*

contrasting keywords: **gluey**

list *verb*

▶ to make a set of the names of things written down one after the other. ***List** all the books you need from the library, and I'll try to get them for you.*

index
To **index** means to make an alphabetical list of names, places, or subjects in a book, showing their page numbers. *If you write a thesaurus, it is a good idea to index all the words you have included and put it at the back.*

tabulate
To **tabulate** means to make a plan or chart listing things that are related to one another. *We tabulated the results of our experiment to show how we reached our conclusions.*

itemize
To **itemize** means to give details about each part of an overall group. *We itemize our monthly expenses so that we can figure out how much money to budget for each.*

enumerate
To **enumerate** means to name things one by one or make them clear in a list. *Let's enumerate the arguments for and against buying a new computer.*

similar keywords: **arrange, record**

live *verb*

▶ to be alive. *I will never forget you as long as I **live**.*

exist
To **exist** can mean to have life or be real. *Do you think ghosts really exist?*

be
To **be** can mean to live or have reality. *I'm afraid he is no more.*

breathe
To **breathe** can mean to **exist** or have life. *The wise one told us that everything that breathes is sacred.*

survive
To **survive** means to stay alive or in existence, especially after someone's death or the end of something. *Three people were killed in the accident, and two survived.*

remain
To **remain** can mean to stay alive. *Of my grandmother's five brothers and sisters, now only two remain.*

contrasting keywords: **die**

lively *adjective*

▶ full of energy or spirit. *We had a **lively** party with lots of dancing and laughter.*

frisky	**Frisky** means jumping around in a lively way. *The horses were very frisky after their long rest in the paddocks.*
vivacious	**Vivacious** means lively and energetic. *We have a vivacious teacher who makes our classes interesting and fun.*
playful	**Playful** means full of fun. *The playful puppy loved to run after the ball.*
frolicsome	**Frolicsome** means enjoying happy or energetic play. *The playground was full of frolicsome children.*
jaunty	**Jaunty** means lively and confident. *She walked into the room with a jaunty step.*

> similar keywords: **energetic, busy**
> contrasting keywords: **lethargic, lazy**

lonely *adjective*

▶ without friendly company. *He was **lonely** when his best friend was away.*

alone	**Alone** means by yourself. *Were you alone in the house?*
lone	**Lone** means unaccompanied or not with anyone. *They could see a lone traveller coming toward them.*
solitary	**Solitary** means quite **alone** or without any companions. *I went on a solitary walk when I wanted time to think.*
reclusive	**Reclusive** means wanting to live by yourself and not see other people. *He is reclusive by nature, but his relatives try to visit him often.*
secluded	**Secluded** means quiet and private. *She lives a secluded life, far away from civilization.*

> similar keywords: **shy**
> contrasting keywords: **friendly**

loot   *verb*

▶ to take property or goods by stealing. *The thieves **looted** the vacant homes during the fire.*

plunder	To **plunder** means to steal by open force. *The enemy army plundered the farmers' storehouses.*
pillage	To **pillage** is so similar to **plunder** that you can usually use either. *The soldiers pillaged the empty village.*
raid	To **raid** means to carry out a surprise attack. *The children raided the kitchen, looking for cookies.*
ransack	To **ransack** can mean to search thoroughly for goods to steal. *The raccoons ransacked the garbage cans in search of food.*
ravage	To **ravage** means to destroy or lay waste. *Swarms of locusts ravaged the farmer's field.*

similar keywords: **attack**

loud   *adjective*

▶ producing a lot of sound so that you can hear it easily. *The **loud** noise startled me.*

blaring	**Blaring** means producing a loud, harsh sound. *It was hard to relax at the beach because there were so many blaring tape players.*
deafening	**Deafening** means so loud that it could make someone deaf. *The jackhammers were deafening, so the workers had to wear ear plugs.*
raucous	**Raucous** means harsh-sounding. *We heard raucous laughter coming from the party.*
shrill	**Shrill** means loud and piercing. *The locomotive's shrill whistle echoed through the canyon.*
resonant	**Resonant** can mean deep and booming. *The opera singer's resonant baritone voice can be heard all through the auditorium.*

contrasting keywords: **quiet**

love   *verb*

▶ to feel strong affection for another person. *I **love** my parents, my brothers, and my sisters.*

adore	To **adore** means to feel very strong love for someone or something. *The children adored their puppy.*
dote on	To **dote on** means to love someone or something so much that you appear to be silly. *He dotes on his hamster and talks about it all the time.*
cherish	To **cherish** means to care tenderly about someone or something. *I cherish your friendship.*
care for	To **care for** means to have a fondness for someone or something. *I don't care for beef.*

> similar keywords: **like, worship**
> contrasting keywords: **hate**

loving   *adjective*

▶ feeling or showing love. *His **loving** father always tries to do the best for him.*

affectionate	**Affectionate** means having and showing feelings of love toward someone. *The affectionate puppy kept licking my hand.*
fond	**Fond** means having warm feelings toward someone. *I have fond memories of the people we met during our trip.*
tender	**Tender** can mean loving in a romantic way. *The film ended with a tender embrace.*
devoted	**Devoted** means showing a very strong attachment to something or someone. *She is devoted to her pets and spends hours caring for them.*

> similar keywords: **friendly, kind, faithful**
> contrasting keywords: **unfriendly, unkind, mean, cruel**

lucky *adjective*

▶ having good luck or good fortune. *We were **lucky** to find a parking spot so close to the arena.*

fortunate **Fortunate** means being lucky or having good fortune. *You were fortunate to find the earring you lost.*

happy **Happy** can mean **fortunate** or lucky for everyone concerned. *It was a happy coincidence to meet you at the movies.*

promising **Promising** means likely to turn out well. *The weather looks promising, so perhaps we could have a picnic.*

charmed **Charmed** can mean living as if under a magic spell. *She seems to lead a charmed life, being healthy, happy, and very successful.*

auspicious **Auspicious** means favourable or showing signs of success. It is a rather formal word. *All the signs were auspicious, so our parents decided to set up their own business.*

contrasting keywords: **unlucky**

M, m

mad *adjective*

▶ mentally ill or unbalanced. *The dog went **mad** because it had rabies.*

crazy   **Crazy** is so similar to **mad** that you can usually use either. It is not a kind term. *The book is about a crazy person who really thinks he can fly.*

insane   **Insane** means mentally ill. It is similar to **mad** and **crazy**, but is often used in a more serious way. *The arctic explorer almost went insane from loneliness and starvation.*

disturbed   **Disturbed** can mean emotionally or mentally unstable. *The doctor told the disturbed patient to relax and rest for a few weeks.*

> contrasting keywords: **sane**

main *adjective*

▶ most important or biggest. *My **main** reason for training so hard is to get on the Olympic swimming team.*

major   **Major** means greater in importance or size. *Her major interest is playing the guitar.*

chief   **Chief** means most important or main. *My chief function in the club is to organize charity fund raising.*

key   **Key** means main or important. *The goalie is a key member of the hockey team.*

fundamental   **Fundamental** means most important or basic. *You have to learn the fundamental rules of the road before you can get a licence to drive.*

primary   **Primary** means first in order of importance. *My primary concern is finding enough food to feed all of the guests.*

> similar keywords: **significant, best**
> contrasting keywords: **minor**

make *verb*

▶ to bring something into being. *Paul and I are **making** a batch of cookies.*

manufacture To **manufacture** means to make or produce something by hand or machine, especially in large numbers. *Mom works for a company that manufactures furniture.*

form To **form** means to make or produce something. *The children piled up sand to form a sand castle.*

prepare To **prepare** means to make something ready. *I am practising every day to prepare myself for the performance.*

whip up To **whip up** means to make something quickly. *Mom and Dad had to whip up a meal when their friends paid a surprise visit.*

> similar keywords: **create, build, produce, cause**
> contrasting keywords: **destroy**

male *noun*

▶ a man or a boy. This is a formal word that often is used in discussions about medicine and biology. *Our research task was to find out why some **males** go bald.*

man A **man** is a mature or adult male. *My father is known to be a friendly man.*

boy A **boy** is a male who has not reached adulthood. *The boys were learning to play soccer.*

young man A **young man** is a male who is almost an adult, or a **boy** who behaves in a mature way. *The principal said she was proud of all the young men and women who were entering high school.*

gentleman **Gentleman** is a courteous term for a man. It is used mainly on formal occasions. *Ladies and gentlemen, thank you for attending this meeting.*

> similar keywords: **female**

manage   *verb*

▶ to be in charge of something or someone. *She was asked to **manage** the store while the owner was away.*

run
: To **run** can mean to conduct or administer something, such as a business or an experiment. *My parents run a small printing business.*

direct
: To **direct** can mean to guide something or someone by giving instructions. *Our class teacher will direct the school play this year.*

control
: To **control** means to be in charge of or **direct** someone or something. *The teacher had to control a large group of children on the field trip.*

supervise
: To **supervise** means to keep an eye on and be responsible for someone or something. *The principal supervised my class the day the French teacher was absent.*

> similar keywords: **rule**

manager   *noun*

▶ someone who runs a business or other organization, or supervises other people. *My **manager** gave me an outline of my duties for the month.*

director
: A **director** can be someone who shares the management of a company or other organization. *The board of directors meets once a month to review the progress of the project.*

superintendent
: A **superintendent** is someone who is in charge of work being done. *The building superintendent is in charge of all the repairs carried out in our apartment.*

administrator
: An **administrator** is someone who directs or manages something, according to set rules or ways. *She was a good administrator, and the other club members were happy to follow her directions.*

official
: An **official** is someone who has the authority to do a particular job, usually in connection with government. *The municipal official said she would ensure that the recycling trucks kept to a regular schedule.*

> similar keywords: **boss**

manner *noun*

▶ a way of behaving or of doing things. *The doctor has a good bedside* **manner**.

attitude	An **attitude** can be the way you behave or hold your body. *The students have a positive attitude about school.*
bearing	Your **bearing** is the way you behave or stand. *She had the flexibility and the strong bearing of an athlete.*
carriage	Your **carriage** is the way you hold your head and body when you walk or stand. *The butler in the movie had a very dignified carriage and a polite manner.*
stance	Your **stance** is the position of your body when you are standing. *The musician's confident stance showed that she was used to performing in public.*
posture	Your **posture** is the particular position of your body at any time. *Studying yoga helped improve my attitude as well as my posture.*

> similar keywords: **appearance**

march *verb*

▶ to walk like a soldier, with swinging arms and even steps. *The band members* **marched** *in time to the drum beat.*

parade	To **parade** means to march, often in a procession or for display. *Our band paraded into the auditorium for the assembly.*
stride	To **stride** means to walk with long, bold steps. *She strode quickly along the street without looking left or right.*
strut	To **strut** means to walk in a proud or conceited way, with your back straight and your head held high. *The actor strutted across the stage to accept the award.*
swagger	To **swagger** means to walk in a conceited way, hoping to draw attention to yourself. *He was so proud of his new clothes that he swaggered along when he wore them.*

> similar keywords: **frolic**
> contrasting keywords: **limp, walk, trudge**

mark *noun*

▶ a scratch, stain, or cut. *The wet glass left a **mark** on the wooden table.*

stain
: A **stain** is a discoloured spot made by a substance that leaves marks. *It was hard to remove the grape juice stain from the carpet.*

blot
: A **blot** is a spot or a **stain**, often one caused by ink. *Remember to put the cap on your pen so that you won't get an ink blot on your shirt pocket.*

scratch
: A **scratch** is a mark left by something sharp. *The scratch on the floor was made by a skate that dropped.*

blemish
: A **blemish** is a **stain** or a defect. *There is a blemish in the paintwork on my new bike.*

dent
: A **dent** is a small hollow in a hard surface, caused by pressure or a heavy blow. *The dent in the car fender was caused when he got too close to a pillar in an underground garage.*

meal *noun*

▶ food eaten at more or less fixed times each day. *Breakfast is my favourite **meal**.*

snack
: A **snack** is a small quick meal. *I have fruit as a snack every afternoon after school.*

feast
: A **feast** is a magnificent meal set out for many guests. *Everyone enjoyed the delicious feast after the ceremonies.*

spread
: A **spread** can be a large meal for many people. It is more suited to everyday language. *They put on a wonderful spread to welcome their relatives from Quebec.*

feed
: A **feed** is a meal or something to eat. It is more suited to everyday language. *We sat down to a great feed of fresh corn on the cob.*

> similar keywords: **food**

mean *adjective*

▶ bad-tempered and cruel. *It was **mean** of that neighbour to yell at the children for cutting across the lawn.*

unkind
Unkind means not very friendly or warm-hearted. *It would be unkind not to help someone in trouble.*

shabby
Shabby can mean unfair or mean. *That's a shabby way to treat anyone.*

contemptible
Contemptible means **despicable**, disgraceful, and mean. *Tripping the other runner was a contemptible thing to do.*

despicable
Despicable means disgraceful and deserving contempt and scorn. *It was despicable of you to cheat them.*

miserable
Miserable can mean unpleasant and nasty. *It will make you miserable if you act selfishly all the time.*

> similar keywords: **resentful, cruel, evil, nasty**
> contrasting keywords: **kind, decent, loving**

meaning *noun*

▶ something that is intended to be said or shown. *The teacher explained the **meaning** of the poem.*

gist
Gist is the most important part of something. *I understood the gist of her message, so I can explain it to you.*

drift
Drift can be the general meaning of something. *Did you get the drift of that argument?*

significance
Significance can be so similar to **meaning** that you can usually use either. *The museum guide explained the significance of the sculpture.*

sense
Sense can be the particular meaning of a word, a statement, or a passage in a book. *In what sense is the poet using that word?*

essence
Essence is the basic nature or character of someone or something. *The artist has caught the essence of Mother Teresa in that portrait.*

measure *verb*

▶ to determine the size or quantity of something by using a special instrument, such as a ruler. *We **measured** the length of rope we would need.*

gauge **Gauge** means to measure the size, capacity, amount, or force of certain things. *Airports have instruments to gauge the rate at which the wind is blowing.*

estimate To **estimate** means to measure or work out roughly the quantity, size, or amount of something. *We estimated how much wood we would need to build the cabin.*

survey To **survey** can mean to find out the form and boundaries of land by measuring it. *Rosa surveyed the new area and marked the corners of the lot.*

rate To **rate** means to measure by comparing one thing with another. *The swimming coach records our times so that our progress can be rated.*

> similar keywords: **judge, calculate, examine**

mediocre *adjective*

▶ neither good nor bad. *It was a **mediocre** movie, but we still watched it to the end.*

indifferent **Indifferent** can mean neither good nor bad in quality or character. *I am an indifferent chess player.*

second-rate **Second-rate** can mean mediocre, or not very good. *He's a second-rate actor and is often out of work.*

banal **Banal** means unoriginal or dull because it has been used too much. *The plot of the TV soap opera was so banal we could guess everything that was going to happen.*

mundane **Mundane** means ordinary, dull, or boring. *We rejected his mundane suggestion when Sarah made a better one.*

> similar keywords: **ordinary, inferior**
> contrasting keywords: **superior, excellent**

meet *verb*

▶ to come face to face with someone or something. *I **meet** my friend Shamun on the way to school each morning.*

encounter
To **encounter** means to meet unexpectedly. It is slightly more formal than meet. *We encountered some difficulties when we began to rebuild the barn.*

come across
To **come across** means to meet by chance. *Whom do you think I came across yesterday?*

run into
To **run into** means to meet by chance. It is similar to **bump into** and **come across**. *Denise ran into her uncle at the carnival.*

bump into
To **bump into** is so similar to **come across** and **run into** that you can usually use any one of these. *I bumped into Amardip at the art gallery.*

join up with
To **join up with** means to meet someone by arrangement. *I will join up with you at your place after dinner.*

meeting *noun*

▶ an arrangement to come together for a purpose. *Next week's **meeting** of the science club will be on Wednesday.*

appointment
An **appointment** can be an arrangement made between people to meet to do something. *My brother has a dental appointment this afternoon.*

date
A **date** is an **appointment**, usually made with a friend to do something enjoyable. *Anna and I have a date to go to the movies.*

rendezvous
A **rendezvous** is a meeting arranged beforehand. *They have agreed to be at our rendezvous at seven o'clock tonight.*

assignation
An **assignation** is usually an **appointment** between two people. This is a rather formal word. *In the movie, the spy and his contact had an assignation in a secluded part of the park.*

tryst
A **tryst** is a **rendezvous**, especially between two people who are romantically involved. *Romeo and Juliet arranged a secret tryst in the garden.*

mess *noun*

▶ a dirty or untidy state. *The garage was a **mess** after I took apart my bike.*

muddle   A **muddle** is a confused mess. *I left my locker in a muddle because I was late for gym class.*

clutter   A **clutter** is an untidy group or pile of things. *Working our way through all the clutter, we found a few treasures in the attic.*

shambles   **Shambles** means any place or thing that is in confusion or disorder. *My bedroom was a shambles after my little brother finished playing in it.*

disarray   **Disarray** is confusion and disorder. *The messy party guests left our living room in a state of disarray.*

litter   **Litter** is garbage scattered about. *I never litter when I go on a camping trip.*

message *noun*

▶ information sent to one person from another. *Please take a **message** if Katherine telephones while I'm away.*

letter   A **letter** is a written or printed message addressed and sent to someone. *We received a long letter from David when he went to Hong Kong.*

note   A **note** is a short letter. *I sent a thank-you note to my teacher and classmates when they sent flowers to me in the hospital.*

memo   A **memo** is a brief **note**. It is the short form of the word "memorandum." *The principal sent a memo to the teachers, asking them to attend a meeting.*

dispatch   A **dispatch** is an official message sent by a messenger. *Captain Collins sent a dispatch to the general, asking for reinforcements.*

communiqué   A **communiqué** is an official news report. *After the meeting, the premiers issued a communiqué to the public.*

> similar keywords: **report**

messenger *noun*

▶ someone who carries a message. *Large companies often employ* **messengers** *to take letters to their customers or to branch offices.*

courier	A **courier** is someone who carries messages, letters, or parcels for other people. *The courier delivered the parcel to the freelance editor.*
letter carrier	A **letter carrier** is someone who takes letters and packages from post offices to the people to whom they are addressed. *Letter carriers walk many kilometres each day.*
envoy	An **envoy** is someone who is sent to represent another person or a country. *The foreign affairs minister sent an envoy to Tibet on a fact-finding mission.*
correspondent	A **correspondent** can be a person employed to contribute news regularly from a particular place. *The news correspondent had information about the earthquake.*

method *noun*

▶ a way of going about something, especially in an orderly way. *If you follow this* **method**, *you will find it easier to organize your computer files.*

approach	An **approach** is a particular way of going about something. *A new approach to student evaluation has been accepted at our school.*
procedure	A **procedure** is a way of doing something. *She followed the correct procedure for applying for a job, and was offered an interview.*
technique	A **technique** is a particular way of doing or performing something. *His tennis instructor taught him a new serving technique.*
style	A **style** is a particular way of behaving or of doing something. *Sharon has her own style of painting.*
means	**Means** can be a method or way used to reach an end or a goal. *Cars, buses, taxis, and subway trains are common means of transportation in cities.*

mimic *verb*

▶ to copy someone's voice or movements. *Some birds can **mimic** human voices.*

imitate   To **imitate** means to copy someone or to use someone as a model. *The parrot is one bird that can imitate a human voice.*

ape   To **ape** means to copy or mimic someone, sometimes without thinking about or realizing what you are doing. It is more suited to everyday language. *He is only four, but he apes his big sister.*

caricature   To **caricature** can mean to mimic someone by exaggerating the person's appearance, voice, or manner. *The actors caricatured the politicians in a very unflattering way.*

impersonate   To **impersonate** means to pretend to be someone else. *The comedian impersonated a famous rock star.*

similar keywords: **copy**

minimize *verb*

▶ to make something seem as small or unimportant as possible. *We should not **minimize** the value of people's efforts to help others.*

lessen   To **lessen** can be so similar to **minimize** that you can usually use either. *In his description, the guide deliberately lessened the hardships of the trip so we would not be worried.*

trivialize   To **trivialize** means to make something important seem unimportant. *That book trivializes their contributions to scientific research.*

play down   To **play down** means to treat something as unimportant in order to keep attention away from it. *She played down the amount of help she had given.*

make light of To **make light of** means to treat something as unimportant or amusing. *We made light of our injuries so Mom wouldn't worry about us.*

similar keywords: **decrease**
contrasting keywords: **emphasize**

minor   *adjective*

▶ lesser in importance or size. *The new plan had only a few* **minor** *faults.*

secondary   **Secondary** means next after the first in order of importance. *My dad said that winning is secondary to the enjoyment of playing the game.*

trivial   **Trivial** means of very little importance. *Trivial worries seem to take up more time than they are worth.*

trifling   **Trifling** is so similar to **trivial** you can usually use either word. *She said her problem was a trifling matter that could wait.*

petty   **Petty** means of little importance. *We ignored petty complaints about the way we decorated the gym.*

slight   **Slight** can mean minor or small. *There is a slight change in our plans to go away next week.*

> similar keywords: **insignificant, subordinate**
> contrasting keywords: **main, significant, important**

miracle   *noun*

▶ an occurrence that is surprising because it is thought to be very unlikely or impossible. *It is a* **miracle** *that you weren't hurt when you fell from the ladder.*

wonder   A **wonder** is a surprising or odd event. *It's a wonder that Yoshiko telephoned me just when I was thinking about her.*

marvel   A **marvel** is a strong surprise or astonishing thing or event. *The acrobats performed one marvel after another.*

sensation   A **sensation** can be an event that causes surprise or excitement. It is more suited to everyday language. *The new dance was a real sensation!*

curiosity   A **curiosity** can be an odd event. *The strange disappearance of my socks in the dryer was a curiosity.*

phenomenon   A **phenomenon** can be an event that seems extraordinary. *It's a phenomenon that Miranda's and my birthday and first name are the same.*

miserable *adjective*

▶ very unhappy. *We were **miserable** because our trip was cancelled.*

depressed   **Depressed** means feeling extremely sad or miserable. *Tim was depressed when he realized he had forgotten about the concert.*

forlorn   **Forlorn** means miserable because you are left all alone. *The sick child was forlorn when he couldn't go on the class trip.*

heart-broken   **Heart-broken** means crushed with sadness or grief. *He was heart-broken when his dog died.*

blue   **Blue** means sad or **depressed**. It is more suited to everyday language. *I was blue when everyone went to the movie except me.*

down   **Down** means feeling down-hearted or in low spirits. It is more suited to everyday language. *She felt down when she realized that she had no chance of taking part in the marathon.*

> similar keywords: **sad, glum, grumpy**
> contrasting keywords: **happy, joyful, glad**

misery *noun*

▶ great unhappiness. *They caused their parents **misery** when they were arrested for shoplifting.*

sorrow   **Sorrow** means grief or sadness. *Families feel great sorrow when a loved one dies.*

anguish   **Anguish** is very great **sorrow** or worry. *The parents of the lost child suffered terrible anguish.*

melancholy   **Melancholy** is a feeling of sadness or **depression**. *Her melancholy was so deep for a while that it seemed nothing could cheer her up.*

gloom   **Gloom** can be a feeling of unhappiness or **depression**. *Gloom fell on us all when we heard about our classmate's accident.*

> contrasting keywords: **happiness**

misfortune *noun*

▶ bad luck. *Losing your lunch money was a **misfortune**, but certainly not a tragedy.*

accident
An **accident** is an unwanted or unlucky happening. *Careless cycling was the cause of the accident.*

mishap
A **mishap** is an unfortunate **accident**. *I had a mishap on my way to school: I fell and scraped my knee.*

hardship
Hardship means bad luck or suffering in the way you live. *Many Canadians endured hardship during the Great Depression.*

blow
A **blow** is a sudden shock or misfortune. *It was a blow to our team when our top player changed schools.*

evil
An **evil** is something that can cause suffering, misfortune, or disaster. *The pollution of our oceans is an evil we can prevent.*

similar keywords: **disaster**

misrepresent *verb*

▶ to describe or show something in an incorrect or false way. *Unfortunately, their actual comments were **misrepresented** in the newspaper article.*

twist
To **twist** can mean to change the meaning of something on purpose. *The reporter twisted what they said to make it sound more controversial.*

distort
To **distort** can mean to misrepresent or **twist** something. *The article distorted the facts, so it was difficult to know the truth.*

slant
To **slant** can mean to present or tell something in a way that makes one particular thing seem more important. *They slanted the report to make their candidate for mayor seem to be the best choice.*

exaggerate
To **exaggerate** means to say more than is true about something to make it sound better. *He exaggerated the story until it sounded as though he alone was responsible for winning the game.*

falsify
To **falsify** means to represent something in a false or incorrect way. *The accountant falsified the records to cover up her bad investments for the company.*

mistake *noun*

▶ something someone has done wrongly. *I made three **mistakes** in my spelling test.*

error   An **error** is so similar to **mistake** that you can usually use either word. *I saw my error and corrected it.*

slip   A **slip** can be so similar to **mistake** and **error** that you can usually choose any of them. *I made a slip in adding up the bill.*

blunder   A **blunder** is a silly mistake. *What a blunder to give you the wrong date for the meeting!*

misunder-standing   A **misunderstanding** is a mistake of meaning, or a misinterpretation. *A misunderstanding occurred because he did not receive the whole message.*

faux pas   A **faux pas** is an embarrassing **slip** in speech or behaviour; a social **blunder**. It is a French term that has been adapted into the English language. *It was a faux pas to invite them both to the same party, since they dislike each other.*

mix *verb*

▶ to combine or blend things together. *I **mixed** the eggs, sugar, salt, baking powder, milk, oil, and flour to make pancakes.*

mash   To **mash** means to mix something by pounding or crushing. *I mashed the potatoes until they were soft and creamy.*

emulsify   To **emulsify** means to mix things together so that they form a liquid that looks like milk and is often rather oily. *I shook the jar of salad dressing to emulsify the oil and vinegar.*

stir   To **stir** can mean to mix something by moving a spoon or something similar around in it. *When you make a sauce, you have to stir it all the time it is cooking.*

fold   To **fold** can mean to mix one thing with another by gently turning over with a rubber spatula or something similar. *The cook folded the beaten egg whites into the mixture to make a cake.*

> similar keywords: **combine**
> contrasting keywords: **separate**

moderate   *adjective*

▶ keeping within proper bounds, or not extreme. *We put a **moderate** price on the goods at our bake sale and sold everything.*

reasonable   **Reasonable** means fair or moderate. *We made a reasonable profit at the garage sale.*

modest   **Modest** can mean of medium value, quality, or amount. *I paid a modest amount for a used saxophone when I was learning to play.*

restrained   **Restrained** means controlled or kept in check. *There was polite but restrained applause for the amateur singer.*

middle-of-the-road   **Middle-of-the-road** means moderate or not going to extremes in thought or behaviour. *The politician's opinions on overfishing are middle-of-the-road.*

> similar keywords: **ordinary**
> contrasting keywords: **intense**

modern   *adjective*

▶ belonging to or used in the present time. ***Modern** airplanes are much bigger and faster than the early ones.*

contemporary   **Contemporary** can mean modern or existing now. *The apartment was decorated in a contemporary style.*

current   **Current** means belonging to the present time. *We read about many of the current problems of the world in the newspaper.*

up-to-date   **Up-to-date** means modern or having to do with new ideas and styles. *We used only the most up-to-date books as resources for our report.*

recent   **Recent** means made or done not long ago. *I've been too busy to go to any recent movies.*

late   **Late** can mean new or **recent**. *The late model of car offers added safety features.*

> similar keywords: **new, chic**
> contrasting keywords: **old-fashioned, old**

momentary *adjective*

▶ lasting for a very short space of time. *There was a **momentary** flash of lightning before the storm died down.*

brief
    Brief can mean short in time. *We are having a brief rest before finishing our work.*

fleeting
    Fleeting means passing swiftly away. *We had a fleeting view of the racing cars as they went around the bend.*

passing
    Passing can mean **brief** or going by quickly. *My mother hopes my passion for very loud music is only a passing phase.*

transitory
    Transitory means continuing only for a brief time. *Fame for most professional athletes is transitory.*

> similar keywords: **temporary, brief**
> contrasting keywords: **permanent**

move *verb*

▶ to change from one place or position to another. *My dog was so comfortable on the couch that he didn't want to **move**.*

shift
    To **shift** means to move from one place or position to another. This is a more informal word than move. *Shift your weight from your left foot to your right as you do the exercise.*

stir
    To **stir** can mean to move gently or in a slight way. *The leaves of the tree stirred in the gentle breeze.*

budge
    To **budge** means to move away. This is usually used with the word "not" or "can't." *We tried to push the truck out of the ditch, but it would not budge.*

give way
    To **give way** can mean to move or yield. *We all pushed the heavy rock and it finally gave way.*

relocate
    To **relocate** means to locate your business or home in a new place. *The company relocated its head office to Vancouver.*

> similar keywords: **carry, send**

moving *adjective*

▶ changing from place to place. *The **moving** shadows on the child's bedroom wall frightened him.*

mobile   **Mobile** means able to move or be moved. *After two weeks in bed with a broken leg, Timothy is mobile again.*

manoeuvrable   **Manoeuvrable** means easy to move about. *The small car was very manoeuvrable in busy traffic.*

dynamic   **Dynamic** means having to do with the power that causes movement. *A battery is the dynamic force in many portable electronic devices.*

kinetic   **Kinetic** means having to do with movement. *A hanging mobile is an example of kinetic art.*

> contrasting keywords: **steady, still**

musical *adjective*

▶ harmonious, pleasing to your ears, and like music. *The **musical** tones of the robins drifted through the meadow.*

tuneful   **Tuneful** means full of or producing pleasant and agreeable sounds. *We enjoyed the tuneful folk music on the CD.*

melodious   **Melodious** means tuneful and sweet-sounding. *We were wakened by the melodious singing of birds.*

lyrical   **Lyrical** means having the form and musical quality of a song. *His reading of the lyrical poem was very emotional.*

mellow   **Mellow** can mean having a very deep and rich sound. *The last mellow notes of the French horn echoed throughout the concert hall.*

sweet   **Sweet** can mean light and pleasant to your ears. *The baby fell asleep to the sweet sounds of the lullaby.*

N, n

naive *adjective*

▶ having little understanding of the ways of the real world. *His **naive** comment showed us that he had no idea how serious the situation was.*

simple **Simple** can mean lacking knowledge; being ignorant or unaware. *He was a simple individual, who wanted nothing more than to tend his garden and his animals.*

unworldly **Unworldly** means having little or no knowledge of the ways of the world. *The scientist was an unworldly person whose main concern was research.*

gullible **Gullible** means easily fooled or cheated. *People used to play practical jokes on him because he was so gullible.*

innocent **Innocent** can mean having the simplicity of a person who isn't experienced in the ways of the world. *The students felt very innocent after reading about the lives of the runaways.*

name *noun*

▶ what something or someone is called. *What **name** will you give your new kitten?*

title A **title** is a name that shows an occupation or rank in society. *She earned the title "Doctor" after studying hard for her medical degree.*

pseudonym A **pseudonym** is a made-up name used instead of a writer's real name. *He decided to use a pseudonym so his family wouldn't know he had written the book.*

pen name A **pen name** is the same as a **pseudonym**. *"George Sand" was the pen name of the French author Amandine Aurore Lupin.*

alias An **alias** is a made-up name used instead of a person's real name. *The criminal gave an alias in order to get a new passport.*

nickname A **nickname** is a name people call you, usually in a friendly way, instead of your real name. *Her nickname is "Spike," because she's a great volleyball player.*

name *verb*

▶ to give a name to someone or something. *They **named** the baby Lakshmi.*

call To **call** can be so similar to **name** that you can usually use either word. *They called the kitten "Whiskers."*

title To **title** means to give a name to a book, story, play, movie, and so on. *What have you titled your new poem?*

dub To **dub** can mean to give someone a nickname. *We dubbed him "The Fox."*

tag To **tag** can mean to use a special word or phrase to describe someone. *They tagged her a genius.*

term To **term** means to name someone or something, or to give a label to someone or something. *According to this fitness chart, you would be termed "very healthy."*

narrow *adjective*

▶ not wide. *The path through the garden was very **narrow**.*

tight **Tight** can mean fitting closely, especially too closely. *We all got into the van, but it was a tight squeeze.*

close **Close** can mean narrow or **tight**. *During the train trip, we'll be living in close quarters.*

small **Small** can mean narrow or not great in extent. *The rabbit squeezed through a small hole in the fence.*

confined **Confined** means restricted to a very small space. *In Tokyo "tube" hotels, people stay overnight in very confined spaces with just enough room for one small bed.*

cramped **Cramped** can mean narrow or not having enough space. *The room was cramped after we put all of our furniture in it.*

> similar keywords: **thin**
> contrasting keywords: **wide, spacious, thick**

narrow-minded *adjective*

▶ lacking in understanding of other people's ideas. *They are so **narrow-minded** that they don't even listen to the opinions of others.*

intolerant | **Intolerant** means unwilling to let other people have or express opinions different from your own. *I do not like it when people are intolerant of others who have different tastes in music, clothes, or books.*

bigoted | **Bigoted** means holding an unreasonable opinion and being **intolerant** of others. *The bigoted neighbours said rude and foolish things.*

biased | **Biased** can mean having a strong opinion that stops you from seeing the other side of an argument. *The soccer player was too biased in favour of her sport to see any good in baseball.*

prejudiced | **Prejudiced** means influenced without a sensible or balanced reason. *The dog-show judge was prejudiced in favour of the Airedale because he has one himself.*

contrasting keywords: **broad-minded, neutral**

nasty *adjective*

▶ unpleasant or disgusting. *I got a **nasty** cut on my thumb when the glass broke.*

awful | **Awful** can mean very bad or unpleasant. *We had an awful mess to clean up when the paint spilled.*

repulsive | **Repulsive** means dreadful or disgusting. *The food was so repulsive that it made us feel ill.*

revolting | **Revolting** means disgusting or **repulsive**. *The milk tasted revolting because it had turned sour.*

vile | **Vile** means disgustingly bad. *I hate it when my friends use vile language.*

gross | **Gross** can mean disgusting or coarse. It is more suited to everyday language. *There is a really gross scene in that crummy horror movie.*

similar keywords: **bad, horrible**
contrasting keywords: **nice, agreeable, good**

naughty *adjective*

▶ behaving in an annoying or irritating way. *The kindergarten child was purposely being* **naughty** *in order to get attention from the teacher.*

badly behaved   **Badly behaved** means not behaving properly. *My younger sister was badly behaved because she felt she was too old to need a babysitter.*

mischievous   **Mischievous** means behaving in a way that is naughty without meaning serious harm. *The mischievous toddler threw his socks in the bath.*

incorrigible   **Incorrigible** means showing that you intend to continue doing what you like, even though it's naughty. *The incorrigible child had every intention of pouring juice all over the kitchen floor.*

uncooperative   **Uncooperative** means not helpful, or unwilling to work together. *The work will take longer if you are uncooperative and don't help us.*

devilish   **Devilish** means full of mischief. *She was in a devilish mood, ready to play a prank on the next person who walked into the room.*

> similar keywords: **disobedient, mean**
> contrasting keywords: **well-behaved, obedient**

nautical *adjective*

▶ having to do with ships, sailors, or sailing. *If you are interested in sailing, you will want to learn the proper* **nautical** *terms.*

seafaring   **Seafaring** means travelling on the sea. *Portugal has been a seafaring nation for generations.*

seagoing   **Seagoing** means designed for or able to sail on the open sea. *They have bought a seagoing launch and are going to sail around the world.*

maritime   **Maritime** means having to do with ships or the sea. *International maritime law states that a nearby ship must go to the aid of a ship in trouble.*

seaworthy   **Seaworthy** means in a fit condition to sail at sea. *The inspector said the boat was seaworthy, and they could start as soon as they wished.*

naval   **Naval** means having to do with armed forces ships. *The naval vessels sailed to prevent the foreign boats from overfishing the Grand Banks.*

near *adjective*

▶ not distant. *The library is quite **near**, and we should be there in five minutes.*

close
: **Close** can have almost the same meaning as **near**. *Teresa's house is close, so we'll drop her off first.*

next
: **Next** means nearest in place or position. *I'll be in the next room, so just shout if you want me.*

adjacent
: **Adjacent** means lying near or alongside something. *The school bought the adjacent lot to give the students a bigger playground.*

neighbouring
: **Neighbouring** means living or placed near something or someone. *We went to a play at the neighbouring school.*

warm
: **Warm** sometimes means being quite near to something you're looking for, usually in a game. It is often used in everyday language. *Keep looking—you're very warm now.*

contrasting keywords: **distant**

necessary *adjective*

▶ unable to be done without. *Water is **necessary** for life.*

essential
: **Essential** means absolutely necessary. *Flour is an essential ingredient in bread.*

vital
: **Vital** can be so similar to **essential** that you can often use either. *Careful preparations are vital if this project is to be a success.*

crucial
: **Crucial** means of the greatest importance. *Checking the air tanks before you go scuba diving is crucial.*

imperative
: **Imperative** means necessary or not to be avoided. *It was imperative that our boat reach the shore before the storm came.*

obligatory
: **Obligatory** means necessary, required, or considered as binding. *Wearing a uniform will be an obligatory part of this job.*

contrasting keywords: **extra**

neglect *verb*

▶ to pay no attention to something, usually by ignoring it. *He **neglected** his appearance when he was on vacation.*

overlook
: To **overlook** means to miss or ignore someone or something. *I overlooked one spot on the ceiling when I painted my room.*

leave out
: To **leave out** means to forget about or ignore someone or something. *He did well on the test even though he left out one question.*

omit
: To **omit** means to **leave out** or fail to do something. *They omitted to tell us some of the more interesting details.*

disregard
: To **disregard** means to fail to pay any attention or thought to something or someone. *She disregarded her friend's negative comments and successfully reached her goal.*

forget
: To **forget** can mean to fail to remember someone or something, sometimes on purpose. *Forget about going to the movies and come with me to the park instead.*

> contrasting keywords: **remember**

negotiate *verb*

▶ to deal with someone in order to prepare some kind of agreement. *Canada, the U.S.A., and Mexico have recently **negotiated** free trade agreements.*

decide
: To **decide** can mean to settle something in doubt. *Let's ask the teacher to decide for us.*

arbitrate
: To **arbitrate** means to judge or settle a disagreement between other people. *Will you arbitrate for us, because we can't agree?*

mediate
: To **mediate** means to come between people who are arguing to try to help them to agree. *The consumer affairs official mediated between the car dealership and the dissatisfied customer.*

intervene
: To **intervene** means to step in, in order to solve a problem. *When the union and management couldn't agree, the government intervened.*

intercede
: To **intercede** means to speak or act on behalf of someone in trouble. *The lawyer interceded for the tenants in their disagreement with the property management.*

nervous *adjective*

▶ worried or frightened, especially about something that might happen in the future. *I am **nervous** about going to my new karate class.*

anxious	**Anxious** means very worried or uneasy. *We were anxious when the hikers didn't get back before dark.*
apprehensive	**Apprehensive** means afraid of what might happen. *I was apprehensive about meeting my new instructor.*
edgy	**Edgy** means nervous and irritable. *It makes some people edgy to be caught in a traffic jam.*
jumpy	**Jumpy** means so nervous that you are likely to make sudden uncontrolled movements. *I'm jumpy if I'm alone in the house at night.*
jittery	**Jittery** means nervous or **jumpy**. *We were quite jittery waiting for the race to start.*

> similar keywords: **frightened, upset, fearful**
> contrasting keywords: **calm, patient**

neutral *adjective*

▶ not taking one side or the other. *I was still **neutral** after hearing them debate the issue.*

even-handed	**Even-handed** means neither favouring nor preferring one side to the other. *The referee was known for her even-handed treatment of players.*
disinterested	**Disinterested** means not directly involved in something. *They called for a disinterested outsider to help them settle the dispute.*
noncommittal	**Noncommittal** means not giving your decision or opinion so you can't be held to it. *Your noncommittal answer could have meant anything.*
detached	**Detached** means remaining apart, or not being concerned with or involved in something. *Tamara maintained a detached attitude throughout the whole disagreement.*

> similar keywords: **fair**
> contrasting keywords: **unfair, narrow-minded**

new *adjective*

▶ recently arrived, obtained, or come into being. *This is the first episode of the **new** TV series.*

novel
: **Novel** means new or different, usually in an unusual way. *He had a novel way of holding his golf club.*

original
: **Original** can mean newly thought up or invented, and not like anything else. *The unusually shaped bicycle won a prize for the most original design.*

innovative
: **Innovative** means completely new in a clever or creative way. *We admired the innovative projects they displayed in the classroom during Education Week.*

fresh
: **Fresh** can mean new or different. *That is a very fresh approach to our problem.*

> similar keywords: **modern, chic**
> contrasting keywords: **old-fashioned, old**

nice *adjective*

▶ pleasing or delightful. *Several guests admired the children's **nice** manners.*

pleasant
: **Pleasant** means agreeable or pleasing. *We all had a pleasant day at the provincial park.*

enjoyable
: **Enjoyable** means pleasing or to your liking. *The party was enjoyable because everyone chatted happily together.*

lovely
: **Lovely** can mean very **pleasant** or good. *The weather was lovely while we were away.*

acceptable
: **Acceptable** means satisfactory to the person receiving it. *The meal was acceptable, even though the helpings could have been larger.*

> similar keywords: **agreeable, good**
> contrasting keywords: **nasty, pathetic, annoying, horrible**

noise *noun*

▶ any kind of sound, especially a sound that is too loud or that you don't like. *Please stop making that **noise**; it's difficult to concentrate on my reading.*

din
: A **din** is a loud noise that goes on and on. *The children made a terrible din when they were playing with the metal garbage can lids.*

hubbub
: A **hubbub** is a loud confused noise, like that made by many voices. *There was a hubbub in the room as everyone talked at once.*

racket
: A **racket** can be a loud confused noise. *The carpenter building our shelves couldn't help making a racket as she sawed the wood and drilled the screw holes.*

uproar
: An **uproar** is a noisy disturbance. *The fans were in an uproar when the home team came from behind to win the game in the final few seconds.*

pandemonium
: **Pandemonium** means a scene of wild and noisy disorder. *Pandemonium broke out when the concert tickets finally went on sale.*

> similar keywords: **commotion**
> contrasting keywords: **whisper**

nonsense *noun*

▶ words that are silly or without meaning. *The book's ending seemed like **nonsense** to me.*

drivel
: **Drivel** can be so similar to **nonsense** that you can usually use either. *That's the kind of drivel you would expect from an uninformed person.*

rubbish
: **Rubbish** can be so similar to **drivel** and **nonsense** that you can usually use any of them. *You won't convince me if you keep talking rubbish.*

hogwash
: **Hogwash** means meaningless or insincere talk. It is more suited to everyday language. *We were unconvinced by the argument because we thought it was utter hogwash.*

gibberish
: **Gibberish** is meaningless words. *She listened to her brother speak gibberish in his sleep.*

number *noun*

▶ a word or symbol used to indicate an amount or the position of something. *Please take a **number** at the counter, and then wait your turn.*

figure A **figure** is a symbol that stands for a number. *Write the figure 3 next to the circle with three crosses in it.*

numeral A **numeral** is a word, figure, or group of figures that stands for a number. *The Roman numeral for 100 is C.*

digit A **digit** is any of the **numerals** from 0 to 9. *There are only 10 digits.*

integer An **integer** is any whole number. *We made a list of all the integers up to 100 that could be divided evenly by 3.*

fraction A **fraction** is a part of a whole number. *The decimal 0.75 equals the fraction $\frac{3}{4}$.*

numerous *adjective*

▶ very many. *The pennies in the jar were too **numerous** to count quickly.*

multiple **Multiple** means having or involving many parts. *The question on the science test had multiple parts.*

multitudinous **Multitudinous** means forming a great number or crowd. This is a rather formal word. *The multitudinous waves swamped the seafarer's vessel.*

profuse **Profuse** means very many or plentiful. *They offered profuse apologies for forgetting about our meeting.*

innumerable **Innumerable** means more than can be counted. *As soon as we started our hike, innumerable mosquitoes descended on us.*

legion **Legion** means great in number. This is an old-fashioned word. *Joan of Arc's followers were legion.*

> similar keywords: **countless, abundant, various**
> contrasting keywords: **scarce, single**

O, o

obedient *adjective*

▶ following someone else's wishes or orders. *The **obedient** puppy is being trained as a guide dog.*

docile
: **Docile** means quiet and easy to manage. *The children learned to ride on the docile pony.*

tractable
: **Tractable** means easily managed. *Animals with tractable natures make ideal pets.*

law-abiding
: **Law-abiding** means obeying the laws. *The law-abiding citizens helped the police in their search.*

compliant
: **Compliant** means agreeing with someone else readily or willingly. *I don't think it's good to be so compliant that you seem to have no mind of your own.*

> similar keywords: **well-behaved, submissive**
> contrasting keywords: **disobedient, naughty, defiant**

obey *verb*

▶ to carry out commands. *The children **obeyed** the traffic rules.*

heed
: To **heed** means to pay attention to someone or something. *We decided to heed the "No Lifeguard on Duty" notice at the lake and not go swimming after all.*

observe
: To **observe** can mean to obey or **follow** rules or laws. *You must observe the traffic rules when riding a bicycle on the road.*

follow
: To **follow** can mean to accept someone or something as a guide. *I'll follow your instructions.*

comply with
: To **comply with** means to act according to the rules, laws, or requests. *The audience complied with the request to remain in their seats.*

> similar keywords: **behave**
> contrasting keywords: **disobey**

obsession *noun*

▶ a strong idea or feeling that controls someone's behaviour. *She had an **obsession** about video games and played them every day.*

hang-up	A **hang-up** is something that worries you and that you can't get off your mind. This is more suited to everyday language. *He had a hang-up about wearing his glasses when he first got them.*
complex	A **complex** is so similar to **hang-up** that you can usually use either. It is more suited to everyday language. *I had a complex about speaking in public.*
phobia	A **phobia** is an overpowering fear. *Some people have phobias about heights or enclosed places.*
fetish	A **fetish** is an obsession that is usually expressed by repeated behaviour. *He had a fetish about cleanliness and washed his hands three or four times an hour.*
passion	A **passion** is a very strong feeling about someone or something. *Her passion for golf takes up most of her free weekends and afternoons.*

obstacle *noun*

▶ something that is in your way or that holds you up. *We could see that the **obstacle** holding up the traffic was a fallen tree.*

hindrance	A **hindrance** is something that slows you down or hinders your progress. *Lack of money has been a real hindrance to our school's plans to buy more computers.*
hitch	A **hitch** is something that obstructs or makes things difficult. *The one hitch to going on the camping trip was getting my parents' permission.*
handicap	A **handicap** is any disadvantage that makes success harder. *Wearing uncomfortable shoes turned out to be a handicap for him in the walkathon.*
drawback	A **drawback** is a disadvantage or an inconvenience. *The plan is great except for one drawback—we don't have enough helpers.*
barrier	A **barrier** is anything that bars or blocks the way. *Not being able to speak the same language doesn't have to be a barrier between people.*

obvious *adjective*

▶ easily seen. *It was **obvious** from his happy smile that he had enjoyed the ride.*

evident | **Evident** means obvious or easily understood. *It's evident from your expression that you liked the ride, too.*

plain | **Plain** can mean clearly seen. It can be very similar to **evident**. *It is plain to me that you don't like zucchini.*

seeming | **Seeming** means apparent or **evident**, but only in appearance. *The more experienced figure skater is at a seeming advantage, but you can never be sure of the final results.*

perceptible | **Perceptible** means easily recognized or noticed. *There was no perceptible difference between the copy and the original.*

distinct | **Distinct** can mean obvious and unmistakable. *Don't worry, you will see a distinct difference between the twins.*

> similar keywords: **visible, clear**

offer *noun*

▶ something that is presented for consideration or acceptance. *I made him an **offer** of $50 for the bike, but he refused.*

proposal | A **proposal** is a plan or scheme offered to someone for approval. *We presented our proposal for the new swimming pool to the committee.*

proposition | A **proposition** is a plan or subject suggested as something to be acted upon or discussed. *Your idea is an interesting proposition, but I don't think it's practical right now.*

bid | A **bid** is an offer of money for something, especially one made at an auction. *She made a bid of $200 for the antique table.*

tender | A **tender** is an offer to do a job for a certain price. *The contractor with the lowest tender will get the job of building the arena.*

submission | A **submission** can be something that is presented, often a **proposal** or a report. *I submitted my design for the new school logo.*

> similar keywords: **suggestion**

offspring   *noun*

▶ the baby animal or child of a particular parent. *A lion's* ***offspring*** *is called a cub.*

young   **Young** can be offspring, usually of animals. *The female kangaroo carries its young in a pouch.*

issue   **Issue** can be offspring, usually of people. This is a rather formal word. *The king's first male issue was the heir to the throne.*

descendant   A **descendant** is an offspring or a person who has descended from a particular ancestor. *I'm a descendant of a family who came from India more than a hundred years ago.*

progeny   **Progeny** means the offspring or **descendants** of people or animals. This is a rather formal word. *Before long, I won't have any more room for my pet rabbits' progeny.*

kid   A **kid** is a young person, or child. It is more suited to everyday language. *My aunt and uncle have three kids.*

> contrasting keywords: **ancestor**

old   *adjective*

▶ of or from an earlier time. *In the* ***old*** *days there were hardly any cars on the roads.*

ancient   **Ancient** means of, happening, or living a very long time ago. *We saw photographs of the ancient temples in Angkor, Cambodia.*

antique   **Antique** means dating from earlier times. *They found some antique dishes in the farmhouse attic.*

prehistoric   **Prehistoric** means belonging to the time before history was written or records were kept. *We saw the fossils of a prehistoric shellfish in the museum.*

vintage   **Vintage** can mean from a time in the past. *We saw some vintage airplanes at the air show.*

> similar keywords: **old-fashioned**
> contrasting keywords: **modern, new**

old-fashioned *adjective*

▶ belonging to a time in, or style of, the past. *We dressed up in **old-fashioned** clothes and pretended we were early settlers.*

out-of-date
Out-of-date means not in fashion or no longer used. *You need a modern computer to replace that out-of-date one.*

obsolete
Obsolete means no longer used because something newer and more fashionable has replaced it. *My computer is so obsolete that it belongs in a museum.*

antiquated
Antiquated means old-fashioned or **out-of-date**. *That antiquated book has some interesting diagrams that show how people once thought the human body worked.*

archaic
Archaic means very old-fashioned or belonging to the very distant past. *"Thee" and "thou" are archaic words that are not used very often today.*

dated
Dated means **out-of-date**. *In the play, the actor wore dated clothes that were popular ten years ago.*

> similar keywords: **old**
> contrasting keywords: **modern, new, chic**

opaque *adjective*

▶ not able to be seen through. *I couldn't see who was there because the glass in the door is **opaque**.*

dense
Dense can mean too thick to see through. *The airport was closed because of the dense fog.*

thick
Thick can often be used instead of **dense**. *The smoke was so thick we couldn't see where we were going.*

cloudy
Cloudy can mean not clear. *We added ammonia, and now the water is cloudy.*

muddy
Muddy can mean not clear. *The water was too muddy for us to see the bottom of the creek.*

> contrasting keywords: **transparent**

opinion *noun*

▶ what you think or decide. *What is your **opinion** about the upcoming election?*

attitude	An **attitude** can be the way you behave toward or the way you feel about something. *She had very little experience, but she had a great attitude to the new job.*
outlook	An **outlook** is an **attitude** or point of view. *Indra will go a long way with her optimistic outlook on life.*
viewpoint	A **viewpoint** is a way of considering or thinking about something or someone. *They asked for our viewpoint about extending the school year.*
stand	A **stand** can be a definite opinion that you declare openly. *The students took a strong stand on fighting drug abuse.*
conviction	A **conviction** can be an opinion or belief that you hold strongly. *It is my conviction that we would all be happier if we thought more about others and less about ourselves.*

opposite *adjective*

▶ completely different in every way. *The ending of the movie was **opposite** to what I had expected.*

converse	**Converse** means turned about or opposite in direction, action, or meaning. *We are going in converse directions instead of trying to come to an understanding.*
antithetical	**Antithetical** means completely opposite or in direct contrast. *Which of these two antithetical statements do you think is correct?*
contradictory	**Contradictory** means opposite or not consistent. It is similar to **antithetical**. *The results of the two experiments are contradictory.*
contrary	**Contrary** means opposed to or different from something else, but it may not be exactly opposite. *My viewpoint is contrary to public opinion.*
conflicting	**Conflicting** means clashing, disagreeing, or in opposition. *We were surprised at the conflicting ideas about helping the homeless.*

> contrasting keywords: **similar**

optimistic *adjective*

▶ expecting that things will turn out well. *His **optimistic** outlook helped us all believe that our report would be finished on time.*

positive   **Positive** can mean tending to see what is good or gives hope. *Her positive approach helped her to find a solution to the problem.*

confident   **Confident** means having a strong belief, or feeling quite certain about something, usually something that is good or desirable. *I am confident that the pollution in our lake can be cleaned up.*

hopeful   **Hopeful** means looking forward to or expecting something, especially something good. *The mountain climbers were hopeful of reaching the base camp before nightfall.*

buoyant   **Buoyant** means light-hearted and cheerful. *They expressed their buoyant feelings by laughing and joking as they set out.*

happy-go-lucky   **Happy-go-lucky** means unworried and trusting cheerfully to luck. *The happy-go-lucky hikers set off without a map or compass.*

> similar keywords: **joyful**
> contrasting keywords: **pessimistic**

orange *adjective*

▶ having a reddish-gold or reddish-yellow colour. *We planted some seeds and weeks later dug up huge **orange** carrots.*

amber   **Amber** means having a yellowish-brown colour. *Mom slowed the car, ready to stop, when she saw the amber light.*

terracotta   **Terracotta** means having a brownish-red colour. *We have terracotta pots for all of our plants.*

ginger   **Ginger** means having a reddish-brown colour. *I named my cat Ginger because she has ginger-coloured fur.*

peach   **Peach** means having a light pinkish-orange colour. *The early sun cast a peach glow on the water.*

gilt   **Gilt** means having a golden-orange colour. *I bought a picture frame with a gilt-coloured edge.*

order   *noun*

▶ an instruction that you must obey. *The sergeant gave the **order** to march.*

command A **command** is so similar to an **order** that you can usually use either word. *At last the command to stop was heard.*

decree A **decree** is an official order, usually made by a government or someone in a position of power. *By royal decree, the rain always stopped by the time the sun set in the mythical kingdom of Camelot.*

instructions **Instructions** are orders. This is a plural noun. *My instructions are to ask everyone for a ticket.*

summons A **summons** is an order to appear in a certain place, often a law court. *I received a summons to appear as a witness at the trial.*

warrant A **warrant** is a paper given by a justice of the peace to the police, allowing them to arrest someone or search a building. *We have a warrant for your arrest.*

> similar keywords: **demand**

ordinary   *adjective*

▶ usual or normal. *It was just another **ordinary** school day.*

average **Average** can mean usual or ordinary. *An average Monday consists of school, basketball practice, dinner, homework, and TV.*

standard **Standard** can mean normal or ordinary. *Any sports store will have a tire for your bike, because it's a standard size.*

fair **Fair** can mean of an ordinary or moderately good standard. *His marks in the exam were fair.*

so-so **So-so** means ordinary, or neither very good nor very bad. It is more suited to everyday language. *We had a so-so time at the beach, with sunny but cool weather.*

> similar keywords: **mediocre, usual, moderate**
> contrasting keywords: **excellent, unusual**

organization *noun*

▶ a group of people that runs or manages something. *We need to set up a fund-raising* ***organization***.

company	A **company** can be a group of people brought together to run a business. *This book is produced by a publishing company.*
firm	A **firm** is a business organization. It is very similar to **company**. *She went to work for a law firm located in the downtown area.*
corporation	A **corporation** is a business **company**, especially one established by law. *The government set up a broadcasting corporation.*
syndicate	A **syndicate** is a group of business people or business organizations, especially formed to carry out a particular project. *The engineering firms formed a syndicate to build the big new hotel.*
outfit	An **outfit** can be a business organization or group of people working together. *That new home-shopping computer network is a dependable outfit.*

outside *noun*

▶ the outer part or side of something. *We covered the* ***outside*** *of the box with coloured paper.*

exterior	**Exterior** means the outer part of something. *The exterior of the building was in great shape and didn't need painting.*
surface	**Surface** can mean the top or outer side of something. *The workers were repairing the surface of the road because it was full of potholes.*
face	**Face** can mean the main side or front of something. *The face of the cliff was too steep to climb.*
facade	A **facade** is the front of something as seen from the outside, especially of a building. *The historic building had a very attractive facade although the inside was quite plain.*

> similar keywords: **side, edge**
> contrasting keywords: **inside**

outskirts *noun*

▶ the outer areas. This is a plural noun. *There are small farms on the **outskirts** of the town.*

periphery
The **periphery** is the outside edge of an area or thing. *The chairs were arranged around the periphery of the room.*

boundary
The **boundary** is the outside edge that separates one area from another. *The farm hand rode around the boundary of the farm, checking for broken fences.*

perimeter
The **perimeter** is the outside edge of a two-dimensional shape or the **boundary** of an area such as a field. *The lights mark the perimeter of the airfield.*

limit
The **limit** is the outermost point of an area. *The king sent messengers to the limits of his kingdom to find someone who could slay the dragon.*

frontier
A **frontier** is the outer area of known territory or the boundary of a country. *Outer space has been called the final frontier.*

> similar keywords: **edge**
> contrasting keywords: **centre**

outwit *verb*

▶ to trick or fool others by being more intelligent or clever than they are. *I have a brilliant plan that will **outwit** the other team and let us win.*

circumvent
To **circumvent** means to defeat or outwit someone through skillful planning. *The citizens' group, after much preparation, circumvented the township's plans to build a dump site in their neighbourhood.*

get the better of
To **get the better of** means to defeat or be superior to someone. *My fondness for dessert got the better of me, and I had two slices of pie.*

pull a fast one
To **pull a fast one** means to outwit someone in order to achieve an unfair result. This is more suited to everyday language. *The swindler tried to pull a fast one on my grandmother, but she wasn't fooled by him.*

> similar keywords: **deceive, trick**

overturn   *verb*

▶ to turn something over on its side, back, or face. *I **overturned** the wheelbarrow to tip the grass cuttings onto the compost pile.*

invert	To **invert** means to turn something upside down, inside out, or inwards. *The magician inverted the glass of milk without spilling a drop.*
upset	To **upset** can mean to knock or turn something over. *When the cat jumped on my lap, it upset my cup of tea.*
flip	To **flip** can mean to turn something over. *The children flipped the rock over to see what was underneath.*
capsize	To **capsize** is for a boat or ship to overturn. *The canoe capsized in the rapids, but nobody was hurt.*
tip over	To **tip over** means to topple something over. *The cat tipped its milk dish over as it ran out the door.*

> contrasting keywords: **steady**

own   *verb*

▶ to have something that belongs to you. *My parents **own** the condominium we live in.*

possess	To **possess** means to own or have something. *The art gallery possesses several valuable paintings.*
hold	To **hold** can mean to have in your possession. *The producers who hold the rights to the book plan to make a movie version of it.*
have all to yourself	To **have all to yourself** means to have something completely for your own use. *You will have the house all to yourself this weekend because we are going away.*
monopolize	To **monopolize** means to get or have complete control of something. *The new children found it hard to join in because the others had monopolized all the toys.*
occupy	To **occupy** can mean to own or live in a building or home. *Family friends occupy our old apartment.*

P, p

pacify *verb*

▶ to make something or someone quiet or peaceful. *Sarah quickly* **pacified** *the frightened horse.*

mollify To **mollify** means to make someone calmer or less angry. *The finance minister mollified the angry crowd by promising to consider their complaints about high taxation.*

appease To **appease** means to make someone peaceful, quiet, or happy. *The babysitter appeased the crying child by rocking him.*

calm To **calm** means to make someone or something less excited or emotional. *The teacher calmed the excited children by reminding them that the class trip wasn't until the next week.*

defuse To **defuse** can mean to **calm** a tense situation. *When the argument started to get unpleasant, Lin defused the situation by cracking a joke.*

> similar keywords: **comfort, please**
> contrasting keywords: **anger, frighten**

pain *noun*

▶ a feeling of hurt or soreness in a particular part of your body. *My brother had a lot of* **pain** *in his leg after he broke it.*

ache An **ache** is a dull continuous pain. *I had a stomachache from eating too many pickles.*

stitch A **stitch** can be a sudden sharp pain, especially between your ribs. *I had a stitch in my side after my aerobics class.*

cramp A **cramp** is a sudden tightening of a muscle in your body. *My mother suggested that I pull my foot forward when I had a cramp in my leg.*

spasm A **spasm** is an uncontrolled movement of your muscles. *I had a spasm in my leg after the cross-country run.*

pardon *noun*

▶ a formal declaration of forgiveness for a crime. *The government gave the prisoner a* **pardon** *because he was too old and sick to be in jail.*

release   A **release** can be the act of setting someone free from imprisonment, arrest, or other confinement. *Because there was not enough evidence against her, she was given a release from prison.*

stay   A **stay** is a delay in carrying out an order of a court of law. *There was a stay of the trial decision while the appeal was heard.*

amnesty   An **amnesty** is a pardon given to a group of people, especially for offences against the government. *An amnesty was granted to all political prisoners.*

parole   **Parole** is the release from prison, subject to certain conditions, before the full sentence has been served. *On account of good behaviour, she was granted parole after eight of the ten years of her sentence.*

acquittal   An **acquittal** is a declaration of innocence. *The man's acquittal by the jury was due to the lack of evidence against him.*

part *noun*

▶ a piece or fragment of something. *Sunita sawed* **part** *of the shelf off to make it fit.*

portion   A **portion** is a part or share of something. *I left my lunch at home, so George gave me a portion of his.*

section   A **section** is a part or division of something. *I play the trumpet in the brass section of our school orchestra.*

segment   A **segment** is a piece or a **section**. *I divided my orange and gave each of my friends a segment.*

proportion   A **proportion** is a part of something compared with the whole of it. *Enrico did a larger proportion of the work than anyone else.*

fraction   A **fraction** can be a small amount or piece. *Andrea finished her composition in a fraction of the time it took the rest of the class.*

similar keywords: **share, piece**

pass *verb*

▶ to go by or move past something. *We waved from the car when we **passed** your house yesterday.*

overtake	To **overtake** means to catch up with and pass someone or something. *The police overtook the speeding driver and made her stop.*
outstrip	To **outstrip** can mean to pass someone or something and to leave them behind when running or travelling quickly. *I outstripped my nearest competitor in the 100-m sprint.*
beat	To **beat** can mean to defeat or do better than someone. *She beat him in the race.*
surpass	To **surpass** means to exceed or go beyond someone or something. *Our dinner at the restaurant surpassed everyone's expectations.*
lap	To **lap** can mean to get ahead of other competitors by a complete round of a racing track or length of a swimming pool. *The winning car lapped the others halfway through the race and never gave up the lead.*

past *adjective*

▶ gone by in time. *Ms. Ortiz is a **past** member of three committees.*

former	**Former** means coming before someone or something else in time, or from an earlier or past time. *The former principal of our school came back to visit us.*
bygone	**Bygone** means past or gone by. It is a slightly old-fashioned word. *We read stories about bygone days when people travelled on horseback.*
sometime	**Sometime** means **former** or in the past. *Anna was a sometime speed skater and now coaches younger athletes.*
late	**Late** can mean having recently died. *The princess took over the throne of her father, the late king.*
previous	**Previous** means earlier or **former**. *Please go back and reread the previous directions.*

contrasting keywords: **future**

pathetic *adjective*

▶ causing feelings of pity or sadness. *The picture of the starving children on TV was a **pathetic** sight.*

pitiful	**Pitiful** means causing or deserving pity. *The mouse made a pitiful attempt to escape as the cat pounced on it.*
wretched	**Wretched** means **pitiful** and causing misery. *The homeless people were living in wretched conditions in an abandoned warehouse.*
sorrowful	**Sorrowful** means full of, or feeling, sadness. *The sorrowful children missed their dead pet.*
dismal	**Dismal** means feeling or causing deep sadness. *Our plan to raise a lot of money was a dismal failure.*
woeful	**Woeful** means **wretched** and deserving pity. *Your woeful expression nearly made me cry.*

> similar keywords: **bad, miserable**
> contrasting keywords: **nice, happy**

patient *adjective*

▶ waiting quietly and calmly. *The **patient** customer waited for his turn.*

tolerant	**Tolerant** means putting up with or allowing things that you may not like or feel happy about. *The babysitter was very tolerant of the children playing with their noisy toys.*
long-suffering	**Long-suffering** means continually putting up with something that annoys or hurts you. *My long-suffering friend puts up with my moodiness.*
persistent	**Persistent** means to keep on doing something until you have finished, no matter how hard it is. *We were so persistent that we worked through lunch to complete the job.*
stoical	**Stoical** means behaving in a patient and calm way that shows you have courage. *We were impressed by your stoical behaviour while you were waiting to be rescued.*

> contrasting keywords: **nervous**

p a y *noun*

▶ the money you are paid for the work you do. *Most people try to save some of their* ***pay***.

salary	A **salary** is the money you earn, especially for office work. *The bank manager earns a bigger salary at the new branch.*
wage	A **wage** is the money you are paid for working, especially in a factory or as a labourer. *The mechanic earned a good wage.*
fee	A **fee** is the money charged for a service or privilege. *The phone company charges a $5 fee each month for its call-answering service.*
income	**Income** is all the money you get from your work and investments. *You may have to pay tax on your total income.*
commission	**Commission** is the **fee** or percentage earned by someone who sells things for an employer. *The salesperson earned a 10% commission on each car sold.*

similar keywords: **profit**

p a y *verb*

▶ to give money or something similar in return for goods or services. *How much did you* ***pay*** *for your new skates?*

spend	To **spend** means to pay out money, wealth, or something similar. *I spent a lot of my savings at the craft show.*
expend	To **expend** can mean to pay out or **spend** money, usually large amounts. *We expended nearly all our available money on the new farm machinery.*
invest	To **invest** means to put money into something such as a business, hoping that you will make more money from the deal. *She invested her inheritance in real estate and before long became a millionaire.*
fund	To **fund** means to provide money for a certain purpose. *Our taxes will help fund the new museum.*

similar keywords: **buy, repay**

peaceful *adjective*

▶ calm and free from trouble or strife. *We enjoyed living in the **peaceful** country town where people were so friendly.*

serene   **Serene** means peaceful or showing no signs of stress or strife. *The stress therapist has a serene personality that helps people relax.*

tranquil   **Tranquil** means peaceful, calm, or free from disturbance. *We found a tranquil spot on the bank of the river to have a rest.*

quiet   **Quiet** can mean calm and peaceful. *We enjoyed a quiet evening at home after a hard day at school.*

harmonious   **Harmonious** means showing agreement in feeling or action. *The harmonious atmosphere returned when the club president helped the arguing members to reach an agreement.*

> similar keywords: **calm**
> contrasting keywords: **violent, aggressive**

perfect *adjective*

▶ with nothing missing and no faults. *It was a **perfect** day to play baseball.*

faultless   **Faultless** means without any mistakes or blemishes. *They gave a faultless performance at the concert.*

impeccable   **Impeccable** means completely free from any faults. It is very similar to **faultless**. *His manners were impeccable during his visit.*

flawless   **Flawless** means perfect. It is very similar to **faultless**. *The jeweller said the diamond was flawless.*

ideal   **Ideal** means a perfect example of something. *Margaret will make an ideal captain for the team.*

complete   **Complete** can mean perfect in every way. *Our happiness was complete as we paddled down the river.*

> similar keywords: **excellent, precise**
> contrasting keywords: **defective**

permanent *adjective*

▶ lasting forever or for a very long time. *She was very happy to finally get a* **permanent** *job with the company.*

everlasting   **Everlasting** means lasting or continuing for a long time or forever. *At the end of the story, the hero discovers everlasting joy.*

eternal   **Eternal** means lasting forever or seeming not to have any end. *There is an eternal flame at the peace memorial.*

immortal   **Immortal** means lasting or living forever. *In Greek mythology, the gods and goddesses are powerful and immortal beings.*

perpetual   **Perpetual** means without a fixed end or lasting, or seeming to last, forever. *My watch has a perpetual calendar that always shows me the correct day and date.*

perennial   **Perennial** means continually coming back each year or lasting for a long time. *The perennial flowers in our garden bloom every spring.*

> similar keywords: **countless**
> contrasting keywords: **temporary, momentary**

permission *noun*

▶ agreement to let someone do something. *I have* **permission** *to leave school early today.*

leave   **Leave** can mean **permission** to do something, but is a more formal word. *"I beg leave to go," she said to the queen.*

approval   **Approval** can mean permission or **consent**. *We had to get the approval of the coach before we chose our team jackets.*

clearance   A **clearance** can be official permission to go ahead with something. *They needed clearance from the town council to add an extra storey to their house.*

consent   **Consent** means permission or agreement to do something. *Dr. Lam asked for her patient's consent before operating.*

persist *verb*

▶ to continue or keep on with something, even when people oppose you. *She **persisted** with her research even though her associates thought it was pointless.*

persevere
To **persevere** means to continue with something you have started, even though it may be difficult. You can often use it instead of **persist**. *Although I am tired, I will persevere with my work.*

last the distance
To **last the distance** means to keep on with a difficult task or some physical activity until you have finished. *He knew he couldn't win the race, but he was determined to last the distance.*

hang in
To **hang in** can mean to **persevere** or to keep on trying, even though you may want to give up. This is more suited to everyday language. *We'll just hang in until this job is finished.*

stick to your guns
To **stick to your guns** means to keep your position in an argument when people oppose you. This is more suited to everyday language. *My friends tried to talk me out of choosing such a difficult project, but I stuck to my guns.*

similar keywords: **continue, endure, extend, advance**
contrasting keywords: **quit**

persistence *noun*

▶ the fact or action of continuing to do something in spite of difficulty. *Because of his **persistence** in practising every day, he finally made the basketball team.*

perseverance
Perseverance is the determination to continue to do something in spite of difficulty. *We admired Mariko's perseverance in doing the painful exercises after her accident.*

tenacity
Tenacity means the stubborn determination to continue to do something. *The ant's tenacity in dragging the huge crumb to its nest amazed us.*

stamina
Stamina is physical strength or power, especially to fight off sickness or tiredness. *The cross-country race will test your stamina.*

grit
Grit can mean courage or strength of character. *My uncle showed a lot of grit in overcoming the difficulties of life in a wheelchair.*

persistent *adjective*

▶ continuing in spite of opposition. *We watched with interest the spider's* **persistent** *attempts to put its web across the path we use every day.*

tenacious **Tenacious** means stubbornly persistent. *The detective's tenacious questioning of the witness finally got her the evidence she needed.*

dogged **Dogged** means unflinching, or resolved not to give in. *Anthony's parents were proud of his dogged attempts to learn to swim.*

single-minded **Single-minded** means showing you have decided or resolved to succeed in a particular thing. *Amanda is single-minded about saving her pocket money to buy a bicycle.*

unflagging **Unflagging** means not weakening or giving up. *They were unflagging in their efforts to raise money for the disaster relief fund.*

> similar keywords: **patient, stubborn**

persuade *verb*

▶ to cause someone to do or believe something by advising, arguing with, or influencing him or her. *It took three of us to* **persuade** *him to see that movie.*

convince To **convince** means to make someone believe or feel sure about something. *Her poor report card convinced her to work harder.*

talk into To **talk into** means to persuade others to do something by talking to them. *No matter what they say, people can't talk me into doing things that are foolish and dangerous.*

coax To **coax** means to persuade someone gently and patiently. *Sofia coaxed her sick little brother to eat.*

lobby To **lobby** means to try to get political support for a particular issue or cause. *The environmental group lobbied various politicians on the issue of banning automobiles from the city centre.*

> similar keywords: **influence, encourage**
> contrasting keywords: **discourage**

pessimistic *adjective*

▶ expecting that things will turn out badly. *We were **pessimistic** about our chances of winning the championship.*

discouraging **Discouraging** means making things appear in the worst possible way. *The artist kept on with her work in spite of the critics' discouraging remarks.*

disheartening **Disheartening** means **discouraging**, or causing a loss of good spirits. *It took me a while to get over the disheartening news that my friend was moving to Ontario.*

gloomy **Gloomy** means causing great unhappiness or depression. *Our gloomy situation didn't look so bad the next morning.*

depressing **Depressing** means causing gloom or misery. *We finally told them to keep their depressing comments to themselves.*

negative **Negative** can mean tending to see what is bad or hopeless about a situation. *A negative attitude may keep you from finding a solution to the problem.*

contrasting keywords: **optimistic, joyful**

piece *noun*

▶ a bit or part of something. *I cut off a **piece** of my new dress material to show Pat.*

scrap A **scrap** is a small piece. *Maria made a toy car out of a scrap of wood.*

fragment A **fragment** is a part that has been broken off. *He cut his foot on a fragment of broken bottle lying in the grass.*

morsel A **morsel** is a very small piece or amount. *I was too tired to eat more than a morsel of food before I fell asleep.*

particle A **particle** is a very small bit. *A particle of dust got in her eye and made it very sore.*

sliver A **sliver** is a small, thin piece. *We used a sliver of wood as a wedge to stop the window from rattling.*

similar keywords: **trace, part**

pity *noun*

▶ a feeling of sorrow for the suffering of others. *We looked at the poor beached whale with **pity**.*

sympathy   **Sympathy** can mean a feeling of sorrow you share with someone else who is sad or in trouble. *We felt great sympathy for our neighbours when their house burned down.*

compassion   **Compassion** means pity together with a feeling that you want to help. *We were asked to show compassion for the homeless victims of the flood by donating food and blankets.*

tenderness   **Tenderness** means a feeling of care and consideration. *The father cared for his sick baby with tenderness.*

mercy   **Mercy** is the pity or kindness you show when you don't punish someone for doing something wrong. *The lawyer asked the judge to show mercy on the young man because it was his first offence.*

> similar keywords: **comfort**

place *noun*

▶ an area, part of a space, position, or location. *We're going to try a new **place** for our dinner out this weekend.*

position   A **position** is a particular place. *I chose a position near the window.*

spot   A **spot** can be a less formal word for a place. *Pick a good spot for the barbecue.*

location   A **location** can be a particular place or area. *The bank machine has been moved to a new location in the mall.*

site   A **site** is a particular place where something has happened or is going to happen, or the place where something is or will be built. *We want to build a house on a site overlooking the lake.*

venue   A **venue** is a place where a particular event is held. *The venue for the concert will be the community centre.*

place   *verb*

▶ to put something in a particular position. *When Paul finished drinking his tea, he* ***placed*** *his cup back on its saucer.*

set
To **set** can be so similar to **place** that you can usually use either word. *James set the vase on the table.*

rest
To **rest** can mean to lie or lean one thing against another. *Mei rested the ladder against the wall.*

deposit
To **deposit** can mean to put something down. *Judy deposited her backpack on the bed.*

stick
To **stick** can mean to place something. *I'm going to stick all my old games in the attic.*

similar keywords: **position**

plan   *verb*

▶ to make preparations for doing something. *We* ***planned*** *the camping trip carefully so that we wouldn't forget anything.*

arrange
To **arrange** can mean to prepare or plan something. *We arranged a party for the last day of school.*

organize
To **organize** can mean to **arrange** something or make plans for it. *We organized the campaign for the student council election.*

engineer
To **engineer** means to plan or **arrange** something in a clever way. *Everyone was surprised when she engineered a friendly meeting between the two opponents.*

mastermind
To **mastermind** means to plan and direct something in a skillful, clever way. *Not a thing went wrong when Helene masterminded the food drive.*

schedule
To **schedule** means to plan the times when certain events should or will happen. *Our music teacher scheduled a band practice for Monday at four in the afternoon.*

similar keywords: **plot**

please *verb*

▶ to make someone happy. *The gift **pleased** them very much.*

delight   To **delight** means to give someone great pleasure. *Receiving the good citizen award delighted me.*

charm   To **charm** can mean to please very much. *Her intelligent remarks charmed me.*

appeal to   To **appeal to** means to have the ability to **attract** or interest someone. *This book appeals to me.*

attract   To **attract** means to **appeal to** someone because of your personality, behaviour, and so on. *Your smile attracts me.*

satisfy   To **satisfy** can mean to please or make someone happy. *My test results satisfied me.*

> similar keywords: **pacify**
> contrasting keywords: **disgust, irritate, annoy**

plot *noun*

▶ a secret plan or idea, often to harm someone. *The captain discovered that there was a **plot** for a mutiny.*

conspiracy   A **conspiracy** is similar to a **plot**. It always involves more than one person. *The RCMP arrested the people involved in the conspiracy.*

scheme   A **scheme** can be a secret plan. *They worked out a scheme to kidnap the millionaire's favourite horse.*

intrigue   An **intrigue** can be a secret plan made by dishonest or sly people. *Political intrigue caused the downfall of the government.*

ruse   A **ruse** is a dishonest trick or plan. *Her father saw through her ruse to avoid mowing the lawn.*

stratagem   A **stratagem** is a plan or trick for deceiving an enemy. *The Greeks' stratagem for conquering the city of Troy was to hide inside a wooden horse.*

> similar keywords: **trick**

plot   *verb*

▶ to plan secretly, especially something harmful or evil. *They **plotted** to overthrow the government.*

scheme To **scheme** can mean to plot or make up a secret plan. *We schemed all night, planning his surprise party.*

conspire To **conspire** means to plan secretly with another person or group of people. *The terrorists conspired to hijack a plane.*

collude To **collude** means to **conspire** to cheat people. *The ship's captain colluded with the smugglers to deceive the customs officers.*

connive To **connive** can mean to work together secretly. *The industrial spy connived with the scientist to steal the secret plans for the new computer chip.*

> similar keywords: **plan**

poisonous   *adjective*

▶ containing a substance that may kill you or make you very sick if you swallow it, or it pierces your skin. *Accidentally eating the **poisonous** mushroom was the cause of his illness.*

venomous **Venomous** means producing a poisonous substance that can kill you or make you very sick. It is used about some snakes and spiders. *The rattlesnake is a venomous reptile.*

toxic **Toxic** can mean poisonous, or acting as a poison. *The toxic waste from the mill was killing the fish in the river.*

noxious **Noxious** means harmful to your health. *Many people were taken to the hospital when noxious gas filled the Tokyo subway station.*

carcinogenic **Carcinogenic** means able to cause cancer in your body. *Any known carcinogenic chemicals and food additives are banned by law.*

virulent **Virulent** means extremely infectious, malignant, or poisonous. *The Black Death was a virulent form of plague that attacked Europe and much of Asia during the 14th century.*

polish *verb*

▶ to make something smooth and bright by rubbing. *He **polished** the soapstone carving until it shone.*

shine	To **shine** can mean to polish or make something sparkle or glisten. *Dad decided to shine all the silver cutlery in the drawer.*
buff	To **buff** means to polish metal or give a smooth, bright glow to other surfaces. *Danella buffed the brass knocker on the door.*
burnish	To **burnish** means to make something glistening and bright by rubbing. It is similar to **buff**. *He burnished the copper kettle, too.*
furbish	To **furbish** can mean to polish or **burnish** armour or weapons. It is a rather old-fashioned word. *The Samurai furbished his sword and put it carefully into its sheath.*

similar keywords: **smooth**
contrasting keywords: **roughen**

polite *adjective*

▶ having good manners. *What a **polite** girl you are to offer the elderly man your seat on the bus.*

courteous	**Courteous** is so similar to **polite** that you can usually use either word. *Rajih asked in such a courteous way that we all agreed to help him.*
gracious	**Gracious** means very kind and **courteous**. *Irene was a gracious host and thanked everyone for coming to her party.*
respectful	**Respectful** means to show politeness and respect. *The children speak to the older neighbour in a respectful manner.*
gallant	**Gallant** means helpful and brave. *The gallant warrior preferred to win over the enemy with words rather than the sword.*
mannerly	**Mannerly** means showing good manners. *They shook hands and greeted the new guests in a mannerly way.*

similar keywords: **well-behaved, kind**
contrasting keywords: **rude, bold, vulgar, abrupt**

pompous   *adjective*

▶ showing too much sense of your own importance. *The **pompous** politician gave commands to the other people in the group.*

pretentious   **Pretentious** means having an exaggerated outward show of importance, wealth, and so on. *The pretentious actor always talked about the important people he knew and the expensive cars he bought.*

affected   **Affected** can mean behaving in an artificial way to impress people. *That lawyer is very affected, especially in the way she speaks.*

snooty   **Snooty** means **snobbish**, proud, or arrogant. It is more suited to everyday language. *Don't get snooty just because you are captain of the team.*

snobbish   **Snobbish** means looking down on people who are not as wealthy, important, or clever as you. *You have been snobbish ever since you won the award.*

> similar keywords: **proud, conceited**
> contrasting keywords: **humble**

ponder   *verb*

▶ to consider or think deeply or carefully about something. *I **pondered** the question of whether I should try out for the track team.*

contemplate   To **contemplate** means to consider something thoughtfully. *He contemplated the meaning of the poem for several minutes.*

weigh   To **weigh** can mean to consider carefully by thinking about all aspects of something. *I need lots of time to weigh my interests and skills before making a career decision.*

reflect on   To **reflect on** means to think carefully about something. *I reflected on the moral of the story.*

pore over   To **pore over** means to read or study something very carefully. *The students pored over their books before the exam.*

> similar keywords: **concentrate**

poor *adjective*

▶ having little money, property, or means of producing wealth. *Just because people seem **poor** to others doesn't mean they are always unhappy.*

needy **Needy** means very poor or not having enough money or belongings. *There are many organizations that help needy people to get the proper training for a better job.*

impoverished **Impoverished** means having been made very poor. *The farmers were impoverished after many years of drought.*

disadvantaged **Disadvantaged** can mean not having a reasonable standard of living because you don't have enough money or the means of making it. *During the Great Depression, disadvantaged people travelled across the country looking for work.*

hard up **Hard up** means in need of money. It is more suited to everyday language. *I was so hard up that I had to borrow some money from my brother.*

> similar keywords: **broke**
> contrasting keywords: **wealthy**

position *noun*

▶ a job or duty for which you are paid. *Mr. Singh began his career in the bank with a **position** as a teller.*

post A **post** is a job or a duty. *My sister has a teaching post.*

situation A **situation** can be a position or job. This is a rather formal word. *The butler looked for a new situation after his employer died.*

standing A **standing** can be a position or rank. *Britta's standing in the company has earned her great respect.*

office An **office** is a position of trust or power, usually in the government or a business. *She has the office of press secretary to the Prime Minister.*

appointment An **appointment** is a job or special position someone is given. *We were pleased at his appointment as general manager of the company.*

position   *verb*

▶ to put in a particular place. *He positioned his chair right in front of the television.*

locate

To **locate** means to put something in a particular position or area. *The residents protested the township's plan to locate the new dump site in their neighbourhood.*

situate

To **situate** means to place something in a certain position. It is very similar to **locate**. *They situated the new hospital on the other side of town.*

station

To **station** means to place something in a position for a particular reason. *The concert promoters stationed security guards at every entrance.*

install

To **install** means to put something into place so it can be used. *Mom installed a new washerless faucet in the kitchen sink.*

establish

To **establish** means to set up. *They established the new school exactly where the old one had been.*

> similar keywords: **place**

possible   *adjective*

▶ able to be done or used. *It is possible to walk there in less than ten minutes.*

feasible

Feasible means likely to work. *I think your plan is feasible.*

viable

Viable means **feasible** or able to survive. *Solar energy is a viable alternative to nuclear energy in some parts of the world.*

workable

Workable means able to be put into operation. *I have thought of a workable plan.*

practicable

Practicable means **feasible** or able to be done or put into practice because it is sensible or uses what you have. *It will be more practicable for us to go there by bus.*

> similar keywords: **likely, useful, believable, practical**
> contrasting keywords: **impossible, useless**

poverty *noun*

▶ the condition of having little money, few possessions, or no means of producing wealth. *The farmers lived in **poverty** for a year after the crops failed.*

want	**Want** is the condition of not having the necessities of life. It is similar to **poverty**, but slightly more formal. *There are people living in want in all our big cities.*
need	**Need** can mean a situation when you are short of the necessities of life. *They were in great need when they lost all their belongings in the fire.*
destitution	**Destitution** means the state of extreme poverty. *Their relatives sent them gifts of food and clothing to relieve their destitution.*
deprivation	**Deprivation** can mean the state of being without many of the things you need because you have no money. *Although she was unemployed, the money she had saved kept her from deprivation.*

> contrasting keywords: **wealth**

powerful *adjective*

▶ having great force, authority, or influence. *They are among the most **powerful** nations in the world. She is one of the most **powerful** speakers I have ever heard.*

mighty	**Mighty** means having or showing power, force, or ability. It is a rather old-fashioned word. *The Dalai Lamas of Tibet were mighty but kindly rulers.*
forceful	**Forceful** means strong, powerful, and able to influence people. *Prime Minister Laurier was a forceful speaker.*
potent	**Potent** can mean strong or having great power. *There are potent arguments against building the new airport so close to the city.*
dominant	**Dominant** means the most important or powerful. *The dominant group at the meeting was the one that supported the mayor.*

> similar keywords: **hardy, strong**
> contrasting keywords: **powerless, fragile, weak, decrepit**

powerless *adjective*

▶ not having the power or ability to do things. *With his hands and feet tied up, the magician seemed **powerless** to escape.*

impotent **Impotent** is similar to **powerless**. *The townspeople wanted to prevent the flooding, but they were impotent against the force of the tidal wave.*

incapacitated **Incapacitated** means having been made powerless or unable to do something. *The ambulance carried the incapacitated victims of the chemical leak to the hospital.*

feeble **Feeble** means lacking in force, strength, or effectiveness. *The tired survivors could only make feeble attempts to cry for help.*

pathetic **Pathetic** can mean showing a great lack of ability. *I made such a pathetic attempt at writing my report that I decided to try again.*

> similar keywords: **useless, decrepit, fragile, vulnerable, weak**
> contrasting keywords: **powerful**

practical *adjective*

▶ sensible and facing things as they really are. *It is not **practical** to try to build the fence in one day.*

realistic **Realistic** means facing life as it really is. *She has realistic ideas about the fight against automobile pollution.*

down-to-earth **Down-to-earth** means practical and sensible. *I try to be down-to-earth in the way I solve my problems.*

matter-of-fact **Matter-of-fact** means dealing with facts, or being so sensible that it is rather uninteresting. *He gave a matter-of-fact talk rather than an imaginative one.*

pragmatic **Pragmatic** means practical or thinking about the results or usefulness of your actions. *The pragmatic politician planned a successful election campaign.*

> similar keywords: **sensible, possible**

practice *noun*

▶ a performance or action that is repeated regularly to improve skill. *With* **practice**, *you will get better at playing field hockey.*

drill
: A **drill** can be an exercise or a strict way of training that is repeated regularly. *We have a fire drill once a month.*

training
: **Training** can be a session to develop fitness or a time to practise certain physical skills. *The singers took voice training twice a week.*

run-through
: A **run-through** is a quick trial or practice, usually before the official performance. *I had a run-through of what I was going to perform for my balance-beam routine.*

warm-up
: A **warm-up** is a short period of preparation for a sporting event, or a musical or theatrical performance. *The band had a warm-up before the performance.*

rehearsal
: A **rehearsal** is a practice before giving a public performance. *We had several rehearsals before the opening night of our school play.*

praise *verb*

▶ to say that you admire or approve of someone or something. *Although we didn't win the game, the coach* **praised** *our efforts.*

compliment
: To **compliment** means to praise or say that you admire someone or something. *Oba complimented me on my positive attitude.*

commend
: To **commend** means to say that you admire and approve of someone or something. *I commend you for your hard work this year.*

speak well of
: To **speak well of** means to say very good or complimentary things about someone or something. *I heard your teacher speak well of your friend.*

congratulate
: To **congratulate** means to express happiness at someone's accomplishments or good fortune. *I will congratulate Meghan on her victory in the election.*

glorify
: To **glorify** means to praise someone or something very highly. *The statue was built to glorify the idea of understanding among all peoples.*

> similar keywords: **approve**
> contrasting keywords: **disapprove of, fault, slander**

precise *adjective*

▶ absolutely right in every detail. *Do you know the **precise** time?*

exact **Exact** can mean completely right. It is very similar to **precise**. *It is vital to use the exact address in sending computer E-mail.*

accurate **Accurate** can mean careful and **exact**. *Is that an accurate copy of the original?*

specific **Specific** means clear and **accurate**. *Her directions were very specific, so we didn't get lost.*

definite **Definite** means precise and clearly stated. *I found your definite instructions to be very helpful.*

meticulous **Meticulous** means paying attention even to the smallest detail. *Michael gives every part of his work meticulous attention.*

> similar keywords: **perfect, thorough**
> contrasting keywords: **vague**

predict *verb*

▶ to tell what is going to happen in the future. *The journalists tried to **predict** which party would win the election.*

foresee To **foresee** means to see what is going to happen before it does. *I foresaw trouble when the kitten got into the knitting basket.*

forecast To **forecast** is similar to **predict** and you can often use either word. *The weather bureau has forecast rain for next weekend.*

prophesy To **prophesy** means to tell what you believe is going to happen. *The economist prophesied that prosperity would return next year.*

foretell To **foretell** means to predict. *Do you think that someone can foretell your future by examining the lines on your palm?*

divine To **divine** means to **foretell** by using supposed supernatural powers, or to locate underground water or minerals with a divining rod. *The farmer's friend used a tree branch to divine a water source for the new well.*

> similar keywords: **warn, calculate, examine**

prefer *verb*

▶ to regard one thing or person as better than another. *I **prefer** pesto sauce to meat sauce on my spaghetti.*

favour To **favour** can mean to prefer someone or something. *I favour dogs over cats.*

single out To **single out** means to pick or choose someone or something ahead of others. *They singled Chun out for a special award because of her athletic skill.*

opt for To **opt for** means to choose one thing instead of another or other things. *I opt for the subway because it's faster than the streetcar.*

elect To **elect** can mean to pick out or choose something. *I elected to try out for the gymnastics team.*

> similar keywords: **choose**

press *verb*

▶ to act upon something with mass or force. *We **pressed** the button at the pedestrian crossing and waited for the "walk" sign.*

compress To **compress** means to press things together, or force something into less space. *Lawrence was able to compress the air mattress into a small bag.*

jam To **jam** can mean to push or force something into a space tightly. *I jammed the books into the small bookcase.*

squeeze To **squeeze** can mean to press hard in order to remove something. *Let's squeeze some oranges so that we can have fresh juice.*

squash To **squash** means to flatten or crush something. *The car's wheel squashed my tennis ball.*

trample To **trample** means to crush or tread heavily on something or someone. *The neighbour's dog trampled the flowers in our garden.*

> similar keywords: **push**

pretty   *adjective*

▶ pleasant or pleasing to look at, especially in a dainty or graceful way. *I bought a* **pretty** *vase.*

fair
> **Fair** can mean very pretty or beautiful. This is a rather old-fashioned use of the word. *The fair Maid Marian is a character in the legend of Robin Hood.*

good-looking
> **Good-looking** means pleasant to look at. *I think it is more important to be kind than to be good-looking.*

handsome
> **Handsome** means having a fine or pleasant appearance. *People have different opinions on what makes a person handsome.*

attractive
> **Attractive** means quite pleasing to look at. *The living room has been redecorated in an attractive colour scheme.*

cute
> **Cute** means pleasing in a pretty, charming, or dainty way. It is more suited to everyday language. *What a cute little kitten!*

> similar keywords: **beautiful**
> contrasting keywords: **ugly**

prevent   *verb*

▶ to keep or hinder something or someone from doing something. *We'll build a dike to* **prevent** *the floodwaters from ruining our crops.*

stop
> To **stop** can mean to prevent, restrain, or hinder someone or something from doing something. *I can help you to stop biting your nails.*

prohibit
> To **prohibit** can mean to prevent or hinder. *Smoking is prohibited in stores, theatres, and many other places.*

suppress
> To **suppress** can mean to keep something hidden or from being known or published. *The government tried to suppress freedom of speech by controlling the newspapers, TV, and radio.*

forbid
> To **forbid** can mean to prevent or make it impossible for someone to do something. *His parents forbade him to stay out late on school nights.*

> similar keywords: **hinder, block, ban, exclude**
> contrasting keywords: **allow**

price *noun*

▶ the amount of money for which something is bought or sold. *I'll buy it if the **price** is right.*

cost	The **cost** is the price to be paid for something. *What's the cost of the bike with the black handlebars?*
charge	The **charge** is the price or **cost** of something. *There's a charge of 75¢ each time you use your telephone calling card at a phone booth.*
expense	The **expense** is the amount of money to be paid for something. *We couldn't go by plane because the expense was too great.*
rate	The **rate** is a specially worked out **charge** or payment for something. *The lawyer's rate was $250 per hour.*
outlay	An **outlay** is the amount of money spent in getting something. *The money for the videos was a fairly small outlay.*

prison *noun*

▶ a place where criminals are kept locked up. *The bank robber was sent to **prison** for ten years.*

jail	A **jail** is so similar to a **prison** that you can usually use either word. *He spent ten years in jail.*
penitentiary	A **penitentiary** is a prison for people who have committed serious crimes. *The penitentiary had high walls and was heavily guarded.*
compound	A **compound** can be a closed-off area with buildings where people can be kept. *The soldiers guarded the captured pilots in a compound for prisoners-of-war.*
detention centre	A **detention centre** is a small prison, often attached to a police station, where accused offenders are kept until they appear in court. *After her appearance in bail court, the accused was released from the detention centre.*
cell	A **cell** can be a small room in a prison. *Each evening, the prisoners were returned to their cells.*

prisoner *noun*

▶ someone who is kept somewhere against his or her will. *The **prisoners** were locked in their cells after dinner.*

captive   A **captive** is someone who has been taken prisoner. *The kidnappers kept the captives locked up for almost a month.*

convict   A **convict** is someone who has been found guilty of a crime and is serving a prison sentence. *The police quickly arrested the escaped convict.*

inmate   An **inmate** is someone who has to stay in an institution such as a prison. *She counselled the inmates to prepare them for life outside prison.*

hostage   A **hostage** is a person held as security until certain demands are met. *The bank robbers seized a hostage and demanded that the police let them make a getaway.*

> similar keywords: **criminal**
> contrasting keywords: **escapee**

prize *noun*

▶ a reward for winning something, such as a race or competition. *The winner's **prize** was a free trip to a popular skiing resort.*

trophy   A **trophy** is a prize won in a contest, usually a silver cup or something similar. *My trophy for winning the race was a cup with my name on it.*

award   An **award** is a prize won for good work or achievement. *Katina was given an award for her brave action.*

medal   A **medal** is a flat piece of metal given as a prize or an **award** for bravery or some other achievement. *The figure skater won an Olympic bronze medal.*

pennant   A **pennant** is a triangular flag, often given as a prize in a sporting event. *Our baseball team has won three pennants.*

ribbon   A **ribbon** is a narrow strip of fabric, sometimes representing a medal. *The poodle won a blue ribbon at the dog show.*

produce   *verb*

▶ to bring something or someone into being. *This soil **produces** good crops.*

bear
To **bear** can mean to produce by natural growth or to give birth to a child. *This tree bears oranges. Taluta bore a son who grew up to look exactly like his father.*

yield
To **yield** can mean to produce or **bear** something. It is not used to refer to animals or people. *The crops will yield a good harvest this year.*

breed
To **breed** can mean to produce young under particular conditions. *They breed prize sheep.*

grow
To **grow** means to develop or cause to come into being. *We grew these plants from seeds.*

spawn
To **spawn** can mean to give birth to or produce a large number. *The salmon spawn each spring. Our first meeting spawned some outstanding ideas.*

similar keywords: **make, cause, create**
contrasting keywords: **destroy**

profession   *noun*

▶ an occupation in which special knowledge is needed. *My sister is an architect by **profession**.*

craft
A **craft** is a skill or an art for which you need special abilities or training. *His craft is pottery.*

trade
A **trade** is a particular kind of work using your hands, for which you need special training. *Lee decided that carpentry was the best trade to learn.*

apprenticeship
An **apprenticeship** is a time during which someone learns a trade or an art by working for someone with experience. *My apprenticeship with the glass sculptor lasts two years.*

livelihood
A **livelihood** is a way or means of earning a living. *She earns a livelihood by driving a bus.*

similar keywords: **job, position**

profit   *noun*

▶ money made by selling something for more than it cost to produce or buy. *The umbrella factory made a big profit this year.*

proceeds	**Proceeds** means the money you get when you sell something. *The proceeds from the used book sale were used to help the homeless.*
return	A **return** can be the extra money you receive as a profit from an investment. *My mother was pleased with the return on her Canada Savings Bonds.*
dividend	A **dividend** is a share in the profit made by a business. *The software company paid a good dividend to its stockholders.*
bonus	A **bonus** can be extra money paid to an employee as a reward for good work. *Each worker received a bonus because sales had been high.*
royalty	A **royalty** is money paid to writers, composers, or inventors as a share of the profits made from their work. *The composer of that song receives a royalty each time it is played on the radio, on TV, or in a public performance.*

> similar keywords: **pay**

promise   *noun*

▶ a statement telling someone that you will be sure to do or stop doing something. *The child made a promise to be good.*

pledge	A **pledge** is a promise made very seriously. *She made a pledge that she would not be late again.*
vow	A **vow** is a solemn promise. It is very similar to a **pledge**. *The secret agent took a vow not to reveal any confidential information.*
oath	An **oath** can be a promise that what you are about to say is true. *When you give evidence in court, you take an oath to tell the truth.*
word	Your **word** is a serious promise that means what you say can be trusted. It is an abbreviation of the expression "word of honour." *I give you my word that I won't do it again.*
pact	A **pact** is a solemn promise or agreement between people. *We made a pact that we would always be friends.*

pronounce   *verb*

▶ to make the sound of a word or letter. *I **pronounced** the word slowly so that my parrot could learn to say it.*

enunciate

To **enunciate** can mean to pronounce words or sounds clearly. *He enunciates his words very well although he is only three.*

articulate

To **articulate** means to speak words or sounds clearly, or to express thoughts effectively. *She was so articulate that everyone could understand what she was explaining.*

sound

To **sound** can mean to speak, pronounce, or express words or sounds clearly. *The teacher asked the little boy to sound out the word.*

voice

To **voice** means to express a thought or feeling out loud. *I voiced my opinion about the play.*

utter

To **utter** means to speak or pronounce. *The judge uttered the decision so that everyone could hear.*

property   *noun*

▶ something that is owned by a person or group of people. *Everything with my name on it is my **property**.*

possessions

Possessions are the things someone owns. *We hired a van to move all our possessions to our new house.*

belongings

Belongings are things that you own. It is very similar to **possessions**. *I had to decide where to put my belongings in my new bedroom.*

paraphernalia

Paraphernalia means **belongings**, especially things you use in a particular activity. *We didn't realize how much paraphernalia we had collected until we began to pack up for the camping trip.*

assets

Assets are things you own, especially things that are valuable. *Our house and car are our most expensive assets.*

gear

Gear can be equipment used for a particular purpose. *We packed our camping gear in two knapsacks.*

protect *verb*

▶ to keep something or someone from injury, danger, or annoyance. *I brush with fluoride toothpaste to* **protect** *my teeth from cavities.*

guard
To **guard** means to protect or to keep something or someone safe from harm. *Our dog guards our house and barks at strangers.*

defend
To **defend** means to protect or to keep something or someone safe, especially from attack. *Antibodies in the blood defend our bodies from harmful infections.*

shield
To **shield** can mean to protect someone or something with anything that acts as a shield. *I used my body to shield my small brother from the freezing wind.*

screen
To **screen** can mean to protect or shelter someone or something with anything that acts as a screen. *The gigantic beach umbrella screened us from the sun.*

secure
To **secure** means to make something safe from harm or danger. *We used ropes to secure the boat to the dock.*

> contrasting keywords: **endanger**

protrude *verb*

▶ to stick out or stretch out more than is usual. *I need braces on my teeth because the top row* **protrudes**.

jut
To **jut** means to stick out sharply. *Watch out for the shelf that juts from the wall.*

project
To **project** can mean to stand out or stick out or **jut**. *The antenna on top of the tower projects two metres from the top of the main structure.*

bulge
To **bulge** means to stick out as a rounded mass or hump. *The squirrel's cheeks were bulging with nuts.*

swell
To **swell** means to **bulge** out. *After I sprained my ankle, I put ice on it so that it wouldn't swell too much.*

billow
To **billow** means to **bulge** out because of being filled with air. *The clothes on the line flapped and billowed in the strong breeze.*

proud *adjective*

▶ thinking well of yourself. *I am **proud** that I won the wheelchair race.*

self-confident **Self-confident** means believing strongly in your own ability to do something. *Isabel is a self-confident reporter because she has years of experience.*

self-reliant **Self-reliant** means counting on your abilities to accomplish something. *We need a self-reliant person who can work without supervision.*

smug **Smug** means showing or feeling that you are very pleased with yourself. *I gave a smug smile when I won first prize.*

arrogant **Arrogant** means showing that you think you are very important. *Peter was arrogant until Carla defeated him in the debate.*

haughty **Haughty** means **arrogant** or proud in a boastful way. *The famous conductor has a very haughty manner, even when not onstage.*

> similar keywords: **pompous, conceited**
> contrasting keywords: **humble**

prove *verb*

▶ to show something to be true or genuine. *The jeweller's appraisal of my gold necklace **proves** its true value.*

confirm To **confirm** can mean to strengthen or make more certain someone's belief in something. *The newspaper article confirmed my suspicions that the factory would close.*

corroborate To **corroborate** means to make something more certain by giving additional, similar information about it. *The information I gave the police officer corroborated Geoffrey's report of what had happened.*

substantiate To **substantiate** means to prove something by producing evidence. *You will have to substantiate your accusation that they stole your book.*

verify To **verify** means to prove something is true or correct. *You can verify the spelling of a word by looking it up in a dictionary.*

bear out To **bear out** means to prove someone or something is right. *The facts you have given him bear me out.*

public *adjective*

▶ used by or having to do with the people of a community or the people as a whole. *Many people use **public** transportation to go downtown so that they won't have to worry about finding a parking space.*

general	**General** means concerning all or most people. *The general feeling at the meeting was that the school dance should be postponed.*
popular	**Popular** means widely liked by a particular group or by people in general. *Lots of people listen to this radio station because it plays popular music.*
collective	**Collective** means having to do with a group of people taken as a whole. *The job will be done more quickly if we make a collective effort.*
communal	**Communal** means shared by several people. *The apartments have lockers and a communal laundry room in the basement.*
common	**Common** means shared by two or more people. *The two friends shared a common interest in stamp collecting.*

publication *noun*

▶ something that has been printed for distribution to the public. *This section of the library contains only Canadian **publications**.*

newspaper	A **newspaper** is a publication that is produced daily or weekly and contains news reports, feature articles, reviews, advertisements, and so on. *We read the newspaper every day so that we know what's happening in Canada and in the rest of the world.*
magazine	A **magazine** is a publication that comes out at regular intervals and contains articles, stories, pictures, and so on. *This monthly magazine is available in both a paper-bound and an electronic edition.*
journal	A **journal** is a **magazine** that is issued regularly by a professional or learned group, especially for readers who are members of that group. *The teacher always reads the monthly educational journals.*
pamphlet	A **pamphlet** is a very small stapled or unbound book. *The garden composter came with a pamphlet filled with useful suggestions on recycling.*

similar keywords: **book**

publish *verb*

▶ to make something known to the public. *The newspaper **published** the story about the daring rescue.*

report To **report** means to describe or give an account of something. *At the meeting, Amardip reported that the student council had made some changes to the election rules.*

declare To **declare** means to announce something or make something known officially. *The government declared that the economic recession was finally over.*

proclaim To **proclaim** means to announce something publicly. *The prime minister proclaimed a new civic holiday.*

broadcast To **broadcast** means to spread information, especially by radio or TV. *The radio station broadcasts the latest news every hour.*

> similar keywords: **inform, reveal**

pull *verb*

▶ to move something by tugging it toward you. *I **pulled** my fishing line into the boat, but the bait was gone.*

haul To **haul** means to pull something hard. *We hauled the anchor into the boat.*

drag To **drag** means to pull something slowly or heavily along. *We dragged the sports equipment across the gym floor.*

draw To **draw** means to pull, move, or take something in a particular direction. *I quickly drew my hand away from the fire.*

tow To **tow** means to **drag** or pull something behind you using a rope or chain. *The tractor towed our car out of the flooded river.*

lug To **lug** means to pull or carry something along with a great deal of effort. *We lugged our heavy hockey equipment bags into the dressing room.*

> contrasting keywords: **push**

punish *verb*

▶ to make someone suffer in some way because of a crime or an offence. *The teacher* **punished** *the bullies by making them stay in at lunch time.*

discipline
To **discipline** means to punish in a way that is supposed to teach someone not to do the same thing again. *They disciplined us for being careless by making us pay for the new window.*

chastise
To **chastise** means to punish or scold someone. *Their father chastised the children for being late for dinner.*

penalize
To **penalize** means to give a person a punishment. *The hockey player was penalized for high-sticking.*

correct
To **correct** can mean to punish someone or scold someone, especially a child, to try to improve his or her behaviour. *She corrected her son when he snatched the ball from the other child without asking for it.*

> similar keywords: **scold**

purple *adjective*

▶ coloured dark reddish-blue. *Do you prefer green or* **purple** *grapes?*

magenta
Magenta means coloured reddish-purple. *In full-colour magazines and books, all the colours in pictures are made up of small dots of magenta, yellow, blue, and black.*

mauve
Mauve means coloured light purple. *If you mix purple and white paint you get a mauve colour.*

violet
Violet means coloured bluish-purple. *Violet is the colour seen at the end of a rainbow.*

lilac
Lilac means coloured pale reddish-purple. *The flowers on a lavender bush are a lilac colour.*

indigo
Indigo means coloured a deep violet blue. *Blue jeans get their colour from indigo dye.*

push *verb*

▶ to move something by pressing or leaning against it. *Julian likes to **push** the stroller with his baby brother in it.*

shove To **shove** means to push something roughly. *Someone shoved me from behind, but I didn't fall over.*

thrust To **thrust** means to force or push something hard. *David thrust the knife into the watermelon to cut it.*

drive To **drive** means to make someone or something go forward. *The sheepdog drove the sheep into the pen.*

ram To **ram** can mean to push or **drive** something with great force. *Nasima rammed the earth down around the fence posts.*

propel To **propel** means to push or **drive** something forward energetically. *The rowers propelled their boat across the finish line.*

> similar keywords: **press**
> contrasting keywords: **pull**

puzzle *verb*

▶ to make someone uncertain or unable to understand. *The signpost **puzzled** me because the name of the street was spelled differently from the one on the map.*

perplex To **perplex** means to make someone confused and uncertain. It is very similar to **puzzle**. *That exam question perplexed me because we never learned how bees find their way home.*

baffle To **baffle** means to puzzle or confuse someone. *The disappearance of the millionaire baffled the relatives.*

bewilder To **bewilder** means to confuse someone hopelessly. *I was bewildered by the question and couldn't think of a reply.*

mystify To **mystify** means to confuse someone completely with something that seems strange or unusual. *The mark on the wall mystified her until she realized there was a secret sliding door there.*

> similar keywords: **confuse**
> contrasting keywords: **explain**

Q, q

question   *verb*

▶ to ask someone for information about something. *The doctor **questioned** her patient about his symptoms.*

inquire	To **inquire** can mean to question or to ask about. *Milana inquired about the cost of the table.*
interrogate	To **interrogate** means to question someone closely in order to find out something. *The police interrogated the suspect for several hours.*
interview	To **interview** means to meet with someone formally in order to ask particular questions. *For my class project, I interviewed my grandmother about life on the Prairies when she was a young girl.*
quiz	To **quiz** means to ask someone many questions. *My mother quizzed me on all the material I had studied for my test.*

> similar keywords: **ask**
> contrasting keywords: **answer**

quiet   *adjective*

▶ free from, or making little, noise or sound. *This is a **quiet** street because there is no heavy traffic.*

soft	**Soft** can mean making little sound. *We could hardly hear his soft voice in the crowded restaurant.*
faint	**Faint** can mean lacking loudness or strength. *We could hear the faint sound of singing in the distance.*
low	**Low** can mean not loud. *The owl gave a low hoot.*
muffled	**Muffled** means deadened or made less in sound, usually because of being covered by or wrapped in something. *Because of the muffled voice, it was difficult to tell whether the kidnapper was male or female.*

> contrasting keywords: **loud**

quit *verb*

▶ to give up or leave something. *Dad* **quit** *his job when he got a better offer.*

evacuate   To **evacuate** means to leave a place in order to escape danger. *We evacuated the building when the fire alarm sounded.*

vacate   To **vacate** means to leave a place, such as a building or a room, usually because someone else wants it. *We had to vacate the hotel room before noon.*

abandon   To **abandon** means to leave a place and intend to stay away. *We had to abandon the leaking ship.*

desert   To **desert** means to leave a place where you are on duty and not come back. *The soldier deserted his post.*

forsake   To **forsake** means to give up someone or something. *She decided to forsake her career in advertising in order to study art.*

similar keywords: **leave**

R, r

rain *verb*

▶ to come down from the sky in drops of water. *We won't have to water the garden because it **rained** all night.*

shower	To **shower** can mean to fall in light, scattered drops. *It showered on and off, while the sun was trying to come out.*
sprinkle	To **sprinkle** can mean to rain lightly. *Let's keep walking, because it's only sprinkling.*
drizzle	To **drizzle** means to rain gently and steadily in fine drops. *I wish the sun would come out, because it has been drizzling for days.*
pour	To **pour** means to rain heavily. *It started to pour and we got soaked coming home from school.*
teem	To **teem** means to rain very hard. *It has been teeming all day and the roads are very slippery.*

ramble *verb*

▶ to talk or write without keeping to the subject. *He **rambled** on and on about things that I didn't understand.*

wander	To **wander** can mean to move or turn idly toward another thing. *His mind wandered off the subject of cows, and he started to talk about his new computer.*
stray	To **stray** can mean to turn aside from the subject you were talking or writing about. *I strayed from the topic of my essay and wrote about horses instead.*
digress	To **digress** means to **wander** away from the main subject when writing or speaking. *I started to lecture on the effects of drinking, but I'm afraid I have digressed from my topic.*
diverge	To **diverge** can mean to **wander** off or turn aside from a plan, discussion, and so on. *We have diverged from the main points of the meeting, and I'd like to return to them.*

similar keywords: **rave**

rash   *adjective*

▶ acting too quickly and without thought of possible danger or trouble. *Diving into the shallow creek was a **rash** act.*

reckless **Reckless** means not caring about danger, often in a foolish way. *Riding a bike without lights at night is a reckless thing to do.*

foolhardy **Foolhardy** means foolishly adventurous or not thinking about danger. It is quite similar to **reckless**. *You were foolhardy to explore the abandoned house by yourself.*

impetuous **Impetuous** means acting quickly and thoughtlessly, but not necessarily in a dangerous way. *The impetuous little boy rushed off without hearing the rest of what his mother was saying.*

hasty **Hasty** means acting in a hurry and without thinking. *I try not to make hasty decisions about important matters.*

harebrained **Harebrained** means **reckless** or not sensible. *It was their harebrained idea to go skiing at midnight.*

> similar keywords: **careless, sudden**
> contrasting keywords: **wary, careful**

rave   *verb*

▶ to talk wildly, making little sense, especially when you are very ill. *The delirious patient was **raving**, so the nurse gave him a sedative to put him to sleep.*

babble To **babble** means to speak words quickly and unclearly. *The nervous boy babbled his response to her question.*

jabber To **jabber** means to speak words quickly, unclearly, or foolishly. *The student jabbered on and on about why her homework wasn't finished.*

prattle To **prattle** means to talk in a careless, childlike manner. *He prattled on about little things that didn't mean much to us.*

talk nonsense To **talk nonsense** means to say something that is silly or has no meaning. *Don't talk nonsense.*

> similar keywords: **talk, ramble**

reaction *noun*

▶ something done as a result of an action by someone else. *Our **reactions** to the play were very favourable.*

response A **response** is a reaction caused by something that provokes it. *Donna's response to her kind words was a smile.*

reply A **reply** can be similar to a **response**, and you can often use either word. *Would you please reply to my request for more information.*

answer An **answer** can be a **reply** or a **response**. *His answer to the insult was simply to ignore it.*

feedback **Feedback** can be information passed back about something that has been done or said. This is more suited to everyday language. *My editing partner gave me a lot of useful feedback on my new story.*

acknowledgment An **acknowledgment** can be a thing done or given to show that you are grateful or think highly of something. *My friends took me to a movie in acknowledgment of the help I had given them.*

read *verb*

▶ to look at and understand writing or printing. *My father **reads** a story to my little sister every night.*

browse through To **browse through** means to glance through a book in a casual and leisurely way. *I browsed through a magazine while I was waiting to see the dentist.*

leaf through To **leaf through** means to turn the pages of a book, or something similar, quickly. *I leafed through the book to make sure it would help me in researching my science report.*

skim To **skim** can mean to glance over something without taking everything in. *I skimmed the chapter titles in the book to see whether it had the information I needed.*

study To **study** can mean to look at something closely. *The lawyer studied all the documents for the case.*

peruse To **peruse** is to read through something thoroughly. *Takeo perused the magazine carefully, reading each article.*

ready *adjective*

▶ in the right condition for immediate action or use. *I'm always* **ready** *to leave for school at 8:00 a.m.*

prepared	**Prepared** means made ready for something. *When you go camping, you should be prepared for any kind of weather.*
equipped	**Equipped** means provided with whatever is needed to do something. *The plumber was equipped for a very difficult job.*
available	**Available** means easily attainable or ready. *The dry cleaning will be available for you to pick up tomorrow afternoon.*
outfitted	**Outfitted** means provided or supplied with all the clothing, equipment, furniture, or other things you need. *We were outfitted for a two-week fishing trip to northern British Columbia.*
primed	**Primed** can mean prepared for a particular purpose. *The hikers said they were primed and ready to go.*

realize *verb*

▶ to find out or come to understand clearly. *At last I* **realized** *what she meant.*

discover	To **discover** can mean to find out something you didn't know before. *They finally discovered the meaning of the coded message.*
learn	To **learn** can mean to find out or come to know something. *Zaira was surprised when she learned what a good swimmer David was.*
ascertain	To **ascertain** means to find out or make sure of something. *I am trying to ascertain the truth.*
glean	To **glean** can mean to gather something slowly and with difficulty, one bit at a time. *It took them many weeks to glean all the information they needed.*
catch on	To **catch on** can mean to understand something, often something you should have understood earlier. It is more suited to everyday language. *It didn't take Sophie long to catch on to the problem, and soon she had the motor fixed.*

similar keywords: **sense, understand**

rebel *verb*

▶ to fight against the government or resist those who rule or have power. *The people rebelled against the dictator and exiled her.*

mutiny
To **mutiny** means to rebel against someone in authority. It is usually used about sailors or soldiers. *The crew mutinied because of their captain's unfair treatment.*

revolt
To **revolt** means to rebel against those who have power over you. *The American colonists revolted against their British rulers.*

riot
To **riot** means to take part in a violent disturbance caused by mobs. *During the French Revolution, mobs of dissatisfied poor people rioted in the streets.*

rampage
To **rampage** is to behave in a furious, violent manner. *The crazed inmates overpowered the guards and rampaged through the prison.*

> similar keywords: **disobey**
> contrasting keywords: **give in**

rebellion *noun*

▶ a refusal to obey someone who is in charge or who has power over you. *William Lyon Mackenzie led a rebellion in Upper Canada in 1837 to protest the behaviour of the government.*

revolt
A **revolt** is so similar to **rebellion** that you can usually choose either word. *Many people fled to the United States after the unsuccessful revolt of 1837.*

uprising
An **uprising** is a rebellion against the government or other authority by a large number of people. *The dictator fled Haiti following uprisings throughout the country.*

coup
A **coup** is a sudden successful move, especially against a government. *The Greek generals were in power for several years following the army coup.*

mutiny
A **mutiny** is a rebellion against authority, especially by sailors or soldiers against their officers. *The sailors set the ship's captain adrift in a rowboat during the mutiny.*

record   *verb*

▶ to write down information so that it can be kept. *I'll use my journal to* **record** *all the events of the trip.*

note
: To **note** means to write something down, usually so you can remember it. *Halima noted on the calendar the time of her appointment to see the doctor.*

register
: To **register** means to have something written down on a list that is kept as a record. *We're going to get to the pool early so that we can register for swim class.*

enter
: To **enter** can mean to write something on a list. *Luke entered his name on the list of volunteers.*

transcribe
: To **transcribe** means to write spoken words. *I transcribed the taped interview and used some of the quotes in my newspaper article.*

log
: To **log** can mean to write down important details of a voyage or flight. This is usually done by the captain of a ship or plane. *The captain logged the weather information as soon as she received it.*

> similar keywords: **list**

recover   *verb*

▶ to get well again after being sick. *Pedro has now* **recovered** *from his accident.*

recuperate
: To **recuperate** is so similar to **recover** that you can usually use either word. *My little sister Miriam is recuperating from the measles.*

convalesce
: To **convalesce** means to grow stronger after an illness. *Sunita is convalescing at home after her appendix operation.*

rally
: To **rally** can mean to recover or gain fresh strength, often after an illness. *We were relieved when she rallied so quickly after the operation.*

brighten
: To **brighten** can mean to become more lively or cheerful, especially if you haven't been feeling well. *Miguel gradually brightened as his fever went down.*

> contrasting keywords: **deteriorate**

red *adjective*

▶ coloured like a ripe tomato. *The **red** peppers brightened up the green spinach salad.*

crimson	**Crimson** means coloured a deep, purplish-red. *We wore crimson poppies on Remembrance Day.*
scarlet	**Scarlet** means coloured a bright red. *The guards at Buckingham Palace wear scarlet coats.*
ruby	**Ruby** means rich red-coloured, like the precious stone called a ruby. *The stoplight shone ruby red through the mist.*
maroon	**Maroon** means having a dark brownish-red colour. *Amardip held the chestnut up to the light to admire its rich maroon colour.*
pink	**Pink** means having a pale red colour. *The pink roses were less expensive than the long-stemmed red ones.*

refresh *verb*

▶ to fill someone with new energy and strength. *You'll be ready to work again after you **refresh** yourself with a short rest.*

revive	To **revive** can mean to bring someone or something back into a lively state. *A drink of cool water will revive me after that long walk.*
renew	To **renew** can mean to restore someone or something to the way it was before. *The rain renewed the grass, and it turned green again.*
invigorate	To **invigorate** means to fill someone with life and energy. *Jane's morning swim invigorated her and made her feel wide awake.*
stimulate	To **stimulate** can mean to encourage someone to feel lively or interested. *The cheering fans stimulated us into fighting back to score another goal.*
rejuvenate	To **rejuvenate** means to make someone feel young or energetic again. *Ali felt rejuvenated after a good night's sleep.*

refuge *noun*

▶ a place giving shelter or protection from danger or trouble. *The cave was a perfect* ***refuge*** *during the storm.*

shelter
A **shelter** is a place that provides protection or safety. *The bus shelter can be crowded on a chilly morning.*

haven
A **haven** can be a place of safety and protection. *The fishing boats used the sheltered bay as a haven whenever the sea became too rough.*

asylum
An **asylum** can be any refuge offering safety or care. *The refugees from that war-torn country are seeking asylum in Canada.*

retreat
A **retreat** is a private place where people go to find peace and quiet. *They go to the retreat in the mountains nearly every year.*

sanctuary
A **sanctuary** can be a place protected by law where plants and animals cannot be harmed. *The wildlife sanctuary was a perfect place to see animals living in their natural state.*

refuse *verb*

▶ to say you will not accept something offered to you. *He* ***refused*** *my help and said he could manage by himself.*

decline
To **decline** can mean to refuse to accept something in a polite way. *She declined my invitation to the party.*

reject
To **reject** means to refuse to accept or use something, usually because it isn't satisfactory. *The newspaper contest rejected my story because it was too long.*

renounce
To **renounce** means to refuse to accept something that you are entitled to have. *The man renounced his legal right to the money.*

turn down
To **turn down** can mean to refuse or **reject** something. This is more suited to everyday language. *Mom turned down their offer to buy our house because the price was too low.*

rebuff
To **rebuff** means to refuse to accept something in a definite and strong way. *He rebuffed all her attempts to be friendly.*

> similar keywords: **prevent, ban, repel, resist**
> contrasting keywords: **allow**

rejoice   *verb*

▶ to be glad or delighted. *The whole family **rejoiced** when the baby was born.*

celebrate   To **celebrate** means to have a party for a special reason. *When the exams are over, we are going to celebrate.*

revel in   To **revel in** means to take great pleasure in something. *Ben revelled in the attention he received after winning the songwriting contest.*

exult   To **exult** means to rejoice greatly. *The lottery winners exulted in their good fortune.*

whoop it up   To **whoop it up** means to have a party or celebration. This is more suited to everyday language. *Miranda really whooped it up on her birthday.*

> contrasting keywords: **grieve**

related   *adjective*

▶ of a similar kind or having something in common. *Geography and geology are **related** subjects of study.*

connected   **Connected** can mean thought of as related. *Last night's robbery may be connected to a similar one across town.*

associated   **Associated** means related to or **connected** with something in your mind or thoughts. *Major accomplishments and their associated pleasures are memories you may have all your life.*

allied   **Allied** can mean joined together in reality or in your thoughts. *Running and its allied sport, hurdling, interest me a lot.*

relevant   **Relevant** means related to what is being discussed. *Her remark about people landing on Mars was relevant to the topic of space exploration.*

affiliated   **Affiliated** means associated or united with an organization, political party, or some other body. *The mayor said that she was not affiliated with any political party.*

> similar keywords: **similar**
> contrasting keywords: **unrelated**

reliable *adjective*

▶ trusted or able to be relied on. *Joe is such a **reliable** friend, I know he will keep his promise.*

responsible   **Responsible** means reliable, or able to accept and be trusted with special responsibilities or duties. *We need a responsible person to be in charge of the sports equipment.*

dependable   **Dependable** is so similar to **reliable** that you can usually use either word. *We asked Sabira to place the want ad because she is always dependable.*

conscientious   **Conscientious** means reliable because you are very careful and particular in what you do. *We gave the most important jobs to Paolo because he is such a conscientious worker.*

dutiful   **Dutiful** means always doing what you think is right. *We elected Lisa again because she had been such a dutiful club president.*

> similar keywords: **faithful, steadfast, honest**
> contrasting keywords: **fickle**

religion *noun*

▶ any particular system of worship that usually involves belief in and respect for a supernatural power. *When we studied different **religions** in school, we learned that each **religion** has a number of values and morals that followers accept.*

faith   **Faith** can mean a particular religion with its collection of principles and teachings. *Ahmed was brought up in the Islamic faith.*

belief   **Belief** can be very similar to **faith**. *Avinder's family is of the Sikh belief.*

denomination   **Denomination** means a large, organized religious group, especially in the Christian church. *Kim belongs to the Baptist denomination.*

theology   **Theology** means the collection of beliefs held by a particular religion. *In the theology of the ancient Greeks, there were many gods and goddesses.*

creed   A **creed** is a formal statement of religious or other beliefs. *She is tolerant of others, regardless of creed.*

religious   *adjective*

▶ believing in a particular religion. *Daksa is **religious** and observes the Hindu festivals each year.*

pious | **Pious** means showing religious devotion and respect. *Tamar is very pious and will not carry out any business activities on Shabbat.*

devout | **Devout** means very religious and devoted to your religious commitments. *Hiroshi is a devout Buddhist who meditates and chants every day.*

reverent | **Reverent** means showing deep respect. *Mary's reverent behaviour in church was unusual for someone so young.*

faithful | **Faithful** can mean true to your belief in your religion. *Like all faithful Muslims, I fast from sunrise to sunset each year during Ramadan.*

similar keywords: **holy**

remains   *noun*

▶ what is left. This is a plural noun. *Dad used the **remains** of the chicken to make soup.*

remnants | **Remnants** are parts or amounts that are left. This is a plural noun. *I patched my jeans using the remnants of an older pair.*

odds and ends | **Odds and ends** are scraps or **remnants**. This is a plural noun. *We made toys out of odds and ends from our parents' workshops.*

residue | **Residue** is something that is left. This is a singular noun. *Most of the grass cuttings went into the catcher of the lawn mower, and I raked up the residue.*

leftovers | **Leftovers** are things that remain or were not used, especially from a meal. This is a plural noun. *He made a delicious stew from the leftovers of the turkey.*

balance | **Balance** can mean the amount left over. This is a singular noun. *After I took out $20 from my bank account, my balance was down to $300.*

similar keywords: **excess**

remember *verb*

▶ to bring something back to, or to keep it in, your mind. *I **remember** the way to solve that math problem.*

recollect To **recollect** is very similar to **remember** and you can often choose either word. *I tried to recollect how to say that in French.*

recall To **recall** means to remember or **recollect** something. These three words are so similar that you can usually use any of them. *Alex does well on tests because he can recall information very easily.*

place To **place** can mean to connect someone or something in your mind with certain places, events, or other things. *I could only place Nicole when I heard her sing the same song she sang at our last concert.*

recognize To **recognize** means to know someone or something again at a later time. *I recognized Mario right away, even though we had met more than a year ago.*

remove *verb*

▶ to take something off or away. *I always **remove** my shoes before coming inside the house.*

withdraw To **withdraw** means to take something out. *I withdrew some money from the bank.*

extract To **extract** means to pull or take something out. *The dentist extracted my brother's wisdom tooth.*

excise To **excise** means to cut something out. *It didn't hurt when the doctor excised the wart from my finger.*

dislodge To **dislodge** means to remove something from its existing position. *When the workers were pruning the tree, they accidentally dislodged a bird's nest.*

erase To **erase** means to remove all trace of something or to rub it out. *We erased the writing from the board.*

contrasting keywords: **insert, add**

repair   *verb*

▶ to bring something back into good condition. *I'm going to* **repair** *my brother's old bike instead of buying a new one.*

mend
To **mend** means to put something into working order. *Dad is going to help me mend my torn jeans.*

fix
To **fix** means to repair or **mend** something. These three verbs are so similar that you can usually use any one of them. *I will have to fix the loose hand brakes.*

restore
To **restore** means to bring something back to its original condition. *The Historical Society wants to restore the first house built in our town.*

renovate
To **renovate** means to repair something so that it is like new. *We are going to renovate our house.*

patch up
To **patch up** means to repair something, especially in a hasty or makeshift way. *When the car broke down, we patched it up until we could get it fixed properly.*

> similar keywords: **improve, correct**
> contrasting keywords: **damage**

repay   *verb*

▶ to pay back or return something. *I want to* **repay** *the money you lent me.*

reimburse
To **reimburse** means to pay back money that someone spent on something for you. *I'll reimburse you for the concert tickets you bought.*

compensate
To **compensate** means to make something up to someone. *I will compensate you for delivering those newspapers for me when I was sick.*

refund
To **refund** means to give or pay back money. *The theatre refunded the cost of our tickets when the concert was cancelled.*

reward
To **reward** can mean to give something to someone in return for work or help. *The neighbours rewarded me for shovelling their snow.*

> similar keywords: **pay**

repeated *adjective*

▶ done again and again. *They were exhausted after making **repeated** attempts to pull the boat up onto the beach.*

regular	**Regular** means following a rule or pattern, especially at fixed times. *Regular eating and sleeping habits help keep you healthy.*
periodic	**Periodic** means happening or appearing at regular intervals. *It is a good idea to pay periodic visits to your dentist.*
recurrent	**Recurrent** means happening or appearing again and again. *She has recurrent attacks of asthma in January and February.*
rhythmical	**Rhythmical** means happening in a regular pattern of timing. *The rhythmical beat of the music was what made our ice dancing routine so special.*
frequent	**Frequent** means happening often. *They make frequent visits to the ski slopes during the winter.*

repel *verb*

▶ to drive away or force back. *Our bug spray **repelled** the blackflies.*

repulse	To **repulse** is so similar to **repel** that you can usually use either. *The picnickers repulsed the attack of the angry bees.*
scare off	To **scare off** means to frighten someone or something away. *We remained very quiet so we wouldn't scare off the nesting heron.*
dispel	To **dispel** means to drive or send something away in all directions. *Mom's explanation of what the noise really was dispelled all my little brother's fears.*
spurn	To **spurn** means to refuse to have anything to do with someone or something because you are scornful. *At the ball, the prince spurned Cinderella's wicked sisters.*

> similar keywords: **refuse, resist, prevent**
> contrasting keywords: **attract**

report *noun*

▶ an account of the important facts, especially of a meeting, an event, or progress at work or school. *Please write a **report** on how your committee will be set up.*

document A **document** is a paper, giving information or evidence. *I keep my birth certificate and other important documents in a safe place.*

statement A **statement** is something spoken or written that presents facts or details about something or someone. *The officer told us that we'd have to make a statement at the police station after the accident.*

dossier A **dossier** is a bundle of documents containing information about a person or subject. *The government intelligence agency kept a dossier on the spy.*

brief A **brief** is an outline of information or instructions on a subject, especially for use by a lawyer conducting a legal case. *The legal assistant prepared a brief on the case for the lawyer.*

bulletin A **bulletin** is a short written or spoken report or account, especially of news or events. *Did you see the TV bulletin about the peace talks?*

similar keywords: **summary, message**

resentful *adjective*

▶ having a feeling of jealousy, hurt, or anger. *The jealous co-workers were **resentful** of his rapid success.*

bitter **Bitter** can mean filled with harsh, unpleasant, or sour feelings. *She is bitter because her friend would not help her.*

spiteful **Spiteful** means having a wish to annoy or hurt someone else. *The spiteful child hit his playmate for no reason.*

vindictive **Vindictive** means paying someone back for something that has been done to you. *They could be vindictive when others cheated them.*

vengeful **Vengeful** means wanting to get even. *Although I didn't agree with their actions, I could understand the vengeful feelings of the victim's friends.*

similar keywords: **angry, mean, jealous**

reside *verb*

▶ to have your home in a particular place. It is a fairly formal word. *We **reside** in Halifax now.*

live To **live** can mean the same as **reside**. It is a much less formal word. *I live in Prince George.*

dwell To **dwell** means to **live** in a particular place or condition. It is a rather old-fashioned word. *They dwell in peace and harmony.*

inhabit To **inhabit** means to **live** in or occupy a place. *Bears inhabit these woods.*

board To **board** means to pay for the use of a room and for meals. *He has to board at school because his parents live in the country.*

squat To **squat** can mean to **live** without permission on land or in a property you don't own. *The city let the homeless families squat in the deserted building until they could find a better place to live.*

> similar keywords: **inhabit**

resist *verb*

▶ to stand up to or fight against something or someone. *My body successfully **resisted** the invading virus because I had received my flu shot.*

defy To **defy** can mean to resist someone or something boldly. *They defied the icy blizzard and walked home after their car broke down.*

oppose To **oppose** means to disagree with and resist someone or something. *Our town was opposed to the plan to build the shopping mall so close to the park.*

withstand To **withstand** means not to give way to something or someone. *The small fishing boat somehow withstood the pounding waves during the storm.*

obstruct To **obstruct** can mean to interfere with or **oppose** something or someone. *The tall trees obstructed our view of the sea.*

> similar keywords: **repel, ban, refuse**
> contrasting keywords: **give in**

respect *noun*

▶ a feeling of admiration. *I have the greatest* **respect** *for people who help others.*

regard	**Regard** can be a respect for, or a favourable opinion of, someone or something. *I have a very high regard for Mom's knowledge in these matters.*
esteem	**Esteem** is the good opinion you have of someone. *Tony's hard work earned him the esteem of the whole class.*
honour	**Honour** can mean respect or **esteem**. *The scientist was treated with honour when she visited her old school.*
veneration	**Veneration** means a feeling of deep respect and love. This is a rather formal word. *We were filled with veneration for the wise shaman.*
devotion	**Devotion** can be loyalty or great affection. *Ms. Tsui was an excellent manager and won the devotion of her associates.*

contrasting keywords: **scorn**

rest *noun*

▶ a time of ease or recovery. *I think I'll have a* **rest** *after I finish my homework.*

break	A **break** is a short rest. *They took a break from work.*
recess	A **recess** is a period of rest from work. *The judge said we would take a two-hour recess before continuing with the trial.*
pause	A **pause** can be a brief period of inactivity or rest. *They took a pause from climbing in order to catch their breath.*
leisure	**Leisure** is time that is free from work. *We were given a day of leisure to do whatever we wanted.*
breather	A **breather** is a short break that allows you to catch your breath. It is more suited to everyday language. *It's time to take a breather from your studies.*

contrasting keywords: **work**

rest   *verb*

▶ to refresh yourself by taking a nap or a quiet break. *Little children often **rest** in the afternoon.*

relax   To **relax** means to rest and feel at ease. *You can sit down and relax for an hour.*

recline   To **recline** means to rest by lying back. *After a long day, Ingrid reclined in her favourite chair and closed her eyes for ten minutes.*

wind down   To **wind down** means to rest after working very hard. *Reading a science-fiction novel helps me wind down after a stressful game.*

put your feet up   To **put your feet up** means to sit or lie down and have a rest. This is more suited to everyday language. *What a strenuous workout! Let's put our feet up and listen to some music.*

take it easy   To **take it easy** means to have a restful time. This is more suited to everyday language. *You should take it easy after running such a long cross-country race.*

> similar keywords: **laze**
> contrasting keywords: **work**

restaurant   *noun*

▶ a place where you can buy and eat a meal. *That **restaurant** serves both Korean and Japanese food.*

café   A **café** is a restaurant that serves coffee, tea, and small meals. *We had lunch in an outdoor café.*

bistro   A **bistro** is a small restaurant or wine bar. *Let's meet in the French bistro on the corner.*

cafeteria   A **cafeteria** is an inexpensive self-service restaurant. *Is there a cafeteria in this office building?*

snack bar   A **snack bar** is a counter where beverages and small meals are served. *There is a snack bar in this arena where we can get a sandwich.*

diner   A **diner** is a small inexpensive restaurant. *She parked her truck and went into the diner for a quick meal.*

result   *noun*

▶ something that springs or proceeds from an action or event. *The success of the play was the **result** of our group's terrific effort.*

outcome
: An **outcome** is something that results from what has happened previously. *The plot was so exciting that I couldn't wait to discover the outcome.*

effect
: An **effect** is a result, or something that is produced by some cause. *Wrinkles are an effect of aging.*

consequence
: A **consequence** is the inevitable or expected result of something. *I was grounded as a consequence of not phoning to say that I would be home late.*

conclusion
: **Conclusion** can mean a final result. *The signing of an agreement was the conclusion of the peace talks.*

sequel
: A **sequel** can be anything that follows or results from something. *The author wrote a sequel to her popular novel.*

retaliate   *verb*

▶ to strike back. *If others tease you, it is pointless to **retaliate** by insulting them.*

reciprocate
: To **reciprocate** means to act in a similar way in return. *If you are rude to him, he will reciprocate by being rude to you.*

take revenge
: To **take revenge** means to cause hurt or damage because of something someone has done to you. *When they spoiled our game, we took revenge by hiding their bikes.*

get even
: To **get even** means to **take revenge**. This is more suited to everyday language. *The wise teacher said that things get worse, not better, when people try to get even with their enemies.*

avenge
: To **avenge** means to **take revenge** for something. *You might avenge the murder of a friend, but it won't bring him or her back.*

settle a score
: To **settle a score** means to **get even** for a wrong done to you. This is more suited to everyday language. *She settled a score with the company that fired her by taking it to court for wrongful dismissal.*

reticent *adjective*

▶ not inclined to talk a lot or openly. *He was **reticent** about what was bothering him, so I convinced him to talk with a counsellor.*

reserved   **Reserved** means inclined to keep your feelings or thoughts to yourself. It is similar to **reticent**. *She seemed unfriendly, but she was only being reserved.*

quiet   **Quiet** can mean shy and not inclined to talk. *The new student in class was rather quiet until he knew everyone.*

taciturn   **Taciturn** means not inclined to communicate by talking. *I can be rather taciturn when I am in a bad mood.*

laconic   **Laconic** means using few words when talking. *She is sometimes laconic in her replies.*

secretive   **Secretive** means liking to keep things to yourself. *People can often mistrust you if they think you are too secretive.*

> similar keywords: **shy**
> contrasting keywords: **talkative**

retrieve *verb*

▶ to bring back or to get again. *My dog **retrieved** the ball after I threw it.*

fetch   To **fetch** can mean to go after and bring back. *Our dog fetches the newspaper every morning.*

reclaim   To **reclaim** can mean to change the natural condition of land so that it may be used by humans. *The developers drained the land, eventually reclaiming it from the swamp.*

recover   To **recover** can mean to get back something that has been lost or stolen. *They finally recovered the stolen bicycles.*

repossess To **repossess** means to take back something because the money owed for it is overdue. *The car dealership let him make smaller, more frequent payments so that it would not have to repossess his van.*

cash in   To **cash in** means to turn something in for cash. This is more suited to everyday language. *She cashed in her Canada Savings Bonds to help her daughter go to college.*

reveal   *verb*

▶ to uncover something or make it known. *They **revealed** the secret door to the Pharaoh's hidden tomb.*

disclose   To **disclose** can mean to tell something or allow it to be known. *He disclosed the history of the castle.*

show   To **show** can mean to demonstrate or explain something or make it clear. *She showed me how to mix the chemicals correctly to make the experiment work.*

expose   To **expose** can mean to reveal something that has been hidden from most people. *His book exposed the many anonymous good deeds his family had done in the past.*

unfold   To **unfold** can mean to reveal or explain something little by little. *As he unfolded the whole saga, I began to understand his pride in his family's history.*

> similar keywords: **admit, publish, inform, blab**
> contrasting keywords: **hide**

reverse   *verb*

▶ to turn back or go backward. *We came to a dead end and had to **reverse** our direction.*

back into   To **back into** means to move backward. *Dad backed the car into the garage.*

recede   To **recede** means to move back and become more distant. *As we sailed away, the harbour receded into the distance.*

ebb   To **ebb** means to flow back or away. *We waited until the tide ebbed before we walked around the rocks.*

rebound   To **rebound** means to bounce or spring back. *The puck rebounded off the boards.*

> similar keywords: **overturn**
> contrasting keywords: **advance**

rhythm   *noun*

▶ the pattern of regularly repeated groups of strong and weak stresses or accents in music, poetry, or speech. *They clapped to the* **rhythm** *of the music.*

beat

Beat can be the units of time in a piece of music, or the rate at which accents or stresses follow one another, giving a feeling of pattern or regularity. *I like music that has a strong, regular beat.*

time

Time can be the speed of movement of a piece of music. *This music is marked to be played in waltz time.*

tempo

Tempo is the speed at which you perform a piece of music, and is usually indicated for you. It is very similar to **time**. *This song has a fast, lively tempo.*

swing

Swing can be a steady marked rhythm or movement in music or speech. *Everything the big band played had a swing to it.*

cadence

Cadence can be another word for rhythm. *They marched to the cadence of the drums.*

ridiculous   *adjective*

▶ so silly or funny that people feel like laughing, often in a scornful way. *Why are you wearing that* **ridiculous** *costume?*

absurd

Absurd can mean ridiculous or foolish. *I'm wearing these absurd rabbit ears because I thought it was a costume party.*

nonsensical

Nonsensical means foolish or making no sense. *We found ourselves in a nonsensical situation that no one could explain.*

ludicrous

Ludicrous means so ridiculous that no one could take it seriously. *Your suggestion that we walk from Vancouver to Edmonton is ludicrous.*

preposterous

Preposterous means annoyingly ridiculous. *Don't come to me with any more of your preposterous suggestions.*

farcical

Farcical means so ridiculous that it doesn't seem like a real situation. *It was almost farcical the way that we kept on running into each other.*

similar keywords: **silly**
contrasting keywords: **sane**

ring   *verb*

▶ to make or give out a clear musical sound. *The bells are **ringing**.*

peal	To **peal** means to ring loudly and for a long time. *The bells pealed to celebrate the crowning of the new queen.*
chime	To **chime** can mean to make the sound of a bell that has been struck. *This clock chimes every hour.*
knell	To **knell** means to ring slowly and with a sad sound. *The church bells knelled for the miners' funeral.*
toll	To **toll** means to ring with single, slow, sad, sounds, usually at a funeral. It is similar to **knell**. *My dad is reading a book called* For Whom the Bell Tolls.
tinkle	To **tinkle** can mean to make light jingling sounds. *The wind chime tinkled in the breeze.*

room   *noun*

▶ a part of a building separated by walls from other parts. *Our apartment has five **rooms**.*

chamber	A **chamber** is a private room, usually a bedroom. It is an old-fashioned word. *The sick duke received visitors in his chamber.*
den	A **den** can be a quiet, cozy, private room. *My mother likes to read in the den.*
compartment	A **compartment** can be a room or separate section in a railway car or ship. *We shared our railway compartment with two other passengers.*
cubicle	A **cubicle** is a very small, partly enclosed room. *We studied in a quiet library cubicle.*
cell	A **cell** can be a small room in a prison, a convent, or a monastery. *The monks meditated and read in their cells each evening.*

r o t   *verb*

▶ to go bad. *The green vegetables are **rotting** because of the hot weather.*

decay
To **decay** can be so similar to **rot** that you can usually use either. *The apples fell from the tree and decayed on the ground.*

decompose
To **decompose** means to break up as it rots. *The leaves decomposed and fertilized the forest floor.*

putrefy
To **putrefy** can mean to rot with a very unpleasant smell. *If we don't get the fridge working, the meat will putrefy.*

fester
To **fester** means to go bad and form pus. This is mostly used about a wound or a sore. *Put some ointment on that cut before it festers.*

perish
To **perish** can mean to rot or **decay**. *When the refrigeration unit broke down, the food perished in the shipping container.*

> similar keywords: **deteriorate, spoil**

r o u g h   *adjective*

▶ feeling uneven or not smooth. *The wooden table top I made was quite **rough** until I sanded it.*

bumpy
Bumpy means having a lumpy or uneven surface. *It was a rough ride over the bumpy road.*

gnarled
Gnarled can mean rough and worn by old age or the weather. *The gnarled driftwood made an interesting decoration.*

coarse
Coarse means thick or not having a fine, smooth feel. *This breed of dog has coarse hair.*

shaggy
Shaggy can mean rough and matted. *The pony's coat was so shaggy that I couldn't brush it easily.*

bristly
Bristly means rough because of having short, stiff hairs. *The baby liked touching her dad's bristly chin before he'd had a shave.*

> contrasting keywords: **smooth**

roughen *verb*

▶ to make something feel worn or not smooth. *Hard work has **roughened** their hands.*

coarsen	To **coarsen** can mean to make something feel rough or no longer fine. *Too much sun can coarsen your skin.*
chap	To **chap** means to make your skin cracked, red, and rough. *We put salve on our lips so the cold wind wouldn't chap them.*
chafe	To **chafe** means to wear down or make something sore by rubbing it roughly. *The saddle chafed the horse's back.*
rasp	To **rasp** means to scrape something with a rough tool. *The carpenter rasped the piece of wood with a file.*
ruffle	To **ruffle** means to disturb or spoil the smoothness of something. *Birds ruffle their feathers when they are cleaning themselves.*

> contrasting keywords: **smooth**

rubbish *noun*

▶ useless leftover material or matter. *We took our **rubbish** to the dump.*

garbage	**Garbage** is so similar to **rubbish** that you can often use either word. *Our household garbage is collected every week and taken away in trucks.*
refuse	**Refuse** is **garbage** or waste material. *Rain washed the refuse off the sidewalks into the gutters.*
debris	**Debris** is the rubbish left when something is broken or destroyed. *The rescuers had to clear away piles of debris to get to the victims of the earthquake.*
junk	**Junk** means old and unwanted things. *We are going to clean out all the junk from our garage tomorrow.*
trash	**Trash** is rubbish or anything that you think is worthless or useless. *We put our pile of trash out to be collected, but we were pleased to see people take things they could use.*

rude *adjective*

▶ bad-mannered or not behaving politely. *I think it is **rude** to butt in ahead of people who are lined up for the bus.*

impolite　　**Impolite** is so similar to **rude** that you can usually choose either word. *It's impolite to talk when someone else is speaking.*

impudent　　**Impudent** means rude and disrespectful. *The teacher was disappointed with the student's impudent behaviour.*

insolent　　**Insolent** means boldly and openly rude and disrespectful. *We were surprised by their insolent attitude to their parents.*

insulting　　**Insulting** means showing rudeness by saying hurtful things. *I ignored their insulting remarks about my hairstyle.*

presumptuous　　**Presumptuous** means being too bold or taking for granted that you know more than somebody else. *It was presumptuous of you to correct your father's pronunciation.*

> similar keywords: **bold, vulgar, abrupt**
> contrasting keywords: **polite**

rule *noun*

▶ an instruction telling you what to do. *I'll read out the **rules** of the game.*

law　　A **law** is a rule made by a government or a ruler for all the people to follow. *The law says you must wear your seat belt in a car.*

regulation　　A **regulation** is a rule made by an authority, such as a school, city, or town. *Local regulations forbid you to post advertisements on bus shelters.*

convention　　A **convention** can be a rule, often not written down, that everyone understands and follows. *It is a convention here to say "hello" when you answer the telephone.*

precept　　A **precept** is a general rule or saying about behaviour. *"Look before you leap" is a wise precept.*

formula　　A **formula** can be a rule or recipe that you should follow. *Looking for the good things even when times are tough can be a formula for happiness.*

rule *verb*

▶ to have or exercise power over something or someone. *The queen **ruled** her subjects wisely.*

reign
To **reign** means to rule or use authority as a king or queen does. *Victoria reigned as queen of Great Britain and Ireland and empress of India from 1837 to 1901.*

preside
To **preside** means to have control over something. *The chairperson's job was to preside over the meeting.*

officiate
To **officiate** means to perform the duties that accompany a particular position. *The student council president officiated at the mock trial.*

dominate
To **dominate** can mean to rule or control because you have the most power. *Our group was successful because we shared ideas and individuals didn't dominate the discussion.*

command
To **command** can mean to give orders or be in charge. *The major commanded the sergeant to control the soldiers.*

> similar keywords: **manage**

run *verb*

▶ to move quickly on your feet. *Jennifer can **run** very fast in her new athletic shoes.*

sprint
To **sprint** means to run as fast as possible, but usually only for a short distance. *We sprinted from the car to the house to avoid getting too wet in the rainstorm.*

trot
To **trot** means to run at a slow, even pace. *The ballplayers trotted out onto the playing field.*

jog
To **jog** means to run at a continuously even pace, usually for exercise. *We jog around the track every morning and every evening without fail.*

gallop
To **gallop** means to move very fast. *He galloped down the street and around the corner to catch up with his friends.*

> similar keywords: **march, hurry, speed, jump**
> contrasting keywords: **dawdle, walk, trudge**

S, s

sacrifice *verb*

▶ to give up something you like or want for a particular purpose. *I **sacrificed** my leisure time on Saturday to help out at the charity carwash.*

relinquish — To **relinquish** means to give up or let go of something. It is a rather formal word. *Nadia relinquished her seat on the bus to a man with a cast on his foot.*

forgo — To **forgo** means to sacrifice or **do without** something. *He decided to forgo his holiday to save money for his first year in community college.*

do without — To **do without** means to get along without something you would like to have. *I've decided I can do without a more trendy coat this fall.*

resign — To **resign** means to **relinquish** something, especially a job or position. *Ahmed resigned as president of the club so that he could spend more time on his schoolwork.*

sad *adjective*

▶ sorrowful or miserable. *I was **sad** when my best friend left town.*

unhappy — **Unhappy** means not cheerful or happy. *Tim was unhappy when he couldn't go on the class trip.*

homesick — **Homesick** means **unhappy** because you are not at home. *The children were homesick during their first few days at summer camp.*

low — **Low** can mean **unhappy** or sad. *I was in low spirits when I was unable to finish the marathon.*

hurt — **Hurt** can mean sad because someone has been unkind to you. *My feelings were hurt when she didn't invite me to her birthday party.*

upset — **Upset** means feeling sad or **hurt**. *She was upset when she wasn't picked for the team.*

> similar keywords: **miserable, glum**
> contrasting keywords: **happy, joyful, glad**

safe *adjective*

▶ free from danger or risk. *We knew we were* **safe** *when the wind and waves died down.*

protected **Protected** means guarded or shielded from danger or harm. *I was protected as I huddled in the tiny cave away from the storm.*

sheltered **Sheltered** means **protected** from bad weather, danger, and so on. *We planted the seedlings in a sheltered corner of the garden.*

secure **Secure** means safe or free from danger. *We were secure knowing we had a map and compass to help us find our way home.*

immune **Immune** means free or **protected** from danger, harm, or disease. *Tina was immune from mosquito bites as long as she wore repellent.*

unharmed **Unharmed** means not hurt, although the possibility existed. *Everyone survived the crash miraculously unharmed.*

contrasting keywords: **vulnerable, dangerous**

sag *verb*

▶ to hang loosely. *His blue jeans* **sagged** *over his hips.*

droop To **droop** means to sink or hang down. *Her eyes drooped in sadness until her friend cheered her up.*

collapse To **collapse** can mean to fall down suddenly, often from weakness. *The exhausted children collapsed onto their beds.*

loll To **loll** can mean to hang loosely, or sink down. *The dog's tongue lolled from its mouth as it panted.*

slump To **slump** means to drop heavily and loosely. *I slumped into the chair.*

slouch To **slouch** means to sit, walk, or stand in a drooping manner. *Our gym teacher told us it was bad for our backs to slouch too much.*

similar keywords: **drop, fall**

said *verb*

▶ spoken or told. This word is the past tense of say and is often used with dialogue, or conversation requiring quotation marks. *She **said**, "I am going fishing."*

whispered **Whispered** means spoken without vibrating your vocal cords, saying something so no one except the person spoken to can hear. *"Don't look now," I whispered, "but your brother and his friend are headed this way."*

cried **Cried** can mean said loudly or in an excited way. *"Watch out, Bob!" I cried, when I saw the speeding car approaching.*

exclaimed **Exclaimed** means spoken with strong feeling. *"Don't walk along the edge of the cliff!" he exclaimed.*

stated **Stated** means said in a neutral way. *The diplomat stated her country's policy on disarmament at the United Nations' meeting.*

> similar keywords: **describe, pronounce, shout, shriek**

sail *verb*

▶ to travel in a ship or boat. *Last summer we visited Ontario and **sailed** around Georgian Bay.*

cruise To **cruise** means to sail from place to place, especially for pleasure. *We cruised among the islands, looking at the beautiful scenery.*

glide To **glide** can mean to move slowly and easily across water. *The sailboat glided across the calm lake.*

skim To **skim** can mean to move lightly across the surface of the water. *The canoe skimmed across the still lake.*

navigate To **navigate** can mean to control the direction of a ship or boat. *Louisa navigated the boat along the coast.*

float To **float** means to move gently on top of water. *We floated on our raft for a couple of hours, reading and enjoying the sunshine.*

s a n e *adjective*

▶ sensible or based on common sense. *When we realized that we were lost, we knew the only **sane** thing to do was to find shelter for the night.*

sound Sound can mean sure or reliable. *Mom always gives me sound advice when I'm in trouble.*

well-balanced Well-balanced can mean sane or sensible. *This is a well-balanced approach to the problem.*

logical Logical can mean based on sensible or correct reasoning. *The logical course of action, now that it's pouring, is to go inside.*

lucid Lucid can mean rational or sane. *That was a very lucid explanation of why you were so late, Paul.*

rational Rational can mean having full control of your mind. *Aziza gave a rational argument to support her point of view.*

> similar keywords: **sensible**
> contrasting keywords: **irrational, mad**

s a t i s f i e d *adjective*

▶ pleased and happy because your wishes or needs are fulfilled. *Catherine looked at her test results with a **satisfied** smile.*

content Content means satisfied with what you have. *I am very content in our new home.*

complacent Complacent means satisfied or quietly pleased, especially with yourself. *The committee members are too complacent to realize that they should be working harder.*

comfortable Comfortable can mean having enough to be satisfied. *They live a comfortable life.*

satiated Satiated means satisfied to such a great extent that you are bored or tired. *I won't be going to an amusement park for a while, because our weekend at Marineland left me satiated.*

> similar keywords: **glad**
> contrasting keywords: **dissatisfied, greedy**

save *verb*

▶ to keep, free, or deliver someone or something from danger or harm. *Their life jackets* ***saved*** *them from drowning.*

rescue To **rescue** means to save someone or something from danger. *Anita climbed up the tree and rescued the terrified kitten.*

preserve To **preserve** can mean to keep something or someone safe. It is a slightly old-fashioned word. *Our guide preserved us from any dangers along the trail.*

safeguard To **safeguard** means to protect or to keep something or someone from harm. *We all took turns watching the bird's nest, safeguarding it from wild animals.*

salvage To **salvage** means to save or recover something, especially from a shipwreck or fire, or something similar. *The sailors salvaged most of the cargo before the ship sank.*

> similar keywords: **protect**
> contrasting keywords: **endanger**

saying *noun*

▶ something that is often said. *My mother seems to have a humorous* ***saying*** *for every situation.*

adage An **adage** is a wise saying. *"More haste, less speed" is a common adage.*

proverb A **proverb** is a short, popular, and usually wise saying that has been used by people for a long time. *"A stitch in time saves nine" is a sensible proverb.*

epigram An **epigram** is a short witty saying that goes straight to the point of a matter. *"Speech is silver, but silence is golden" is a well-known epigram.*

maxim A **maxim** is a saying containing a general truth or rule. *"Look before you leap" is a wise maxim.*

motto A **motto** is a short saying, often taken as summing up the aims or beliefs of a particular organization or group. *The motto of the Scouts is "Be Prepared."*

scant *adjective*

▶ barely enough of something. *There was only enough water for a **scant** mouthful each.*

sparse	**Sparse** can mean of small amount, especially when what exists is thinly spread out or scattered. *Shade trees were sparse along the hot, dusty trail.*
skimpy	**Skimpy** can mean having less thickness, size, or amount than you would like. *My skimpy coat barely kept me warm during those fall evenings at the cottage.*
meagre	**Meagre** means of a small amount or of poor quality. *We gulped down a meagre breakfast of toast as we raced to catch the bus.*
measly	**Measly** means having an annoyingly small amount of something. It is more suited to everyday language. *There was only a measly two cents left in my piggy bank.*

> similar keywords: **insufficient**
> contrasting keywords: **extra, abundant, sufficient**

scarce *adjective*

▶ not often seen or found. *Some forms of wildlife are becoming **scarce** as their natural habitats are destroyed.*

rare	**Rare** means unusual or uncommon. *Vaccination has made polio a rare disease today.*
infrequent	**Infrequent** means not happening very often. *Our grandparents' visits to us have become infrequent since they moved to the city.*
sporadic	**Sporadic** means irregular and not very frequent. *You could tell he was not a hockey fan by his sporadic attendance at the games.*
occasional	**Occasional** means happening or appearing sometimes. *I've only received an occasional letter from Sara since she went to the United States.*

> similar keywords: **unusual**
> contrasting keywords: **numerous, countless**

scatter *verb*

▶ to throw something loosely about. *I **scattered** crumbs around for the birds to eat.*

strew To **strew** means to scatter or throw things everywhere. *The wind strewed the leaves all over the lawn.*

distribute To **distribute** can mean to put or scatter something around. *Daphna distributed the compost over the lawn.*

disperse To **disperse** can mean to scatter something around. *The wind dispersed my pile of leaves and blew them into the air.*

spread To **spread** can mean to scatter something or send it around. *Cover your mouth when you cough or you will spread your germs to everyone else.*

dissipate To **dissipate** can mean to scatter or disappear. *The large crowd dissipated in many directions when the police arrived.*

> contrasting keywords: **gather, store**

scholar *noun*

▶ a learned person. *Taluta is a **scholar** in First Nations history, having written important books and lectured at many universities on the subject.*

intellectual An **intellectual** is someone who shows great mental ability. *Peter Mark Roget was an intellectual who devised the first English thesaurus.*

philosopher A **philosopher** is someone who searches for truth and wisdom. *The philosopher has written many books containing her thoughts on the meaning of life.*

sage A **sage** is a very wise person. *As well as being an actor and a poet, Chief Dan George was a sage who wrote about preserving our natural environment.*

genius A **genius** is an unusually talented or clever person. *Everyone regards the great artist, Leonardo da Vinci, as a genius.*

> similar keywords: **student**

scold   *verb*

▶ to find fault with, and angrily criticize, someone. *They **scolded** me for being so careless.*

rebuke To **rebuke** means to scold or to show that you disapprove of someone's behaviour. *He rebuked us for failing to carry out our obligation.*

reprimand To **reprimand** means to scold or **rebuke** someone, especially in a formal way. *The bus driver reprimanded them for standing on the seats.*

reproach To **reproach** means to find fault with or blame someone. *If you try to be polite and unselfish, people will have no reason to reproach you.*

admonish To **admonish** means to warn or caution someone not to do something. *We admonished the children not to be too noisy when others were trying to nap.*

chide To **chide** means to scold or nag someone. *He chided them for not putting their clothes away.*

> similar keywords: **fault**
> contrasting keywords: **praise**

scorn   *noun*

▶ a complete and obvious lack of respect. *I showed my **scorn** for his offensive remark by turning my back on him.*

contempt **Contempt** is the feeling that you have for someone or something mean, worthless, and disgraceful. *I have nothing but contempt for anyone who is cruel to animals.*

disrespect **Disrespect** is rudeness and lack of respect. *The demonstrators showed their disrespect for the new president by heckling him.*

disdain **Disdain** is a feeling of dislike for something or someone you think is unworthy. *She gave the rude young man a look of disdain.*

ridicule **Ridicule** is words or actions meant to cause scornful laughter at a person or thing. *Their ridicule of her shyness made the young child cry.*

> contrasting keywords: **respect**

scratch   *verb*

▶ to mark or cut something roughly. *The knife **scratched** the plastic counter top.*

nick

To **nick** means to cut something slightly. *She nicked her hand with the craft knife.*

scrape

To **scrape** means to rub a surface with a rough or sharp object. *The little boy scraped his knee when he fell on the rough pavement.*

score

To **score** can mean to make a deep scratch, especially in wood or metal. *The screwdriver slipped and scored the wood.*

graze

To **graze** can mean to scratch your skin. *Samira grazed her hand against the wall.*

claw

To **claw** can mean to scratch or dig with claws or as if using claws. *The prisoners of war clawed their way to freedom by digging under the fence using only their hands.*

> similar keywords: **cut, tear**

scruffy   *adjective*

▶ dirty, shabby, and uncared-for. *But I want my jean jacket to look **scruffy**.*

unkempt

Unkempt means in an uncared-for or untidy condition. *She got the job in spite of her unkempt appearance.*

dishevelled

Dishevelled means untidy and disordered. *We looked dishevelled after working in the yard all afternoon.*

bedraggled

Bedraggled means wet, dirty, and hanging limply. *Their clothes were bedraggled when they came out of the storm.*

shabby

Shabby means worn or threadbare. *Your old running shoes are starting to look shabby.*

ragged

Ragged means torn or shabby. *The old man was wearing a ragged winter coat.*

> similar keywords: **untidy**
> contrasting keywords: **tidy**

secret   *adjective*

▶ done or made without others knowing. *I discovered the **secret** plan to ruin the game.*

confidential   **Confidential** means secret or not public. *Don't let anyone else read this confidential letter.*

classified   **Classified** can mean known or used by only a few people, and not made public, especially top-secret military or government information. *Lock the classified files away where no one else can read them.*

private   **Private** can mean secret or not public. *That computer file is private, so I use a password to access it.*

hush-hush   **Hush-hush** means extremely secret. It is more suited to everyday language. *Their meeting was so hush-hush they wouldn't even tell us what it was about.*

> similar keywords: **secretive**

secretive   *adjective*

▶ liking to keep things secret or to yourself. *Ever since the reporter wrote a misleading story, the scientists have been **secretive** about their research work.*

stealthy   **Stealthy** means done or made in a hidden or sly, secretive way in the hope that it won't be discovered. *We knew something was wrong when we heard a faint, stealthy movement in the next room.*

furtive   **Furtive** means done or acting in a **stealthy** or secretive way. *He gave a quick, furtive look around and then disappeared through the hole in the fence.*

surreptitious   **Surreptitious** means made, done, or behaving in a secret or **stealthy** way. *He didn't notice our surreptitious glance as we walked past him.*

underhanded   **Underhanded** means secret and sly, usually in regard to things that are not very honest or honourable. *They met in the middle of the night to discuss their underhanded plot to discredit their political opponent.*

> similar keywords: **secret, cunning**
> contrasting keywords: **frank**

see *verb*

▶ to look at or take things in with your eyes. *I see the cows coming across the field.*

observe   To **observe** means to see or look at something. *Dylan observed the hooded men go into the bank, and he immediately called the police.*

view   To **view** means to look at or see something. *We went to the art gallery to view the collection of Inuit sculpture.*

notice   To **notice** means to see or take note of something. *I noticed she was using a new camera.*

watch   To **watch** means to look at something attentively. *The students watched a TV show about the Special Olympics.*

witness   To **witness** means to be present at and see something. *We witnessed the historic events.*

> similar keywords: **inspect**

seek *verb*

▶ to try to find or get something. *Many explorers sought a route to China through the Northern Passage.*

hunt for   To **hunt for** means to look for something. *I hunted for my binder everywhere, but I couldn't find it.*

search for   To **search for** means to look for something thoroughly. *I searched for a four-leafed clover all day, but I never found one.*

pursue   To **pursue** can mean to try hard to find something. *In* The Wizard of Oz, *Dorothy helped the tin man pursue his goal of getting a heart.*

quest after   To **quest after** means to look for or seek. It is the sort of old-fashioned word that you might find in poetry. *Jason and the Argonauts quested after the Golden Fleece.*

strive for   To **strive for** means to try very hard or make a great effort to find or get something. *Pablo is striving for top marks.*

> similar keywords: **follow**
> contrasting keywords: **avoid**

selfish   *adjective*

▶ thinking only of your own interests. *The **selfish** child never shared his toys with the other children.*

self-centred   **Self-centred** means being interested only in yourself. *I try to be kind and generous and not act self-centred.*

inconsiderate   **Inconsiderate** means not caring about other people's rights or feelings. *It would be inconsiderate to play loud music when the baby is sleeping.*

spoiled   **Spoiled** means selfish because you are used to getting your own way. *Don't pout like a spoiled child just because you can't see a movie tonight.*

possessive   **Possessive** means wanting to have or control something all by yourself. *Don't be so possessive! Let the others play with the kitten, too.*

> similar keywords: **ungrateful, conceited**
> contrasting keywords: **kind, generous**

sell   *verb*

▶ to give up something in exchange for money. *I **sold** my old skates at the yard sale.*

auction   To **auction** means to sell something by holding a public sale where items are sold to the person who offers the highest amount of money. *The police auctioned lost bicycles that had not been claimed by their owners.*

wholesale   To **wholesale** means to sell large quantities of goods to store owners rather than directly to the public. *Mom's company manufactures and wholesales furniture.*

peddle   To **peddle** means to take things around from place to place in order to sell them. *He was peddling brooms from house to house.*

retail   To **retail** means to sell in small quantities directly to the consumer. *Christina retails her pottery from her small craft shop.*

> contrasting keywords: **buy**

seller   *noun*

▶ someone who sells something, or gives up goods in exchange for money. *The **seller** of the second-hand piano was moving to a small apartment.*

vendor	A **vendor** is someone who sells things. *Everyone crowded around the frozen yogurt vendor on the beach.*
retailer	A **retailer** is someone, such as a storekeeper, who sells things directly to the public. *My uncle is a jewellery retailer.*
merchant	A **merchant** is someone who buys goods wholesale and sells them to the public to make a profit. *The Tibetan handicrafts merchant had a booth at the crafts fair.*
dealer	A **dealer** is someone who buys and sells things. *That antiques dealer is a specialist in old furniture.*
broker	A **broker** is someone who buys or sells things for someone else. *They hired a broker to sell their house.*

contrasting keywords: **buyer**

send   *verb*

▶ to cause something to go somewhere. *I'll **send** you a postcard from Montreal.*

dispatch	To **dispatch** means to send something off. *I dispatched a fax notifying them of my new address.*
forward	To **forward** means to send something on. *Will you forward my mail to me while I'm away?*
pass on	To **pass on** can mean to send something or give it to someone. *Would you like me to pass on your message when Caitlin gets home?*
relay	To **relay** means to pass or send something on. *They used their radio to relay the storm warning to the ship.*
transmit	To **transmit** means to send something over or along to a person or place. *I transmitted my membership request by computer E-mail.*

similar keywords: **carry**
contrasting keywords: **get**

sense *verb*

▶ to notice, feel, or be aware of something. *You could **sense** the excitement at the start of the race.*

experience To **experience** can mean to feel something, or to have something happen to you that you can sense. *Amanda experienced a lot of friendliness during her visit.*

feel To **feel** can mean to sense or **experience** something. *He doesn't like winter because he feels the cold. They felt joyous when they heard the good news.*

perceive To **perceive** means to come to know or realize something through one of the senses of sight, hearing, touch, taste, or smell. *Brian perceived a faint smell of roast chicken wafting out of the house.*

recognize To **recognize** can mean to realize or understand something clearly. *I recognized my mistake in time to do something about it.*

similar keywords: **realize, understand**

sensible *adjective*

▶ able to act with good judgment. *The **sensible** children made sure the cars had stopped before they stepped into the crosswalk.*

wise **Wise** can mean showing good judgment. *Yasmin made a wise decision to take no notice of that stupid dare.*

level-headed **Level-headed** means being calm and sensible, with good judgment. *The level-headed teacher quickly got the class out of the room when the fire started.*

sage **Sage** means sensible or **wise**, especially as a result of learning or experience. *The sage woman advised the young couple to find out what had really caused their quarrel.*

prudent **Prudent** means showing you are careful and sensible in a practical way. *Prudent people always lock their doors when they go out.*

similar keywords: **shrewd, sane, practical**
contrasting keywords: **silly**

separate *verb*

▶ to put things apart. *Rebekah **separated** her pencils from her markers.*

divide To **divide** means to split up or separate into parts. *A river divides the city into two areas.*

disconnect To **disconnect** means to separate two things that are usually connected to each other. *Osama disconnected the VCR from the television.*

detach To **detach** means to separate or unfasten one thing from another. *Please detach the top section of the form and keep it for yourself.*

break off To **break off** means to separate one thing from another, using force. *The storm broke off a large branch of the tree.*

free To **free** can mean to separate one thing from another with difficulty. *Nicole's grip was so strong that I couldn't free my hand.*

contrasting keywords: **join, combine, mix**

series *noun*

▶ a number of things or events arranged or happening in a certain order. *The doctor ordered a **series** of tests for his patient.*

sequence A **sequence** is a series of things following each other. *Jenny solved the math problem by doing the calculations in the proper sequence.*

chain A **chain** can be a series of connected things. *The movie presented a strange chain of events that helped us figure out who the murderer was.*

succession A **succession** can be a number of people or things following one another in order. *Mom had a succession of people coming to see her today at the office.*

course A **course** is a set series of things. *My course of studies begins with introductory lessons.*

cycle A **cycle** is a series of events happening in a regular repeating order. *The seasons continually come and go in their usual cycle.*

sew *verb*

▶ to join, using a needle and thread. *I am going to **sew** a patch on my jeans.*

stitch   To **stitch** is very similar to **sew** and you can often use either word. *Karen stitched the rip in her pocket.*

embroider   To **embroider** means to sew decorative patterns on something. *I embroidered a dragon on my new shirt.*

work   To **work** can mean to sew or **embroider** something. *I worked a design of roses on the handkerchief.*

darn   To **darn** means to mend something with crossing rows of stitches. *Dad darned the hole in my sock.*

tack   To **tack** means to sew loosely with large stitches. *Fatima tacked up the hem before she tried on the dress.*

shadowy *adjective*

▶ seeming faint, dim, and unreal. *There was a **shadowy** outline of a statue behind the white curtain.*

nebulous   **Nebulous** means cloudy or vague. *Rob has only the most nebulous idea of how he should be doing the job.*

ghostly   **Ghostly** means looking or appearing like a ghost. *The trees were ghostly shapes in the fog.*

ethereal   **Ethereal** means light, airy, or not solid. *The clouds made ethereal patterns in the sky.*

intangible   **Intangible** means not able to be touched or seen. *Happiness is the intangible reward for helping others.*

contrasting keywords: **actual**

shake   *verb*

▶ to move backward and forward with short, quick movements. *The branches of the trees shook as the wind blew.*

vibrate   To **vibrate** means to keep on moving quickly up and down or to and fro. *The hummingbird's wings vibrated as it drank the flower's nectar.*

tremble   To **tremble** means to shake or quiver, especially from cold, weakness, or fear. *Trevor's icy-cold hands trembled as he tried to take off his snow-covered boots.*

shudder   To **shudder** means to shake suddenly from horror, cold, or fear. *Kate shuddered when she saw that the cars couldn't avoid a collision.*

quake   To **quake** means to shake or **tremble**. *The teller quaked with fear when he saw the robbers come into the bank.*

rock   To **rock** means to move from side to side or to and fro. *The boat was rocking on the waves.*

> similar keywords: **sway**

shape   *noun*

▶ the way something looks or appears from its outline. *The children cut the construction paper into squares, circles, and other shapes.*

form   A **form** is the shape or appearance of something. *The instructor folded the origami paper into the form of a beautiful swan.*

design   **Design** can mean the shape or outline of something. *I like the futuristic design of our new lamp.*

structure   **Structure** can be the way something is put together and gets its shape. *This model shows the bone structure of the tyrannosaurus rex.*

build   Your **build** is the way your body is shaped or structured. *The runner had a slim, athletic build.*

figure   Your **figure** is the shape of your body. *It doesn't really matter what your figure looks like.*

share *noun*

▶ the part of something given to or owned by someone. *We each received a **share** of the reward money.*

quota   A **quota** is the share that you are entitled to, or are required to meet. *The workers easily completed their quota of work last week.*

allocation An **allocation** is a portion of something set apart for a special purpose. *There was a special allocation of funds for library books in the school's budget.*

allotment   An **allotment** is something handed out or distributed. *We received our allotment of books in September.*

cut   A **cut** can be a share of profits made. It is more suited to everyday language. *My cut from the sale of homemade toys was $40.*

helping   A **helping** is a share of food. *May I please have a second helping of noodles?*

> similar keywords: **part**

share *verb*

▶ to distribute parts of something, with each person receiving a part. *The children **shared** the raisins among themselves.*

divide   To **divide** means to separate anything into parts. *I divided the books among the children.*

split   To **split** can mean to separate something into parts in any way. *After our lunch at the restaurant, we split the bill among the four of us.*

apportion   To **apportion** is to divide among or assign different sizes or shares. *We apportioned the tasks according to the abilities of the children.*

dole out   To **dole out** means to give something out in small quantities. *Juan doled out the pieces of fruit until we all had some.*

divvy up   To **divvy up** means to share something out. This is more suited to everyday language. *The thieves divvied up the stolen cosmetics.*

> similar keywords: **distribute**

shine *verb*

▶ to give out light. *The sun **shone** all day.*

beam To **beam** means to send out rays of light. *The searchlight beamed over the ocean.*

glow To **glow** can mean to shine like something very hot. *The forest was full of insects that glowed in the dark.*

burn To **burn** can mean to shine brightly. *The lights in the house burned all night.*

blaze To **blaze** can mean to shine brightly like a flame or fire. *The headlights of the truck blazed into my eyes and I couldn't see anything.*

flare To **flare** can mean to shine brightly and suddenly. *All was dark, and then the fireworks flared.*

> similar keywords: **sparkle**

shining *adjective*

▶ giving out or reflecting bright light. *Tara looked at me with **shining** eyes when I told her the good news.*

gleaming **Gleaming** means giving out flashes or beams of light. *The rooms of the castle were lit up by gleaming torches.*

flaming **Flaming** can mean shining very brightly. *We sat and watched the flaming logs in the fireplace.*

luminous **Luminous** means radiating light or full of light. *The luminous stars lit up the prairie sky.*

incandescent **Incandescent** means shining or white with heat. *I replaced the incandescent bulb with an energy-saving fluorescent one.*

phosphorescent **Phosphorescent** means giving out light with little or no heat. *A special substance called phosphorus is used to make a phosphorescent light.*

> similar keywords: **shiny, bright**
> contrasting keywords: **dull**

shiny *adjective*

▶ having a bright, shining surface. *Erik polished the table until it was* **shiny**.

glossy **Glossy** is so similar to **shiny** that you can usually use either. *I chose glossy paint for the window trim.*

lustrous **Lustrous** can mean shiny or with a glistening sheen like silk. *We chose a porcelain bowl that had a lustrous blue glaze.*

sleek **Sleek** means shiny and smooth. *One dog is shaggy, and the other has a very sleek coat.*

satin **Satin** means shiny and very smooth like the cloth called satin. *This photograph has a satin finish.*

silky **Silky** means shiny and soft like silk. *The ad claims you will have silky hair if you use this shampoo.*

> similar keywords: **shining**
> contrasting keywords: **dull**

shock *verb*

▶ to cause someone to feel great surprise, sometimes with horror or disgust. *The scene where the monster jumps out from the closet really* **shocked** *me.*

appall To **appall** can mean to shock, displease, or dismay someone. *We were appalled by the terrible way they treated their dog.*

startle To **startle** can mean to disturb or surprise someone suddenly. *The loud boom of thunder startled the children.*

astound To **astound** means to shock or amaze someone either with wonder or surprise. *We were astounded to hear how quickly he had recovered.*

take aback To **take aback** means to cause someone great surprise and confusion. *My best friend's cold attitude toward me really took me aback.*

bowl over To **bowl over** means to surprise, upset, and confuse someone. This is usually more suited to everyday language. *I was bowled over when I heard the cost of the camera repairs.*

> similar keywords: **frighten**

shore   *noun*

▶ the land at the edge of an ocean, sea, lake, or other body of water. *There are pine trees all along the **shore** of this beautiful lake.*

coast
A **coast** is the land at the edge of an ocean or sea. *Halifax is built on the coast of Nova Scotia.*

beach
A **beach** is a stretch of shore that is flat and made up of sand or small stones or shells. *After our swim, we played volleyball on the beach.*

seaside
Seaside is similar to **coast**. *Let's go down to the seaside and watch the sailboats.*

waterfront
A **waterfront** is the part of a city or town that borders on a body of water. *They tore down the old docks and warehouses and built a park along the waterfront.*

shorten   *verb*

▶ to make something short or shorter. *Can you please **shorten** the discussion? I'm really getting tired.*

condense
To **condense** can mean to say or write something in fewer words. *Atepa condensed his story into just a few pages.*

abbreviate
To **abbreviate** means to make a word, phrase, or story shorter by leaving out some letters or words. *We abbreviate "Avenue" to "Ave." to save space.*

abridge
To **abridge** means to shorten a book, interview, and so on, by leaving out some parts. *Sometimes a writer abridges a famous novel to make it easier for children to read.*

summarize
To **summarize** means to say or write something in a short and clear way, giving the main points only. *The coach summarized the rules of the game for the new players.*

sum up
To **sum up** means to give only the main points of something that has already been said or done. *I will sum up everything I just said so that we all understand the plan.*

contrasting keywords: **expand**

shout *verb*

▶ to call or cry out loudly. *My sister **shouted** with happiness when our team won the game.*

yell
To **yell** is so similar to **shout** that you can usually use either. *I yelled to the boy crossing the road, warning him to watch out for the car.*

bellow
To **bellow** means to shout out angrily. *The sergeant bellowed at the troops when they disobeyed orders.*

roar
To **roar** can mean to make the kind of loud, deep sound that a lion makes. *The fans roared when we scored the tying goal.*

whoop
To **whoop** means to yell loudly. *We all whooped with happiness when we were told about our prize.*

bawl
To **bawl** means to cry noisily. *The little boy bawled when he fell over.*

> similar keywords: **shriek**

show *verb*

▶ to cause or allow something to be seen. *Nazir **showed** his drawing to his friends.*

display
To **display** means to show something so that it can be clearly seen. *We displayed our prize pumpkins at the county fair.*

exhibit
To **exhibit** means to show something in a place where the public can go to see it. *The young artist was asked to exhibit her paintings in the town hall.*

demonstrate
To **demonstrate** means to show something clearly and plainly. *Alan demonstrated his skill at gymnastics before an astonished crowd.*

parade
To **parade** means to show by making something move or march in an orderly way. *The farmer paraded the prize cow round the ring.*

flaunt
To **flaunt** means to show something off boldly. *Jane flaunted her trophy until we were sick of her bragging.*

> contrasting keywords: **hide**

show-off *noun*

▶ someone who says or does things in order to make people pay attention or give praise. *She's such a show-off that she wants everyone to watch her do handstands.*

braggart
A **braggart** is someone who boasts about his or her accomplishments. *I try not to be a braggart when I do really well on a test.*

peacock
A **peacock** can be someone who constantly shows off his or her looks and appearance. *Someone should tell that peacock that he's not nearly as terrific as he thinks.*

know-it-all
A **know-it-all** is someone who thinks he or she knows everything. *Only a know-it-all corrects people every time they make a little slip-up.*

smart aleck
A **smart aleck** is someone who is both conceited and rude. This is more suited to everyday language. *Stop being such a smart aleck and let me have a try!*

shrewd *adjective*

▶ clever at making good judgments. *The shrewd shopper realized that the old chair was a valuable antique.*

astute
Astute means able to understand things clearly and quickly. *The astute manufacturer saw how good my invention was.*

sharp
Sharp can mean mentally quick and alert. *The sharp security guard wrote down the licence number of the getaway car.*

canny
Canny can mean shrewd or wise. *The canny businessperson always bought her supplies at the lowest possible price.*

ingenious
Ingenious means clever and often inventive. *You have an ingenious way of using words in your poetry.*

resourceful
Resourceful means clever and quick at dealing with difficult or unexpected situations. *The resourceful campers used branches and leaves to build a shelter after their tent was lost in the canoeing accident.*

> similar keywords: **clever, sensible, cunning**
> contrasting keywords: **silly**

shriek *verb*

▶ to make a loud, sharp, high-pitched cry or noise. *The fans* **shrieked** *with delight when the band appeared onstage.*

screech   To **screech** means to make a harsh high-pitched cry or noise. *The tires screeched on the wet pavement when the car stopped suddenly.*

squeal   To **squeal** means to make a high-pitched cry. *The children squealed with delight as they rolled in the mud.*

yelp   To **yelp** means to give a quick, sharp cry. *The dog yelped when it hurt its paw.*

scream   To **scream** means to make a loud piercing cry or sound. *The sirens screamed as the fire engines raced to the fire.*

squawk   To **squawk** means to make a loud, unpleasant cry. *The chickens squawked when the fox chased them.*

> similar keywords: **shout**

shrink *verb*

▶ to become smaller. *Your wool sweater has* **shrunk** *in the hot water.*

shrivel   To **shrivel** can mean to shrink and wrinkle. *The plant shrivelled and died when it wasn't watered.*

wither   To **wither** can mean to dry up. It is very similar to **shrivel**. *You'd better water the ferns or they'll wither.*

atrophy   To **atrophy** means to lose size or strength. *Muscles atrophy if they aren't used for a long time.*

dwindle   To **dwindle** means to become smaller or fewer in number. *Enrollments in our local school dwindled last year.*

contract   To **contract** can mean to become smaller in size. *Metal contracts as it gets colder.*

> similar keywords: **decrease**
> contrasting keywords: **increase, enlarge**

shy   *adjective*

▶ uncomfortable, timid, not relaxed with other people. *I'm often **shy** until I get to know people.*

bashful   **Bashful** means easily embarrassed. *They were bashful the first time they performed in public.*

modest   **Modest** means having a level-headed opinion of yourself and your abilities. *Debbie was modest about her success in the art competition.*

demure   **Demure** means **modest** and shy. *We were surprised that a child who seemed so demure was such an aggressive athlete.*

diffident   **Diffident** means not confident or sure of yourself. *Jamie is diffident about being in the school play.*

> similar keywords: **reticent, lonely**
> contrasting keywords: **bold, friendly**

sick   *adjective*

▶ having a disease or being unwell. *I was so **sick** that my mother took me to the doctor.*

ill   **Ill** is so similar to **sick** that you can usually use either word. *"You are too ill to get out of bed," the doctor said.*

ailing   **Ailing** means not being very well, even though you may not have anything specifically wrong with you. *I told him I had been ailing for several weeks.*

indisposed   **Indisposed** means just slightly sick. This is a rather formal word. *Tanya told me on the phone that she was indisposed with a cold.*

not yourself   **Not yourself** means not feeling or looking as healthy or energetic as usual. *I'm not myself today because I didn't sleep well last night.*

under the weather   **Under the weather** means in poor health. This is more suited to everyday language. *The flu has left me feeling under the weather.*

> contrasting keywords: **healthy**

side *noun*

▶ one of the outer parts, edges, or lines of something, usually not the top, bottom, front, or back. *You walk past the **side** of the building to get the right door.*

flank	The **flank** can mean the side of anything. *The warriors made plans to attack the enemy's flank.*
wing	A **wing** can be a side part, especially a side building joined to a central building. *They decided to add a new wing to the library.*
jamb	A **jamb** is the side part of a doorway, window, or other such opening. *We used pine to make the jambs for the windows and doors.*
profile	A **profile** is the outline of someone's face as seen from the side. *Martina asked me to look straight ahead for the first photo, and then she photographed my profile.*

similar keywords: **outside, edge**

sign *noun*

▶ a mark, figure, or other indicator used to stand for a word, idea, or mathematical value. *The **signs** for addition (+) and subtraction (–) were first used in print only 500 years ago.*

symbol	A **symbol** is something that stands for or represents something else. *The tree is a symbol of life in many cultures.*
emblem	An **emblem** is a badge or something that serves as a sign or **symbol**. *The maple leaf is the emblem of Canada.*
token	A **token** is a sign or **symbol** of something, usually given to someone. *A red rose is a token of love.*
totem	A **totem** is something, often an animal, used as a **token** or **emblem** of a family or group. *The Haida carve their totems onto tall poles of wood.*

significant *adjective*

▶ important and likely to have great effect on something. *Your twenty-first birthday will be a **significant** event in your life.*

momentous　**Momentous** means of great importance. *The signing of the Canadian Charter of Rights and Freedoms was a momentous occasion.*

memorable　**Memorable** means worth remembering. *My sister's graduation was a memorable occasion.*

critical　**Critical** can mean having to do with an important or dangerous time. *Rajan had to make a critical decision about his career plans.*

fateful　**Fateful** means important because of the seriousness of the things that happened as a result. *The world will always remember the fateful day when the first atomic bomb was dropped on Hiroshima.*

serious　**Serious** can mean important, weighty, or needing a lot of care. *I have brought you here to discuss a very serious matter.*

> similar keywords: **main, important**
> contrasting keywords: **insignificant, minor**

silly *adjective*

▶ without sense. *He gave a **silly** answer.*

foolish　**Foolish** is so similar to **silly** that you can usually use either word. *That seems like a foolish thing to do.*

senseless　**Senseless** means without good sense. It is similar to **silly** and **foolish**. *The plan they suggested couldn't work because it was senseless.*

idiotic　**Idiotic** means extremely silly. *I won't listen to any more of your idiotic ideas.*

inane　**Inane** means silly or not intelligent. *I'm sick of your inane chatter.*

stupid　**Stupid** means not intelligent. *It would be really stupid to climb that rusty old ladder.*

> similar keywords: **ridiculous, irrational, mad**
> contrasting keywords: **sensible, sane**

similar *adjective*

▶ having a likeness, especially in a general or not specific way. *Kevin and Mei drew* **similar** *pictures of the accident scene.*

alike	**Alike** means the same as similar, but is used at the end of a sentence, rather than before the noun. *The twins' faces are alike.*
comparable	**Comparable** means similar enough for it to be sensible to compare them. *If Katrina can beat Clare, she can probably beat Jeanette, because Clare and Jeanette are comparable runners.*
akin	**Akin** means related or **alike**. *Mules are akin to donkeys.*
corresponding	**Corresponding** means similar or matching. *A provincial premier and a state governor are corresponding positions.*
synonymous	**Synonymous** means similar or nearly the same in meaning. *This thesaurus groups synonymous words together.*

> similar keywords: **equal, related**
> contrasting keywords: **various, unlike**

simple *adjective*

▶ not having complicated or unnecessary parts. *We like* **simple** *home cooking best.*

plain	**Plain** can mean simple and not fussily decorated. *I bought some plain blue material to make curtains.*
natural	**Natural** can mean real and in its original state. *This is the natural look of wool before it is dyed.*
unadorned	**Unadorned** means **plain** and without decorations or ornaments. *How bare the unadorned room looked after the party decorations had been taken down.*
unobtrusive	**Unobtrusive** means not very noticeable. *Maya looked very elegant in her simple black dress and unobtrusive silver jewellery.*
quiet	**Quiet** can mean toned down and not done up for show. *The house was decorated in quiet tones of beige.*

> contrasting keywords: **gaudy, spectacular**

simplify *verb*

▶ to make something easier to understand, do, or use. *I will* **simplify** *the rules of the game for the kindergarten children.*

streamline To **streamline** can mean to simplify something in order to make it more efficient. *We will get the work done more quickly if we streamline the way we do it.*

sort out To **sort out** can mean to simplify and understand something by separating it into parts and solving each one. *We'll soon sort out our problems.*

unravel To **unravel** can mean to make something less complicated and easier to understand. *I eventually unravelled his explanation and understood what he was saying.*

disentangle To **disentangle** can mean to work something out by simplifying it. It is very similar to **unravel**. *I think I've disentangled the mystery by talking to each person involved.*

> similar keywords: **explain, solve**
> contrasting keywords: **confuse**

singer *noun*

▶ someone who can make musical sounds with the voice, often someone who has been specially trained. *There are thirty* **singers** *in the choir.*

vocalist A **vocalist** is so similar to a **singer** that you can usually choose either word. *My sister is the lead vocalist in a rock group.*

soloist A **soloist** can be someone who sings alone. *The soloist sang a beautiful song at the concert.*

minstrel A **minstrel** was a musician in the Middle Ages who sang or said poetry while playing a musical instrument. *The minstrel entertained the crowd of people at the castle by playing a flute and singing.*

troubadour A **troubadour** was a poet, singer, or songwriter in medieval France, Italy, and Spain. *The troubadour sang for the king and queen at the castle.*

single *adjective*

▶ one alone. *My **single** reason for going is to see the new calves.*

only	**Only** means single or just one. *The only task I haven't finished is my math homework.*
sole	**Sole** means single or **only**. *Lianne is the sole member of the team who was sidelined by an injury.*
exclusive	**Exclusive** can mean single or **sole**. *His concert in Vancouver is his exclusive performance in Canada on the world tour.*
unique	**Unique** means different from all others or having no equal. *Each person's fingerprints are unique.*
lone	**Lone** can mean single or **sole**. *She is the lone surviving member of that historic Olympic team.*

contrasting keywords: **numerous, double**

skillful *adjective*

▶ very good or expert at doing something. *Efra is a **skillful** debater and rarely loses an argument.*

adept	**Adept** means extremely skillful. *My tennis instructor is an adept player and has won many tournaments.*
deft	**Deft** means skillful, especially at doing something with your hands. *The deft fingers guided the tiny device into place.*
dexterous	**Dexterous** is so similar to **deft** that you can usually use either word. *You are so dexterous that you could be a surgeon one day.*
adroit	**Adroit** is very similar to **dexterous** and **deft**. *The musician's adroit fingers moved quickly over the keyboard.*
handy	**Handy** can mean skillful at constructing things. *If you're handy, you'll find it easy to replace that faucet yourself.*

similar keywords: **competent**
contrasting keywords: **clumsy, incompetent**

slander *verb*

▶ to make a false spoken statement that harms someone's good name. This is often a legal word. *The reporter **slandered** the politician when she spoke about him on the radio.*

defame   To **defame** means to damage someone's good name, especially when the person is well known. *The newspaper story defamed the sports star.*

libel   To **libel** means to make statements that damage someone's reputation. This is often a legal word. *The athlete sued the newspaper that libelled her.*

malign   To **malign** means to speak unfavourably or badly of someone. *You maligned me when you said I lied.*

smear   To **smear** can mean to damage someone's good name, usually without any proof. *His nasty stories smeared my reputation, and I had to resign as leader.*

> similar keywords: **insult**
> contrasting keywords: **worship, praise**

sleep *verb*

▶ to rest the body and mind with your eyes closed. *How long did you **sleep** last night?*

slumber   To **slumber** means to sleep peacefully. *Please be quiet, because the baby is slumbering.*

doze   To **doze** means to sleep lightly or off and on. *The cat is dozing in front of the fire.*

nap   To **nap** means to sleep for a short time. *I think I will nap for forty-five minutes or so.*

snooze   To **snooze** means to sleep lightly for a short time. It is similar to **doze** and **nap**. *It's not wise to snooze on the couch after a big meal.*

drowse   To **drowse** means to feel like sleeping or to be half-asleep. *Did you see me drowsing during that boring movie?*

slight   *adjective*

▶ small and thin. *If you want to be a jockey, it helps to have a **slight** build.*

petite
: **Petite** means very small and slim. It is usually used to describe a woman or girl. *This store sells smaller-sized clothes designed for petite people.*

dainty
: **Dainty** can mean small and fine in appearance or movement. *We saw a collection of dainty glass ornaments.*

delicate
: **Delicate** can mean so small and fragile as to seem likely to be easily hurt or broken. *Those old china cups seem quite delicate.*

elfin
: **Elfin** means someone being so small and **dainty**, or having such a mischievous appearance, that you are reminded of an elf. *That little boy has an elfin grin.*

puny
: **Puny** can mean small and weak. *Most sea creatures are puny when compared with the blue whale.*

> similar keywords: **thin, small, fragile**
> contrasting keywords: **fat, heavy, stocky, hardy**

slope   *noun*

▶ a direction or line that goes up or down at an angle or to one side rather than being flat or completely upright. *Roofs are usually built with a **slope** to let the rainwater run off.*

slant
: **Slant** is so similar to **slope** that you can usually use either word. *Please fix these awnings so that they have a slight slant.*

tilt
: A **tilt** is a slope or a leaning to one side. *The post has such a tilt that it will probably fall over.*

incline
: An **incline** is a surface that has a slope. *We walked down the incline of the hill.*

gradient
: The **gradient** is the rate at which something slopes or rises. *What is the gradient of this road?*

pitch
: The **pitch** is the degree of slope. It is similar to **gradient**. *This roof requires a steep pitch because it snows a lot here.*

slope *verb*

▶ to have a direction or line that is neither flat nor upright. *Our garden **slopes** down toward a creek.*

slant   To **slant** is so similar to **slope** that you can usually use either word. *Please draw a line that slants to the left.*

lean   To **lean** means to be in a sloping position. *In the Italian city of Pisa, there is a famous tower that leans to one side.*

tilt   To **tilt** means to move into a sloping position. *The fence began to tilt as the children climbed over it.*

tip   To **tip** means to fall to one side. *Be careful that your glass doesn't tip.*

list   To **list** means to **tip** or **tilt** to one side. It is usually used about ships. *The huge wave made the ship list toward the starboard side.*

slow *adjective*

▶ taking a long time or not moving or acting quickly. *It was such a **slow** trip that we didn't arrive till after dark.*

leisurely   **Leisurely** means pleasantly slow or without haste. *After lunch we went for a leisurely stroll by the river.*

unhurried   **Unhurried** means slow or without any rush. *We packed a picnic lunch and had an unhurried meal by the river.*

plodding   **Plodding** means moving in a slow and heavy way. *I could tell by her plodding steps that she was tired*

lazy   **Lazy** can mean slow-moving or inactive. *We spent a lazy afternoon reading by the fireplace.*

> similar keywords: **lethargic**
> contrasting keywords: **fast**

small *adjective*

▶ not very big or very large. *The car was too **small** for everyone to fit into.*

little	**Little** means small in size. *These little puppies are only two weeks old.*
tiny	**Tiny** means very small or **little**. *We still have the tiny shoes you wore when you were a baby.*
minute	**Minute** means extremely small. *The insect was so minute that we could hardly see it.*
miniature	**Miniature** means being a very small copy of something. *There were miniature astronauts in the toy spacecraft.*
short	**Short** can mean not very tall. *The child was too short to get a drink from the water fountain.*

similar keywords: **slight**
contrasting keywords: **big, huge**

smell *noun*

▶ the quality of something that you sense through your nose. *I like the **smell** of freshly cut hay.*

odour	**Odour** is so similar to **smell** that you can usually use either word. *There is a woodsy odour in this old cabin.*
scent	A **scent** is a pleasant smell. *These roses have a lovely strong scent.*
fragrance	**Fragrance** is a sweet smell. It is similar to **scent**. *We could all smell the fragrance of his cologne.*
aroma	An **aroma** is a special, usually pleasant, smell of something. *The kitchen was filled with the wonderful aroma of curried chicken.*
bouquet	A **bouquet** can be an **aroma**. *The herbs gave the stew a beautiful bouquet.*

smelly *adjective*

▶ giving out a strong or unpleasant smell. *Please take that **smelly** can of garbage away.*

stinking   **Stinking** means very unpleasantly smelly. *There was a bag of stinking garbage in the pail.*

rank   **Rank** can mean having a strong, unpleasant smell. *The streets were rank during the garbage strike.*

putrid   **Putrid** means having the smell of something rotting or going bad. *A bad egg has a putrid smell.*

foul   **Foul** can mean bad-smelling and is similar to **putrid**. *This meat is foul.*

fetid   **Fetid** means having a stale, sickening smell. *The shed was filled with hot, fetid air.*

smile *verb*

▶ to show you are happy or amused by widening your mouth and turning it up at the corners. *I **smiled** when I saw my sister coming down the street.*

grin   To **grin** means to smile broadly. *I grinned at my friend across the classroom.*

smirk   To **smirk** means to smile in a smug, self-satisfied way that annoys people. *He smirked when the teacher praised him.*

giggle   To **giggle** means to laugh in a silly way. *We giggled when she made a funny face.*

snicker   To **snicker** means to **giggle** in a rude, disrespectful way. *The villain snickered at the hero's misfortune.*

titter   To **titter** means to **giggle** or **snicker** in a quiet way. *The audience tittered when the actor accidentally tripped on his robe.*

---

similar keywords: **laugh**
contrasting keywords: **frown**

---

smooth *adjective*

▶ feeling even and without bumps or lumps. *This pear has such a **smooth** skin.*

polished
: **Polished** means made smooth and shiny by rubbing. *I slipped on the polished floor.*

slippery
: **Slippery** means too smooth to get a hold on. *The slippery material slid through her fingers.*

silken
: **Silken** means smooth and soft like silk. *My friend has silken hair.*

glassy
: **Glassy** means feeling or looking smooth and transparent like glass. *We rowed across the glassy-looking lake.*

creamy
: **Creamy** can mean feeling rich and smooth like cream. *I spread the creamy lotion all over my skin.*

> similar keywords: **shiny**
> contrasting keywords: **rough**

smooth *verb*

▶ to make something even or level. *Adigan **smoothed** the comforter on his bed.*

iron
: To **iron** means to press the creases out of clothes with a heated iron. *I don't need to iron this cotton shirt before I wear it.*

level
: To **level** means to make even or to flatten. *They will have to level the ground before they build the house.*

sand
: To **sand** means to smooth something by rubbing it with sandpaper. *Lisa sanded the wooden bookends before varnishing them.*

grind
: To **grind** means to make something smooth by rubbing it with something rough. *The optician ground the lenses before putting them in the eyeglasses frame.*

plane
: To **plane** means to smooth wood using a special tool called a plane. *The carpenter planed the pieces of wood before fitting them together.*

> similar keywords: **polish**
> contrasting keywords: **roughen**

soak *verb*

▶ to wet something thoroughly, especially by leaving it in a liquid for a long time. *I soaked the clothes in the tub to loosen the stain.*

drench	To **drench** means to make something very wet. *The rain drenched our hair and clothes.*
saturate	To **saturate** can mean to **drench** or to wet something as completely as possible. *Even our socks were saturated from the heavy rainfall.*
flood	To **flood** can mean to flow over, fill, or cover something with water. *After the heavy rains, the river rose and flooded many houses along its banks.*
inundate	To **inundate** can be so similar to **flood** that you can often use either word. *The tidal wave inundated the village on the island.*
swamp	To **swamp** can mean to cover something with water. It is similar to **flood**. *A wave swamped the boat, nearly sinking it.*

similar keywords: **wet**

soft *adjective*

▶ having a flexible surface and usually pleasant to touch. *I kneaded the dough until it was soft. My quilt is very soft.*

downy	**Downy** means fluffy and soft, as fine hair or feathers are. *Andrew let his head sink into the downy pillow.*
silky	**Silky** means smooth and shiny like silk. *Kwan brushed her dog's silky hair.*
velvet	**Velvet** can mean soft and smooth like fur. *The kitten padded through the house on its velvet paws.*
spongy	**Spongy** means soft, light, and squashy like a sponge. *We walked carefully over the spongy ground.*
tender	**Tender** means not tough or hard. *I made a salad from tender young lettuce leaves.*

contrasting keywords: **hard**

soften   *verb*

▶ to make or become less firm to the touch. *I **softened** the dried beans by soaking them in water.*

thaw	To **thaw** means to make something that is frozen melt or become softer. *Liam took the strawberries out of the freezer and thawed them slowly.*
mash	To **mash** means to crush or beat something into a soft mass. *Please mash the sweet potatoes.*
squash	To **squash** means to crush until soft or flat. *I squashed the grape when I accidentally stepped on it.*
pulp	To **pulp** means to make into a soft, wet mass. *Paper mills pulp wood and other materials to make paper.*
tenderize	To **tenderize** means to make something less tough or hard. *We tenderized the meat with lemon before we cooked it.*

contrasting keywords: **harden**

solemn   *adjective*

▶ sincere or earnest. *I made a **solemn** promise to help him through his difficulties.*

serious	**Serious** means solemn and really meaning what you say. *I will give you some serious advice.*
grave	**Grave** means solemn and without humour. *Dianne's expression was grave as she listened to the details of the accident.*
sober	**Sober** can mean solemn and quiet. *The sad news put us in a sober mood.*
stern	**Stern** can mean solemn and severe. *The instructor gave them a stern warning not to misbehave again.*
dour	**Dour** can mean gloomily solemn, **stern**, or severe. *Your dour manner is rather discouraging.*

contrasting keywords: **happy**

solve   *verb*

▶ to explain or find the answer to something. *We've **solved** the mystery.*

work out
To **work out** can mean to solve something, using a great deal of effort. *It took me ages to work this math problem out.*

crack
To **crack** can mean to find the answer to a code, a puzzle, or other problem. It is more suited to everyday language. *They cracked the spy's code.*

untangle
To **untangle** means to work something out by careful study or effort. *We finally untangled the clue for the cryptic crossword.*

figure out
To **figure out** means to solve or understand something. *I can't figure out what the inscription on this monument means.*

resolve
To **resolve** means to solve or settle something. *We resolved the disagreement by making a compromise.*

similar keywords: **simplify**

song   *noun*

▶ a short musical composition with words. *Craig wrote the music and I made up the lyrics for our new **song**.*

tune
A **tune** is a simple musical composition. *Zahra played a familiar tune on her guitar.*

anthem
An **anthem** is a song written for a country or organization and sung on special occasions. *The national anthems for both countries were sung before the World Series game.*

ballad
A **ballad** is a simple poem that tells a story and is often set to music and sung. *Sean sang a sad ballad about a ship that was lost at sea.*

dirge
A **dirge** is a song of sadness and mourning. *If you play that music any slower it will sound like a funeral dirge.*

lullaby
A **lullaby** is a soft gentle song, sung to put a baby to sleep. *The baby finally fell asleep as her father rocked her and sang a lullaby.*

sorry *adjective*

▶ feeling sad because you have done something wrong. *I'm* **sorry** *I yelled at them.*

apologetic   **Apologetic** means admitting you were wrong and expressing your regret. *James was extremely apologetic for arriving so late.*

ashamed   **Ashamed** means feeling sorry or guilty for what you have done. *I was ashamed that I didn't call you on your birthday just because we had argued.*

remorseful   **Remorseful** means feeling deeply sorry for your wrongdoing. *They were so remorseful that they had trouble sleeping last night.*

repentant   **Repentant** means deeply sorry and **apologetic** for having done something wrong. *They were repentant for having shoplifted the shoes.*

contrite   **Contrite** means feeling or showing that you are sorry or sad, especially from guilt. This is a slightly formal word. *We knew she was contrite when she apologized in such a humble way.*

> contrasting keywords: **unashamed**

sour *adjective*

▶ having a sharp taste such as that of lemons. *These grapes are* **sour** *because they are not ripe.*

acid   **Acid** means having a very sharp taste. It is similar to **sour**. *Vinegar has an acid taste.*

bitter   **Bitter** means having an unpleasantly harsh or sharp taste. *This coffee is very bitter.*

tart   **Tart** means sour or sharp in taste. *This applesauce needs more sugar; it is too tart.*

tangy   **Tangy** means having a strong and sometimes biting taste. *Camembert cheese is mild, while Danish blue cheese is sharp and tangy.*

green   **Green** can mean not ripe and therefore tasting sour. *These plums are too green to eat.*

> contrasting keywords: **sweet**

souvenir *noun*

▶ something you keep as a memory of a place or an event. *I kept the concert program as a **souvenir** of Sarah's first piano recital.*

memento A **memento** is something that acts as a reminder of the past. *Aunt Daphne gave them a book as a memento of her visit.*

keepsake A **keepsake** is something you keep in order to remember a person or event. *Glen gave Mika a beautiful shell as a keepsake of their day at the beach.*

remembrance A **remembrance** can be a **memento** or **keepsake**. *We compiled a scrapbook as a remembrance of our trip across Canada.*

trophy A **trophy** can be a souvenir of a victory. *This lacrosse trophy reminds us that team effort pays off.*

token A **token** is a sign or symbol of something you want to remember. *They exchanged rings as tokens of friendship.*

spacious *adjective*

▶ ample room or having a lot of space. *We will use this room for the party because it is **spacious**.*

roomy **Roomy** is so similar to **spacious** that you can usually use either. *They live in a roomy apartment.*

commodious **Commodious** means conveniently spacious. It is a rather formal word. *The chairperson said that he required a more commodious office.*

wide **Wide** can mean having plenty of space from side to side. *The kindergarten room is big and wide.*

open **Open** can mean not limited or blocked. *We had a lovely open view from the verandah.*

expansive **Expansive** means **open** and widespread. *Their townhouse has an expansive garden.*

similar keywords: **big**
contrasting keywords: **narrow**

sparkle   *verb*

▶ to give out little flashes of light. *The raindrops **sparkled** in the sunshine.*

glitter	To **glitter** means to sparkle brightly, as gold or silver does. *Laura's dress glittered with rhinestones.*
shimmer	To **shimmer** means to give out a soft light that comes and goes. *The still surface of the lake shimmered in the moonlight.*
glimmer	To **glimmer** means to give out a faint light that comes and goes. *The lamp glimmered in the distance.*
twinkle	To **twinkle** means to sparkle softly. *The stars twinkled brightly in the night sky.*
flicker	To **flicker** means to give out an unsteady light. *The candle flickered in the evening breeze.*

similar keywords: **shine**

spectacular   *adjective*

▶ excitingly or impressively unusual and attracting people's notice. *The audience clapped and cheered at the **spectacular** display of ice dancing.*

eye-catching	**Eye-catching** means noticeable or attracting attention because of an unusual or attractive appearance. *The window dresser put the most eye-catching clothes in the store display.*
resplendent	**Resplendent** means splendidly bright and noticeable. *The carnival bands were resplendent in their multicoloured costumes as they paraded down the street.*
opulent	**Opulent** means spectacular and richly decorated with gold, jewels, and finery. *The opulent castle of King Ludwig is a great tourist attraction.*
flamboyant	**Flamboyant** means dazzlingly bright and noticeable. *That rock star set a new fashion trend with his flamboyant style of dress.*

similar keywords: **gaudy**
contrasting keywords: **simple, drab**

speed *verb*

▶ to move very quickly. *Carmen **sped** away on her bike, as fast as she could go.*

race To **race** can mean to run or move very quickly. *I raced to the station, only to see the train pull out.*

hurtle To **hurtle** means to rush noisily. *The rickety old train hurtled straight through the quiet stations.*

tear To **tear** can mean to move with a great rush. *We tore out of the house to see what the excitement was all about.*

fly To **fly** can mean to move swiftly. *The children flew down the hill on their toboggan.*

streak To **streak** can mean to move extremely quickly and suddenly. *Before I could stop him, the dog streaked across the road.*

> similar keywords: **hurry, dart**
> contrasting keywords: **dawdle, walk**

spin *verb*

▶ to turn around and around. *The wheels of the car **spun** around on the ice.*

gyrate To **gyrate** means to move around in a circle. *The sails of the windmill gyrated slowly in the light breeze.*

whirl To **whirl** means to turn around or spin rapidly. *We whirled faster and faster in time to the music.*

whirr To **whirr** can mean to spin around quickly with a low buzzing noise. *The propellers of the helicopter whirred as it took off from the landing pad.*

twirl To **twirl** means to spin rapidly. *We twirled and twirled until we were so dizzy we fell over.*

swirl To **swirl** means to move or turn around in a whirling way. *The water swirled around the rocks in the middle of the river.*

> similar keywords: **turn**

spoil   *verb*

▶ to ruin something or make it go bad. *The milk* **spoiled** *because it was left out over the weekend.*

taint	To **taint** means to spoil something slightly. *The bad smell in the refrigerator tainted the cheese.*
contaminate	To **contaminate** means to make something dirty or impure. *Improper canning contaminated the Franklin Expedition's food.*
pollute	To **pollute** means to spoil something by adding dirty or damaging things to it. *They cleaned up the garbage that was polluting the lake.*
foul	To **foul** means to make something dirty and unpleasant. *The automobile fumes fouled the city air.*

similar keywords: **damage, rot**

star   *noun*

▶ someone who is excellent in something or who is famous in an art or profession. *The* **star** *of a TV show spoke about careers in the media at our school.*

celebrity	A **celebrity** is a famous or well-known person. *The audience clapped and cheered when the celebrity finished her cello recital.*
idol	An **idol** is someone who is adored or admired excessively. *The basketball captain became the idol of the school when the team won for the third time in a row.*
hero	A **hero** is someone who has done something brave or outstanding. *Indihar was the hero of the hour when she saved the little boy from drowning.*
household name	A **household name** is someone almost everybody has heard about. *Kim Campbell was once a household name in Canadian politics.*
leading light	A **leading light** is someone who is well known or outstanding in a particular area. This is more suited to everyday language. *The mayor is also one of the leading lights of the musical society.*

similar keywords: **expert**

stare   *verb*

▶ to look at directly for a long time, usually with your eyes wide open. *I **stared** at the magnificent exhibit of African art.*

gaze
To **gaze** means to look long and steadily. *The artist gazed at the scene she was about to paint.*

gape
To **gape** means to stare with your mouth wide open. *They all gaped at the shattered windows.*

goggle
To **goggle** means to stare with your eyes opened wide. *We goggled at the magician's amazing tricks.*

peer
To **peer** means to look closely at something, as if searching. *Chet peered into every room trying to find the kitten.*

gawk
To **gawk** means to stare stupidly. It is more suited to everyday language. *They all gawked at the burning fence but no one did anything about it.*

start   *noun*

▶ the first part of something. *Everyone was lined up for the **start** of the wheelchair race.*

beginning
Beginning is so similar to **start** that you can usually use either word. *We arrived just in time to see the beginning of the play.*

commencement
Commencement is very similar to **start** and **beginning**. It is usually used in more formal language, such as in written reports. It is also used for a graduation ceremony, which marks the start of the next part of your life. *The commencement of the festival was marked by a display of fireworks.*

outset
Outset means the very start of something. *From the outset of the game, we knew our team would win.*

onset
Onset means the start of a particular thing. *The onset of the disease was sudden, but it didn't last long.*

origin
An **origin** is the place where something starts or comes from. *The origin of fireworks was ancient China.*

contrasting keywords: **end**

start *verb*

▶ to set something moving or take the first step in something. *I **started** as soon as it was light enough to see.*

activate   To **activate** can mean to make something active or to set it in motion. *In the old days, someone had to give an airplane propeller a spin to activate its motor.*

get going   To **get going** means to start or make haste. This is more suited to everyday language. *If you don't hurry up and get going, we'll never make it on time.*

set out   To **set out** means to start on a journey. *Michelle set out to work before the sun rose.*

fire away   To **fire away** means to start speaking, usually when someone tells you to. This is more suited to everyday language. *I'm listening, so fire away.*

> similar keywords: **begin, initiate**
> contrasting keywords: **end, finish, stop**

steadfast *adjective*

▶ constant and unchanging. *The two brothers have a **steadfast** love for each other.*

staunch   **Staunch** means loyal and steadfast. *Alex and Kam are staunch friends who have had many adventures together.*

firm   **Firm** can mean strong, definite, and unchanging. *They were firm supporters of recycling long before it became popular.*

enduring   **Enduring** means lasting or permanent. *Our enduring friendship has not been spoiled by occasional arguments.*

stout-hearted   **Stout-hearted** means brave and determined. *Although we had no chance of winning, our stout-hearted team didn't give up until the final whistle blew.*

> similar keywords: **faithful, reliable, honest**
> contrasting keywords: **fickle**

steady *adjective*

▶ firmly placed so that it won't move. *Make sure the ladder is **steady** before you climb it.*

stable   **Stable** can mean not likely to fall or move. *You need a stable foundation to build a house on.*

firm   **Firm** can mean steady or not likely to move or shake. *We made sure the rock was firm before we climbed onto it.*

secure   **Secure** can mean firmly fastened in place. *We checked that the boat's mooring was secure before we went ashore.*

well-balanced   **Well-balanced** can mean placed in a steady position or not likely to fall over. *Not even the strongest wind could blow down the well-balanced tree house.*

fixed   **Fixed** can mean so firmly or securely placed that it cannot move. *We set the ladder in a fixed position so we could always reach our attic.*

> similar keywords: **still**
> contrasting keywords: **moving**

steady *verb*

▶ to make something firm so that it won't move. ***Steady** the boat so it doesn't tip over while they're getting in.*

secure   To **secure** means to make something firm, usually by fastening it in some way. *We secured our bikes to the fence so they wouldn't be stolen.*

fix   To **fix** can mean to make something firm or to put it securely in place. *You need to fix the poles in the ground before you put up the tent.*

support   To **support** can mean to provide support, so that someone or something won't fall. *Get ready to support me when I do my handstand.*

stabilize   To **stabilize** means to make something firm or steady. *We stabilized the freighter canoe by changing the position of the cargo.*

> similar keywords: **strengthen**
> contrasting keywords: **overturn**

steal   *verb*

▶ to take something that does not belong to you. *I left my bike unlocked and someone **stole** it.*

pilfer	To **pilfer** means to steal things that are small or not worth much. *Stop pilfering cookies from the jar.*
pinch	To **pinch** means to steal or take something without asking. It is more suited to everyday language. *Did someone pinch my rice crackers when I wasn't looking?*
rob	To **rob** means to steal from or take forcibly. *I carried only a small amount of cash just in case someone tried to rob me.*
embezzle	To **embezzle** means to steal money entrusted to your care. *The dishonest teller was arrested for embezzling money from the bank.*

> similar keywords: **abduct, take, cheat**

still   *adjective*

▶ free from movement. *The mountains were reflected in the **still** waters of the lake.*

motionless	**Motionless** means not showing any movement. *The antelope was unaware of the motionless lion waiting to pounce.*
stationary	**Stationary** means standing still. *The van was stationary at the red light.*
immobile	**Immobile** means not moving or able to be moved. *This cast will make sure the broken bones in your arm are immobile while they heal.*
sedentary	**Sedentary** means requiring a sitting position with little movement. *Word processing is a sedentary job.*
stagnant	**Stagnant** means not running or flowing. It is used to describe water and air. *Mosquitoes breed in stagnant water.*

> similar keywords: **steady**
> contrasting keywords: **moving**

stocky *adjective*

▶ short, solid, and strong in the way you are built. *The **stocky** football player was placed in the front line.*

thickset
Thickset means having a very thick and solid build. *Weightlifting has made her thickset and powerful.*

stout
Stout can mean tough and strongly built. *That stout old oak tree has withstood many storms.*

squat
Squat means short and thick. It can describe things as well as people. *The squat old buildings were left standing next to the new skyscraper.*

stubby
Stubby means short and thick. *What stubby fingers you have!*

burly
Burly means big and solidly built. *His burly figure was just right for a sumo wrestler.*

> similar keywords: **fat, heavy**
> contrasting keywords: **thin, slight**

stone *noun*

▶ a piece of the hard substance that makes up part of the earth. *Please don't throw **stones** near the boats.*

rock
A **rock** is a large mass of stone. *We climbed the rocks in the park.*

boulder
A **boulder** is a very large rounded **rock**. *We tried to move the boulder that was blocking the entrance to the cave.*

pebble
A **pebble** is a small rounded stone. *Our garden path is made of pebbles.*

cobble
A **cobble** is a specially shaped stone used in paving streets. *The horse's hooves clattered on the cobbles in the old town.*

gravel
Gravel is a mixture of small stones, pebbles, and, sometimes sand. *We ordered a load of gravel to surface the driveway.*

stop *verb*

▶ to end or finish. *It's time to **stop** watching TV.*

quit
To **quit** means to finish or give up. *It was difficult, but my mom finally quit smoking.*

halt
To **halt** means to stop moving. *After hiking five kilometres, we halted and took a rest.*

pause
To **pause** means to stop or rest for a short time. *Lana paused to look out the window before she sat down to do her homework.*

stall
To **stall** means to stop, especially when you don't want to. It can also mean putting off or delaying a job, a decision, and so on. *The car stalled at the lights. You can't stall any longer, so start writing your first draft now.*

hesitate
To **hesitate** means to wait or **pause**, as if you are not sure whether or not you should go on. *Aaron hesitated before he came into the room.*

> similar keywords: **end, finish**
> contrasting keywords: **start, begin, initiate**

store *verb*

▶ to put something aside or away so that it will be ready when you need it. *The squirrels were busily **storing** acorns for winter.*

save
To **save** can mean to keep something, or to put it aside for when you need it. *I saved my money so that I could buy a camera.*

stockpile
To **stockpile** means to save up large amounts of something for when you need it. *We stockpiled wood to burn during the winter.*

stow
To **stow** means to put something somewhere, or to pack it away. *Stow your bags under your seats where no one can trip over them.*

hoard
To **hoard** means to save something up and hide it away where no one else can find it. *We hoarded cookies so we could have a midnight feast.*

> similar keywords: **gather, keep**
> contrasting keywords: **scatter, discard**

strange *adjective*

▶ unusual or extraordinary. *We did not enjoy the movie because the story was rather* **strange**.

odd	**Odd** is so similar to **strange** that you can usually use either word. *Everyone wondered whether you were feeling all right because your behaviour seemed odd.*
peculiar	**Peculiar** is so similar to **strange** and **odd** that you can usually use any of them. *We noticed a peculiar smell as we walked past the science room.*
abnormal	**Abnormal** means different from the usual, often not in a desirable way. *The extreme heat is abnormal for this time of the year.*
bizarre	**Bizarre** means very strange. *That multicoloured car is bizarre.*
weird	**Weird** means extremely strange. *We were frightened by the weird sounds coming from the park last night.*

> similar keywords: **unconventional, unusual**
> contrasting keywords: **usual**

strengthen *verb*

▶ to make something or someone stronger. *I used examples to* **strengthen** *my argument.*

reinforce	To **reinforce** means to strengthen something by adding to it. *Reinforce the poster by backing it with cardboard.*
brace	To **brace** can mean to make something stronger and firmly fixed in place. *Mei braced the ceiling with long pieces of wood.*
prop up	To **prop up** can mean to strengthen something by giving support to it. *They worked harder in order to prop up the failing business.*
fortify	To **fortify** means to strengthen something against attack or damage. *They fortified the castle by building a moat around it.*

> similar keywords: **steady**
> contrasting keywords: **weaken**

strict *adjective*

▶ demanding that you behave well and obey the rules. *My karate teacher is very **strict** about following the correct procedures.*

rigid	**Rigid** can mean strict and not changing from what you have decided or believe. *They have very rigid principles that they stick to.*
firm	**Firm** can mean strong, definite, and unchanging in what you have decided, have agreed to, or believe. *Once they have made a decision, they are quite firm about it.*
straitlaced	**Straitlaced** means strict and unbending in the way you behave. *Sometimes they seem a bit too straitlaced and old-fashioned.*
austere	**Austere** can mean strict or severe in the way you live or discipline yourself. *The monks followed an austere lifestyle.*
harsh	**Harsh** means strict in a cruel or unpleasant way. *Those were harsh words to use on a child who meant no harm.*

> contrasting keywords: **broad-minded, lenient**

strong *adjective*

▶ having great bodily power or energy. *You are **strong** because you work on a farm.*

robust	**Robust** means strongly or solidly built. *Marinna is a robust little baby.*
hearty	**Hearty** means strong, healthy, and energetic. *My mother is a hearty woman who loves rock climbing.*
brawny	**Brawny** means having well-developed muscles. *The lifeguard had a brawny build.*
husky	**Husky** can mean big and strong. *The husky lumberjack soon chopped down the tree.*
wiry	**Wiry** can mean thin and strong. *Karen looks weak, but she is wiry.*

> similar keywords: **hardy, powerful**
> contrasting keywords: **weak, powerless, fragile, decrepit**

stubborn *adjective*

▶ determined not to give way or change your mind. *We tried to talk him into wearing another tie, but he was **stubborn** and wore the bright orange one.*

obstinate   **Obstinate** means stubborn, even though you know you may be wrong. *Victoria is obstinate and insists on doing everything her way.*

pig-headed   **Pig-headed** means stupidly stubborn. *It is no use trying to talk sense to a pig-headed person.*

adamant   **Adamant** means staying firm in what you decide. *David was adamant that he would not give up.*

inflexible   **Inflexible** can mean not changing your mind under any circumstances. *We begged him to try again, but he was completely inflexible.*

uncompromising   **Uncompromising** means having your mind made up without taking much notice of other people's opinions or trying to fit in with them. *"No" was her uncompromising answer.*

> similar keywords: **persistent**

student *noun*

▶ someone who is learning something in a systematic way, usually in a school. *There are six **students** in my research group.*

pupil   A **pupil** is someone who is being taught by another person. It is very similar to **student**. *The pupils learned about geography and history from the exchange teacher.*

apprentice   An **apprentice** is someone who is learning a trade or craft from someone who is already an expert. *The apprentice is going to be a carpenter by the summer.*

rookie   A **rookie** is a beginner at something. *With practice, the rookie on our team will be an excellent volleyball player.*

disciple   A **disciple** is a follower of a teacher or leader. *The brilliant professor has many disciples who support all of her theories.*

> similar keywords: **scholar**

subdue *verb*

▶ to overcome someone or something, usually by force. *The new treatment **subdued** the harmful effects of the disease.*

overpower
To **overpower** means to subdue someone using your greater strength. *The kung fu instructor overpowered the thug who tried to mug her on the street.*

repress
To **repress** means to keep something or someone under control by effort or force. *Richard repressed his hunger by sheer willpower.*

oppress
To **oppress** can mean to be cruel to someone in your power. *The cruel dictator oppressed the people until they revolted.*

persecute
To **persecute** means to **oppress** others, usually for their religious or political beliefs. *The persecuted people fled to another country where they were able to freely practise their beliefs.*

> similar keywords: **force, abuse, defeat**
> contrasting keywords: **free**

submissive *adjective*

▶ giving in obediently, without questioning. *The sick animal was **submissive** when we approached it.*

subservient
Subservient means very submissive. *George was often subservient to his strong-minded older sister.*

weak-willed
Weak-willed means giving in to others because you have a weak character. *They were so weak-willed that they obeyed every order, no matter how unfair.*

servile
Servile means weakly allowing others to control you. *I want you to do what you are asked, but I do not expect you to be servile.*

downtrodden
Downtrodden means governed or ruled so harshly that you are frightened not to obey. *The downtrodden people finally overthrew the corrupt government.*

> similar keywords: **obedient**
> contrasting keywords: **defiant, argumentative, aggressive**

subordinate *adjective*

▶ placed in or belonging to a lower order or rank. *The overworked manager asked a* **subordinate** *employee to help prepare the report.*

junior
Junior can mean of a low rank. *His sister is a junior officer in the armed forces.*

subsidiary
Subsidiary means of a secondary order or rank. *Mrs. Perera manages a subsidiary company, and she reports to the head office each month.*

common
Common can mean of the ordinary rank. *Bill Cosby's wit and good timing showed that he was no common comedian.*

lowly
Lowly means of very low or humble position or rank. *The owner's son started at a lowly job in the company.*

auxiliary
Auxiliary means playing a helping or supporting role. *The hospital has an auxiliary electrical system in case of a power failure.*

> similar keywords: **insignificant, minor, inferior**
> contrasting keywords: **superior, significant**

subtract *verb*

▶ to take away a part from a whole, or one number or quantity from another. *If you* **subtract** *27 from 356, you get 329.*

deduct
To **deduct** means to take away or subtract one quantity from another. *My father has money deducted from each pay cheque to pay his taxes.*

dock
To **dock** can mean to cut off or take away a part of something. *Mom docked my allowance to pay for the window I broke.*

diminish
To **diminish** means to make something smaller. *The fact that I had read the book didn't diminish my enjoyment of the movie.*

curtail
To **curtail** means to cut something short. *We curtailed our trip and came home a week early.*

> similar keywords: **remove**
> contrasting keywords: **add**

succeed *verb*

▶ to do or accomplish what you have attempted. *Virginia **succeeded** in learning to play the violin.*

shine	To **shine** can mean to be very good at something. *Hari shines at long-distance running.*
make the grade	To **make the grade** means to reach the standard that has been set. This is more suited to everyday language. *In sports, if you don't practise regularly you may not make the grade.*
triumph	To **triumph** means to have a victory or success. *Ralph triumphed as usual in his tennis match.*
win	To **win** means to gain a victory. *The competition was a hard one, but Daksa won.*
prevail	To **prevail** can mean to succeed or to win. *We finally prevailed in getting our friend to change his mind.*

> similar keywords: **thrive, accomplish, flourish**
> contrasting keywords: **fail**

sudden *adjective*

▶ happening quickly and without warning. *We all jumped at the **sudden** noise.*

abrupt	**Abrupt** means sudden and unexpected. *Their abrupt departure made us wonder what had happened.*
impulsive	**Impulsive** means acting on a sudden desire. *Bik reached out her hand in an impulsive gesture of friendship.*
snap	**Snap** means done quickly or suddenly. *They made a snap decision to go to town.*
meteoric	**Meteoric** can mean swift or happening quickly, like a meteor's fall. *Laura is a brilliant architect, and her progress in her career has been meteoric.*

> similar keywords: **rash**

sufficient *adjective*

▶ having as much as is needed or wanted. *Julie bought* **sufficient** *wallpaper to cover the living room and dining room walls.*

enough
: **Enough** means the same as sufficient. You can usually use either word. *There is only enough pie for one piece each.*

adequate
: **Adequate** means **enough** or sufficient for the purpose. *I hope our clothes are adequate for the cold weather.*

satisfactory
: **Satisfactory** means fulfilling all the requirements or demands. *Mom wouldn't pay for the repairs until she was sure the work was satisfactory.*

decent
: **Decent** can mean sufficiently big to fulfill a particular need. *The hungry hikers had not had a decent meal in days.*

appropriate
: **Appropriate** means suitable for a particular purpose. *Is this computer software appropriate for the type of work you do?*

> similar keywords: **abundant, extra**
> contrasting keywords: **insufficient, scant**

suffocate *verb*

▶ to be prevented from breathing. *Don't ever let children put plastic bags over their faces, because it could* **suffocate** *them.*

choke
: To **choke** means to stop breathing because something is caught in the throat. *You can learn how to dislodge something from a person's throat if they are choking.*

smother
: To **smother** means to suffocate by blocking the supply of air to the nose and mouth. *The long wool scarf wrapped around the child's face made him feel as if he were smothering.*

asphyxiate
: To **asphyxiate** means to suffocate or cause a loss of consciousness. It is a more formal, medical word. *We heard on the news that the smoke had nearly asphyxiated the firefighters.*

stifle
: To **stifle** means to **smother** or make it difficult for someone to breathe. *The lack of air in this stuffy room is stifling me.*

suggestion   *noun*

▶ an idea brought to someone to consider and possibly do something about. *My* **suggestion** *to dress up made all the children happy.*

recommendation A **recommendation** can be a suggestion about what to do, or how to do something. *The council made several recommendations on where the shopping mall should be built.*

piece of advice A **piece of advice** is an opinion suggested or offered by someone who thinks it is worth following. *Let me give you a piece of advice: making good friends is more important than making good money!*

pointer A **pointer** can be a helpful suggestion. *The hockey coach gave me a few pointers on how to improve my slapshot.*

tip A **tip** can be a piece of useful information. *My sister gave me a tip on how to solve the math problem.*

> similar keywords: **offer**

suit   *verb*

▶ to be satisfactory or convenient. *It's a casual party, so wear something that* **suits** *the occasion.*

serve To **serve** can mean fit to be used for a particular purpose. *The tree served as a shelter for the birds.*

suffice To **suffice** means to be enough to be satisfactory. *Do you think thirty egg rolls will suffice for the party?*

qualify To **qualify** means to make or show yourself fit for something. *Ron qualified for the finals by winning the heat.*

satisfy To **satisfy** can mean to suit a purpose. *Will this type of container satisfy your requirements?*

fill the bill To **fill the bill** means to be entirely suitable for a particular purpose. This is more suited to everyday language. *I think Tadashi will fill the bill as student council president.*

summary *noun*

▶ a short statement in speech or writing giving the main points of something.
*I gave the group a **summary** of the book's plot.*

précis
A **précis** is a brief piece of writing containing the main points of a longer piece. *Robin wrote a précis of the article on whales.*

synopsis
A **synopsis** is a written **outline** or summary of a longer piece of writing. *Ali wrote a synopsis of the novel to persuade us to read it.*

outline
An **outline** is a short description that gives only the most important points of something. *We were all given an outline of what had to be done.*

résumé
A **résumé** is a summary of a person's education and work experience. *I applied for the job by faxing a letter and a copy of my résumé.*

plan
A **plan** can be an outline of your method for doing something. *In the spring, I sketched a plan of the vegetable garden I wanted to plant.*

> similar keywords: **report**

superior *adjective*

▶ of a higher grade than usual. *I am only interested in buying **superior** products.*

high-class
High-class is so similar to **superior** that you can usually use either. *High-class restaurants are usually very expensive.*

quality
Quality can mean excellent or of superior grade. *The fruit and vegetable stand had a sign saying "Only quality produce sold here."*

deluxe
Deluxe means of expensive and luxurious quality. *I would expect a deluxe hotel to have an outstanding restaurant and beautifully decorated rooms.*

choice
Choice can be similar to **quality**. *That store is expensive, but it sells only choice meats and the freshest fish.*

> similar keywords: **excellent, best, great**
> contrasting keywords: **inferior, subordinate**

sure *adjective*

▶ having no doubt about something. *I am **sure** of what I am saying.*

certain | **Certain** is so similar to **sure** that you can usually use either word. *I am certain my answer is correct.*

positive | **Positive** can mean absolutely sure. *I am positive you are wrong.*

confident | **Confident** means having a strong belief about something. *Rema was confident that she had passed the test.*

clear | **Clear** can mean not able to be doubted. *Manuel achieved a clear win in the race.*

definite | **Definite** means **clear** and **certain**. *It is a definite advantage to be able to do arithmetic in your head.*

contrasting keywords: **confused, uncertain**

surroundings *noun*

▶ everything that is around or near someone or something. *We are all affected by our **surroundings**.*

environment | Your **environment** is made up of the surrounding things and conditions of your life. *We grew up in a country environment.*

habitat | A **habitat** is the surroundings in which a particular plant or animal naturally grows or lives. *These tropical fish need a very warm habitat.*

environs | **Environs** are the surrounding districts of a place. *This is a map of Montreal and its environs.*

setting | A **setting** is the environment or surroundings of something. *The house had a pretty country setting.*

scene | A **scene** can be the place or surroundings in which an event happens. *The police investigated the scene of the crime.*

sway   *verb*

▶ to move or swing from side to side. *I **swayed** in time with the music.*

wave	To **wave** means to move loosely to and fro or up and down. *The pennants waved in the strong wind.*
wobble	To **wobble** means to move unsteadily from side to side. *When I first got inline skates, I wobbled all over the sidewalk.*
waddle	To **waddle** means to walk with short steps, swaying from side to side. *The duck, followed by its ducklings, waddled across to the pond.*
reel	To **reel** means to stagger or sway, especially from giddiness or a blow. *My little sister, Tina, reeled across to us when she got off the merry-go-round.*
lurch	To **lurch** means to move suddenly and unsteadily. *The boat lurched across the choppy lake.*

similar keywords: **shake**

sweet   *adjective*

▶ having a pleasant taste, like that of honey or sugar. *This ripe peach is **sweet** and juicy.*

sugary	**Sugary** means tasting too sweet because of having too much sugar. *I don't like this sugary soft drink.*
candied	**Candied** means cooked in sugar or having a crust of sugar. *Where my family comes from, candied yams and grits is a favourite dish.*
syrupy	**Syrupy** means thick and sweet, like syrup. *The chocolate candy had a syrupy filling.*
fruity	**Fruity** means having the flavour or aroma of fruit. *The incense we burned in the living room had a lovely fruity fragrance.*
sickly	**Sickly** can mean so sweet that it makes you feel sick. *Don't eat any more of those sickly doughnuts.*

contrasting keywords: **sour**

T, t

take *verb*

▶ to get or receive something. *Will you **take** a cheque instead of cash?*

confiscate	To **confiscate** means to take something and keep it. *The teacher confiscated the student's comic book.*
appropriate	To **appropriate** means to take something because you want to use it yourself. *The dishonest treasurer appropriated some of the club's money to pay his own bills.*
borrow	To **borrow** means to take or get something on the understanding that you have to return it. *I borrowed three books from the library this week.*
adopt	To **adopt** means to choose or take something or someone as your own. *We adopted a new motto for our team.*

> similar keywords: **get, grab, steal, abduct**
> contrasting keywords: **give**

talk *noun*

▶ an exchange of thoughts using spoken words, especially in a friendly or informal way. *We had a good **talk** after dinner.*

conversation	**Conversation** is so similar to **talk** that you can usually use either. *Please don't interrupt our conversation.*
discussion	A **discussion** is a talk in which you consider something from all sides. *Our family had a discussion about what to do on the long weekend.*
debate	A **debate** is an organized talk in which the reasons for and against something are considered. It is similar to **discussion**. *The debate in parliament went on all through the night.*
interview	An **interview** is a talk in which someone is asked questions about something. *The actor gave an interview about her latest movie.*
dialogue	**Dialogue** means a talk between two or more people, especially in a play or story. *The dialogue in the first part of the movie was not very interesting.*

talk *verb*

▶ to speak together. *The children **talked** all the way to school.*

converse To **converse** means to talk with someone else. It is used in rather formal language. *We conversed about music and art.*

confer To **confer** means to have a discussion about something. *I will have to confer with the other group members about that.*

chat To **chat** means to talk in a friendly way, not about a serious subject. *The children chatted about their hobbies.*

gossip To **gossip** means to talk about other people's business. *Some of the neighbours gossiped about the new family on the street.*

discuss To **discuss** means to talk over. *Our class discussed the outcome of the upcoming elections.*

> similar keywords: **ramble, rave**

talkative *adjective*

▶ liking to talk a lot. *My brother finds it hard to keep quiet in class because he is very **talkative**.*

loquacious **Loquacious** is similar to **talkative**. It is a rather formal word. *I am loquacious when I talk on the phone.*

voluble **Voluble** means talking with a ready and continuous flow of words. *Nilan was voluble in his retelling of the final minutes of the game.*

communicative **Communicative** means liking to share or pass on thoughts, opinions, or information by talking. *Hiroko was in a friendly, communicative mood.*

chatty **Chatty** means liking to chat. *You can hear all the neighbourhood gossip from that chatty clerk at the corner store.*

garrulous **Garrulous** means very talkative, often in an annoying way. *I think he is so garrulous because he is lonely.*

> similar keywords: **lengthy**
> contrasting keywords: **reticent, abrupt**

tall   *adjective*

▶ of more than average height. *Angeline can reach the box on top of the cupboard because she is quite **tall**.*

high
: **High** can mean stretching a long way upwards. *We have a high fence around our backyard to keep the dog in.*

lofty
: **Lofty** means reaching high into the air. *The lofty mountains seemed to touch the clouds.*

towering
: **Towering** means very tall or **lofty**. *The city seemed full of towering buildings.*

lanky
: **Lanky** means tall in an ungraceful way. *Although lanky, he plays basketball with grace and style.*

elevated
: **Elevated** means raised up, generally above the ground. *The stage was elevated so that the whole audience could see.*

> similar keywords: **big**

task   *noun*

▶ a piece of work you are expected to do. *We were each given a **task** so we would be ready to leave on time.*

chore
: A **chore** is a task you have to do that is not very exciting or that you don't like much. *I have to finish my chores before I can go to the park.*

errand
: An **errand** is a small task you are sent to do. *Dad sent me into town on an errand for him.*

assignment
: An **assignment** is a particular task you are given to do. *Our assignment was to make a model of our solar system.*

duty
: A **duty** is something you have to do because of your position. *It is her duty as coach to decide the batting order.*

mission
: A **mission** is a special task someone is sent to carry out. *Their mission was to discover the secret hideout.*

> similar keywords: **job, undertaking**

tasteless *adjective*

▶ lacking in taste or flavour. *The food at that restaurant is dull and **tasteless**.*

plain

Plain means not rich or strong in taste. *Dad believes in cooking old-fashioned, plain meals.*

bland

Bland means pleasant and easy to digest, but lacking a strong or interesting taste. *Spices can change a bland meal into a tasty one.*

mild

Mild can mean easy to digest and not strong, spicy, or sharp in taste. *I like hot curries and jerk chicken, but my friend Da-chun likes his food mild.*

insipid

Insipid means too tasteless to be pleasant. *I think this watery soup is insipid.*

flat

Flat can mean disappointingly tasteless. *I used all the ingredients in the recipe, but the turkey stew tasted flat.*

contrasting keywords: **tasty**

tasty *adjective*

▶ full of flavour. *Pad Thai is a very **tasty** noodle dish.*

spicy

Spicy means strong-tasting because of being flavoured with a spice, such as pepper or cinnamon. *Hot and sour soup is usually very spicy.*

sharp

Sharp can mean having a strong, biting taste. *This blue cheese is too sharp for me.*

pungent

Pungent means having a biting taste or smell. *This is a pungent grapefruit juice.*

piquant

Piquant means having a pleasantly strong, biting taste. *This pasta sauce has a piquant flavour.*

appetizing

Appetizing means appealing to the appetite or stimulating your taste buds. *That green mango salad looks really appetizing.*

contrasting keywords: **tasteless**

teach *verb*

▶ to assist someone in learning a skill or series of related skills, or to give knowledge of something. *Ms. Levine **teaches** our class. My father **teaches** music.*

instruct To **instruct** means to teach or to explain something to someone. *The dentist instructed us on how to care for our teeth.*

train To **train** means to teach a person or an animal to know or do something. *Our voice coach trained us to sing loudly and clearly.*

drill To **drill** can mean to **train** someone by giving repeated exercises. *Ms. Levine drilled us until we knew all our lines for the play.*

coach To **coach** means to **train** or teach people in small groups or on their own. *My friend David coached me in math so I could understand the new work.*

> contrasting keywords: **learn**

teacher *noun*

▶ someone who instructs other people. *The **teacher** showed us how to mix the paints to make a new colour.*

tutor A **tutor** is someone who is hired to teach a single person or people in small groups. *A tutor helped Oren with his schoolwork while he was in the hospital.*

instructor A **instructor** is a teacher. *My music instructor is pleased with my progress.*

lecturer A **lecturer** teaches very large groups of people, usually at a college or university. *When the room was full, the lecturer began telling the students about the new theory.*

trainer A **trainer** is someone who helps athletes stay fit and teaches them the skills they need to do well in their sport. *Maria's trainer gave her a program to follow in preparation for the big race.*

> similar keywords: **adviser**
> contrasting keywords: **student**

tear *verb*

▶ to pull something apart, leaving rough edges. *I **tore** the paper in two.*

rip	To **rip** means to tear something in a rough way. *Carl ripped his shirt on the barbed-wire fence.*
slash	To **slash** means to cut something violently and unevenly. *Vandals have slashed the subway seats.*
slit	To **slit** means to make a long, straight cut or opening in something. *Dad slit the envelope open and took out the letter.*
gash	To **gash** means to make a long, deep cut in something. *Sinëad accidentally gashed her hand with the linoleum knife.*
lacerate	To **lacerate** means to cut or tear something roughly. *The broken glass lacerated my brother's foot.*

similar keywords: **cut, scratch**

tease *verb*

▶ to make fun of or pester someone in a lighthearted, but annoying way. *We **teased** them about arriving too early for the dance.*

taunt	To **taunt** means to insult or tease someone in a cruel way. *It was cruel to taunt her for missing the empty net.*
rib	To **rib** can mean to tease, **ridicule**, or make fun of someone. It is more suited to everyday language. *We ribbed Andrew about always being first in line for lunch.*
heckle	To **heckle** means to torment and bother a speaker with annoying questions and comments. *Some members of the audience heckled the politician at the election meeting.*
ridicule	To **ridicule** means to make fun of someone or something in a scornful way. *Kim ridiculed my first attempt to paddle a canoe.*

similar keywords: **insult**

tell   *verb*

▶ to give someone an account or description of something. *Grandfather,* **tell** *us the old tales about Coyote, the Trickster.*

narrate   To **narrate** means to tell a particular story in speech or writing. *On my sister's tape of* Peter and the Wolf, *a famous actor narrates the story.*

relate   To **relate** means to tell or **narrate** something, usually a story. *Grandmother related the story of how she had found the lost gold mine.*

recount   To **recount** means to tell about something, giving as much information as you can. *Please recount everything that happened after I left you.*

outline   To **outline** means to tell about something briefly, giving only the main points. *Lin outlined the plan for us again.*

> similar keywords: **inform, explain, describe**

temporary   *adjective*

▶ lasting for a short time. *Robin had a* **temporary** *summer job delivering newspapers.*

provisional **Provisional** means temporary or just for the time being. *The school's discipline policy was provisional until it was discussed at the PTA meeting.*

interim   **Interim** means temporary or lasting for a short time between events. *They appointed an interim president until new elections could be held.*

makeshift   **Makeshift** means temporary or used for only a short time. *These makeshift tents will have to do until the supplies arrive.*

casual   **Casual** can mean employed occasionally. *The manager hired two casual labourers when we were busy.*

part-time   **Part-time** means working for only part of the regular hours. *Gill has a part-time job delivering pizzas.*

> similar keywords: **momentary**
> contrasting keywords: **permanent, continuous**

test *noun*

▶ a set of questions to answer, or some other method of evaluation, designed to show how much you know about something or what your abilities are. *The **test** included some true-or-false and some longer questions.*

examination
An **examination** is a test of knowledge or skill that often has to be passed before the next stage of learning begins. *My sister worked really hard to pass the college entrance examinations.*

quiz
A **quiz** is a short or informal test. *We had a surprise geography quiz today.*

trial
A **trial** can be an experiment or test carried out in order to prove something. *They ran several trials on the new drug to make sure that it had no harmful side effects.*

audition
An **audition** is a special test or hearing to see how suitable an actor or performer is for a particular part. *Elsa is going for an audition for a part in the new play.*

checkup
A **checkup** is a test designed to make sure that all is in order, especially your health. *Dad went to the doctor for his yearly checkup.*

test *verb*

▶ to attempt to find out a particular thing about something or someone. *I **tested** the water to see if it was drinkable.*

try
To **try** can mean to test something, often by using it yourself. *I am going to try my new skis today.*

sample
To **sample** means to test or judge something by eating or using some of it. *The judges sampled all the pies before they announced the winner of the baking contest.*

check
To **check** means to find out about or to investigate something. *Ron checked the car battery before we set off on our trip.*

screen
To **screen** means to examine or test a number of people or things. *The crown attorney and defence counsel screened each jury candidate to make sure she or he was suitable.*

similar keywords: **examine, investigate, question**

theme   *noun*

▶ the central subject of a talk, a discussion, or a piece of writing. *Our next **theme** in science is the environment.*

topic
: The **topic** is the main subject of a speech, a discussion, a composition, and so on. *The topic of my essay is the value of the rain forest.*

focus
: The **focus** can be the main or central point of interest of something. *The story wanders off the topic because it lacks a strong focus.*

moral
: The **moral** is the lesson that someone is supposed to learn from a story or an event. *The moral of this story is that friendship is more important than fame and fortune.*

point
: The **point** can be the main purpose of a speech, a discussion, a composition, and so on. *It took her ten minutes to get to the point of her story.*

thick   *adjective*

▶ measuring rather a lot from one surface to another, or being closely packed or heavy. *I have a lovely, **thick** blanket on my bed in winter.*

dense
: **Dense** means thick or closely packed. *The jungle was very dense and hard to walk through.*

heavy
: **Heavy** can mean thicker or greater than usual. *Lucia drew a heavy line under the title of her story.*

solid
: **Solid** can mean thick or **dense**. *Solid fog filled the valley, making travel hazardous.*

compact
: **Compact** means **dense** or firmly packed. *The wet snow was perfect for making heavy, compact snowballs.*

contrasting keywords: **thin, narrow**

thicken *verb*

▶ to become thicker or more dense. *The recipe says to stir the mixture until it* ***thickens***.

clot	To **clot** means to thicken by forming solid lumps. *After you have been bleeding for a while, your blood clots and stops flowing out.*
coagulate	To **coagulate** means to change from a liquid into a thick mass. *The egg white coagulated in the hot frying pan.*
congeal	To **congeal** means to thicken by becoming solid. It is similar to **coagulate**. *Gravy congeals as it cools.*
curdle	To **curdle** means to go lumpy. It is used particularly about milk that has been treated with an acid or has not been refrigerated. *The milk curdled when it was left out in the sun.*
condense	To **condense** means to become thicker and less in volume. *The tomato sauce condensed to half its original volume after it simmered on the stove for two hours.*

thief *noun*

▶ someone who steals. *A **thief** must have taken my new portable CD player.*

robber	A **robber** is a thief, often one who uses force or violence. *A robber attacked the tourist and stole his money.*
burglar	A **burglar** is someone who steals by breaking into a home or building. *Our house has an alarm to scare away burglars.*
shoplifter	A **shoplifter** is someone who steals from a store while pretending to be shopping. *The store's policy is to report all shoplifters to the police.*
pickpocket	A **pickpocket** is someone who steals from the pockets or handbags of people in public places. *My father's wallet was stolen by a pickpocket at the parade.*
kleptomaniac	A **kleptomaniac** is someone who feels an uncontrollable urge to steal things. *So many things have been disappearing that I think there must be a kleptomaniac in the school.*

similar keywords: **bandit, criminal**

thin *adjective*

▶ measuring very little from one surface to the other. *I like nice **thin** toast.*

slim
: **Slim** means pleasantly thin. This can be used about people or things. *Antonio was reading a slim book about iguanas.*

slender
: **Slender** is so similar to **slim** that you can usually choose either word. *The furniture had graceful, slender proportions.*

skinny
: **Skinny** means very thin. This is usually only used about people or animals. *The poor, skinny old horse was pulling a heavy cart.*

lean
: **Lean** can mean thin, but usually also fit and strong. *The lean long-distance runner completed the marathon in record time.*

spindly
: **Spindly** means long or tall and **slender**, but usually also weak or frail. *The spindly young shrubs needed plenty of care to make them grow strong and thick.*

> similar keywords: **slight, narrow**
> contrasting keywords: **thick, stocky**

think *verb*

▶ to form or have an idea of something in your mind. ***Think** about the different things you did during the summer.*

suppose
: To **suppose** can mean to think or believe something without having any actual knowledge. *Do you suppose Yaakov would mind if I borrowed his book?*

suspect
: To **suspect** can mean to think that something is very likely to be true. *I suspect that he will find it very easy to use the new computer.*

reckon
: To **reckon** can mean to think or **suppose**. It is more suited to everyday language. *I reckon Jenny is the only one who knows about this.*

guess
: To **guess** can mean to think or believe something. *I guess you had a good reason to miss the hockey practice.*

> similar keywords: **believe, conclude, ponder, imagine**

thorough *adjective*

▶ complete, careful, or without missing anything. *We gave our closets a **thorough** cleaning.*

comprehensive **Comprehensive** means including nearly everything. *The newspaper gave a comprehensive report of the opening of the peace conference.*

detailed **Detailed** means looking at every little part of something. *The lab technician made a detailed examination of the blood sample.*

exhaustive **Exhaustive** means dealing with something in detail. *After an exhaustive search, the volunteers finally found the missing child.*

intensive **Intensive** means done with a lot of attention or work. *The nurses and doctors gave my friend Matt intensive care after his accident.*

in-depth **In-depth** means thorough or dealing with something completely. *They had an in-depth discussion about free speech.*

> similar keywords: **whole, careful, precise, perfect**
> contrasting keywords: **incomplete**

thought *noun*

▶ something that has come into your mind as a result of thinking. *I suddenly had the **thought** that a swim would make me cooler.*

idea An **idea** is a thought or a picture in your mind. *He had a clear idea about how the room could be decorated.*

brainstorm A **brainstorm** can be a sudden brilliant thought. *Ahmed's brainstorm gave us the solution to the whole problem.*

notion A **notion** is an **idea** or belief, often imaginary. *I have a notion of what travelling through space might be like.*

theory A **theory** is an explanation based on thought or opinion. *They presented a different theory about how the stars were formed.*

concept A **concept** is a general **idea** or understanding of something. *I do have a pretty clear concept of computer programming.*

thread   *noun*

▶ a thin, slender string that has been spun from a material such as cotton, silk, or nylon. *I pulled the loose* **thread**, *and my button fell off.*

filament   A **filament** is a very slender thread, or something like it. *Under a microscope, a filament of wool from my sweater looked rough and jagged.*

fibre   A **fibre** is a **filament** of natural or manufactured material. *They used glass fibres to replace the wire telephone cables.*

strand   A **strand** is one of the threads that a cord, rope, or cable is made from. *When a rope unravels, it splits up into strands.*

tendril   A **tendril** is a threadlike part of a plant that twists around something to support the plant. *The tendrils of the vine clung to the bars of the railing.*

threaten   *verb*

▶ to tell someone, using words or some other sign, that you intend to harm him or her. *The leader of the gang* **threatened** *the bank teller.*

menace   To **menace** means to take a threatening attitude toward someone. *I felt menaced by the stranger, so I locked the front door.*

intimidate   To **intimidate** means to frighten in order to make someone do something. *The spy tried to intimidate the ambassador's secretary into revealing the secret code.*

blackmail   To **blackmail** means to demand money from someone by threatening to reveal personal secrets. *He tried to blackmail the politician because he knew about her criminal background.*

extort   To **extort** means to force someone to give you something, such as money or information, by using threats. *He extorted money from her by threatening to go to the newspapers with the story.*

> similar keywords: **frighten, force**
> contrasting keywords: **comfort**

thrifty *adjective*

▶ carefully managing or looking after your money or supplies. *The **thrifty** woman always kept a record of how she spent her money.*

frugal   **Frugal** means being careful not to waste anything. *If we are frugal with our supplies, we will have enough for the three-day trip.*

economical   **Economical** can mean not wasting anything. *He found it was more economical to buy his groceries once a week than every day.*

prudent   **Prudent** means carefully managing things like money so that you are prepared for the future. *My grandmother was prudent and had saved enough money for a comfortable retirement.*

stingy   **Stingy** means not generous or not willing to share money or other things. *I hope you won't think I am stingy if I do not treat you to lunch.*

> similar keywords: **cheap**
> contrasting keywords: **generous**

thrive *verb*

▶ to grow strong or to do well. *Our new business is **thriving**.*

prosper   To **prosper** means to be successful. *The farmers have prospered this year because of the abundant crops.*

benefit   To **benefit** means to get better or gain an advantage. *We will all benefit from a vacation in the mountains.*

boom   To **boom** means to do very well suddenly. *During the gold rush, business in the Yukon towns was booming.*

blossom   To **blossom** can mean to develop or turn out well. *Tamar has blossomed into a fine musician.*

bloom   To **bloom** can mean to be healthy and full of life. *The sickly child bloomed during his stay at summer camp.*

> similar keywords: **succeed, flourish**
> contrasting keywords: **fail**

throb   *verb*

▶ to pound regularly and more strongly than usual. *The doctor asked if my injured arm was* ***throbbing***.

beat	To **beat** can mean to throb. *Sakina's heart beat wildly as she raced for the finish line.*
pulsate	To **pulsate** means to throb or **beat** like your heart. *We could hear the drums pulsating in the distance.*
palpitate	To **palpitate** means to **beat** much faster than usual. *The children's hearts palpitated at the eerie sounds of the forest.*
flutter	To **flutter** can mean to beat faster and more irregularly than usual. *Gunnar's heart fluttered with excitement as the judges named the winner.*
buzz	To **buzz** means to make a low humming sound. *The sounds of the insect-infested swamp buzzed in my ears.*

throw   *verb*

▶ to send something through the air. *Mandy* ***threw*** *the ball to Aziz.*

toss	To **toss** means to throw something, often in a casual way. *Virginia tossed her backpack on the floor.*
fling	To **fling** means to throw something, usually forcefully or impatiently. *John flung the book angrily onto the table.*
hurl	To **hurl** means to throw something with great force or strength. *Indihar hurled the ball across the field.*
pitch	To **pitch** means to throw something, often taking careful aim. *Pitch the ball low so that the little child can hit it.*

tidy *adjective*

▶ having everything in its right place. *If you have a **tidy** room, it is easy to find things.*

neat **Neat** means tidy and well-ordered. *Lee's homework was neat and easy to read.*

orderly **Orderly** means arranged in a tidy manner. *The books were in orderly rows on the shelves.*

meticulous **Meticulous** means giving attention to the smallest detail. *My brother is so meticulous that he arranges his videotapes in alphabetical order.*

shipshape **Shipshape** means **neat** and tidy. *We made the house shipshape before my cousins came to visit us.*

methodical **Methodical** means acting or done in a careful, **orderly** way. *Dad is methodical in his habits, and he always hangs up his clothes.*

> similar keywords: **clean**
> contrasting keywords: **untidy, scruffy**

tire *verb*

▶ to reduce your strength, becoming sleepy or weak. *The long walk **tired** the children.*

fatigue To **fatigue** means to tire in the body or mind. *The climb up the steep hill fatigued us.*

weary To **weary** is so similar to **tire** and **fatigue** that you can usually use any of these. *The constant noise and bustle of her office sometimes wearies my sister.*

exhaust To **exhaust** means to tire or wear someone out to a great extent. *Track-and-field practice exhausts me.*

tax To **tax** means to burden or **exhaust** someone or something. *Nursing taxed him much more than he had expected.*

drain To **drain** can mean to use up your strength gradually. *We felt drained as we swam to the other side of the lake.*

> similar keywords: **weaken**

tired *adjective*

▶ weak from effort or hard work and needing sleep. *The children were **tired** and ready for bed by the end of the busy day.*

weary   **Weary** means tired out in your mind or body as a result of hard work, or something similar. *We were very weary after our long hike.*

worn out   **Worn out** can mean very tired. *Justine was worn out after the archery finals.*

exhausted   **Exhausted** means greatly tired or drained of strength and energy. *The runners were all exhausted after the cross-country race.*

bushed   **Bushed** means very tired or **exhausted**. It is usually used in rather informal language. *I was bushed by the time I finished my workout.*

fatigued   **Fatigued** means very tired or drained of energy as a result of physical or mental effort. *The medical students were fatigued after the three-hour examination.*

> similar keywords: **lethargic, weak**
> contrasting keywords: **energetic, lively**

toast *verb*

▶ to brown something by heat or a flame. *We sat around the campfire and **toasted** marshmallows.*

grill   To **grill** means to toast or cook food, usually on a rack. *For breakfast we grilled some sausages.*

barbecue   To **barbecue** means to cook food on a rack over a flame or heated coals in a specially built fireplace or metal container. *At the picnic we barbecued chicken and corn on the cob.*

bake   To **bake** means to cook something in an oven. *Turn the oven on and bake the frozen pizza for eight minutes.*

roast   To **roast** means to cook something over a fire or to **bake** it in an oven. *When you roast a turkey, the delicious smell spreads all through the house.*

top *noun*

▶ the highest point or surface of anything. *From the **top** of the cliff, we could see the whole valley stretching out below us.*

peak A **peak** is the pointed top of anything, usually a mountain. *Mount Robson is the highest peak in the Canadian Rockies.*

pinnacle A **pinnacle** is the highest point of anything, usually a mountain. *No one has ever climbed that treacherous rocky pinnacle.*

summit A **summit** is the top or highest point of something. *We reached the summit of the hill after a steep climb.*

apex An **apex** is the tip, point, or highest part of anything. *Only one tree grew on the apex of the mountain.*

crest A **crest** is the very top of something. *The sunlight bounced off the crests of the waves.*

> contrasting keywords: **bottom**

touch *verb*

▶ to put your hand or finger on something. *I **touched** the CD with dirty hands and left smudges on it.*

feel To **feel** means to examine something by touching. *I felt the grass to see how wet it was.*

handle To **handle** means to use your hands to examine or touch something. *The vet gently handled the injured puppy to see if he could find any broken bones.*

caress To **caress** is to touch in a gentle, affectionate way. *The little girl caressed the kitten.*

stroke To **stroke** means to pass your hand gently over something. *The rider stroked the frightened horse to calm it.*

pat To **pat** means to **stroke** something lightly with your hand. *Fatima patted the chair to show me where to sit.*

touchy *adjective*

▶ irritable or easily offended. *He's so **touchy** sometimes that you have to be careful what you say to him.*

thin-skinned **Thin-skinned** means touchy. *Some people are too thin-skinned to listen to any criticism of their work.*

moody **Moody** means changeable in mood or feelings. *If you are going to be moody, you might as well stay at home by yourself.*

prickly **Prickly** can mean easily made angry. *He's always prickly when he's tired.*

sensitive **Sensitive** can mean easily affected by something. *My friend has a sensitive nature and is easily hurt.*

> similar keywords: **grumpy, annoyed, fickle**
> contrasting keywords: **agreeable**

trace *noun*

▶ a very small amount. *There is only a **trace** of vitamin A in this frozen dinner.*

drop A **drop** can be a very small amount of a liquid. *I put two drops of water into the test tube.*

dash A **dash** can be a small unmeasured amount of something. It is often used in cooking. *Add just a dash of pepper to the stew.*

pinch A **pinch** can be the very small amount of something you can pick up between your thumb and first finger. *The recipe says to add only a pinch of salt.*

hint A **hint** can be such a tiny amount of something that you can hardly tell it is there. *There was just a hint of warmth in the air.*

whisper A **whisper** can be a **hint** or suggestion. *There isn't a whisper of truth in that rumour.*

> similar keywords: **piece**

tradition *noun*

▶ a belief or way of doing something that is handed down from generation to generation. *Our family has a **tradition** of getting together at my grandparents' house on the first long weekend of every summer.*

custom
A **custom** is a usual way of doing something. *Is it your custom to eat a large breakfast?*

habit
A **habit** is a regular pattern of behaviour, usually done without much thought. *He had a habit of taking his shoes off at the front door.*

convention
A **convention** is a custom or rule that has become established. *It is a convention to put the date at the top of a letter.*

practice
A **practice** can be so similar to a **custom** that you can usually use either word. *It's my practice to go for a run twice a week.*

usage
Usage is the customary way of using words in a particular language or dialect. *This book on English usage will explain the difference between "compare with" and "compare to."*

transparent *adjective*

▶ allowing light to pass through so something can be seen. *I traced the map using **transparent** paper.*

clear
Clear can mean transparent or able to be seen through. *I covered my book with clear plastic so that I could still see the title.*

sheer
Sheer means so thin that it can be seen through. *We could see our visitors through the sheer curtains.*

limpid
Limpid means transparent and **clear**, like glass. *We could see the shellfish on the sandy bottom of the limpid pool of water.*

crystal
Crystal can mean transparent and **clear**, like glass. *The powerboat's wake disturbed the crystal surface of the still lake.*

translucent
Translucent means allowing some light to come through without being completely transparent. *Soft light came through the translucent frosted window.*

contrasting keywords: **opaque**

travel *verb*

▶ to go from one place to another. *We had only **travelled** a little way when my brother got hungry.*

journey To **journey** means to travel, usually a long way. *We journeyed right across Canada.*

roam To **roam** can mean to travel with no special purpose. *Hans spent his spare time roaming through the woods.*

wander To **wander** means to go about with no special purpose or place in mind. *I wandered a long way from the farm, trying to decide where to go.*

rove To **rove** is very similar to **roam** and **wander**. *My aunt roved around the world, visiting any place that sounded interesting.*

venture To **venture** can mean to travel somewhere as part of an adventure. *The travellers ventured to such out-of-the-way places as Bhutan and Sikkim in the Himalayas.*

traveller *noun*

▶ someone who goes about from place to place. *After my grandparents retired, they became world **travellers** for a year.*

tourist A **tourist** is someone who travels or tours for pleasure. *The tourists brought home many souvenirs of their holiday in Mexico.*

sightseer A **sightseer** is someone who travels to see places of interest or beauty. *Peggy's Cove in Nova Scotia is a popular place for sightseers.*

wayfarer A **wayfarer** is a traveller, especially one on foot. This is a rather old-fashioned word. *There were rest stations set up where the wayfarers could stop along the way.*

pilgrim A **pilgrim** is someone who travels to a holy place, especially to carry out a religious duty. *Every Muslim hopes to be a pilgrim to Mecca at least once in a lifetime.*

commuter A **commuter** is someone who travels regularly between home and work. *The Vancouver Skytrain is filled with commuters every morning and evening.*

trick *noun*

▶ something done to deceive someone. *Let's play a **trick** on Micah and hide under the bed.*

hoax	A **hoax** is a trick or practical joke. *The crop circles in Britain weren't really made by extraterrestrials—they were only a hoax.*
prank	A **prank** is a playful trick. *Debbie is full of pranks and mischief.*
ruse	A **ruse** is a dishonest trick or scheme. *They carefully planned a ruse to make everyone think they were still in the house.*
swindle	A **swindle** is a trick that cheats someone out of something. *The swindle was discovered when they found the envelope contained pieces of paper instead of money.*

similar keywords: **plot, joke**

trick *verb*

▶ to outwit, deceive, or cheat someone. *We managed to **trick** Dad on April Fool's Day when we hid the newspaper in the refrigerator.*

fool	To **fool** means to trick someone or to make someone think or believe something that isn't true. *It's really difficult to fool my parents.*
bluff	To **bluff** means to trick or deceive someone by pretending to be very bold. It is more suited to everyday language. *We thought Nema had good cards, but she was only bluffing.*
kid	To **kid** can mean to trick or tease someone, especially in a good-humoured way. *We kidded my little brother by telling him that spaghetti grows on trees.*
hoax	To **hoax** means to deceive someone by playing a trick or practical joke. This is a rather old-fashioned word. *Andrea even hoaxed her father with her clever disguise.*

similar keywords: **deceive, cheat, outwit, betray**

trickery   *noun*

▶ the tricking, cheating, or fooling of someone. *We were so used to Uncle Jack's* **trickery** *that we never knew when to believe him.*

subterfuge   **Subterfuge** means a trick, plan, or excuse used in order to avoid something. *Our subterfuge worked when they followed the false trail down to the river.*

deceit   **Deceit** means a dishonest trick or the act of lying or cheating. *Fiona was guilty of deceit when she lied about where the money came from.*

cunning   **Cunning** means the use of a clever plan to trick or deceive someone. *The fox's cunning was rewarded when it escaped without being seen.*

guile   **Guile** means cleverness or **cunning** in the way you cheat someone. *The con artist used charm and guile to trick them into giving him their savings.*

fraud   **Fraud** means trickery aimed at cheating someone or something. *The con artist was eventually arrested for committing fraud.*

trudge   *verb*

▶ to walk heavily and slowly. *We* **trudged** *through the mud in our rubber boots.*

tramp   To **tramp** means to tread or walk heavily and steadily. *Hour after hour, the soldiers tramped through the jungle.*

plod   To **plod** means to walk or move in a slow, steady, and unexciting way. *We plodded through the heavy snow.*

toil   To **toil** can mean to walk or move with difficulty. *We toiled through thick mud and reeds before we finally reached the river.*

slog   To **slog** can mean to keep trudging along. *The weary hikers slogged up yet another long, steep hill.*

lumber   To **lumber** means to move clumsily or heavily, especially because of great size or weight. *The elephants lumbered along the road.*

---

similar keywords: **walk, march, limp**
contrasting keywords: **frolic, dart**

---

true *adjective*

▶ full of truth, or not false. *Is it **true** that your cousin is a famous opera singer?*

right
> **Right** can mean free from error or agreeing with the truth or the facts. *I'm sure your information about reptiles is right.*

correct
> **Correct** means free from mistakes. *All the answers Keiko gave were correct.*

accurate
> **Accurate** means free from error. *The reporter said that your account of the incident was accurate.*

valid
> **Valid** means made with good reasons. *The teacher thought that Edward had a valid reason for being late for school.*

certain
> **Certain** can mean accepted as true or sure. *Trudy was certain that she could identify the thief.*

> similar keywords: **actual, genuine**
> contrasting keywords: **incorrect**

turn *verb*

▶ to make something move around or partly around in a circle. *Very slowly, Rob **turned** the knob and opened the door.*

rotate
> To **rotate** means to turn something around in a circle. *Rotate the handle in a clockwise direction.*

wind
> To **wind** means to tighten something, usually a spring, by turning it around. *You have to wind up the music box before it will play.*

screw
> To **screw** means to turn something, usually to tighten or seal it. *I poured myself a glass of juice, then screwed the lid back on the bottle.*

twist
> To **twist** can mean to combine two or more things by **winding** them together. *Louise twisted pieces of string together to make a thick, strong rope.*

reel
> To **reel** can mean to **wind** something onto a reel, a cylinder, or a wheel. *As soon as I felt a bite, I reeled in my fishing line.*

> similar keywords: **spin, bend**

twisted *adjective*

▶ curved, bent, or having a spiral form. *The **twisted** old tree was just right for climbing.*

coiled **Coiled** means curled around into loops. *The snake was coiled, ready to strike.*

winding **Winding** means curving, bending, or turning first one way and then another. *We had to cycle slowly down the winding mountain roads.*

entangled **Entangled** means tangled up, twisted up, or caught in. *My fishing line became entangled with the propeller of the boat.*

wavy **Wavy** means curving first one way and then the other. *Jason has thick, wavy hair.*

sinuous **Sinuous** means **winding** or having many curves and bends. *We followed the sinuous path up and down and round about, until we ended up where we started!*

tyrannical *adjective*

▶ severely cruel or harsh. *The people hated their **tyrannical** king for his cruelty toward them.*

oppressive **Oppressive** means unjustly cruel. *The oppressive government put people in prison without granting them a trial.*

repressive **Repressive** means forcefully keeping people under control. *Some repressive governments control the newspapers, TV, and radio and deny their people freedom of speech.*

despotic **Despotic** means like a ruler who has total power, especially one who is cruel and unjust. *The president dissolved the elected assembly and became a despotic ruler.*

totalitarian **Totalitarian** means having to do with a government that has complete control and does not allow any opposition. *East Germany had a totalitarian government until the people rebelled.*

similar keywords: **bossy, cruel**
contrasting keywords: **submissive**

U, u

ugly *adjective*

▶ unpleasant to look at. *The child was frightened by the **ugly** monster mask.*

hideous   **Hideous** means extremely ugly. *The film was about a hideous monster.*

repulsive   **Repulsive** can mean so unpleasant to look at that you feel sick or disgusted. *Some people find spiders repulsive.*

grotesque   **Grotesque** means ugly in a way that is odd or unnatural. *They used special makeup to give him the grotesque appearance of an alien creature.*

foul   **Foul** can mean very ugly or nasty. This is a rather unusual way of using this word today. *The brave princess was not afraid of the foul dragon.*

> contrasting keywords: **beautiful, pretty**

unashamed *adjective*

▶ not feeling shame, sorrow, or embarrassment. *I am **unashamed** to be associated with this cause, even though it is unpopular.*

impenitent   **Impenitent** means not feeling sorry for doing wrong and not being willing to put things right. *The judge sentenced the impenitent criminal to ten years in jail.*

unrepentant   **Unrepentant** means not showing regret or sorrow for doing wrong. It is very similar to **impenitent**. *They were unrepentant in spite of the trouble they caused for everyone else.*

unremorseful   **Unremorseful** means not feeling any regret for doing wrong. *My parents were angry because I was unremorseful when I got home so late.*

unapologetic   **Unapologetic** means not wanting to say you are sorry. *They said the accident was not their fault and were quite unapologetic.*

> similar keywords: **bold**
> contrasting keywords: **sorry**

unbelievable   *adjective*

▶ not able to be believed or accepted as true. *Your tale of your odd adventure seems* ***unbelievable****.*

incredible	**Incredible** can be so similar to **unbelievable** that you can usually use either. *This book is full of incredible tales.*
unlikely	**Unlikely** means not likely to be true. *It was an unlikely coincidence, but it really happened.*
improbable	**Improbable** means probably not true. It is very similar to **unlikely**. *I've never heard such an improbable story.*
implausible	**Implausible** means seeming not to be true or reasonable. It is similar to **unlikely** and **improbable**. *Their explanation for not attending class was implausible.*
far-fetched	**Far-fetched** means seeming to be too exaggerated to be true. *I prefer a movie to be realistic rather than far-fetched.*

> similar keywords: **impossible**
> contrasting keywords: **believable, possible, likely**

uncertain   *adjective*

▶ not known for sure. *The time of the train's arrival is still* ***uncertain****.*

doubtful	**Doubtful** can mean causing doubt or uncertainty. *He gave such a doubtful answer that I wondered if he had really read the book.*
questionable	**Questionable** means open to doubt or argument. *It is questionable whether this is true.*
debatable	**Debatable** means open to argument. It is very similar to **questionable**. *It is highly debatable that this is the year's best movie.*
open	**Open** can mean not completed or decided. *The ending of the novel was left open for the reader to decide what happened to the main character.*

> similar keywords: **vague**
> contrasting keywords: **sure**

unconscious *adjective*

▶ having fainted or lost consciousness. *Jack tumbled down the hill and was lying* **unconscious** *at the bottom.*

comatose | **Comatose** means in a coma or unconscious because of sickness or an injury. *After the accident, Shashi was comatose for two days.*

stunned | **Stunned** can mean being briefly unconscious or unaware of your surroundings. *Aran was stunned for a moment by the blow to his head.*

dazed | **Dazed** means made confused or almost unconscious. *My sister was dazed by the crash and tried to remember how it had happened.*

out cold | **Out cold** means unconscious. This is more suited to everyday language. *The baseball player was out cold after the ball hit him on the head.*

unconventional *adjective*

▶ not according to usual or accepted ways of behaviour. *Her wedding dress was* **unconventional** *because it was orange.*

nonconformist | **Nonconformist** means refusing to accept the usual or expected ideas, customs, or ways of living. *People with nonconformist ideas can help create new ways of looking at old problems.*

eccentric | **Eccentric** means not having the usual ideas or ways of behaviour, and considered odd as a result. *In some places, eccentric behaviour is considered charming.*

alternative | **Alternative** can mean existing outside of traditional or established institutions or ways of doing things. *My sister likes to listen to alternative music.*

radical | **Radical** means being in favour of extreme social or political change. *The radical political group demonstrated for tax reforms outside Parliament.*

offbeat | **Offbeat** means unconventional or odd. *Their ideas and their clothes are offbeat, but they do make people listen and look.*

> similar keywords: **strange**
> contrasting keywords: **usual**

understand   *verb*

▶ to take the idea of something into your mind. *I tried to* **understand** *Jan's explanation.*

grasp	To **grasp** can mean to understand or take something into your mind. *Sabira grasped the idea of the game very quickly.*
comprehend	To **comprehend** means to understand the meaning of something. *We tried hard to comprehend our parents' reasons for not wanting us to watch that TV show.*
perceive	To **perceive** can mean to understand or become aware of something with your mind. *John's teacher perceived that he was unhappy about something.*
fathom	To **fathom** means to understand something completely. *I couldn't fathom the instructions for building the model until Leita helped me.*
figure out	To **figure out** means to see or understand something. This is more suited to everyday language. *I figured out a way to solve the riddle.*

> similar keywords: **realize, sense, learn**

undertaking   *noun*

▶ a task or piece of work you promise to do. *Moving all the books from the old library to the new one will be a huge* **undertaking**.

enterprise	An **enterprise** is something that requires effort or courage. *Organizing the yard sale for the neighbourhood was quite an enterprise.*
venture	A **venture** can be something you do that is risky or dangerous. *Both companies were involved in the oil exploration venture.*
project	A **project** is something that is planned or undertaken. *We worked in groups to complete the science project.*
engagement	An **engagement** can mean something you are hired to do, especially only once. *The band had an engagement to play at the dance.*

> similar keywords: **task, job**

uneven *adjective*

▶ not being equally balanced with something else. *The competition between the older and younger students was **uneven**.*

unequal　**Unequal** means not being of the same quantity, amount, quality, and so on. *The customers were upset when they were given unequal servings of dessert.*

unbalanced　**Unbalanced** means not equal or properly balanced. *The teams were unbalanced because two of our players were sick.*

lopsided　**Lopsided** means larger or heavier on one side than the other. *The cake was lopsided, so I put more icing on one side to make the top even.*

asymmetrical　**Asymmetrical** means **lopsided, unbalanced,** or not symmetrical. *An asymmetrical picture arrangement can be more interesting than a symmetrical one.*

> contrasting keywords: **equal**

unfair *adjective*

▶ showing favouritism or not treating everyone the same. *It was **unfair** of them to give Scott the best seat.*

unjust　**Unjust** can mean unfair and is usually used to describe the actions of someone in authority. *It was unjust of the judge not to listen to all the witnesses.*

inequitable　**Inequitable** means unfair or **unjust**. It is a rather formal word. *The crowd booed the referee for her inequitable treatment of the two teams.*

discriminatory　**Discriminatory** means treating one person or group unfairly because you prefer another. *There are laws to prevent discriminatory behaviour.*

prejudiced　**Prejudiced** means behaving unfairly because you have formed an opinion without good reason. *You may not like the team, but don't be prejudiced against the school.*

> similar keywords: **narrow-minded**
> contrasting keywords: **fair, neutral, broad-minded**

unfaithful   *adjective*

▶ not staying true to someone or to what you have promised. *The knight was* **unfaithful** *to his vow to defend the queen.*

disloyal   **Disloyal** means not faithful or true. *The queen accused her advisor of being disloyal for not taking her side in the argument.*

false   **False** can mean not faithful or loyal. *He turned out to be a false friend.*

treacherous   **Treacherous** means **disloyal** or likely to betray someone who has trusted you. *The treacherous soldier gave information to the enemy.*

traitorous   **Traitorous** means betraying a person, a cause, or a country. *The traitorous spy plotted to overthrow the government of his country.*

slippery   **Slippery** can mean not to be depended on. This is a rather informal word. *She was such a slippery businessperson that no one believed she would keep her end of the agreement.*

> similar keywords: **fickle**
> contrasting keywords: **faithful**

unfriendly   *adjective*

▶ not showing friendship, or being unkind. *The book was snatched from me in an* **unfriendly** *way.*

cold   **Cold** can mean lacking friendliness or interest. *Their cold greeting showed they hadn't forgiven us.*

aloof   **Aloof** means not joining in with other people in a friendly way. *People thought Lynn was being aloof, but I knew she was only shy.*

standoffish   **Standoffish** means unfriendly or keeping your distance from other people. It is rather similar to **aloof**. *You don't have to be standoffish with people just because you haven't been introduced to them.*

inhospitable   **Inhospitable** means not welcoming people or showing kindness to others, especially in your own home. *I think it is poor behaviour to be inhospitable to new neighbours.*

> contrasting keywords: **friendly**

ungrateful *adjective*

▶ not showing or feeling gratitude or thanks. *How can you be so **ungrateful** when I spent all afternoon helping you reload your computer software?*

unappreciative **Unappreciative** means not showing or feeling appreciation or gratitude. *The band was upset when the unappreciative audience left the concert before the end.*

thankless **Thankless** means not saying how grateful you are. *That's the last time I go to such trouble for a thankless person like him.*

grudging **Grudging** means unwillingly expressing appreciation or gratitude. *I'd rather have no thanks at all than grudging thanks.*

heedless **Heedless** can mean thoughtless or not being aware of someone else's kindness. *Tracy was quite heedless of our efforts to help her.*

> similar keywords: **selfish**

unlike *adjective*

▶ not the same, or without a likeness. *This gravel road is quite **unlike** the paved highway we were driving on before.*

different **Different** is similar to **unlike**. It is usually used with "from." *Apples are different from oranges in their colour and taste.*

dissimilar **Dissimilar** means unlike. *You would hardly know they are sisters, because their faces have such dissimilar features.*

contrasting **Contrasting** means greatly **different**. *The contrasting photographs showed the house in its run-down condition, and then after it had been fixed up.*

disparate **Disparate** means completely distinct and unlike. This is a rather formal word. *You and I have disparate goals, so I'm not surprised that we disagree about how the project should be done.*

> similar keywords: **various**
> contrasting keywords: **similar, equal**

unlucky *adjective*

▶ ill-fated or not having good luck. *We were rather **unlucky** this month because we all caught the flu.*

unfortunate	**Unfortunate** is so similar to **unlucky** that you can usually use either one. *It was unfortunate that we couldn't get any tickets for the concert.*
hapless	**Hapless** means unlucky and without much hope. It is a slightly old-fashioned word. *The man sleeping in the park looked like a hapless fellow.*
wretched	**Wretched** can mean very unlucky or miserable. *What a wretched thing to happen, just when you were doing so well.*
cursed	**Cursed** can mean so unlucky that it's as if someone has wished misfortune to come your way. *I think that racehorse is cursed because it never wins a race.*
jinxed	**Jinxed** means always unlucky at something and is similar to **cursed**. *He used a new deck of cards, saying that the old one was jinxed.*

contrasting keywords: **lucky**

unmarried *adjective*

▶ not married. *Despite their commitment to each other, they are **unmarried**.*

unwed	**Unwed** is so similar to **unmarried** that you can usually use either word. *Uncle Larry remained unwed for many years.*
single	**Single** can mean unmarried. *My oldest sister is a single parent who works as a lawyer.*
unattached	**Unattached** can mean not engaged or married. *My brother was going out with the same woman for a while, but now he is unattached.*
engaged	**Engaged** can mean promised to be married. *The couple has been engaged for two years, and they plan on marrying after they graduate from medical school.*

unrelated   *adjective*

▶ having no particular relationship or connection. *His question about space travel was* ***unrelated*** *to the road safety talk we listened to.*

irrelevant   **Irrelevant** means having nothing to do with the matter being discussed or thought about. *The speaker made so many irrelevant remarks that it was hard to understand what he was really trying to tell us.*

unconnected   **Unconnected** can mean not thought of as related or connected. *Her educational studies seem unconnected to her ambition to be a professional golfer.*

immaterial   **Immaterial** means unimportant, often to the matter being discussed. *Where the shoes were made was immaterial to him as long as they were comfortable.*

foreign   **Foreign** can mean not belonging. *Getting up early seemed foreign to us after the summer break.*

> contrasting keywords: **related**

untidy   *adjective*

▶ not tidy or neat. *Dad asked us to straighten up our* ***untidy*** *rooms before we went out to play baseball.*

messy   **Messy** means in an untidy and dirty state. *The kitchen was very messy by the time we finished cooking dinner.*

chaotic   **Chaotic** means in total disorder. *The house was chaotic when we were unpacking.*

disorganized   **Disorganized** means in confusion or disorder. *My desk was so disorganized that I couldn't find my homework.*

slovenly   **Slovenly** means untidy and careless, especially in the way you present yourself. *It is foolish to have a slovenly appearance at a job interview.*

> similar keywords: **scruffy, dirty**
> contrasting keywords: **tidy**

unusual   *adjective*

▶ not usual, common, or ordinary. *Diane is generally a punctual person, so it is* ***unusual*** *for her to be this late.*

uncommon
Uncommon means not likely to be found or encountered. *Whistling swans are very uncommon in this part of Canada.*

extraordinary
Extraordinary means beyond what is ordinary. *Luis is a boy of extraordinary intelligence.*

rare
Rare means unusual, **uncommon**, or occurring infrequently. *This coin is valuable because it is rare.*

remarkable
Remarkable means worthy of notice because it is so unusual. *Winning the tournament against so many strong teams was a remarkable accomplishment.*

singular
Singular means out of the ordinary or **remarkable**. *Her career as an actor has been a singular success.*

> similar keywords: **strange, scarce**
> contrasting keywords: **ordinary, usual**

unwilling   *adjective*

▶ not eager, or not happily agreeing, to do something. *The child's father was* ***unwilling*** *to spend such a lot of money on a toy that could break easily.*

reluctant
Reluctant means unwilling or not prepared. *My little cousin is always eager to do crafts, but is often reluctant to clean up afterwards.*

disinclined
Disinclined means unwilling or not wishing to do something. *I'm disinclined to go cycling on such a hot day.*

loath
Loath means unwilling or not inclined. *I am loath to go out into that freezing cold.*

averse
Averse means opposed or very unwilling. *Luckily for us, our teacher is averse to giving us tests every week.*

> contrasting keywords: **enthusiastic**

upset   *adjective*

▶ feeling anxious or unhappy. *I was **upset** when I wasn't chosen for the team.*

agitated   **Agitated** means feeling anxious and unable to be still. *Dad was very agitated when they had not come home by midnight.*

disturbed   **Disturbed** means feeling troubled or unsettled. *We were quite disturbed by the news reports of the earthquakes.*

flustered   **Flustered** means confused, usually because you are nervous. *I was flustered and forgot what to say when I stood up to give my speech.*

uptight   **Uptight** means tense and anxious. It is more suited to everyday language. *Don't get so uptight about your piano exam.*

perturbed   **Perturbed** means very **disturbed** or troubled. *The perturbed pilot looked for a place to land the damaged plane.*

> similar keywords: **nervous**
> contrasting keywords: **calm**

upset   *verb*

▶ to make someone feel sad or disturbed. *Their insults don't **upset** me.*

distress   To **distress** means to cause someone great pain, anxiety, or sorrow. *His plan to leave school before he graduated distressed his parents.*

hurt   To **hurt** can mean to harm someone or cause painful feelings. *Her thoughtlessness hurt him and he turned and walked away.*

disturb   To **disturb** can mean to **upset** or concern someone. *I am disturbed by his loss of interest in his hobbies.*

trouble   To **trouble** means to **disturb** or bother someone. *It's a shame to trouble them when they're tired.*

sadden   To **sadden** means to make someone feel sad or upset. *The news of your illness saddened me.*

> similar keywords: **annoy, worry**
> contrasting keywords: **comfort**

use *verb*

▶ to put something into action for some purpose. *Let's **use** our backpacks to carry the groceries home.*

employ   To **employ** means to use something. It is slightly more formal than use. *I prefer to employ my spare time reading rather than watching TV.*

wield   To **wield** means to use something as a powerful tool. *The principal wields her influence with the parents to raise money for the school.*

exploit   To **exploit** can mean to put something to good use. *They exploited the land well, growing crops for food.*

utilize   To **utilize** means to put something into use. *Many people utilize the wind's energy to generate electricity.*

contrasting keywords: **discard**

useful *adjective*

▶ of use or service. *Don't throw away anything that might be **useful** at another time.*

handy   **Handy** can mean useful or convenient. *That rock made a handy hammer!*

helpful   **Helpful** means able or likely to help or be of use. *The dictionary is helpful when I'm not sure what a word means.*

valuable   **Valuable** can mean of great use or service. *You'd be performing a valuable service by helping the seniors with their gardening.*

beneficial   **Beneficial** means **helpful** or of benefit. *The unusually rainy weather was beneficial for the crops.*

advantageous   **Advantageous** means **helpful** or of advantage to you. *It would be advantageous to get your tickets early so that you get a good seat.*

similar keywords: **possible**
contrasting keywords: **useless**

useless   *adjective*

▶ of no use or serving no purpose. *It is **useless** to try to plug that large hole with that small stopper.*

vain
Vain can have a meaning so similar to **useless** that you can usually use either word. *They made a vain attempt to stop the runaway car before it crashed.*

futile
Futile means not able to produce any result. *The dog made futile leaps at the cat in the tree.*

ineffective
Ineffective means not effective or of little use. *I made an ineffective attempt to mend the broken chair.*

ineffectual
Ineffectual means not able to produce an intended result. *He was an ineffectual leader in our protest against the closing of the park.*

> similar keywords: **impossible**
> contrasting keywords: **useful, possible**

usual   *adjective*

▶ most frequently occurring. *We went to school following the **usual** route, forgetting that the road was closed.*

normal
Normal means standard, common, or regular. *It is normal to have snow at this time of the year.*

conventional
Conventional means relating to standards or rules, often unwritten, that most people accept. *There is a conventional way for tennis players to dress.*

customary
Customary means according to custom or the usual way of acting or doing things. *Shaking hands when you meet someone is customary in this country.*

traditional
Traditional means according to the beliefs, customs, and stories that have been handed down from one generation to another. *In many cultures, it is traditional to eat certain foods on special holidays.*

> similar keywords: **ordinary**
> contrasting keywords: **unusual, unconventional, strange**

V, v

vague *adjective*

▶ not clear or certain. *We had only a **vague** idea of where our cousins lived.*

indefinite   **Indefinite** means doubtful or not definite. *He was indefinite about his future plans.*

hazy   **Hazy** can mean confused or not distinct. *As I was coming out of the anesthetic, everything was hazy.*

faint   **Faint** can mean not clear or distinct. *I have only a faint idea of how to make pancakes.*

approximate   **Approximate** can mean rough or not exact. *I can't give you even an approximate answer.*

> similar keywords: **uncertain, cloudy**
> contrasting keywords: **precise, clear**

various *adjective*

▶ different from one another. *We have **various** kinds of vegetables in the garden.*

diverse   **Diverse** means having many different kinds or forms. *The five of us have diverse interests and abilities.*

mixed   **Mixed** can mean made up of different sorts. *I brought a plate of mixed sandwiches to the picnic.*

assorted   **Assorted** means made up of different kinds. It is similar to **mixed**. *I asked for a box of assorted chocolates.*

miscellaneous   **Miscellaneous** means made up of a mixture of different things. *He had a miscellaneous collection of fishing lures.*

motley   **Motley** means made up of different types or kinds. *It was a motley group of people who answered the appeal for help.*

> similar keywords: **unlike, numerous**
> contrasting keywords: **similar**

view   *noun*

▶ whatever you can see from a particular place. *We all looked at the spectacular* **view** *from the top of the tower.*

landscape
> A **landscape** is a view of scenery on land. *The landscape consisted of a beautiful green valley with a river running through it.*

vista
> A **vista** is a view, especially one seen through an opening or passage. *From the observation tunnels, we gazed at the vista of Niagara Falls.*

outlook
> An **outlook** is what you see when looking out from a place. *My bedroom has a pleasant outlook.*

scene
> A **scene** can be a view, especially one in which something is happening. *The main street of our town is a colourful scene on New Year's Eve.*

panorama
> A **panorama** is an unbroken view of a broad landscape. *Halfway up the mountain, we stopped our car to admire the panoramic scene.*

violence   *noun*

▶ rough, powerful, or damaging force. *The* **violence** *of the earthquake destroyed the village.*

severity
> **Severity** can mean violence, harshness, or sharpness. *The severity of the cold caused us to shiver.*

fury
> **Fury** can mean violence or fierceness. *The hurricane raged with such fury that roofs were ripped off houses.*

vehemence
> **Vehemence** can mean violence or unusual force. *The door was slammed with such vehemence that all the glasses rattled.*

ferocity
> **Ferocity** is savage fierceness. *The rabid dog attacked the letter carrier with ferocity.*

brutality
> **Brutality** is savage cruelty. *The brutality of the storm was evident from all the debris strewn along the shore.*

> similar keywords: **force**

violent   *adjective*

▶ powerful and causing damage. *The **violent** tidal wave capsized many fishing boats and wrecked many houses.*

fierce   **Fierce** can mean violent in force or strength. *Fierce winds buffeted the ship.*

furious   **Furious** means intensely violent or full of rage and anger. *A furious tornado carved a path of destruction through the farmers' fields.*

ferocious   **Ferocious** can mean cruel in a violent way. *The intruders were frightened away by the ferocious guard dog.*

wild   **Wild** can mean violent or **fierce**. *Wild fighting broke out between the rebels and the government forces.*

forceful   **Forceful** can mean full of strength or power. *The forceful blow of the sledgehammer shattered the concrete.*

> similar keywords: **intense, cruel, warlike**
> contrasting keywords: **peaceful**

virtue   *noun*

▶ goodness or moral excellence. *The help Neelam gave us is another sign of her **virtue**.*

decency   **Decency** is good or proper behaviour. *They showed their decency by turning in the wallet full of money.*

character   **Character** can be goodness or integrity. *Your kind actions show that you are a person of good character.*

principle   A **principle** can be a rule on which good behaviour is based. *It is my principle not to lose my temper during a disagreement.*

worth   **Worth** can be the value of a person. *His friends talked about Jose's worth as a human being.*

visible *adjective*

▶ able to be seen. *The lighthouse beacon was **visible** a long way out to sea.*

noticeable   **Noticeable** means able to be seen easily. *The scar was noticeable after the operation, but it soon faded.*

conspicuous   **Conspicuous** means very **noticeable**. *Cindy was conspicuous in her bright orange overalls.*

prominent   **Prominent** means standing out. *Their house was prominent because it was the only one in the street with two storeys.*

exposed   **Exposed** can mean open to view, or not hidden. *When you're photographing wildlife, try to hide in the bushes rather than staying in an exposed spot.*

overt   **Overt** means open, public, or not concealed. *The star wore many gold chains and other expensive jewellery in an overt display of wealth.*

> similar keywords: **obvious**
> contrasting keywords: **invisible**

visit *verb*

▶ to go to see someone or something. *I'm coming to **visit** you on Sunday.*

call   To **call** can mean to make a short visit. *We called at my cousin's house on our way home from school.*

drop by   To **drop by** means to visit someone in an informal or casual way. *We dropped by to see why you missed the soccer practice.*

stop by   To **stop by** means to arrive for a short visit on your way to another place. *We drove from Toronto to Niagara Falls and stopped by to see our friends in Hamilton.*

blow in   To **blow in** means to arrive at some place. This is more suited to everyday language. *My brother just blew in from St. John's.*

attend   To **attend** means to be present somewhere. *Will you attend the meeting?*

> similar keywords: **come**

vulgar *adjective*

▶ ill-mannered, rude, and badly behaved. *They apologized for their **vulgar** conduct.*

common	**Common** can mean vulgar or impolite. *Vandals marked up the wall with common graffiti.*
uncouth	**Uncouth** means behaving in an ill-mannered or rough way. *I wish those uncouth commuters wouldn't push past us like that.*
tasteless	**Tasteless** can mean not showing any sense of what is accepted as polite or correct behaviour. *That is a tasteless way to talk about another person's bad luck.*
crude	**Crude** can mean rude or in such bad taste that some people might be upset. *Nobody laughed at the crude joke.*
coarse	**Coarse** can mean offensive or so rude that it disgusts you. *Such coarse behaviour does not belong in the classroom.*

similar keywords: **rude**
contrasting keywords: **polite**

vulnerable *adjective*

▶ likely or able to be hurt or wounded. *The injured bird was **vulnerable** to attack from other animals because it couldn't fly away.*

insecure	**Insecure** can mean not safe from danger. *I'm in an insecure position at the top of this old ladder.*
exposed	**Exposed** can mean not safe from danger or injury. *We were in an exposed position on the cliff face, and the winds howled around us.*
susceptible	**Susceptible** means easily affected by something, especially something dangerous or harmful. *Because my cousin was so weak after his long illness, he was highly susceptible to colds.*
open	**Open** can mean likely to be affected by danger or harm. *The net was left open when the goalie left to chase the puck.*

similar keywords: **powerless, weak**
contrasting keywords: **safe**

W, w

---

walk *verb*

▶ to move about by placing one foot after the other on the ground. *I missed the bus, so I had to **walk** to school.*

amble To **amble** means to walk at a relaxed, comfortable pace. *It was still early, so we ambled along.*

saunter To **saunter** means to walk in an unhurried, carefree way. *I sauntered down to the beach, munching an apple.*

stroll To **stroll** means to walk in a slow, enjoyable way. *We strolled along the path, listening to the birds and crickets.*

pace To **pace** means to walk with regular steps. *In the old zoo, the tiger paced up and down inside its cage.*

> similar keywords: **march, limp, trudge**
> contrasting keywords: **frolic, dart, hurry, speed**

---

want *verb*

▶ to wish for or have need of something. *Who **wants** lunch?*

desire To **desire** means to wish for something very much. This is a rather formal word. *After the long walk, I desired nothing more than a cool glass of water.*

long for To **long for** means to have a strong wish for something. *Denise longed for a hamburger.*

crave To **crave** means to want or need something desperately. *The day was so hot that Sakda craved a cool drink.*

covet To **covet** means to want to have something very much, especially something that belongs to someone else. *They covet that new bike of yours.*

fancy To **fancy** can mean to feel you want or would like something. *I fancy fish for lunch.*

---

warlike   *adjective*

▶ being ready or eager for fighting or conflict. *The ancient Dravidians were a gentle, not **warlike**, people.*

martial
: **Martial** means having to do with fighting or war. *Some people learn martial arts as a form of exercise and self-discipline.*

militant
: **Militant** means fighting or ready to fight, especially for a cause. *Are those protesters peaceful or militant?*

bellicose
: **Bellicose** means warlike or ready to fight. This is a rather formal word. *The bellicose nation was eager to start a war.*

bloodthirsty
: **Bloodthirsty** means wanting to kill. *The bloodthirsty pirates made the prisoners walk the plank.*

hawkish
: **Hawkish** means favouring a militant attitude toward other nations. It is mostly used about politicians. *We were worried by the diplomat's hawkish attitude at the summit conference.*

> similar keywords: **aggressive, violent**
> contrasting keywords: **peaceful**

warn   *verb*

▶ to tell someone, or to signal to someone, that there may be danger ahead. *They **warned** us that the road was icy.*

caution
: To **caution** is so similar to **warn** that you can usually use either word. *Dad cautioned us not to go swimming alone.*

forewarn
: To **forewarn** means to warn beforehand. *The weather bureau forewarned us about the approaching tornado.*

alert
: To **alert** means to warn someone of a possible attack or danger. *The scout alerted the general about the planned raid on the camp.*

tip off
: To **tip off** can mean to warn someone about probable trouble. This is more suited to everyday language. *The anonymous caller tipped off the police about the planned robbery.*

> similar keywords: **advise, predict**

wary *adjective*

▶ on your guard against danger or trouble. *I was **wary** of the ice on the sidewalk.*

watchful   **Watchful** means looking out carefully for danger or trouble. *I was rescued by the watchful lifeguard.*

cautious   **Cautious** means being very wary when there is danger. *Be cautious when you cross a busy street.*

careful   **Careful** means taking care to avoid risks. *A careful driver rarely causes accidents.*

deliberate   **Deliberate** means carefully thought out. *My slow, deliberate movements calmed the frightened horse.*

discreet   **Discreet** means being careful in your behaviour or speech so that you don't upset people. *Mariko's discreet behaviour made the children trust her.*

> similar keywords: **alert, careful**
> contrasting keywords: **rash, careless**

waste *verb*

▶ to spend or use up something without much result. *Don't **waste** your time being silly when you should be working on your project.*

squander   To **squander** means to spend or use something wastefully. *They had squandered all their money on gambling.*

fritter away   To **fritter away** means to waste something gradually. This is more suited to everyday language. *I try not to fritter away my money on unimportant things.*

blow   To **blow** can mean to waste something or **squander** it, usually all at one time. It is more suited to everyday language. *He blew all his money at the movies and didn't have enough left to pick up the dry cleaning.*

splurge   To **splurge** means to spend money extravagantly or unnecessarily. *I splurged on an expensive dinner for my friends.*

weak   *adjective*

▶ not strong or healthy. *The humane society said that the dog it had rescued was* ***weak*** *but happy.*

frail
Frail means weak and delicate. *Henry helped the frail man up the stairs.*

feeble
Feeble means weak in body or mind. *Great-grandma's body became feeble, but her mind was still sharp.*

invalid
Invalid means weak and sick and finding it difficult to care for yourself. *She is happy to look after her invalid sister.*

helpless
Helpless means so weak that you are unable to do anything for yourself. *I was nearly helpless from laughter.*

debilitated
Debilitated means having a weakened body. *Many people were debilitated during the long famine.*

> similar keywords: **decrepit, fragile, powerless, vulnerable**
> contrasting keywords: **strong, hardy, energetic**

weaken   *verb*

▶ to make someone or something weaker. *The lack of food and water had* ***weakened*** *the poor animal's body, but not its spirit.*

sap
To **sap** means to weaken or destroy something gradually. *Having the flu has sapped all my energy.*

enervate
To **enervate** means to feel drained of energy. *I felt enervated from worrying too much.*

disable
To **disable** means to make someone unfit or unable to use part of their body. *A car accident temporarily disabled her.*

incapacitate
To **incapacitate** is similar to **disable** and you can often use either word. *The flu epidemic incapacitated many people for a short period of time.*

> similar keywords: **tire**
> contrasting keywords: **strengthen**

wealth *noun*

▶ a large store of money and property. *My aunt's **wealth** comes from her successful business ventures.*

money
: Money can mean a person's wealth. *He made his money by inventing a fantastic new computer program.*

fortune
: A **fortune** is a great amount of **money** or property. *Anyone who invented a robot to do homework would make a fortune.*

riches
: Riches means wealth or many and valuable possessions. *We stared at all the queen's riches displayed before us.*

treasure
: Treasure means a store of wealth or **riches**, especially precious metals or money. *They found the stolen treasure hidden in a cave.*

capital
: Capital means the amount of money owned by a business or person. *They used nearly all their capital to buy the apartment building.*

> contrasting keywords: **poverty**

wealthy *adjective*

▶ having a lot of money and valuable belongings. *My friends are **wealthy** enough to live in a large house and travel outside the country every year.*

rich
: Rich means having a lot of money. *You don't have to be rich to be happy.*

prosperous
: Prosperous means successful and wealthy. *The prosperous businessperson worked hard to make the company grow.*

well-off
: Well-off can mean wealthy enough to live a comfortable life. It is usually used in less formal language. *Most of the well-off people in our town drive expensive cars.*

affluent
: Affluent means wealthy and **prosperous**. It can describe things as well as people. *Canada is an affluent country when compared with some other nations.*

> contrasting keywords: **broke, poor**

weight *noun*

▶ a heavy object or mass. *I put a **weight** on the pile of papers so that they wouldn't blow away.*

burden	A **burden** can be something that is carried. *He lifted his heavy burden onto his back.*
load	A **load** is a **burden**, usually a heavy one. *Miranda carried the load of paper into her office.*
pressure	**Pressure** is the force of something that is applied against something or someone. *The water pressure caused the hose to burst.*
ballast	**Ballast** is the heavy material carried by a ship to keep it steady or by a hot-air balloon to control its height. *The cargo of iron bars acted as ballast for the ship.*
encumbrance	An **encumbrance** is a **burden** or something useless that weighs you down. *If you bring all those books, they'll just be an encumbrance.*

well-behaved *adjective*

▶ behaving properly. *All the kindergarten children were **well-behaved**.*

good	**Good** can be so similar to **well-behaved** that you can often use either. *Please be good when the visitors arrive.*
well-mannered	**Well-mannered** means polite or courteous. *Show that you are well-mannered by giving your seat to that woman carrying the baby.*
considerate	**Considerate** means behaving properly and thinking about other people's feelings. *It was considerate of you to let me have first choice.*
cooperative	**Cooperative** means working together with others in a helpful way. *The cooperative students finished their project ahead of schedule.*
as good as gold	**As good as gold** means being as well-behaved as possible. This is more suited to everyday language. *It was an enjoyable outing because all the children were as good as gold.*

> similar keywords: **obedient, polite, kind**
> contrasting keywords: **naughty, disobedient**

wet *adjective*

▶ soaked with water or some other liquid. *My clothes were **wet** because I couldn't find shelter from the rain.*

damp	**Damp** means slightly wet. *We took the damp clothes off the line before the rain started.*
moist	**Moist** is so similar to **damp** that you can usually choose either word. *Kathleen's face was moist with perspiration.*
dank	**Dank** means unpleasantly **moist** or **damp**. *The back of the cave was dank from lack of sun and fresh air.*
soggy	**Soggy** means soaked or thoroughly wet. *The ground was soggy after a week of heavy rain.*
sodden	**Sodden** means completely soaked with liquid. *Our shoes were sodden after walking in the rain.*

> similar keywords: **humid**
> contrasting keywords: **dry**

wet *verb*

▶ to soak something with water or some other liquid. *We **wet** the ground thoroughly before planting the rosebush.*

dampen	To **dampen** means to make something slightly wet. *I dampened the cloth with water and rubbed the dirty mark from my cheek.*
moisten	To **moisten** means to make something moderately wet. *Moisten the sticker before you apply it to the window.*
water	To **water** means to pour water on something. *We water our flower garden every second evening during the hot summer.*
douse	To **douse** means to drench or to soak. *Be sure to douse the campfire when you're through cooking the hot dogs.*

> similar keywords: **soak**

whisper   *noun*

▶ a very soft, quietly spoken sound. *We spoke in a **whisper** so we wouldn't disturb the other people.*

murmur A **murmur** is a whispered conversation or whispering sound. *As the curtain rose at the start of the play, you could still hear the murmur of the audience.*

sigh A **sigh** is the soft sound you make when you let your breath out slowly, usually when you're tired, sad, or relieved about something. *We all gave a sigh of relief when we heard that they had landed safely.*

tinkle A **tinkle** is a short, light, ringing sound. *We heard the tinkle of the door chimes as we entered the room.*

rustle A **rustle** is the very soft sound made when leaves, papers, or something similar rub gently together. *We heard a rustle among the leaves, and a skunk appeared.*

hiss A **hiss** is an "s" sound, like the one a snake makes. *We heard the hiss of the lawn sprinkler.*

> contrasting keywords: **noise**

white   *adjective*

▶ having a colour like milk or snow. *Some big, **white** clouds drifted across the blue summer sky.*

cream **Cream** means having a yellowish-white colour. *We chose white for the ceiling and a rich cream for the walls.*

pale **Pale** can mean having a whitish or colourless appearance. *The moon appeared pale through the clouds.*

ivory **Ivory** means having a creamy white colour. *All we could see were huge, ivory teeth as the shark opened its mouth wide.*

frosted **Frosted** can mean having the appearance of frost. *We could see only shapes through the frosted glass.*

snowy **Snowy** means white like snow. *The old sailor stroked his snowy beard.*

whole   *adjective*

▶ making up the maximum or full quantity, number, or amount of anything. *Marty gave me the **whole** bag of sunflower seeds.*

complete
: **Complete** means having all its parts. *Fiona has a complete set of those new coins.*

full
: **Full** can mean whole or **complete**. *We will probably never know the full story of what happened.*

entire
: **Entire** means having all the parts, whole, or without a break. *We played cards the entire evening.*

total
: **Total** means making up or having to do with the whole of something. *We each put in enough money to make up the total cost of the farewell gift.*

undivided
: **Undivided** means complete and not shared with anything else. *May we please have your undivided attention.*

> similar keywords: **thorough**
> contrasting keywords: **incomplete**

wide   *adjective*

▶ having a large size from side to side. ***Wide** roads are much safer for motorists to drive on.*

broad
: **Broad** means very wide. *The river is broad when it gets nearer the lake.*

extensive
: **Extensive** means large in size. *They own an extensive piece of land near Saskatoon.*

outspread
: **Outspread** means stretched out wide. *Mahmud stood to welcome us with outspread arms.*

far-reaching
: **Far-reaching** means having an effect over a wide area. *Her article about the polluted stream had a far-reaching effect.*

> similar keywords: **big**
> contrasting keywords: **narrow**

winner *noun*

▶ someone who wins something or gains a victory. *Mona was the **winner** of the prize for the most interesting painting.*

victor	A **victor** can be the winner in any game, fight, and so on. *She was the victor in the tennis match.*
champion	A **champion** is someone who holds first place in a sport or contest. *Jacob is the school's chess champion.*
incumbent	An **incumbent** is the current winner or holder of a position. *The incumbent Member of Parliament will be running for re-election.*
hit	A **hit** can be a great success. *Yoshiko has been a hit at parties since she learned to play the guitar.*

wintry *adjective*

▶ cold and stormy like the season of winter. *It was a **wintry** day, with lots of snow left on the mountains.*

chilly	**Chilly** means causing you to shiver or feel cold. *The water was chilly when we first dove in.*
arctic	**Arctic** means extremely cold, like the icy regions north of the Arctic Circle. *We had to dress very warmly to protect ourselves from the arctic winds of Winnipeg in February.*
raw	**Raw** can mean damp and cold. *The air was raw as we climbed higher.*
bleak	**Bleak** means cold or harsh. *It was a bleak, grey day outside.*
glacial	**Glacial** means icy or as cold as ice. *The glacial weather and blizzards made the rescue mission dangerous.*

> similar keywords: **cold**
> contrasting keywords: **fine, hot**

wipe *verb*

▶ to rub lightly in order to dry or clean. *Please **wipe** off the chalkboard for me.*

mop	To **mop** means to remove, clean, or rub something with a mop. *I mopped up the water I had spilled on the floor.*
blot	To **blot** means to dry or to soak something up. *Sean blotted the spilled juice with a cloth.*
sponge	To **sponge** means to wash or wipe something with a sponge or with something similar. *Mrs. Andrus sponged her little boy's dirty hands and face before lunch.*
swab	To **swab** means to clean or wipe with a large mop, or with a piece of sponge, cloth, or cotton batting. *Go and swab the deck! The nurse swabbed the deep cut in my leg before putting a bandage on it.*
towel	To **towel** means to dry or wipe something with a towel. *I towelled my soaking hair until water stopped dripping down my neck.*

wisecrack *noun*

▶ a smart or amusing remark. *Her **wisecracks** are sometimes inappropriate.*

quip	A **quip** is a clever or sarcastic remark. *Dad's quips about the state of my room can be quite amusing.*
gibe	A **gibe** is a taunting or sarcastic remark. *Max made a cruel gibe about my new shirt.*
in-joke	An **in-joke** is a joke understood only by the people involved in a particular situation. *Every family has its in-jokes.*
pun	A **pun** is a play on words that sound alike but are different in meaning. *The baker who was short of money made a pun when he said he would need some dough.*
witticism	A **witticism** is a joke or witty remark. It is a rather formal word. *If you have to make a speech, try to include a few witticisms so people don't get bored.*

similar keywords: **joke**

wish *noun*

▶ something that you want or long for. *It is my **wish** to finish school and become a journalist.*

desire	A **desire** is a strong wish or need for something. *Alex's main desire in life is to help others less lucky than he is.*
craving	A **craving** is an eager or urgent **desire**. *Mountain climbers usually have a craving for excitement in their lives.*
will	Your **will** can be your wish or **desire**. *They were forced to sell their house against their will.*
yen	A **yen** is a strong wish or longing. *Some days I have a real yen for pizza.*
inclination	**Inclination** means a preference or tendency for something. *Lisa has a strong inclination to travel.*

wonderful *adjective*

▶ causing surprise, wonder, happiness, or excitement. *It was a **wonderful** sight to see the spacecraft taking off.*

marvellous	**Marvellous** means wonderful and surprising. *It was marvellous to see the pictures of the galaxies taken with the new telescope.*
fabulous	**Fabulous** means wonderful and very pleasing. It is more suited to everyday language. *We had a fabulous time visiting the science centre.*
incredible	**Incredible** means amazing or hard to believe because it is so surprising. *It is incredible to think that people will someday live in space.*
extraordinary	**Extraordinary** means unusual or remarkable; not ordinary. *Landing spacecraft on distant planets is an extraordinary achievement.*
phenomenal	**Phenomenal** is very similar to **extraordinary** and means beyond what is ordinary or everyday. *What a phenomenal feeling it would be to travel through space!*

> similar keywords: **astonishing, excellent, great**
> contrasting keywords: **bad, horrible, nasty**

work *noun*

▶ something that needs to be done, using your muscles or your mind. *Farming is challenging* **work**.

labour   **Labour** is hard, tiring work. *The people were sweating after their labour in the fields.*

drudgery   **Drudgery** is hard, boring work. *Oskar hated the drudgery of scrubbing the floors.*

effort   **Effort** is the use of physical strength. *Nicole put a lot of effort into building the wall.*

exertion   **Exertion** is similar to **effort**, and you can often use either word. *The exertion of our long swim tired us.*

diligence   **Diligence** is hard, careful, conscientious effort. *David's success on his report card was due to his diligence.*

> similar keywords: **job, task, achievement**
> contrasting keywords: **rest**

work *verb*

▶ to do something that needs an effort of your body or your mind. *You should* **work** *when you're in class.*

labour   To **labour** means to do hard or tiring work. *They laboured for four months building the houses.*

toil   To **toil** means to work hard for a long time. *Each day the people toiled in the fields.*

slog   To **slog** can mean to work hard at a dull task. *We slogged all day, but there was so much garbage we couldn't clear it all away.*

pull your weight   To **pull your weight** means to do your full share of the work. This is more suited to everyday language. *We all have to pull our weight or we won't finish this project on time.*

> contrasting keywords: **rest, laze**

worry *verb*

▶ to feel anxious or uneasy. *I **worry** when I am running behind on an assignment.*

bother
To **bother** means to worry or to give yourself trouble. *Don't bother about making your bed this morning.*

fret
To **fret** means to be worried or annoyed. *Don't fret; I'll show you how to fix it!*

fuss
To **fuss** means to worry or be anxious about unnecessary things. *That's too trivial to fuss about.*

stew
To **stew** can mean to worry constantly about something. *It does no good to stew for days about losing something.*

similar keywords: **fear, upset, annoy**

worship *verb*

▶ to feel love, esteem, and great respect for someone or something, sometimes in a religious way. *The children **worshipped** their grandmother. Many religions **worship** a Supreme Being.*

revere
To **revere** means to feel deep admiration or a high regard for someone, sometimes in a religious way. *Many religions have leaders, prophets, or saints who are revered.*

respect
To **respect** means to hold someone or something in high regard. *We are taught to respect our elders.*

honour
To **honour** means to show admiration or esteem for someone or something. *We honour the founders of our community by holding a parade every year.*

venerate
To **venerate** means to pay honour to someone or something that you respect very much. *The people venerated her for her humanitarian efforts.*

similar keywords: **love**
contrasting keywords: **insult, slander, hate**

write *verb*

▶ to form letters or words with a pen, pencil, or similar thing. *Ines said she would* ***write*** *the results on the chalkboard.*

print To **print** means to write something in separate letters rather than in letters that are joined together. *I printed the names of the streets on my map.*

scribble To **scribble** means to write something hastily or carelessly. *I scribbled a note to Janos to remind him to bring the sandwiches, but he couldn't read it.*

scrawl To **scrawl** means to write something untidily. *The lead singer scrawled her name in my autograph book.*

doodle To **doodle** means to draw something or **scribble** while you are thinking about something else. *I doodled a pattern of triangles and circles while talking on the phone.*

jot To **jot** means to write down or note something quickly. *I'll just jot down the directions to your place.*

Y, y

yard *noun*

▶ a piece of ground that surrounds or is close to a house, school, or other such building. *I looked out my window and saw my friends waiting in the* **yard**.

lawn A **lawn** is a yard that is covered with closely mowed grass. *We watered our front lawn late in the afternoon.*

enclosure An **enclosure** is a piece of ground surrounded by a fence or some other barrier. *Behind the factory was an enclosure where the equipment was locked up.*

pen A **pen** can be an **enclosure** built especially for animals. *The sick calf was put in a pen by itself.*

courtyard A **courtyard** is a fairly small, open piece of land surrounded by walls or buildings. *At the centre of the museum is a courtyard where visitors can sit in the sun.*

yellow *adjective*

▶ having a bright colour like butter. *The sun was like a big,* **yellow** *ball in the sky.*

lemon **Lemon** means having a clear, light-yellow colour. *My favourite roses are the lemon-coloured ones.*

canary **Canary** can mean having a very bright, clear-yellow colour. *My sister's new canary-coloured sports car is easy to spot in a parking lot.*

tawny **Tawny** means having a yellowish-brown colour. *We admired the lion's rich, tawny coat.*

buff **Buff** means having a light-yellow colour. *Pass me the buff folder, please.*

blond **Blond** means having a light-yellow colour. It is commonly used to refer to hair or furniture. *Gunnar's blond hair turns even lighter in the summer sun.*

young *adjective*

▶ being in the early stage of life or growth. *A **young** wolf is called a cub.*

juvenile   **Juvenile** can be very similar to **young**. It is usually used in more formal language. *The movie was too juvenile for my friends and me.*

adolescent   **Adolescent** means being older than a child, but not yet an adult. *We spend most of our adolescent years at high school.*

junior   **Junior** means younger or made up of younger members. *Naja is a top-ranked gymnast at the junior level.*

youthful   **Youthful** means being young, or looking or behaving as you did when you were young. *Their youthful high spirits sometimes led them into a bit of trouble.*

childish   **Childish** means belonging to or behaving like a child, often in a way that is frowned on. *Throwing a tantrum if you do not get your way is childish behaviour.*

contrasting keywords: **adult**

Appendix

Appendix

Mammals
badger
bat
bear
beaver
bighorn sheep
bison
bobcat
buffalo
caribou
chipmunk
coyote
deer
elk
ermine
fisher
fox
gopher
groundhog (woodchuck)
hare
lemming
lynx
marten
mink
mole
moose
mountain goat
mountain lion (cougar)
mouse
musk-ox
muskrat
opossum
otter
porcupine
pronghorn
rabbit
raccoon
rat
sea lion
seal
shrew
skunk
squirrel
vole
walrus
weasel
whale
wolf
wolverine

Fish
(Fresh-water and Salt-water)
arctic char
bass
bowfin
caplin
carp
catfish
cod
eel
flounder
grayling
haddock
halibut
herring

lamprey
mackerel
menhaden
muskellunge
perch
pickerel
pike
salmon
shad
skate
smelt
sole
splake
stickleback
sturgeon
sucker
sunfish
trout
tuna
walleye
whitefish

Birds

blackbird
bluejay
bobwhite
bunting
Canada goose
cardinal
chickadee
cowbird
crow
cuckoo
dove
duck
eagle

eider
falcon
finch
flicker
gannet
goldfinch
grackle
grebe
grosbeak
grouse
guillemot
gull
hawk
heron
hummingbird
kingfisher
kite
kittiwake
loon
mallard
martin
meadowlark
merganser
nuthatch
oriole
osprey
owl
partridge
pelican
pheasant
phoebe
pigeon
ptarmigan
puffin
quail
robin
sandpiper
sapsucker

sparrow
starling
swallow
swan
swift
tanager
teal
tern
thrush
towhee
turnstone
vireo
warbler
whippoorwill
woodcock
woodpecker
wren

Reptiles

Snakes
brown snake
bull (gopher) snake
fox snake
garter snake
hognose snake
milk snake
night snake
queen snake
racer snake
rat snake
rattlesnake
redbelly snake
ribbon snake
ringneck snake
rubber boa
sharptail snake
smooth green snake
water snake

Lizards
eastern short-horned lizard
five-lined skink
northern alligator lizard
northern prairie skink
pigmy horned lizard
western skink

Turtles
Blanding's turtle
box turtle
leatherback turtle
map turtle
musk turtle
painted turtle
snapping turtle
spiny softshell turtle
spotted turtle
wood turtle

Amphibians

Frogs and Toads
American toad
bullfrog
cricket frog
Fowler's toad
Great Plains toad
green frog
grey tree frog
mink frog
northern leopard frog
Pacific tree frog
pickerel frog
red-legged frog
spade-foot toad
spring peeper
striped chorus frog
tailed frog

western spotted frog
western toad
wood frog

Salamanders
blue-spotted salamander
clouded salamander
dusky salamander
eastern newt
Eschscholtz's salamander
four-toed salamander
Jefferson salamander
long-toed salamander
mudpuppy
northwestern salamander
Pacific giant salamander
redback salamander
roughskin newt
smallmouth salamander
spring salamander
tiger salamander
two-lined salamander
yellow spotted salamander

busy as a beaver
busy as a bee
free as a bird
fast as a cheetah
nervous as a colt
slippery as an eel
sly (crafty) as a fox
quick as a hare
sharp as a hawk
gentle (meek) as a lamb
happy as a lark
strong as a lion
quiet as a mouse
stubborn as a mule
wise as an owl
strong as an ox
proud as a peacock
slow as a snail
hungry as a wolf

Mammals

a *shrewdness* of apes
a *sloth* of bears
a *drove* of cattle
a *herd* of elephants
a *skulk* of foxes
a *trip* of goats
a *team* of horses (while pulling)
a *troop* of kangaroos
a *leap* of leopards
a *pride* of lions
a *nest* of mice
a *troop* of monkeys
a *string* of ponies
a *litter* of pups
a *warren* of rabbits
a *flock* of sheep
a *pod* of whales
a *pack* of wolves

Birds

a *raft* of ducks (while swimming)
a *flock* of ducks (while flying)
a *team* of ducks (while flying in line)
a *gaggle* of geese (while standing)
a *skein* (or *wedge*) of geese (while flying)
a *brood* of hens
a *siege* of herons
a *company* of parrots
a *muster* of peacocks
a *colony* of penguins
a *host* of sparrows
a *wedge* (or *skein*) of swans (while flying)

Reptiles/Amphibians

a *knot* of toads
a *bed* of snakes
a *nest* of vipers

Fish

a *school* of fish
a *smack* of jellyfish

Insects

a *colony* of ants
a *swarm* of bees
an *army* of caterpillars
a *cluster* of grasshoppers
a *plague* of locusts

Meat-eating Dinosaurs

albertosaurus
allosaurus
ceratosaurus
compsognathus
tyrannosaurus

Plant-eating Dinosaurs

ankylosaurus
apatosaurus
brachiosaurus
centrosaurus
diplodocus
edmontosaurus
iguanodon
protoceratops
stegosaurus
styracosaurus
triceratops

Sea Reptiles

ichthyosaurus
mesasaurus
plesiosaurus

Flying Reptiles

pteranodon
pterodactyl
rhamphorhynchus

Birds

ichthyornis
teratornis

Mammals

giant ground sloth
giant wombat
mammoth
mastodon
sabre-toothed tiger

Continents
Africa
Antarctica
Asia
Australia
Europe
North America
South America

Oceans
Arctic
Atlantic
Indian
Pacific

Major Mountain Ranges
Alps
Andes
Himalayas
Pyrenees
Rockies
Urals

Largest Islands
Baffin Island
Borneo
Ellesmere
Great Britain
Greenland
Honshu
Madagascar
New Guinea
Sumatra
Victoria Island

Highest Mountains
Cho Oyu
Dhaulagiri
Everest
K2 (Godwin Austen)
Kanchen
Lhotse I
Lhotse II
Makalu
Manaslu I
Nanga

Largest Seas
Andaman Sea
Bering Sea
Black Sea
Caribbean Sea
East China Sea
Mediterranean Sea
Red Sea
Sea of Japan
Sea of Okhotsk
South China Sea

Largest Fresh-water Lakes
Baikal *(Asia)*
Erie *(North America)*
Great Bear *(North America)*
Great Slave *(North America)*
Huron *(North America)*
Michigan *(North America)*
Nyasa *(Africa)*
Superior *(North America)*
Tanganyika *(Africa)*
Victoria *(Africa)*

Principal Rivers
Amazon *(South America)*
Amur *(Asia)*
Chang Jiang *(Asia)*
Congo (Zaire) *(Africa)*
Huang-Ho *(Asia)*
Lena *(Asia)*
Mackenzie *(North America)*
Mekong *(Asia)*
Nile *(Africa)*
Ob-Irtysh *(Asia)*

Provinces/Territories
Alberta
British Columbia
Manitoba
New Brunswick
Newfoundland
Nova Scotia
Ontario
Prince Edward Island
Québec
Saskatchewan
Northwest Territories
Yukon

Capitals
Edmonton
Victoria
Winnipeg
Fredericton
St. John's
Halifax
Toronto
Charlottetown
Québec City
Regina
Yellowknife
Whitehorse

Principal Rivers
Churchill
Columbia
Fraser
Mackenzie
  Athabasca
  Liard
  Peace
  Nelson
Ottawa
Saskatchewan
  North Saskatchewan
  South Saskatchewan
St. Lawrence
Yukon

Largest Lakes

Athabasca
Erie
Great Bear
Great Slave
Huron
Nettiling
Ontario
Reindeer
Superior
Winnipeg

Important Terms

ballot
cabinet
councillor
democracy
department
election
federal government
governor general
house of commons
legislature
lieutenant-governor
mayor
member of the house of assembly
member of the legislative assembly
member of the national assembly
member of parliament
member of provincial parliament
minister
ministry
municipal government
opposition party
parliament
premier
prime minister
provincial government
regional government
senate
senator
speaker of the house
vote

application (program)

bit

byte (megabyte)

CD-ROM

click (using a mouse)

command

compatible

CPU (central processing unit)

cursor

database

desktop

disk

disk drive

document

E-mail (electronic mail)

file

floppy disk

folder

format

graphics

hard disk

hard drive

icon

information highway

Internet

keyboard

memory

menu

microchip

modem

monitor

mouse

multi-media

network

notebook (computer)

on-line

PC (personal computer)

platform

port

printer

processor

program

scrolling

software (program)

startup disk

system

text

trackball

translation

upgrade

version

virus

window

word processing

Our Solar System:

The Planets (and their number of known moons)

Mercury (0)

Venus (0)

Earth (1)

Mars (2)

Jupiter (16)

Saturn (18, with at least 7 more still to be confirmed)

Uranus (15)

Neptune (8)

Pluto (1)

Selected Terms

asteroid

black hole

comet

constellation

dwarf star

galaxy

meteor (shooting star)

meteorite

Milky Way

moon

nebula

neutron star

nova

planet

pulsar

quasar

red giant

satellite

r

ova

avalanche

blizzard

chinook

cyclone

drought

earthquake

flood

fog

hail

hurricane

landslide

lightning

northern lights

rain

rainbow

sleet

smog

snow

storm

tornado

thunder

tidal wave (tsunami)

typhoon

volcano

alpine (downhill) skiing
archery
auto racing
badminton
baseball
basketball
bobsledding
bowling
boxing
cricket
curling
cycling
diving
equestrian sports
fencing
field hockey
fishing
football
golf
gymnastics
handball
hang-gliding
hiking
(ice) hockey
hunting
judo
karate
kayaking
lacrosse
mountain climbing
Nordic (cross-country) skiing
polo
racquetball
roller-skating
rowing
rugby

running
sailing
skating
snowmobiling
soccer
softball
squash
surfing
swimming
table tennis
tennis
track and field
volleyball
water polo
water-skiing
wrestling

Keyboard Instruments
harpsichord
organ
piano (pianoforte)
synthesizer

Stringed Instruments
balalaika
banjo
bass
bouzouki
cello (violincello)
double bass
dulcimer
guitar
harp
koto
lute
lyre
mandolin
samisen
sitar
ukulele
viola
violin (fiddle)
zither

Wind Instruments
accordion
bagpipes
bassoon
clarinet
double bassoon
fife
flute
harmonica (mouth organ)
kazoo
oboe
panpipe
piccolo
recorder
saxophone

Brass Instruments
bugle
cornet
French horn
trombone
trumpet
tuba

Percussion Instruments
Drums
bongo
conga
kettledrum
side drum
snare drum
steel drum
tabor
tambourine
timbal
timpani
tom-tom

Bells, Gongs, and Chimes

carillon
celesta
cowbell
cymbal
glockenspiel
gong
marimba
triangle
vibraphone (vibes)
xylophone

Other Percussion Instruments

castanet
maraca

Some Musical Terms

bar
beat
harmony
key
melody
note
pitch
rest
rhythm
scale
score
tempo
time
tone
volume

Describing Sweet Sounds

concordant
dulcet
harmonious
in tune
lyrical
melodious
musical
rhythmic
tonal
tuneful

Describing Harsh Sounds

atonal
discordant
dissonant
flat
grating
jarring
off-key
off-pitch
out of tune
sharp

affection

amusement

anger

annoyance

anxiety

awe

bliss

boredom

confidence

courage

curiosity

depression

despair

disliking

distress

ecstasy

embarrassment

envy

excitement

fear

fondness

glee

gratitude

grief

happiness

hate, hatred

hope

humility

insecurity

jealousy

joy

liking

loneliness

love

pity

pride

rage

regret

sadness

sorrow

sympathy

wonder

worry

cower
cry
cuddle
dance
embrace
frown
giggle
glower
grimace
grin
gulp
howl
hug
jump
kiss
laugh
pout
scowl
scream
shiver
shout
shriek
shrug
sigh

sing
smile
smirk
sob
squeal
squirm
strut
sulk
titter
tremble
weep
whimper
whine
whistle

Index

Guide to the Index

What do you do when you want to describe a recent holiday and the only word you can think of is "nice"?

Simple! Start at the INDEX, the back section of the book. The index lists all the words in the thesaurus in alphabetical order. At the top of the page you will find the first and last words on that page.

Look at the sample of the index below. You will find "nice" listed twice. These two entries direct you to two different meanings of this word. All the words in bold (darker) type are keywords.

The first time "nice" is listed it is printed in bold (darker) type, along with its part of speech and the page it is on. The bold type tells you that **nice** is a keyword. This means it is the first word in a word group that has the overall meaning of "nice." If you look up that word group on page 281, you will find the related words *pleasant, enjoyable, lovely,* and *acceptable* listed under "nice." "Pleasant" and "enjoyable" would probably be better words than "nice" to describe your holiday.

The second time "nice" is listed, it is printed in normal type, followed by its part of speech, the keyword **kind** in bold type, and its page number. Obviously, a holiday could never be described as "kind," so it wouldn't be necessary to look up this word group. If, however, you wanted to describe a nice person you met on your holiday, you could look up "kind" on page 237. Here you will find other words with the overall meaning "kind." These are *nice, thoughtful, considerate, unselfish,* and *well-meaning.* Any of these words could be used to describe your friend.

So when you look up a word in the index, it guides you to the right meaning of the word as well as to the page on which you will find it.

Index Sample

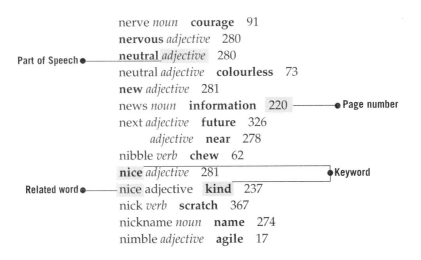

Aa

abandon *verb* **quit** 331

abate *verb* **decrease** 104

abbreviate *verb* **shorten** 379

abduct *verb* 9

abhor *verb* **hate** 195

abide *verb* **endure** 135

able *adjective* **competent** 77

abnormal *adjective* **strange** 409

abode *noun* **home** 204

abolish *verb* **cancel** 56

abominable *adjective* **bad** 34

abominate *verb* **hate** 195

abridge *verb* **shorten** 379

abridged *adjective* **brief** 50

abrupt *adjective* 9

abrupt *adjective* **sudden** 414

abscond *verb* **flee** 162

absconder *noun* **escapee** 139

absent-minded *adjective* **dreamy** 125

absorb *verb* **learn** 243

absurd *adjective* **ridiculous** 353

abundant *adjective* 10

abuse *verb* 10

abysmal *adjective* **bad** 34

accentuate *verb* **emphasize** 132

accept *verb* **believe** 40

acceptable *adjective* **nice** 281

accident *noun* **misfortune** 269

accidental *adjective* 11

accident-prone *adjective* **clumsy** 70

accommodating *adjective* **helpful** 199

accompany *verb* 11

accomplish *verb* 12

accomplishment

     noun **achievement** 13

accumulate *verb* **gather** 178

    verb **increase** 215

accurate *adjective* **precise** 316

    adjective **true** 443

accuse *verb* 12

ace *noun* **expert** 147

ache *noun* **pain** 295

achieve *verb* **accomplish** 12

achievement *noun* 13

acid *adjective* **sour** 398

acknowledge *verb* **admit** 14

acknowledgment *noun* **reaction** 334

acquire *verb* **get** 180

acquittal *noun* **pardon** 296

acquit yourself *verb* **behave** 39

act *noun* **deed** 105

action *noun* **deed** 105

active *adjective* **busy** 53

activate *verb* **start** 404

actor *noun* **entertainer** 137

actual *adjective* 13

adage *noun* **saying** 363

adamant *adjective* **stubborn** 411

adapt *verb* **change** 60

add *verb* 14

add up *verb* **count** 89

additional *adjective* **extra** 148

adept *adjective* **skillful** 388

adequate *adjective* **sufficient** 415

adhesive *noun* **glue** 183

adjacent *adjective* **near** 278

adjourn *verb* **defer** 107

adjudicate *verb* **judge** 234

administrator *noun* **manager** 258

admirable *adjective* **good** 185

admit *verb* 14

admonish *verb* **scold** 366

adolescent *adjective* **young** 479

adopt *verb* **take** 420

adore *verb* **love** 254

adroit *adjective* **skillful** 388

adult *adjective* 15

advance *verb* 15

advance *verb* **further** 177

advantageous *adjective* **useful** 456

adversary *noun* **enemy** 136

advise *verb* 16

advise *verb* **inform** 219

advise against *verb* **discourage** 118

adviser *noun* 16

advocate *verb* **advise** 16

    verb **approve** 25

affected *adjective* **pompous** 310

affectionate *adjective* **loving** 254

affiliated *adjective* **related** 340

affluent *adjective* **wealthy** 467
affront *verb* **insult** 225
afraid *adjective* **frightened** 174
aggravate *verb* **annoy** 22
aggressive *adjective* 17
agile *adjective* 17
agitated *adjective* **upset** 455
agrarian *adjective* **country** 90
agree *verb* 18
agreeable *adjective* 18
aid *noun* **help** 197
    verb **help** 198
aide *noun* **helper** 198
ailing *adjective* **sick** 383
aim *verb* **intend** 226
air-condition *verb* **cool** 86
akin *adjective* **similar** 386
alarm *verb* **frighten** 173
alarmed *adjective* **frightened** 174
alert *adjective* 19
alert *verb* **warn** 464
alias *noun* **name** 274
alien *adjective* **foreign** 169
alight *verb* **land** 240
alike *adjective* **similar** 386
allege *verb* **accuse** 12
alleviate *verb* **comfort** 75
allied *adjective* **related** 340
allocate *verb* **distribute** 123
allocation *noun* **share** 376
allot *verb* **distribute** 123
allotment *noun* **share** 376
allow *verb* 19
allowance *noun* **gift** 181
all right *adjective* **good** 185
all thumbs *adjective* **clumsy** 70
allude to *verb* **hint** 201
alone *adjective* **lonely** 252
aloof *adjective* **unfriendly** 450
alter *verb* **change** 60
altercation *noun* **argument** 26
alternative *noun* **choice** 63
    adjective **unconventional** 447
amalgamate *verb* **combine** 74
amass *verb* **gather** 178
amateur *adjective* **inexperienced** 217

amateurish
    adjective **incompetent** 213
amazed *adjective* **astonished** 29
amazing *adjective* **astonishing** 30
amber *adjective* **orange** 290
ambiguous *adjective* **confusing** 84
ambivalent *adjective* **confused** 83
amble *verb* **walk** 463
ambush *noun* **attack** 30
    verb **catch** 59
amend *verb* **correct** 88
amiable *adjective* **agreeable** 18
amnesty *noun* **pardon** 296
ample *adjective* **abundant** 10
    adjective **big** 42
amplify *verb* **enlarge** 137
    verb **expand** 144
amusing *adjective* **funny** 176
analyze *verb* **examine** 140
ancestor *noun* 20
ancient *adjective* **old** 287
anger *noun* 20
anger *verb* 21
angry *adjective* 21
anguish *noun* **misery** 268
animated *adjective* **energetic** 136
animosity *noun* **dislike** 120
annihilate *verb* **destroy** 112
announce *verb* **inform** 219
annoy *verb* 22
annoyed *adjective* 22
annoying *adjective* 23
annul *verb* **cancel** 56
answer *verb* 23
answer *noun* **reaction** 334
antagonist *noun* **enemy** 136
antagonistic *adjective* **defiant** 108
antecedents *noun* **ancestor** 20
anthem *noun* **song** 397
anthology *noun* **book** 46
anticipate *verb* **expect** 145
anticlimax *noun* **disappointment** 116
antipathy *noun* **dislike** 120
antiquated
    adjective **old-fashioned** 288
antique *adjective* **old** 287

antithetical *adjective* **opposite** 289

anxious *adjective* **enthusiastic** 138

    adjective **nervous** 280

apathetic *adjective* 24

ape *verb* **mimic** 266

aperture *noun* **hole** 203

apex *noun* **top** 437

apologetic *adjective* **sorry** 398

appall *verb* **shock** 378

apparel *noun* **clothing** 68

apparition *noun* **ghost** 181

appeal to *verb* **please** 307

appear *verb* 24

appearance *noun* 25

appease *verb* **pacify** 295

append *verb* **add** 14

appetizing *adjective* **delicious** 109

    adjective **tasty** 423

appointment *noun* **meeting** 263

    noun **position** 311

apportion *verb* **share** 376

appraise *verb* **judge** 234

appreciate *verb* **like** 248

appreciative *adjective* **grateful** 187

apprehend *verb* **capture** 57

apprehensive *adjective* **nervous** 280

apprentice *noun* **student** 411

apprenticeship *noun* **profession** 321

approach *noun* **method** 265

appropriate *adjective* **sufficient** 415

    verb **take** 420

approval *noun* **permission** 301

approve *verb* 25

approximate *adjective* **vague** 458

apt *adjective* **likely** 248

aqua *adjective* **blue** 44

arbitrary *adjective* **irrational** 229

arbitrate *verb* **negotiate** 279

archaic *adjective* **old-fashioned** 288

arctic *adjective* **wintry** 472

arduous *adjective* **difficult** 113

argue *verb* 26

argument *noun* 26

argumentative *adjective* 27

arid *adjective* **dry** 128

arise *verb* **happen** 192

aristocratic

    adjective **distinguished** 123

aroma *noun* **smell** 392

arrange *verb* 27

arrange *verb* **plan** 306

arrest *verb* **capture** 57

arrive *verb* **come** 74

arrogant *adjective* **proud** 325

artful *adjective* **cunning** 97

articulate *adjective* **fluent** 165

    verb **pronounce** 323

ascend *verb* **climb** 67

ascertain *verb* **realize** 335

as good as gold *adjective*

    well-behaved 468

ashamed *adjective* **sorry** 398

ask *verb* 28

aspect *noun* **appearance** 25

asphyxiate *verb* **suffocate** 415

assassinate *verb* **kill** 236

assault *noun* **attack** 30

    verb **attack** 31

assemble *verb* 28

assemble *verb* **combine** 74

assembly *noun* **club** 69

assent *verb* **agree** 18

assess *verb* **examine** 140

assets *noun* **property** 323

assignation *noun* **meeting** 263

assignment *noun* **task** 422

assimilate *verb* **learn** 243

assist *verb* **help** 198

assistance *noun* **help** 197

assistant *noun* **helper** 198

associate *noun* 29

associated *adjective* **related** 340

associate with *verb* **accompany** 11

association *noun* **club** 69

assorted *adjective* **various** 458

assume *verb* **believe** 40

astonished *adjective* 29

astonishing *adjective* 30

astound *verb* **shock** 378

astounded *adjective* **astonished** 29

astounding *adjective* **astonishing** 30

astute *adjective* **shrewd** 381

asylum *noun* **refuge** 339
asymmetrical *adjective* **uneven** 449
athletic *adjective* **agile** 17
atrocious *adjective* **bad** 34
atrophy *verb* **shrink** 382
attach *verb* **add** 14
attack *noun* 30
attack *verb* 31
attack *verb* **attempt** 32
attain *verb* **accomplish** 12
attempt *noun* 31
attempt *verb* 32
attend *verb* **visit** 461
attend to *verb* **concentrate** 80
attentive *adjective* **alert** 19
    adjective **careful** 57
attire *noun* **clothing** 68
attitude *noun* **behaviour** 39
    noun **manner** 259
    noun **opinion** 289
attract *verb* 32
attract *verb* **please** 307
attractive *adjective* 33
attractive *adjective* **pretty** 318
at your peak *adjective* **adult** 15
auction *verb* **sell** 370
audition *noun* **test** 427
augment *verb* **enlarge** 137
auspicious *adjective* **lucky** 255
austere *adjective* **strict** 410
authentic *adjective* **genuine** 180
authority *noun* **expert** 147
authorize *verb* **allow** 19
authorized *adjective* **legal** 244
autocratic *adjective* **bossy** 48
auxiliary *adjective* **subordinate** 413
available *adjective* **ready** 335
avaricious *adjective* **greedy** 188
avenge *verb* **retaliate** 350
average *adjective* **ordinary** 291
averse *adjective* **unwilling** 454
aversion *noun* **dislike** 120
avid *adjective* **enthusiastic** 138
avoid *verb* 33
award *noun* **prize** 320
    verb **give** 182

awareness *noun* **feeling** 157
awful *adjective* **nasty** 276
awkward *adjective* **clumsy** 70
azure *adjective* **blue** 44

Bb

babble *verb* **rave** 333
back into *verb* **reverse** 352
backing *noun* **help** 197
backlog *noun* **excess** 142
bad *adjective* 34
badly behaved *adjective* **naughty** 277
baffle *verb* **puzzle** 329
bake *verb* **toast** 436
balance *noun* **remains** 342
bald *adjective* **bare** 36
ball *noun* 34
ballad *noun* **song** 397
ballast *noun* **weight** 468
balmy *adjective* **fine** 160
ban *verb* 35
banal *adjective* **mediocre** 262
band *noun* **group** 191
bandit *noun* 35
bang *verb* **beat** 37
banish *verb* **expel** 145
bankrupt *adjective* **broke** 52
bar *verb* **ban** 35
    verb **block** 44
barbaric *adjective* **cruel** 96
barbecue *verb* **toast** 436
bare *adjective* 36
bargain for *verb* **expect** 145
barge in *verb* **intrude** 227
barricade *verb* **block** 44
barrier *noun* **obstacle** 285
barrister *noun* **lawyer** 241
base *noun* **bottom** 49
bashful *adjective* **shy** 383
basin *noun* **lake** 239
bat *verb* **hit** 202
battle *noun* **fight** 159

bawl *verb* **cry** 97
    verb **shout** 380
bay *noun* 36
be *verb* **live** 251
beach *noun* **shore** 379
beam *verb* **shine** 377
bear *verb* **produce** 321
bearing *noun* **manner** 259
bear out *verb* **prove** 325
beat *verb* 37
beat *noun* **rhythm** 353
    verb **defeat** 106
    verb **pass** 297
    verb **throb** 434
beat up *verb* **attack** 31
beautiful *adjective* 37
bed *noun* **bottom** 49
bedraggled *adjective* **scruffy** 367
beeline *noun* **course** 92
befriend *verb* 38
beg *verb* **ask** 28
begin *verb* 38
beginning *noun* **start** 403
beguile *verb* **charm** 61
behave *verb* 39
behaviour *noun* 39
beige *adjective* **brown** 52
belief *noun* **religion** 341
believable *adjective* 40
believe *verb* 40
belittle *verb* **insult** 225
bellicose *adjective* **warlike** 464
belligerent *adjective* **aggressive** 17
bellow *verb* **shout** 380
belly *noun* **inside** 223
belongings *noun* **property** 323
be lost in thought *verb* **daydream** 102
bemused *adjective* **dreamy** 125
bend *verb* 41
beneficial *adjective* **useful** 456
benefit *verb* **thrive** 433
bent *adjective* **crooked** 95
beseech *verb* **ask** 28
best *adjective* 41
betray *verb* 42
better *verb* **improve** 212

bewilder *verb* **puzzle** 329
bewildering *adjective* **confusing** 84
bewitch *verb* **charm** 61
bias *verb* **influence** 219
biased *adjective* **narrow-minded** 276
bicker *verb* **disagree** 115
bid *noun* **offer** 286
big *adjective* 42
big-headed *adjective* **conceited** 79
bigoted *adjective* **narrow-minded** 276
billow *verb* **protrude** 324
bistro *noun* **restaurant** 349
bitter *adjective* **resentful** 346
    adjective **sour** 398
bizarre *adjective* **strange** 409
blab *verb* 43
black *adjective* 43
blackmail *verb* **threaten** 432
bland *adjective* **tasteless** 423
blank *adjective* **empty** 132
blanket *verb* **cover** 92
blaring *adjective* **loud** 253
blasé *adjective* **bored** 47
blaze *verb* **shine** 377
blazing *adjective* **hot** 205
bleached *adjective* **colourless** 73
bleak *adjective* **dreary** 126
    adjective **wintry** 472
blemish *noun* **mark** 260
blend *verb* **combine** 74
bless *verb* **approve** 25
blessed *adjective* **holy** 203
blissful *adjective* **joyful** 233
block *verb* 44
blockade *verb* **block** 44
blond *adjective* **yellow** 478
bloodthirsty *adjective* **warlike** 464
bloom *verb* **flourish** 164
    verb **thrive** 433
blossom *verb* **flourish** 164
    verb **thrive** 433
blot *noun* **mark** 260
    verb **wipe** 473
blow *noun* **disappointment** 116
    noun **misfortune** 269
    verb **waste** 465

buccaneer *noun* **bandit** 35
buckled *adjective* **crooked** 95
budge *verb* **move** 272
buff *adjective* **yellow** 478
    verb **polish** 309
build *verb* 53
build *noun* **shape** 375
bulge *verb* **protrude** 324
bulky *adjective* **big** 42
bulldoze *verb* **force** 168
bulletin *noun* **report** 346
bully *verb* **force** 168
bump into *verb* **meet** 263
bumpy *adjective* **rough** 355
bunch *noun* **group** 191
buoyant *adjective* **optimistic** 290
burden *noun* **weight** 468
burglar *noun* **thief** 429
burly *adjective* **stocky** 407
burn *verb* **shine** 377
burnish *verb* **polish** 309
bursting *adjective* **full** 176
bush *noun* **country, the** 91
bushed *adjective* **tired** 436
business *noun* **job** 231
busy *adjective* 53
butter up *verb* **flatter** 162
butt in *verb* **intrude** 227
buy *verb* 54
buyer *noun* 54
buzz *verb* **throb** 434
bygone *adjective* **past** 297

Cc

cadence *noun* **rhythm** 353
café *noun* **restaurant** 349
cafeteria *noun* **restaurant** 349
cajole *verb* **flatter** 162
calamity *noun* **disaster** 117
calculate *verb* 55
call *verb* **name** 275
    verb **visit** 461

callous *adjective* 55
calm *adjective* 56
calm *verb* **pacify** 295
camouflage *verb* **hide** 200
canary *adjective* **yellow** 478
cancel *verb* 56
candid *adjective* **frank** 171
candied *adjective* **sweet** 419
canny *adjective* **shrewd** 381
cantankerous
       adjective **argumentative** 27
capable *adjective* **competent** 77
caper *verb* **frolic** 175
capital *noun* **city** 64
    noun **wealth** 467
capitulate *verb* **give in** 182
capricious *adjective* **fickle** 158
capsize *verb* **overturn** 294
captive *noun* **prisoner** 320
capture *verb* 57
carcinogenic *adjective* **poisonous** 308
career *noun* **job** 231
care for *verb* **love** 254
careful *adjective* 57
careful *adjective* **wary** 465
careless *adjective* 58
caress *verb* **touch** 437
caricature *verb* **mimic** 266
carriage *noun* **manner** 259
carry *verb* 58
cash in *verb* **retrieve** 351
casual *adjective* **careless** 58
    adjective **informal** 220
    adjective **temporary** 426
catastrophe *noun* **disaster** 117
catch *verb* 59
catch on *verb* **realize** 335
catch your eye *verb* **attract** 32
caucus *noun* **council** 88
cause *verb* 59
caution *verb* **warn** 464
cautious *adjective* **wary** 465
cease *verb* **end** 134
celebrate *verb* **rejoice** 340
celebrated *adjective* **famous** 152
celebrity *noun* **star** 402

cell *noun* **prison** 319

    noun **room** 354

cement *noun* **glue** 183

censor *verb* **ban** 35

centre *noun* 60

ceremonial *adjective* **formal** 170

certain *adjective* **sure** 418

    adjective **true** 443

chafe *verb* **roughen** 356

chain *noun* **series** 373

chamber *noun* **room** 354

champion *noun* **winner** 472

    verb **befriend** 38

chance *adjective* **accidental** 11

    noun **fate** 155

change *verb* 60

changeable *adjective* **fickle** 158

channel *noun* **groove** 190

chaotic *adjective* **untidy** 453

chap *verb* **roughen** 356

chaperone *verb* **accompany** 11

character *noun* **virtue** 460

charcoal *adjective* **grey** 189

charge *noun* **price** 319

    verb **accuse** 12

    verb **attack** 31

charisma *noun* **influence** 218

charismatic *adjective* **attractive** 33

charitable *adjective* **generous** 179

charity *noun* **help** 197

charm *verb* 61

charm *verb* **please** 307

charmed *adjective* **lucky** 255

charming *adjective* **agreeable** 18

chase *verb* **follow** 166

chastise *verb* **punish** 328

chat *verb* **talk** 421

chatty *adjective* **talkative** 421

cheap *adjective* 61

cheat *verb* 62

cheat *noun* **crook** 94

check *verb* **test** 427

checkup *noun* **test** 427

cheerful *adjective* **happy** 193

cheerless *adjective* **dreary** 126

cherish *verb* **love** 254

chew *verb* 62

chic *adjective* 63

chicken out *verb* **cower** 93

chide *verb* **scold** 366

chief *adjective* **main** 256

    noun **boss** 48

childish *adjective* **young** 479

chill *verb* **cool** 86

chilly *adjective* **wintry** 472

chime *verb* **ring** 354

chink *noun* **hole** 203

choice *noun* 63

choice *adjective* **superior** 417

choke *verb* **suffocate** 415

chomp *verb* **chew** 62

choose *verb* 64

choose *verb* **intend** 226

chore *noun* **task** 422

chubby *adjective* **fat** 154

chuckle *verb* **laugh** 241

circle *noun* **group** 191

circumvent *verb* **outwit** 293

city *noun* 64

civic *adjective* 65

claim *noun* **demand** 109

clamber up *verb* **climb** 67

clarify *verb* **explain** 147

clash *noun* **conflict** 82

    verb **argue** 26

clasp *verb* **hold** 202

class *noun* **grade** 186

    noun **lesson** 246

classified *adjective* **secret** 368

classify *verb* **arrange** 27

classy *adjective* **distinguished** 123

claw *verb* **scratch** 367

clay *noun* **earth** 129

clean *adjective* 65

clean *verb* 66

cleanse *verb* **clean** 66

clear *adjective* 66

clear *adjective* **sure** 418

    adjective **transparent** 439

    verb **forgive** 169

clearance *noun* **permission** 301

clever *adjective* 67

client *noun* **buyer** 54
climb *verb* 67
climb down *verb* **descend** 111
cling to *verb* **hold** 202
clip *verb* **cut** 98
close *adjective* **humid** 207
    adjective **narrow** 275
    adjective **near** 278
    noun **end** 134
    verb **block** 44
    verb **finish** 161
clot *verb* **thicken** 429
cloth *noun* 68
clothing *noun* 68
cloudy *adjective* 69
cloudy *adjective* **opaque** 288
clout *noun* **influence** 218
club *noun* 69
clumsy *adjective* 70
cluster *noun* **heap** 196
clutch *verb* **hold** 202
clutter *noun* **mess** 264
coach *verb* **teach** 424
coagulate *verb* **thicken** 429
coarse *adjective* **rough** 355
    adjective **vulgar** 462
coarsen *verb* **roughen** 356
coast *noun* **shore** 379
    verb **descend** 111
coat *verb* 70
coating *noun* 71
coax *verb* **persuade** 303
cobble *noun* **stone** 407
coerce *verb* **force** 168
coil *noun* 71
coiled *adjective* **twisted** 444
coin *verb* **invent** 228
coincidental *adjective* **accidental** 11
cold *adjective* 72
cold *adjective* **unfriendly** 450
cold-blooded *adjective* **callous** 55
collaborate *verb* **cooperate** 86
collaborator *noun* **associate** 29
collapse *verb* **fail** 149
    verb **sag** 360
colleague *noun* **associate** 29

collect *verb* **gather** 178
collective *adjective* **public** 326
colloquialism *noun* **language** 240
collude *verb* **plot** 308
colonize *verb* **inhabit** 221
colossal *adjective* **huge** 206
colour *verb* 72
colourful *adjective* 73
colourless *adjective* 73
comatose *adjective* **unconscious** 447
combat *noun* **fight** 159
combative *adjective* **aggressive** 17
combine *verb* 74
combine *verb* **cooperate** 86
come *verb* 74
come *verb* **appear** 24
come about *verb* **happen** 192
come across *verb* **meet** 263
comedian *noun* **entertainer** 137
come to blows *verb* **fight** 159
comfort *noun* 75
comfort *verb* 75
comfortable *adjective* **satisfied** 362
comical *adjective* **funny** 176
command *noun* **order** 291
    verb **rule** 358
commence *verb* **begin** 38
commencement *noun* **start** 403
commend *verb* **praise** 315
commendable *adjective* **good** 185
comment *noun* 76
commission *noun* **pay** 299
commodious *adjective* **spacious** 399
common *adjective* **public** 326
    adjective **subordinate** 413
    adjective **vulgar** 462
commotion *noun* 76
communal *adjective* **public** 326
communicative
    adjective **talkative** 421
communiqué *noun* **message** 264
commuter *noun* **traveller** 440
compact *adjective* **thick** 428
companion *noun* **friend** 172
company *noun* **organization** 292
comparable *adjective* **similar** 386

cove *noun* **bay** 36
cover *verb* 92
cover *verb* **hide** 200
          verb **include** 213
covet *verb* **want** 463
covetous *adjective* **jealous** 231
cowardly *adjective* **fearful** 156
cower *verb* 93
crack *noun* **attempt** 31
          noun **break** 50
          noun **joke** 232
          verb **solve** 397
cradle *verb* **hug** 206
craft *noun* **profession** 321
crafty *adjective* **cunning** 97
crammed *adjective* **full** 176
cramp *noun* **pain** 295
cramped *adjective* **narrow** 275
cranky *adjective* **annoyed** 22
crave *verb* **want** 463
craving *noun* **wish** 474
craze *noun* **fashion** 153
crazy *adjective* **mad** 256
cream *adjective* **white** 470
creamy *adjective* **smooth** 394
create *verb* 93
credible *adjective* **believable** 40
creed *noun* **religion** 341
creepy *adjective* **frightening** 174
crest *noun* **top** 437
crevice *noun* **break** 50
cried *verb* **said** 361
criminal *noun* 94
criminal *adjective* **illegal** 209
crimson *adjective* **red** 338
cringe *verb* **cower** 93
critical *adjective* **significant** 385
criticize *verb* **fault** 155
crook *noun* 94
crooked *adjective* 95
crooked *adjective* **dishonest** 119
cross *verb* 95
crotchety *adjective* **grumpy** 191
crow *verb* **boast** 45
crowd *noun* 96
crowded *adjective* **full** 176

crucial *adjective* **necessary** 278
crude *adjective* **vulgar** 462
cruel *adjective* 96
cruise *verb* **sail** 361
crumbling *adjective* **decrepit** 105
crummy *adjective* **inferior** 218
crust *noun* **coating** 71
cry *verb* 97
crystal *adjective* **transparent** 439
cubicle *noun* **room** 354
cuddle *verb* **hug** 206
cuisine *noun* **food** 167
cunning *adjective* 97
cunning *noun* **trickery** 442
curb *verb* **limit** 249
curdle *verb* **thicken** 429
curiosity *noun* **miracle** 267
curious *adjective* **inquisitive** 222
curl *noun* **coil** 71
        verb **bend** 41
current *adjective* **modern** 271
cursed *adjective* **unlucky** 452
cursor *noun* **indicator** 216
curt *adjective* **abrupt** 9
curtail *verb* **subtract** 413
curve *verb* **bend** 41
custom *noun* **tradition** 439
customary *adjective* **usual** 457
customer *noun* **buyer** 54
cut *noun* 98
cut *verb* 98
cut *noun* **share** 376
cute *adjective* **pretty** 318
cut off *verb* **interrupt** 227
cycle *noun* **series** 373

Dd

dainty *adjective* **slight** 390
dally *verb* **dawdle** 102
dam *noun* **lake** 239
damage *verb* 99
damn *verb* **fault** 155
damp *adjective* **wet** 469

dampen *verb*　**wet**　469
dance *verb*　**frolic**　175
dangerous *adjective*　99
dank *adjective*　**wet**　469
dapper *adjective*　**chic**　63
dare *verb*　100
dark *adjective*　100
dark *adjective*　**black**　43
darken *verb*　101
darn *verb*　**sew**　374
dart *verb*　101
dash *noun*　**trace**　438
　　verb　**hurry**　208
dash off *verb*　**compose**　79
data *noun*　**information**　220
date *noun*　**meeting**　263
dated *adjective*　**old-fashioned**　288
daub *verb*　**coat**　70
dawdle *verb*　102
daydream *verb*　102
daze *verb*　**confuse**　83
dazed *adjective*　**unconscious**　447
dazzling *adjective*　**bright**　51
dead *adjective*　103
deadlock *noun*　**halt**　192
deadly *adjective*　**fatal**　154
deafening *adjective*　**loud**　253
dealer *noun*　**seller**　371
dear *adjective*　**expensive**　146
dearth *noun*　**lack**　239
debacle *noun*　**disaster**　117
debatable *adjective*　**uncertain**　446
debate *noun*　**talk**　420
debilitated *adjective*　**weak**　466
debris *noun*　**rubbish**　356
decay *verb*　**rot**　355
deceased *adjective*　**dead**　103
deceit *noun*　**trickery**　442
deceitful *adjective*　**dishonest**　119
deceive *verb*　103
decency *noun*　**virtue**　460
decent *adjective*　104
decent *adjective*　**sufficient**　415
decide *verb*　**choose**　64
　　verb　**negotiate**　279
declare *verb*　**publish**　327

decline *verb*　**deteriorate**　112
　　verb　**refuse**　339
decompose *verb*　**rot**　355
decrease *verb*　104
decree *noun*　**order**　291
decrepit *adjective*　105
deduce *verb*　**conclude**　81
deduct *verb*　**subtract**　413
deed *noun*　105
defame *verb*　**slander**　389
defeat *verb*　106
defective *adjective*　106
defence *noun*　107
defend *verb*　**befriend**　38
　　verb　**protect**　324
defer *verb*　107
defiant *adjective*　108
deficiency *noun*　**lack**　239
deficient *adjective*　**insufficient**　225
deficit *noun*　**lack**　239
definite *adjective*　**precise**　316
　　adjective　**sure**　418
deflect *verb*　**bend**　41
defraud *verb*　**cheat**　62
deft *adjective*　**skillful**　388
defuse *verb*　**pacify**　295
defy *verb*　**disobey**　121
　　verb　**resist**　347
degenerate *verb*　**deteriorate**　112
dehydrated *adjective*　**dry**　128
delay *verb*　**dawdle**　102
　　verb　**defer**　107
delete *verb*　**exclude**　144
deliberate *adjective*　108
deliberate *adjective*　**wary**　465
delicate *adjective*　**fragile**　170
　　adjective　**slight**　390
delicious *adjective*　109
delight *verb*　**please**　307
delighted *adjective*　**glad**　183
delinquent *adjective*　**disobedient**　120
delirious *adjective*　**excited**　143
deliver *verb*　**carry**　58
　　verb　**free**　172
delude *verb*　**deceive**　103
deluxe *adjective*　**superior**　417

delve into *verb* **investigate** 228
demand *noun* 109
demand *verb* 110
demanding *adjective* **difficult** 113
dematerialize *verb* **disappear** 116
demeanour *noun* **behaviour** 39
demolish *verb* **destroy** 112
demonstrate *verb* **show** 380
demure *adjective* **shy** 383
den *noun* **room** 354
denomination *noun* **religion** 341
denounce *verb* **accuse** 12
dense *adjective* **opaque** 288
    adjective **thick** 428
dent *noun* **mark** 260
depart *verb* **leave** 244
departed *adjective* **dead** 103
dependable *adjective* **reliable** 341
dependant *noun* 110
depict *verb* **describe** 111
deportment *noun* **behaviour** 39
deposit *noun* **layer** 242
    verb **place** 306
depraved *adjective* **indecent** 215
depressed *adjective* **miserable** 268
depressing *adjective* **dreary** 126
    adjective **pessimistic** 304
deprivation *noun* **poverty** 313
deputy *noun* **helper** 198
descend *verb* 111
descendant *noun* **offspring** 287
describe *verb* 111
desert *verb* **quit** 331
deserted *adjective* **empty** 132
design *noun* **shape** 375
    verb **create** 93
desire *noun* **wish** 474
    verb **want** 463
despicable *adjective* **mean** 261
despise *verb* **hate** 195
despotic *adjective* **tyrannical** 444
destiny *noun* **fate** 155
destitute *adjective* **broke** 52
destitution *noun* **poverty** 313
destroy *verb* 112
detach *verb* **separate** 373

detached *adjective* **neutral** 280
detailed *adjective* **thorough** 431
detect *verb* **find** 160
detention centre *noun* **prison** 319
deter *verb* **discourage** 118
deteriorate *verb* 112
determine *verb* **calculate** 55
    verb **conclude** 81
detest *verb* **hate** 195
develop *verb* **create** 93
    verb **expand** 144
devilish *adjective* **naughty** 277
devious *adjective* **cunning** 97
devise *verb* **create** 93
    verb **invent** 228
devoted *adjective* **faithful** 150
    adjective **loving** 254
devotion *noun* **respect** 348
devour *verb* **eat** 130
devout *adjective* **religious** 342
dexterous *adjective* **skillful** 388
dialect *noun* **language** 240
dialogue *noun* **talk** 420
diary *noun* **book** 46
dictatorial *adjective* **bossy** 48
die *verb* 113
differ *verb* **disagree** 115
difference of opinion
        noun **argument** 26
different *adjective* **unlike** 451
difficult *adjective* 113
diffident *adjective* **shy** 383
dig *verb* 114
digest *verb* **learn** 243
digit *noun* **number** 283
dignified *adjective* **grand** 187
digress *verb* **ramble** 332
dilapidated *adjective* **decrepit** 105
diligence *noun* **work** 475
diligent *adjective* **careful** 57
dim *adjective* **dark** 100
    verb **darken** 101
diminish *verb* **decrease** 104
    verb **subtract** 413
din *noun* **noise** 282
diner *noun* **restaurant** 349

dingy *adjective* **drab** 125
dip *verb* **drop** 127
direct *adjective* **frank** 171
    verb **manage** 258
director *noun* **manager** 258
dirge *noun* **song** 397
dirt *noun* **earth** 129
dirty *adjective* 114
dirty *verb* 115
disable *verb* **weaken** 466
disadvantaged *adjective* **poor** 311
disagree *verb* 115
disagreement *noun* **conflict** 82
disappear *verb* 116
disappointed
    adjective **dissatisfied** 122
disappointment *noun* 116
disapprove of *verb* 117
disarray *noun* **mess** 264
disaster *noun* 117
disaster *noun* **failure** 149
disbelieve *verb* **doubt** 124
discard *verb* 118
disciple *noun* **student** 411
discipline *verb* **punish** 328
disclose *verb* **reveal** 352
disconnect *verb* **interrupt** 227
    verb **separate** 373
discontented *adjective* **dissatisfied** 122
discount *adjective* **cheap** 61
discourage *verb* 118
discouraging *adjective* **pessimistic** 304
discover *verb* **find** 160
    verb **realize** 335
discreet *adjective* **wary** 465
discriminatory *adjective* **unfair** 449
discuss *verb* **talk** 421
discussion *noun* **talk** 420
disdain *noun* **scorn** 366
disembark *verb* **land** 240
disentangle *verb* **simplify** 387
disgruntled *adjective* **dissatisfied** 122
disguise *verb* **hide** 200
disgust *verb* 119
disheartening
    adjective **pessimistic** 304

dishevelled *adjective* **scruffy** 367
dishonest *adjective* 119
disinclined *adjective* **unwilling** 454
disinterested *adjective* **neutral** 280
disjointed *adjective* **inarticulate** 212
dislike *noun* 120
dislodge *verb* **remove** 343
disloyal *adjective* **unfaithful** 450
dismal *adjective* **dreary** 126
    adjective **pathetic** 298
dismount *verb* **land** 240
disobedient *adjective* 120
disobey *verb* 121
disorganized *adjective* **untidy** 453
disparate *adjective* **unlike** 451
dispatch *noun* **message** 264
    verb **send** 371
dispel *verb* **repel** 345
dispensable
    adjective **insignificant** 224
dispense *verb* **distribute** 123
disperse *verb* **scatter** 365
display *verb* **show** 380
displeased *adjective* **dissatisfied** 122
dispute *noun* **argument** 26
    verb **disagree** 115
disqualify *verb* **ban** 35
disregard *verb* **neglect** 279
disrespect *noun* **scorn** 366
disrupt *verb* 121
dissatisfied *adjective* 122
dissent *verb* **disagree** 115
dissident *adjective* **defiant** 108
dissimilar *adjective* **unlike** 451
dissipate *verb* **scatter** 365
dissolve *verb* **cancel** 56
    verb **disappear** 116
dissuade *verb* **discourage** 118
distant *adjective* 122
distinct *adjective* **obvious** 286
distinguished *adjective* 123
distort *verb* **misrepresent** 269
distorted *adjective* **crooked** 95
distract *verb* **confuse** 83
distress *verb* **upset** 455
distribute *verb* 123

distribute *verb* **scatter** 365
distrust *verb* **doubt** 124
disturb *verb* **disrupt** 121
    verb **interrupt** 227
    verb **upset** 455
disturbed *adjective* **mad** 256
    adjective **upset** 455
ditch *noun* **groove** 190
    verb **discard** 118
dive *verb* **dart** 101
diverge *verb* **ramble** 332
diverse *adjective* **various** 458
divide *verb* **separate** 373
    verb **share** 376
dividend *noun* **profit** 322
divine *verb* **predict** 316
divulge *verb* **blab** 43
divvy up *verb* **share** 376
docile *adjective* **obedient** 284
dock *verb* **land** 240
    verb **subtract** 413
document *noun* **report** 346
dogged *adjective* **persistent** 303
dole out *verb* **share** 376
dominant *adjective* **powerful** 313
dominate *verb* **rule** 358
donate *verb* **give** 182
donation *noun* **gift** 181
doodle *verb* **write** 477
dossier *noun* **report** 346
dote on *verb* **love** 254
double *adjective* 124
double-cross *verb* **betray** 42
doubt *verb* 124
doubtful *adjective* **uncertain** 446
dour *adjective* **solemn** 396
douse *verb* **wet** 469
do without *verb* **sacrifice** 359
down *adjective* **miserable** 268
down-to-earth *adjective* **practical** 314
downtrodden
    adjective **submissive** 412
downy *adjective* **soft** 395
doze *verb* **sleep** 389
drab *adjective* 125
draft *verb* **compose** 79

drag *verb* **pull** 327
drain *verb* **tire** 435
draw *verb* **attract** 32
    verb **pull** 327
drawback *noun* **obstacle** 285
dread *verb* **fear** 156
dreadful *adjective* **horrible** 205
dream *verb* **imagine** 210
dreamy *adjective* 125
dreary *adjective* 126
drench *verb* **soak** 395
dress *noun* **clothing** 68
dribble *verb* **drip** 127
drift *noun* **meaning** 261
drill *noun* **practice** 315
    verb **teach** 424
drink *verb* 126
drip *verb* 127
drive *verb* **force** 168
    verb **push** 329
drive someone up the wall
    verb **anger** 21
drivel *noun* **nonsense** 282
drizzle *verb* **rain** 332
droll *adjective* **funny** 176
droop *verb* **sag** 360
drop *verb* 127
drop *noun* **trace** 438
    verb **descend** 111
    verb **exclude** 144
drop by *verb* **visit** 461
drowse *verb* **sleep** 389
drudgery *noun* **work** 475
dry *adjective* 128
dual *adjective* **double** 124
dub *verb* **name** 275
dull *adjective* 128
dull *adjective* **boring** 47
    adjective **cloudy** 69
dump *verb* **discard** 118
dupe *verb* **deceive** 103
duplicate *adjective* **double** 124
    noun **copy** 87
    verb **copy** 87
durable *adjective* **hardy** 195
dutiful *adjective* **reliable** 341

duty *noun* **task** 422
dwell *verb* **reside** 347
dwelling *noun* **home** 204
dwindle *verb* **shrink** 382
dye *verb* **colour** 72
dynamic *adjective* **energetic** 136
     adjective **moving** 273

Ee

eager *adjective* **enthusiastic** 138
earth *noun* 129
ease *noun* **comfort** 75
     verb **comfort** 75
     verb **further** 177
     verb **insert** 223
easy *adjective* 129
easygoing *adjective* **informal** 220
eat *verb* 130
ebb *verb* **reverse** 352
ebony *adjective* **black** 43
eccentric *adjective*
         unconventional 447
eclipse *verb* **darken** 101
economical *adjective* **thrifty** 433
ecstatic *adjective* **joyful** 233
edge *noun* 130
edgy *adjective* **nervous** 280
educated *adjective* 131
effect *noun* **result** 350
efficient *adjective* **competent** 77
effort *noun* **achievement** 13
     noun **attempt** 31
     noun **work** 475
effortless *adjective* **easy** 129
egotistic *adjective* **conceited** 79
eject *verb* **expel** 145
elaborate *adjective* **complicated** 78
elastic *adjective* 131
elated *adjective* **joyful** 233
elect *verb* **prefer** 317
elective *noun* **choice** 63
elegant *adjective* **chic** 63
elevate *verb* **lift** 247

elevated *adjective* **tall** 422
elfin *adjective* **slight** 390
elope *verb* **flee** 162
eloquent *adjective* **fluent** 165
elude *verb* **avoid** 33
emancipate *verb* **free** 172
embark on *verb* **begin** 38
embezzle *verb* **steal** 406
emblem *noun* **sign** 384
embrace *verb* **hug** 206
     verb **include** 213
embroider *verb* **expand** 144
     verb **sew** 374
emerald *adjective* **green** 189
emerge *verb* **appear** 24
emigrate *verb* **leave** 244
eminent *adjective* **important** 211
empathy *noun* **comfort** 75
emphasize *verb* 132
employ *verb* **use** 456
empty *adjective* 132
emulsify *verb* **mix** 270
encircle *verb* **enclose** 133
enclose *verb* 133
enclose *verb* **insert** 223
enclosure *noun* **yard** 478
encounter *verb* **meet** 263
encourage *verb* 133
encumbrance *noun* **weight** 468
end *noun* 134
end *verb* 134
endanger *verb* 135
endeavour *noun* **attempt** 31
endless *adjective* **continuous** 85
     adjective **countless** 89
endorse *verb* **approve** 25
endure *verb* 135
endure *verb* **continue** 85
enduring *adjective* **steadfast** 404
enemy *noun* 136
energetic *adjective* 136
enervate *verb* **weaken** 466
enervated *adjective* **lethargic** 246
engaged *adjective* **unmarried** 452
engagement *noun* **undertaking** 448
engineer *verb* **plan** 306

engulf *verb* **flood** 163

enhance *verb* **improve** 212

enjoy *verb* **like** 248

enjoyable *adjective* **nice** 281

enlarge *verb* 137

enormous *adjective* **huge** 206

enough *adjective* **sufficient** 415

enrage *verb* **anger** 21

enrich *verb* **improve** 212

entangled *adjective* **twisted** 444

enter *verb* **record** 337

enterprise *noun* **undertaking** 448

entertainer *noun* 137

enthusiastic *adjective* 138

entice *verb* **charm** 61

entire *adjective* **whole** 471

entreat *verb* **ask** 28

enumerate *verb* **list** 251

enunciate *verb* **pronounce** 323

envelop *verb* **cover** 92

envious *adjective* **jealous** 231

environment *noun* **surroundings** 418

environs *noun* **surroundings** 418

envoy *noun* **messenger** 265

epigram *noun* **saying** 363

equal *adjective* 138

equipped *adjective* **ready** 335

equivalent *adjective* **equal** 138

eradicate *verb* **destroy** 112

erase *verb* **remove** 343

erect *verb* **build** 53

err *verb* 139

errand *noun* **task** 422

erroneous *adjective* **incorrect** 214

error *noun* **mistake** 270

escape *verb* **flee** 162

escapee *noun* 139

escort *verb* **accompany** 11

essence *noun* **meaning** 261

essential *adjective* **necessary** 278

establish *verb* **initiate** 221

    verb **position** 312

established *adjective* **formal** 170

esteem *noun* **respect** 348

estimate *verb* **measure** 262

eternal *adjective* **permanent** 301

ethereal *adjective* **shadowy** 374

ethical *adjective* **decent** 104

ethnic *adjective* **foreign** 169

evacuate *verb* **quit** 331

evade *verb* **avoid** 33

evaluate *verb* **judge** 234

evaporate *verb* **disappear** 116

even *adjective* **equal** 138

    adjective **flat** 161

even-handed *adjective* **neutral** 280

everlasting *adjective* **permanent** 301

evict *verb* **expel** 145

evident *adjective* **clear** 66

    adjective **obvious** 286

evil *adjective* 140

evil *noun* **misfortune** 269

evoke *verb* **cause** 59

exact *adjective* **precise** 316

exaggerate *verb* **misrepresent** 269

examination *noun* **inquiry** 222

    noun **test** 427

examine *verb* 140

example *noun* 141

exasperate *verb* **annoy** 22

exasperating *adjective* **annoying** 23

excavate *verb* **dig** 114

excellent *adjective* 141

exceptional *adjective* **excellent** 141

excess *noun* 142

excessive *adjective* **extra** 148

exchange *verb* 142

excise *verb* **remove** 343

excited *adjective* 143

exciting *adjective* 143

exclaimed *verb* **said** 361

exclamation *noun* **comment** 76

exclude *verb* 144

exclusive *adjective* **single** 388

excursion *noun* **journey** 233

excuse *verb* **forgive** 169

    verb **justify** 235

execute *verb* **kill** 236

exertion *noun* **work** 475

exhaust *verb* **tire** 435

exhausted *adjective* **tired** 436

exhaustive *adjective* **thorough** 431

exhibit *verb* **show** 380
exhilarated *adjective* **excited** 143
exhilarating *adjective* **exciting** 143
exile *verb* **expel** 145
exist *verb* **live** 251
exorbitant *adjective* **expensive** 146
exotic *adjective* **foreign** 169
expand *verb* 144
expand *verb* **enlarge** 137
     verb **increase** 215
expansive *adjective* **spacious** 399
expect *verb* 145
expected *adjective* **likely** 248
expedition *noun* **journey** 233
expel *verb* 145
expend *verb* **pay** 299
expendable
     adjective **insignificant** 224
expense *noun* **price** 319
expensive *adjective* 146
experience *verb* **sense** 372
experienced *adjective* 146
expert *noun* 147
expert *adjective* **competent** 77
expire *verb* **die** 113
     verb **end** 134
explain *verb* 147
explain *verb* **justify** 235
explicit *adjective* **clear** 66
exploit *noun* **deed** 105
     verb **use** 456
explore *verb* **investigate** 228
expose *verb* **endanger** 135
     verb **reveal** 352
exposed *adjective* **bare** 36
     adjective **visible** 461
     adjective **vulnerable** 462
express *adjective* **fast** 153
     verb **describe** 111
exquisite *adjective* **beautiful** 37
extend *verb* 148
extensive *adjective* **wide** 471
exterior *noun* **outside** 292
exterminate *verb* **destroy** 112
extinct *adjective* **dead** 103
extort *verb* **threaten** 432

extra *adjective* 148
extract *verb* **remove** 343
extraordinary *adjective* **unusual** 454
     adjective **wonderful** 474
extravagant *adjective* **generous** 179
exult *verb* **rejoice** 340
eye-catching *adjective* **spectacular** 400

Ff

fabric *noun* **cloth** 68
fabulous *adjective* **wonderful** 474
facade *noun* **outside** 292
face *noun* **outside** 292
facilitate *verb* **further** 177
facsimile *noun* **copy** 87
factual *adjective* **genuine** 180
fad *noun* **fashion** 153
fade *verb* **disappear** 116
faded *adjective* **colourless** 73
fail *verb* 149
failure *noun* 149
faint *adjective* **quiet** 330
     adjective **vague** 458
fainthearted *adjective* **fearful** 156
fair *adjective* 150
fair *adjective* **fine** 160
     adjective **ordinary** 291
     adjective **pretty** 318
faith *noun* **religion** 341
faithful *adjective* 150
faithful *adjective* **religious** 342
fake *adjective* 151
fall *verb* 151
fall *verb* **decrease** 104
     verb **happen** 192
fall apart *verb* **deteriorate** 112
fall through *verb* **fail** 149
false *adjective* **fake** 151
     adjective **incorrect** 214
     adjective **unfaithful** 450
falsetto *adjective* **high-pitched** 200
falsify *verb* **misrepresent** 269
faltering *adjective* **inarticulate** 212

fire away *verb*   **start**   404
firm *adjective*   **hard**   194
     adjective   **steadfast**   404
     adjective   **steady**   405
     adjective   **strict**   410
     noun   **organization**   292
first-rate *adjective*   **great**   188
fissure *noun*   **break**   50
fit *adjective*   **healthy**   196
fix *verb*   **choose**   64
     verb   **repair**   344
     verb   **steady**   405
fixed *adjective*   **steady**   405
fizzle out *verb*   **fail**   149
flabbergasted *adjective*   **astonished**   29
flamboyant *adjective*   **spectacular**   400
flaming *adjective*   **hot**   205
     adjective   **shining**   377
flank *noun*   **side**   384
flap *verb*   **fly**   166
flare *verb*   **shine**   377
flashy *adjective*   **gaudy**   179
flat *adjective*   161
flat *adjective*   **dull**   128
     adjective   **tasteless**   423
flat out *adjective*   **busy**   53
flatter *verb*   162
flaunt *verb*   **show**   380
flawless *adjective*   **perfect**   300
flee *verb*   162
fleece *verb*   **cheat**   62
fleeting *adjective*   **momentary**   272
flesh and blood *noun*   **family**   152
flex *verb*   **bend**   41
flexible *adjective*   163
flicker *verb*   **sparkle**   400
flighty *adjective*   **fickle**   158
flimsy *adjective*   **light**   247
flinch *verb*   **cower**   93
fling *verb*   **throw**   434
flip *verb*   **overturn**   294
flit *verb*   **fly**   166
float *verb*   **sail**   361
flock *noun*   **crowd**   96
flood *verb*   163
flood *verb*   **soak**   395

floor *noun*   **bottom**   49
flop *noun*   **failure**   149
     verb   **fail**   149
floppy *adjective*   **flexible**   163
flourish *verb*   164
flout *verb*   **disobey**   121
flow *verb*   164
flower *verb*   **flourish**   164
fluctuate *verb*   165
fluent *adjective*   165
fluid *adjective*   **liquid**   250
flunk *verb*   **fail**   149
fluster *verb*   **confuse**   83
flustered *adjective*   **upset**   455
flutter *verb*   **fly**   166
     verb   **throb**   434
fly *verb*   166
fly *verb*   **speed**   401
focus *noun*   **centre**   60
     noun   **theme**   428
focus on *verb*   **concentrate**   80
foe *noun*   **enemy**   136
fog *verb*   **darken**   101
foggy *adjective*   **cloudy**   69
fold *verb*   **mix**   270
follow *verb*   166
follow *verb*   **obey**   284
fond *adjective*   **loving**   254
food *noun*   167
fool *verb*   **trick**   441
foolhardy *adjective*   **rash**   333
foolish *adjective*   **silly**   385
foolproof *adjective*   **easy**   129
foot *noun*   **bottom**   49
foray *noun*   **attack**   30
forbid *verb*   **prevent**   318
forbidding *adjective*   **frightening**   174
force *noun*   167
force *verb*   168
forceful *adjective*   **powerful**   313
     adjective   **violent**   460
ford *verb*   **cross**   95
forebear *noun*   **ancestor**   20
forecast *noun*   168
forecast *verb*   **predict**   316
foreign *adjective*   169

foreign *adjective* **unrelated** 453
forerunner *noun* **ancestor** 20
foresee *verb* **expect** 145
    verb **predict** 316
forewarn *verb* **warn** 464
forge ahead *verb* **advance** 15
forget *verb* **neglect** 279
foretell *verb* **predict** 316
forgive *verb* 169
forgo *verb* **sacrifice** 359
forlorn *adjective* **miserable** 268
form *noun* **shape** 375
    verb **make** 257
formal *adjective* 170
former *adjective* **past** 297
formula *noun* **rule** 357
forsake *verb* **quit** 331
forthright *adjective* **frank** 171
fortify *verb* **strengthen** 409
fortunate *adjective* **lucky** 255
fortune *noun* **fate** 155
    noun **wealth** 467
forward *adjective* **bold** 46
    verb **send** 371
foul *adjective* **smelly** 393
    adjective **ugly** 445
    verb **spoil** 402
found *verb* **initiate** 221
fraction *noun* **number** 283
    noun **part** 296
fracture *noun* **break** 50
fragile *adjective* 170
fragment *noun* **piece** 304
fragmentary *adjective* **incomplete** 214
fragrance *noun* **smell** 392
frail *adjective* **fragile** 170
    adjective **weak** 466
frame *verb* **accuse** 12
frank *adjective* 171
fraud *noun* **crook** 94
    noun **trickery** 442
fraudulent *adjective* **illegal** 209
fray *noun* **fight** 159
free *adjective* 171
free *verb* 172
free *verb* **separate** 373

freelance *adjective* **independent** 216
freeze *verb* **cool** 86
    verb **harden** 194
freezing *adjective* **cold** 72
frenzied *adjective* **excited** 143
frequent *adjective* **repeated** 345
fresh *adjective* **bold** 46
    adjective **new** 281
fret *verb* **worry** 476
friction *noun* **conflict** 82
friend *noun* 172
friendly *adjective* 173
frighten *verb* 173
frightened *adjective* 174
frightening *adjective* 174
frightful *adjective* **horrible** 205
frigid *adjective* **cold** 72
frisky *adjective* **lively** 252
fritter away *verb* **waste** 465
frolic *verb* 175
frolicsome *adjective* **lively** 252
frontier *noun* **outskirts** 293
frosted *adjective* **white** 470
frosty *adjective* **cold** 72
frown *verb* 175
frown on *verb* **disapprove of** 117
frugal *adjective* **thrifty** 432
fruity *adjective* **sweet** 419
frustrate *verb* **hinder** 201
frustration *noun* **disappointment** 116
fugitive *noun* **escapee** 139
fulfil *verb* **accomplish** 12
full *adjective* 176
full *adjective* **whole** 471
full-grown *adjective* **adult** 15
fumbling *adjective* **incompetent** 213
function *verb* **behave** 39
fund *verb* **pay** 299
fundamental *adjective* **main** 256
funny *adjective* 176
furbish *verb* **polish** 309
furious *adjective* **angry** 21
    adjective **violent** 460
furrow *noun* **groove** 190
further *verb* 177
furtive *adjective* **secretive** 368

fury *noun*　**anger**　20
　　　noun　**violence**　459
fuse *verb*　**combine**　74
fuss *noun*　**commotion**　76
　　　verb　**worry**　476
fussy *adjective*　**careful**　57
futile *adjective*　**useless**　457
future *adjective*　177

Gg

gag *noun*　**joke**　232
gain *verb*　**get**　180
gallant *adjective*　**polite**　309
gallop *verb*　**run**　358
gambol *verb*　**frolic**　175
game *noun*　**contest**　84
gang *noun*　**group**　191
gangling *adjective*　**clumsy**　70
gangster *noun*　**criminal**　94
gap *noun*　**hole**　203
gape *verb*　**stare**　403
garb *noun*　**clothing**　68
garbage *noun*　**rubbish**　356
garish *adjective*　**colourful**　73
garrulous *adjective*　**talkative**　421
gash *noun*　**cut**　98
　　　verb　**tear**　425
gasp *verb*　178
gather *verb*　178
gather *verb*　**assemble**　28
　　　verb　**conclude**　81
gaudy *adjective*　179
gauge *verb*　**measure**　262
gawk *verb*　**stare**　403
gaze *verb*　**stare**　403
gear *noun*　**property**　323
gelatinous *adjective*　**gluey**　184
general *adjective*　**public**　326
generous *adjective*　179
generous *adjective*　**big**　42
genial *adjective*　**friendly**　173
genius *noun*　**scholar**　365
gentleman *noun*　**male**　257

genuine *adjective*　180
genuine *adjective*　**frank**　171
germinate *verb*　**flourish**　164
get *verb*　180
get a move on *verb*　**hurry**　208
get even *verb*　**retaliate**　350
get going *verb*　**start**　404
get on someone's nerves *verb*　**annoy**　22
get the better of *verb*　**outwit**　293
ghost *noun*　181
ghostly *adjective*　**shadowy**　374
gibberish *noun*　**nonsense**　282
gibe *noun*　**wisecrack**　473
gift *noun*　181
gigantic *adjective*　**huge**　206
giggle *verb*　**smile**　393
gilt *adjective*　**orange**　290
ginger *adjective*　**orange**　290
girl *noun*　**female**　157
gist *noun*　**meaning**　261
give *verb*　182
give away *verb*　**blab**　43
give in *verb*　182
give way *verb*　**move**　272
glacial *adjective*　**wintry**　472
glad *adjective*　183
glare *verb*　**frown**　175
glaring *adjective*　**bright**　51
glassy *adjective*　**smooth**　394
glaze *noun*　**coating**　71
gleaming *adjective*　**shining**　377
glean *verb*　**realize**　335
glide *verb*　**sail**　361
glimmer *verb*　**sparkle**　400
glitter *verb*　**sparkle**　400
gloat *verb*　**boast**　45
globe *noun*　**ball**　34
globule *noun*　**ball**　34
gloom *noun*　**misery**　268
gloomy *adjective*　**drab**　125
　　　adjective　**glum**　184
　　　adjective　**pessimistic**　304
glorify *verb*　**praise**　315
glossy *adjective*　**shiny**　378
glow *verb*　**shine**　377
glower *verb*　**frown**　175

glue *noun*   183
gluey *adjective*   184
glum *adjective*   184
glut *noun*   **excess**   142
gnarled *adjective*   **rough**   355
gnaw *verb*   **chew**   62
goad *verb*   **irritate**   230
go along with *verb*   **agree**   18
gobble *verb*   **eat**   130
goggle *verb*   **stare**   403
good *adjective*   185
good *adjective*   **well-behaved**   468
good-looking *adjective*   **pretty**   318
good-natured *adjective*   **agreeable**   18
gorgeous *adjective*   **beautiful**   37
gossip *noun*   185
gossip *verb*   **talk**   421
gouge *verb*   **dig**   114
grab *verb*   186
gracious *adjective*   **polite**   309
grade *noun*   186
grade *verb*   **arrange**   27
gradient *noun*   **slope**   390
grand *adjective*   187
grant *verb*   **give**   182
grapple *verb*   **fight**   159
grasp *verb*   **hold**   202
    verb   **understand**   448
grasping *adjective*   **greedy**   188
grateful *adjective*   187
grave *adjective*   **solemn**   396
gravel *noun*   **stone**   407
graze *verb*   **scratch**   367
great *adjective*   188
great *adjective*   **important**   211
greedy *adjective*   188
green *adjective*   189
green *adjective*   **inexperienced**   217
    adjective   **jealous**   231
    adjective   **sour**   398
grey *adjective*   189
grey *adjective*   **dreary**   126
grieve *verb*   190
grill *verb*   **toast**   436
grim *adjective*   **frightening**   174
grimace *verb*   **frown**   175

grimy *adjective*   **dirty**   114
grin *verb*   **smile**   393
grind *verb*   **smooth**   394
grip *verb*   **hold**   202
gripe *verb*   **complain**   78
grit *noun*   **persistence**   302
groove *noun*   190
gross *adjective*   **nasty**   276
grotesque *adjective*   **ugly**   445
grouchy *adjective*   **grumpy**   191
ground *noun*   **earth**   129
groundless *adjective*   **irrational**   229
group *noun*   191
group *verb*   **arrange**   27
grow *verb*   **increase**   215
    verb   **produce**   321
grubby *adjective*   **dirty**   114
grudging *adjective*   **ungrateful**   451
grumble *verb*   **complain**   78
grumpy *adjective*   191
grungy *adjective*   **dirty**   114
guard *verb*   **protect**   324
guess *verb*   **think**   430
guffaw *verb*   **laugh**   241
guide *noun*   **adviser**   16
    noun   **example**   141
    noun   **indicator**   216
    verb   **advise**   16
guile *noun*   **trickery**   442
gulf *noun*   **bay**   36
gullible *adjective*   **naive**   274
gulp *verb*   **eat**   130
gummy *adjective*   **gluey**   184
gush *verb*   **flow**   164
guzzle *verb*   **drink**   126
gyrate *verb*   **spin**   401

Hh

habit *noun*   **tradition**   439
habitat *noun*   **surroundings**   418
half-asleep *adjective*   **dreamy**   125
half-hearted *adjective*   **apathetic**   24
hallowed *adjective*   **holy**   203

halt *noun* 192
halt *verb* **stop** 408
hammer *verb* **beat** 37
hamper *verb* **hinder** 201
handicap *noun* **obstacle** 285
handle *verb* **touch** 437
handsome *adjective* **pretty** 318
handy *adjective* **skillful** 388
    adjective **useful** 456
hang around with *verb* **accompany** 11
hanger-on *noun* **dependant** 110
hang in *verb* **persist** 302
hang-up *noun* **obsession** 285
haphazard *adjective* **accidental** 11
hapless *adjective* **unlucky** 452
happen *verb* 192
happiness *noun* 193
happy *adjective* 193
happy *adjective* **lucky** 255
happy-go-lucky *adjective* **optimistic** 290
harbour *noun* **bay** 36
hard *adjective* 194
hard *adjective* **difficult** 113
harden *verb* 194
hard-hearted *adjective* **callous** 55
hardship *noun* **misfortune** 269
hard up *adjective* **poor** 311
hard-working *adjective* **busy** 53
hardy *adjective* 195
harebrained *adjective* **rash** 333
harm *verb* **hurt** 208
harmonious *adjective* **peaceful** 300
harsh *adjective* **strict** 410
hassle *verb* **annoy** 22
hasten *verb* **hurry** 208
hasty *adjective* **rash** 333
hatch *verb* **concoct** 81
hate *verb* 195
hatred *noun* **dislike** 120
haul *verb* **pull** 327
haughty *adjective* **proud** 325
have all to yourself *verb* **own** 294
have in mind *verb* **intend** 226
haven *noun* **refuge** 339
hawkish *adjective* **warlike** 464
hazardous *adjective* **dangerous** 99

hazel *adjective* **green** 189
hazy *adjective* **cloudy** 69
    adjective **vague** 458
head *adjective* **best** 41
    noun **boss** 48
headstrong *adjective* **disobedient** 120
healthy *adjective* 196
heap *noun* 196
hearsay *noun* **gossip** 185
heart *noun* **centre** 60
heart-broken *adjective* **miserable** 268
hearty *adjective* **strong** 410
heave *verb* **gasp** 178
heavy *adjective* 197
heavy *adjective* **thick** 428
heavy-duty *adjective* **hardy** 195
heavy-handed *adjective* **clumsy** 70
heckle *verb* **tease** 425
hectic *adjective* **busy** 53
hedge *verb* **fluctuate** 165
heed *verb* **obey** 284
heedless *adjective* **ungrateful** 451
hefty *adjective* **heavy** 197
heinous *adjective* **evil** 140
help *noun* 197
help *verb* 198
helper *noun* 198
helpful *adjective* 199
helpful *adjective* **useful** 456
helping *noun* **share** 376
helpless *adjective* **weak** 466
herd *noun* **crowd** 96
hermit *noun* 199
hero *noun* **star** 402
heroic *adjective* **brave** 49
hesitant *adjective* **inarticulate** 212
hesitate *verb* **stop** 408
hidden *adjective* **invisible** 229
hide *verb* 200
hideous *adjective* **ugly** 445
high *adjective* **high-pitched** 200
    adjective **tall** 422
high-class *adjective* **superior** 417
highlight *verb* **colour** 72
    verb **emphasize** 132

high-pitched *adjective* 200
high spirits *noun* **happiness** 193
highwayman *noun* **bandit** 35
hijack *verb* **capture** 57
hilarious *adjective* **funny** 176
hinder *verb* 201
hindrance *noun* **obstacle** 285
hint *verb* 201
hint *noun* **trace** 438
hiss *noun* **whisper** 470
hit *verb* 202
hit *noun* **winner** 472
hitch *noun* **obstacle** 285
hoard *verb* **store** 408
hoax *noun* **trick** 441
    verb **trick** 441
hobble *verb* **limp** 249
hogwash *noun* **nonsense** 282
hoist *verb* **lift** 247
hold *verb* 202
hold *noun* **influence** 218
    verb **own** 294
hold on *verb* **continue** 85
hole *noun* 203
hollow *adjective* **empty** 132
hollow out *verb* **dig** 114
holy *adjective* 203
home *noun* 204
homesick *adjective* **sad** 359
honest *adjective* 204
honour *noun* **respect** 348
    verb **worship** 476
honourable *adjective* **honest** 204
hoodwink *verb* **deceive** 103
hop *verb* **jump** 234
hopeful *adjective* **optimistic** 290
hopeless *adjective* **impossible** 211
horizontal *adjective* **flat** 161
horrendous *adjective* **horrible** 205
horrible *adjective* 205
horrify *verb* **disgust** 119
hospitable *adjective* **generous** 179
hostage *noun* **prisoner** 320
hostile *adjective* **aggressive** 17
hostility *noun* **dislike** 120
hot *adjective* 205

household *noun* **home** 204
household name *noun* **star** 402
hover *verb* **fly** 166
howl *verb* **laugh** 241
hub *noun* **centre** 60
hubbub *noun* **noise** 282
huddle *noun* **group** 191
hug *verb* 206
huge *adjective* 206
hullabaloo *noun* **commotion** 76
humane *adjective* **lenient** 245
humble *adjective* 207
humdrum *adjective* **boring** 47
humid *adjective* 207
humiliate *verb* **insult** 225
humorous *adjective* **funny** 176
hunt for *verb* **seek** 369
hurl *verb* **throw** 434
hurry *verb* 208
hurt *verb* 208
hurt *adjective* **sad** 359
    verb **upset** 455
hurtle *verb* **speed** 401
hush-hush *adjective* **secret** 368
husky *adjective* **strong** 410
hygienic *adjective* **clean** 65
hypocritical *adjective* **dishonest** 119

Ii

icy *adjective* **cold** 72
idea *noun* **thought** 431
ideal *adjective* **perfect** 300
identical *adjective* **equal** 138
identify *verb* **label** 238
idiotic *adjective* **silly** 385
idle *adjective* **lazy** 243
    verb **laze** 242
idol *noun* **star** 402
ignorant *adjective* 209
ill *adjective* **sick** 383
illegal *adjective* 209
illicit *adjective* **illegal** 209
illiterate *adjective* **ignorant** 209

inept *adjective* **incompetent** 213
inequitable *adjective* **unfair** 449
inert *adjective* **lethargic** 246
inexpensive *adjective* **cheap** 61
inexperienced *adjective* 217
infer *verb* **conclude** 81
inferior *adjective* 218
infinite *adjective* **countless** 89
infirm *adjective* **decrepit** 105
inflexible *adjective* **hard** 194
        adjective **stubborn** 411
influence *noun* 218
influence *verb* 219
inform *verb* 219
informal *adjective* 220
information *noun* 220
infrequent *adjective* **scarce** 364
infringe *verb* **disobey** 121
infuriate *verb* **anger** 21
infuriated *adjective* **angry** 21
infuriating *adjective* **annoying** 23
ingenious *adjective* **shrewd** 381
inhabit *verb* 221
inhabit *verb* **reside** 347
inheritance *noun* **gift** 181
inhibit *verb* **hinder** 201
        verb **limit** 249
inhospitable *adjective* **unfriendly** 450
initiate *verb* 221
in-joke *noun* **wisecrack** 473
injure *verb* **hurt** 208
inky *adjective* **black** 43
inlet *noun* **bay** 36
inmate *noun* **prisoner** 320
innards *noun* **inside** 223
innocent *adjective* **naive** 274
innovate *verb* **invent** 228
innovative *adjective* **new** 281
innumerable *adjective* **numerous** 283
inquire *verb* **question** 330
inquiring *adjective* **inquisitive** 222
inquiry *noun* 222
inquisitive *adjective* 222
insane *adjective* **mad** 256
insatiable *adjective* **greedy** 188
insecure *adjective* **vulnerable** 462

insensitive *adjective* **callous** 55
insert *verb* 223
inside *noun* 223
insignificant *adjective* 224
insinuate *verb* **hint** 201
insipid *adjective* **tasteless** 423
insist *verb* **demand** 110
insolent *adjective* **rude** 357
insolvent *adjective* **broke** 52
inspect *verb* 224
inspire *verb* **cause** 59
        verb **encourage** 133
install *verb* **position** 312
institute *verb* **initiate** 221
instruct *verb* **inform** 219
        verb **teach** 424
instructions *noun* **order** 291
instructor *noun* **teacher** 424
insubordinate
        adjective **disobedient** 120
insufficient *adjective* 225
insult *verb* 225
insulting *adjective* **rude** 357
insurmountable
        adjective **impossible** 211
intangible *adjective* **shadowy** 374
integer *noun* **number** 283
intellectual *noun* **scholar** 365
intelligence *noun* **information** 220
intelligent *adjective* **clever** 67
intend *verb* 226
intense *adjective* 226
intensive *adjective* **thorough** 431
intentional *adjective* **deliberate** 108
intercede *verb* **negotiate** 279
interfere *verb* **intrude** 227
interfere with *verb* **disrupt** 121
interim *adjective* **temporary** 426
interior *noun* **inside** 223
interject *verb* **intrude** 227
interjection *noun* **comment** 76
interminable *adjective* **continuous** 85
intern *verb* **confine** 82
interpret *verb* **explain** 147
interrogate *verb* **question** 330
interrupt *verb* 227

keepsake *noun* **souvenir** 399
key *adjective* **main** 256
kid *noun* **offspring** 287
    verb **trick** 441
kidnap *verb* **abduct** 9
kill *verb* 236
kin *noun* **family** 152
kind *adjective* 237
kinetic *adjective* **moving** 273
kingdom *noun* **country** 90
kleptomaniac *noun* **thief** 429
knell *verb* **ring** 354
knock *verb* **hit** 202
know-it-all *noun* **show-off** 381
knowledgeable *adjective* **educated** 131

Ll

label *noun* 238
label *verb* 238
labour *noun* **work** 475
    verb **emphasize** 132
    verb **work** 475
lacerate *verb* **tear** 425
lack *noun* 239
lacking *adjective* **insufficient** 225
lacklustre *adjective* **dull** 128
laconic *adjective* **reticent** 351
laden *adjective* **full** 176
lady *noun* **female** 157
lagoon *noun* **lake** 239
lake *noun* 239
lament *verb* **grieve** 190
land *verb* 240
land *noun* **country, the** 91
landscape *noun* **view** 459
language *noun* 240
languid *adjective* **lethargic** 246
lanky *adjective* **tall** 422
lap *verb* **pass** 297
large *adjective* **big** 42
last *verb* **continue** 85
last the distance *verb* **persist** 302

late *adjective* **dead** 103
    adjective **modern** 271
    adjective **past** 297
laugh *verb* 241
laugh *noun* **joke** 232
launch *verb* **initiate** 221
lavish *adjective* **generous** 179
law *noun* **rule** 357
law-abiding *adjective* **obedient** 284
lawful *adjective* **legal** 244
lawn *noun* **yard** 478
lawyer *noun* 241
lax *adjective* **careless** 58
layer *noun* 242
laze *verb* 242
lazy *adjective* 243
lazy *adjective* **slow** 391
leaden *adjective* **heavy** 197
leading *adjective* **best** 41
leading light *noun* **star** 402
leaf through *verb* **read** 334
leak *verb* **drip** 127
lean *adjective* **thin** 430
    verb **slope** 391
leap *verb* **jump** 234
learn *verb* 243
learn *verb* **realize** 335
learned *adjective* **educated** 131
lease *verb* **buy** 54
leave *verb* 244
leave *noun* **permission** 301
leave out *verb* **exclude** 144
    verb **neglect** 279
lecture *noun* **lesson** 246
lecturer *noun* **teacher** 424
leftovers *noun* **remains** 342
legal *adjective* 244
legion *adjective* **numerous** 283
legitimate *adjective* **genuine** 180
    adjective **legal** 244
leisure *noun* **rest** 348
leisurely *adjective* **slow** 391
lemon *adjective* **yellow** 478
lengthy *adjective* 245
lenient *adjective* 245
lessen *verb* **minimize** 266

lesson *noun* 246

let down *verb* **drop** 127

letdown *noun* **disappointment** 116

lethal *adjective* **fatal** 154

lethargic *adjective* 246

let off *verb* **forgive** 169

let out *verb* **blab** 43

letter *noun* **message** 264

letter carrier *noun* **messenger** 265

let your thoughts wander

　　　verb **daydream** 102

level *adjective* **flat** 161

　　　noun **grade** 186

　　　verb **smooth** 394

level-headed *adjective* **sensible** 372

lever *verb* **lift** 247

levy *noun* **demand** 109

liable *adjective* **likely** 248

libel *verb* **slander** 389

liberal *adjective* **broad-minded** 51

liberate *verb* **free** 172

license *verb* **allow** 19

lifeless *adjective* **dead** 103

　　　adjective **dull** 128

lift *verb* 247

light *adjective* 247

light *adjective* **agile** 17

　　　adjective **bright** 51

lighten *verb* **comfort** 75

like *verb* 248

likeable *adjective* **agreeable** 18

likely *adjective* 248

likeness *noun* **copy** 87

lilac *adjective* **purple** 328

limber *adjective* **flexible** 163

lime *adjective* **green** 189

limit *verb* 249

limit *noun* **outskirts** 293

limp *verb* 249

limpid *adjective* **transparent** 439

line *noun* 250

lineup *noun* **line** 250

linger *verb* **dawdle** 102

link *verb* **join** 232

liquid *adjective* 250

list *verb* 251

list *verb* **slope** 391

listless *adjective* **lethargic** 246

literate *adjective* **educated** 131

lithe *adjective* **agile** 17

litter *noun* **mess** 264

little *adjective* **small** 392

live *verb* 251

live *verb* **reside** 347

livelihood *noun* **profession** 321

lively *adjective* 252

livid *adjective* **angry** 21

load *noun* **weight** 468

loaf *verb* **laze** 242

loam *noun* **earth** 129

loath *adjective* **unwilling** 454

loathe *verb* **hate** 195

lobby *verb* **persuade** 303

locate *verb* **find** 160

　　　verb **position** 312

location *noun* **place** 305

lock up *verb* **confine** 82

lofty *adjective* **grand** 187

　　　adjective · **tall** 422

log *verb* **record** 337

logical *adjective* **sane** 362

loll *verb* **laze** 242

　　　verb **sag** 360

lone *adjective* **lonely** 252

　　　adjective **single** 388

lonely *adjective* 252

loner *noun* **hermit** 199

long for *verb* **want** 463

long-suffering *adjective* **patient** 298

long-winded *adjective* **lengthy** 245

look down on *verb* **disapprove of** 117

look forward to *verb* **expect** 145

look over *verb* **inspect** 224

loom *verb* **appear** 24

loop *noun* **coil** 71

　　　verb **bend** 41

loot *verb* 253

lopsided *adjective* **uneven** 449

loquacious *adjective* **talkative** 421

loser *noun* **failure** 149

lose your nerve *verb* **fear** 156

loud *adjective* 253

loud *adjective* **gaudy** 179
lounge *verb* **laze** 242
love *verb* 254
lovely *adjective* **beautiful** 37
　adjective **nice** 281
loving *adjective* 254
low *adjective* **quiet** 330
　adjective **sad** 359
lower *verb* **drop** 127
lowly *adjective* **humble** 207
　adjective **subordinate** 413
loyal *adjective* **faithful** 150
lucid *adjective* **sane** 362
luck *noun* **fate** 155
lucky *adjective* 255
ludicrous *adjective* **ridiculous** 353
lug *verb* **pull** 327
lukewarm *adjective* **apathetic** 24
lullaby *noun* **song** 397
lumber *verb* **trudge** 442
luminous *adjective* **shining** 377
lurch *verb* **sway** 419
lure *verb* **attract** 32
luscious *adjective* **delicious** 109
lustrous *adjective* **shiny** 378
lyrical *adjective* **musical** 273

Mm

mad *adjective* 256
maddening *adjective* **annoying** 23
made-up *adjective* **imaginary** 210
magazine *noun* **publication** 326
magenta *adjective* **purple** 328
magnanimous *adjective* **generous** 179
magnetic *adjective* **attractive** 33
magnetize *verb* **attract** 32
magnificent *adjective* **grand** 187
maim *verb* **hurt** 208
main *adjective* 256
maintain *verb* **keep** 236
majestic *adjective* **grand** 187
major *adjective* **main** 256
make *verb* 257
make *verb* **calculate** 55

make a slip *verb* **err** 139
make believe *verb* **imagine** 210
make headway *verb* **advance** 15
make light of *verb* **minimize** 266
makeshift *adjective* **temporary** 426
make the grade *verb* **succeed** 414
make up *verb* **concoct** 81
male *noun* 257
malign *verb* **slander** 389
malignant *adjective* **fatal** 154
malleable *adjective* **flexible** 163
maltreat *verb* **abuse** 10
man *noun* **male** 257
manage *verb* 258
manager *noun* 258
manipulate *verb* **influence** 219
manner *noun* 259
mannerly *adjective* **polite** 309
manners *noun* **behaviour** 39
manoeuvrable *adjective* **moving** 273
manual *noun* **book** 46
manufacture *verb* **make** 257
mar *verb* **damage** 99
march *verb* 259
margin *noun* **edge** 130
maritime *adjective* **nautical** 277
mark *noun* 260
mark *verb* **label** 238
marker *noun* **indicator** 216
maroon *adjective* **red** 338
martial *adjective* **warlike** 464
marvel *noun* **miracle** 267
marvellous *adjective* **wonderful** 474
mash *verb* **mix** 270
　verb **soften** 396
mask *verb* **hide** 200
massive *adjective* **heavy** 197
mastermind *verb* **plan** 306
masticate *verb* **chew** 62
match *noun* **contest** 84
　verb **copy** 87
material *adjective* **actual** 13
　noun **cloth** 68
materialize *verb* **appear** 24
matte *adjective* **dull** 128
matter-of-fact *adjective* **practical** 314

mature *adjective* **adult** 15

mauve *adjective* **purple** 328

maxim *noun* **saying** 363

meagre *adjective* **scant** 364

meal *noun* 260

mean *adjective* 261

meaning *noun* 261

means *noun* **method** 265

measly *adjective* **scant** 364

measure *verb* 262

medal *noun* **prize** 320

meddle *verb* **intrude** 227

mediate *verb* **negotiate** 279

mediocre *adjective* 262

meek *adjective* **humble** 207

meet *verb* 263

meet *verb* **assemble** 28

meeting *noun* 263

melancholy *noun* **misery** 268

mellow *adjective* **musical** 273

melodious *adjective* **musical** 273

memento *noun* **souvenir** 399

memo *noun* **message** 264

memorable *adjective* **significant** 385

memorize *verb* **learn** 243

menace *verb* **threaten** 432

mend *verb* **repair** 344

mentor *noun* **adviser** 16

merchant *noun* **seller** 371

merciful *adjective* **lenient** 245

mercurial *adjective* **fickle** 158

mercy *noun* **pity** 305

merriment *noun* **happiness** 193

merry *adjective* **happy** 193

mesmerize *verb* **charm** 61

mess *noun* 264

message *noun* 264

messenger *noun* 265

mess up *verb* **disrupt** 121

messy *adjective* **untidy** 453

meteoric *adjective* **sudden** 414

method *noun* 265

methodical *adjective* **tidy** 435

meticulous *adjective* **careful** 57

    adjective **precise** 316

    adjective **tidy** 435

metropolis *noun* **city** 64

metropolitan *adjective* **civic** 65

middle-of-the-road

    adjective **moderate** 271

might *noun* **force** 167

mighty *adjective* **powerful** 313

mild *adjective* **fine** 160

    adjective **lenient** 245

    adjective **tasteless** 423

militant *adjective* **defiant** 108

    adjective **warlike** 464

mimic *verb* 266

mind *verb* **concentrate** 80

mindful *adjective* **alert** 19

mine *verb* **dig** 114

miniature *adjective* **small** 392

minimize *verb* 266

minor *adjective* 267

minstrel *noun* **singer** 387

minute *adjective* **small** 392

miracle *noun* 267

mirth *noun* **happiness** 193

miscalculate *verb* **err** 139

miscellaneous *adjective* **various** 458

mischievous *adjective* **naughty** 277

miserable *adjective* 268

miserable *adjective* **mean** 261

misery *noun* 268

misfortune *noun* 269

mishap *noun* **misfortune** 269

mislead *verb* **deceive** 103

misrepresent *verb* 269

miss *verb* **avoid** 33

mission *noun* **task** 422

mistake *noun* 270

mistake *verb* **err** 139

misty *adjective* **cloudy** 69

misunderstanding *noun* **mistake** 270

mix *verb* 270

mixed *adjective* **various** 458

mix up *verb* **disrupt** 121

mob *noun* **crowd** 96

mobile *adjective* **moving** 273

model *noun* **copy** 87

    noun **example** 141

moderate *adjective* 271

modern *adjective*　271

modest *adjective*　**humble**　207

　　　adjective　**moderate**　271

　　　adjective　**shy**　383

moist *adjective*　**wet**　469

moisten *verb*　**wet**　469

mollify *verb*　**pacify**　295

molten *adjective*　**liquid**　250

momentary *adjective*　272

momentous *adjective*　**significant**　385

money *noun*　**wealth**　467

monk *noun*　**hermit**　199

monopolize *verb*　**own**　294

monotonous *adjective*　**boring**　47

monstrous *adjective*　**bad**　34

moody *adjective*　**glum**　184

　　　adjective　**touchy**　438

mop *verb*　**wipe**　473

mope *verb*　**grieve**　190

mop up *verb*　**clean**　66

moral *adjective*　**decent**　104

　　　noun　**theme**　428

morose *adjective*　**glum**　184

morsel *noun*　**piece**　304

mortar *noun*　**glue**　183

motionless *adjective*　**still**　406

motivate *verb*　**encourage**　133

motley *adjective*　**various**　458

motto *noun*　**saying**　363

mound *noun*　**heap**　196

mount *verb*　**climb**　67

　　　verb　**increase**　215

mourn *verb*　**grieve**　190

mousy *adjective*　**drab**　125

mouth-watering

　　　adjective　**delicious**　109

move *verb*　272

move *noun*　**deed**　105

moving *adjective*　273

mow *verb*　**cut**　98

muddle *noun*　**mess**　264

　　　verb　**confuse**　83

muddy *adjective*　**opaque**　288

muffled *adjective*　**quiet**　330

mug *verb*　**attack**　31

muggy *adjective*　**humid**　207

multiple *adjective*　**numerous**　283

multiply *verb*　**increase**　215

multitudinous

　　　adjective　**numerous**　283

munch *verb*　**chew**　62

mundane *adjective*　**mediocre**　262

municipal *adjective*　**civic**　65

municipality *noun*　**city**　64

murder *verb*　**kill**　236

murky *adjective*　**dark**　100

murmur *noun*　**whisper**　470

muscle *noun*　**force**　167

muse *verb*　**daydream**　102

musical *adjective*　273

mutiny *noun*　**rebellion**　336

　　　verb　**rebel**　336

myriad *adjective*　**countless**　89

mysterious *adjective*　**confusing**　84

mystified *adjective*　**confused**　83

mystify *verb*　**puzzle**　329

mythical *adjective*　**imaginary**　210

Nn

nab *verb*　**grab**　186

nag *verb*　**complain**　78

nail *verb*　**grab**　186

naive *adjective*　274

naked *adjective*　**bare**　36

name *noun*　274

name *verb*　275

nap *verb*　**sleep**　389

narrate *verb*　**tell**　426

narrow *adjective*　275

narrow-minded *adjective*　276

nasty *adjective*　276

nation *noun*　**country**　90

natural *adjective*　**simple**　386

naughty *adjective*　277

nauseate *verb*　**disgust**　119

nautical *adjective*　277

naval *adjective*　**nautical**　277

navigate *verb*　**sail**　361

navy *adjective*　**blue**　44

near *adjective*   278

neat *adjective*   **tidy**   435

nebulous *adjective*   **shadowy**   374

necessary *adjective*   278

need *noun*   **poverty**   313

needy *adjective*   **poor**   311

negative *adjective*   **pessimistic**   304

neglect *verb*   279

negligent *adjective*   **careless**   58

negotiate *verb*   279

neighbouring *adjective*   **near**   278

neighbourly *adjective*   **friendly**   173

nerve *noun*   **courage**   91

nervous *adjective*   280

neutral *adjective*   280

neutral *adjective*   **colourless**   73

new *adjective*   281

news *noun*   **information**   220

newspaper *noun*   **publication**   326

next *adjective*   **future**   177

     adjective   **near**   278

nibble *verb*   **chew**   62

nice *adjective*   281

nice *adjective*   **kind**   237

nick *verb*   **scratch**   367

nickname *noun*   **name**   274

nimble *adjective*   **agile**   17

nippy *adjective*   **cold**   72

noble *adjective*   **distinguished**   123

no-frills *adjective*   **cheap**   61

noise *noun*   282

noncommittal *adjective*   **neutral**   280

nonconformist *adjective*

     unconventional   447

nonplussed *adjective*   **confused**   83

nonsense *noun*   282

nonsensical *adjective*   **ridiculous**   353

normal *adjective*   **usual**   457

nosy *adjective*   **inquisitive**   222

notable *adjective*   **famous**   152

notch *noun*   **cut**   98

note *noun*   **message**   264

    verb   **record**   337

noted *adjective*   **famous**   152

notice *verb*   **see**   369

noticeable *adjective*   **visible**   461

notify *verb*   **inform**   219

notion *noun*   **thought**   431

notorious *adjective*   **famous**   152

not pull your weight *verb*   **laze**   242

not yourself *adjective*   **sick**   383

nourishment *noun*   **food**   167

novel *adjective*   **new**   281

noxious *adjective*   **poisonous**   308

nucleus *noun*   **centre**   60

nude *adjective*   **bare**   36

number *noun*   283

number *verb*   **count**   89

numeral *noun*   **number**   283

numerous *adjective*   283

nurse *verb*   **help**   198

Oo

oath *noun*   **promise**   322

obedient *adjective*   284

obese *adjective*   **fat**   154

obey *verb*   284

objective *adjective*   **fair**   150

obligatory *adjective*   **necessary**   278

oblige *verb*   **help**   198

obliged *adjective*   **grateful**   187

obliging *adjective*   **helpful**   199

obscure *adjective*   **dark**   100

    verb   **darken**   101

observant *adjective*   **alert**   19

observation *noun*   **comment**   76

observe *verb*   **obey**   284

    verb   **see**   369

obsession *noun*   285

obsolete *adjective*   **old-fashioned**   288

obstacle *noun*   285

obstinate *adjective*   **stubborn**   411

obstruct *verb*   **block**   44

    verb   **resist**   347

obvious *adjective*   286

obvious *adjective*   **clear**   66

occasional *adjective*   **scarce**   364

occupation *noun*   **job**   231

occupy *verb* **inhabit** 221
    verb **own** 294
occur *verb* **happen** 192
odd *adjective* **strange** 409
odds and ends *noun* **remains** 342
odour *noun* **smell** 392
off *adjective* **inedible** 217
off base *adjective* **incorrect** 214
offbeat *adjective* **unconventional** 447
offend *verb* **disgust** 119
offender *noun* **criminal** 94
offer *noun* 286
office *noun* **position** 311
official *adjective* **formal** 170
    noun **manager** 258
officiate *verb* **rule** 358
offspring *noun* 287
okay *verb* **approve** 25
old *adjective* 287
old-fashioned *adjective* 288
olive *adjective* **green** 189
omen *noun* **forecast** 168
omit *verb* **neglect** 279
only *adjective* **single** 388
onset *noun* **start** 403
onslaught *noun* **attack** 30
ooze *verb* **drip** 127
opaque *adjective* 288
open *adjective* **free** 171
    adjective **spacious** 399
    adjective **uncertain** 446
    adjective **vulnerable** 462
    verb **begin** 38
operate *verb* **behave** 39
opinion *noun* 289
opponent *noun* **enemy** 136
oppose *verb* **resist** 347
opposite *adjective* 289
oppress *verb* **subdue** 412
oppressive *adjective* **humid** 207
    adjective **tyrannical** 444
opt for *verb* **prefer** 317
optimistic *adjective* 290
option *noun* **choice** 63
opulent *adjective* **spectacular** 400

orange *adjective* 290
orb *noun* **ball** 34
orbit *noun* **course** 92
order *noun* 291
order *verb* **demand** 110
orderly *adjective* **tidy** 435
ordinary *adjective* 291
organization *noun* 292
organize *verb* **plan** 306
origin *noun* **start** 403
original *adjective* **new** 281
oscillate *verb* **fluctuate** 165
ostracize *verb* **isolate** 230
out cold *adjective* **unconscious** 447
outcome *noun* **result** 350
outdoors *noun* **country, the** 91
outfit *noun* **organization** 292
outfitted *adjective* **ready** 335
outgoing *adjective* **friendly** 173
outlaw *noun* **criminal** 94
    verb **ban** 35
outlay *noun* **price** 319
outline *noun* **summary** 417
    verb **tell** 426
outlook *noun* **opinion** 289
    noun **view** 459
outlying *adjective* **distant** 122
out-of-date
        adjective **old-fashioned** 288
outset *noun* **start** 403
outside *noun* 292
outskirts *noun* 293
outspread *adjective* **wide** 471
outstanding *adjective* **excellent** 141
outstrip *verb* **pass** 297
outwit *verb* 293
overabundance *noun* **excess** 142
overbearing *adjective* **bossy** 48
overcast *adjective* **cloudy** 69
overlook *verb* **neglect** 279
overpower *verb* **subdue** 412
oversupply *noun* **excess** 142
overt *adjective* **visible** 461
overtake *verb* **pass** 297
overturn *verb* 294

overweight *adjective* **fat** 154
overwhelm *verb* **flood** 163
own *verb* 294

Pp

pace *verb* **walk** 463
pacify *verb* 295
pack *noun* **crowd** 96
packed *adjective* **full** 176
pact *noun* **promise** 322
pad *verb* **expand** 144
pain *noun* 295
painless *adjective* **easy** 129
paint *verb* **colour** 72
pal *noun* **friend** 172
pale *adjective* **colourless** 73
    adjective **white** 470
palpitate *verb* **throb** 434
pamphlet *noun* **publication** 326
pandemonium *noun* **noise** 282
panic *verb* **fear** 156
panicky *adjective* **frightened** 174
panorama *noun* **view** 459
pant *verb* **gasp** 178
parade *verb* **march** 259
    verb **show** 380
paralegal *noun* **lawyer** 241
paraphernalia *noun* **property** 323
parasite *noun* **dependant** 110
parched *adjective* **dry** 128
pardon *noun* 296
pardon *verb* **forgive** 169
parliament *noun* **council** 88
parole *noun* **pardon** 296
part *noun* 296
partial *adjective* **incomplete** 214
particle *noun* **piece** 304
partner *noun* **associate** 29
part-time *adjective* **temporary** 426
pass *verb* 297
pass away *verb* **die** 113
passing *adjective* **momentary** 272

passion *noun* **obsession** 285
passionate *adjective* **intense** 226
passive *adjective* **apathetic** 24
pass on *verb* **send** 371
past *adjective* 297
paste *noun* **glue** 183
pastel *adjective* **colourless** 73
pastoral *adjective* **country** 90
pat *verb* **touch** 437
patch up *verb* **repair** 344
path *noun* **course** 92
pathetic *adjective* 298
pathetic *adjective* **powerless** 314
patient *adjective* 298
pattern *noun* **example** 141
pause *noun* **rest** 348
    verb **stop** 408
pave *verb* **coat** 70
pay *noun* 299
pay *verb* 299
peaceful *adjective* 300
peach *adjective* **orange** 290
peacock *noun* **show-off** 381
peak *noun* **top** 437
peal *verb* **ring** 354
pebble *noun* **stone** 407
peculiar *adjective* **strange** 409
peddle *verb* **sell** 370
peer *verb* **stare** 403
peeve *verb* **irritate** 230
pen *noun* **yard** 478
    verb **compose** 79
penalize *verb* **punish** 328
penitentiary *noun* **prison** 319
pen name *noun* **name** 274
pennant *noun* **prize** 320
perceive *verb* **sense** 372
    verb **understand** 448
perceptible *adjective* **obvious** 286
perception *noun* **feeling** 157
perennial *adjective* **permanent** 301
perfect *adjective* 300
perfect *verb* **improve** 212
perforation *noun* **hole** 203
perform *verb* **behave** 39

prepare *verb* **make** 257
prepared *adjective* **ready** 335
preposterous *adjective* **ridiculous** 353
presence *noun* **appearance** 25
present *noun* **gift** 181
    verb **give** 182
preserve *verb* **keep** 236
    verb **save** 363
preside *verb* **rule** 358
press *verb* 317
press *verb* **hug** 206
pressure *noun* **weight** 468
prestigious *adjective* **important** 211
presume *verb* **believe** 40
presumptuous *adjective* **rude** 357
pretend *verb* **imagine** 210
pretentious *adjective* **pompous** 310
pretty *adjective* 318
prevail *verb* **succeed** 414
prevent *verb* 318
previous *adjective* **past** 297
price *noun* 319
pricey *adjective* **expensive** 146
prickly *adjective* **touchy** 438
primary *adjective* **main** 256
primed *adjective* **ready** 335
principal *adjective* **best** 41
principle *noun* **virtue** 460
print *verb* **write** 477
prison *noun* 319
prisoner *noun* 320
private *adjective* **secret** 368
prize *noun* 320
probable *adjective* **believable** 40
    adjective **likely** 248
probe *verb* **investigate** 228
procedure *noun* **method** 265
proceed *verb* **advance** 15
proceeds *noun* **profit** 322
proclaim *verb* **publish** 327
procrastinate *verb* **dawdle** 102
procure *verb* **get** 180
prodigy *noun* **expert** 147
produce *verb* 321
produce *verb* **cause** 59
production *noun* **concert** 80

profession *noun* 321
professional
    adjective **experienced** 146
proficient *adjective* **competent** 77
profile *noun* **side** 384
profit *noun* 322
profound *adjective* **intense** 226
profuse *adjective* **numerous** 283
progeny *noun* **offspring** 287
prognosis *noun* **forecast** 168
progress *verb* **advance** 15
prohibit *verb* **prevent** 318
project *noun* **undertaking** 448
    verb **protrude** 324
prolific *adjective* **abundant** 10
prolong *verb* **keep** 236
prominent *adjective* **important** 211
    adjective **visible** 461
promise *noun* 322
promising *adjective* **lucky** 255
promote *verb* **further** 177
pronounce *verb* 323
propaganda *noun* **information** 220
propel *verb* **push** 329
proper *adjective* **decent** 104
    adjective **legal** 244
property *noun* 323
prophecy *noun* **forecast** 168
prophesy *verb* **predict** 316
proportion *noun* **part** 296
proposal *noun* **offer** 286
propose *verb* **advise** 16
proposition *noun* **offer** 286
prop up *verb* **strengthen** 409
prospective *adjective* **future** 177
prosper *verb* **thrive** 433
prosperous *adjective* **wealthy** 467
protect *verb* 324
protected *adjective* **safe** 360
protection *noun* **defence** 107
protégé *noun* **dependant** 110
protest *verb* **complain** 78
protrude *verb* 324
proud *adjective* 325
prove *verb* 325
proven *adjective* **genuine** 180

radical *adjective*　**unconventional**　447

rag *noun*　**cloth**　68

rage *noun*　**anger**　20

ragged *adjective*　**scruffy**　367

raid *verb*　**attack**　31

　　verb　**loot**　253

rain *verb*　332

raise *verb*　**lift**　247

rake in *verb*　**gather**　178

rally *verb*　**assemble**　28

　　verb　**recover**　337

ram *verb*　**push**　329

ramble *verb*　332

rambling *adjective*　**lengthy**　245

rampage *verb*　**rebel**　336

rampart *noun*　**heap**　196

random *adjective*　**accidental**　11

rank *adjective*　**smelly**　393

　　noun　**grade**　186

　　noun　**line**　250

ransack *verb*　**loot**　253

rapacious *adjective*　**greedy**　188

rapid *adjective*　**fast**　153

rapturous *adjective*　**joyful**　233

rare *adjective*　**scarce**　364

　　adjective　**unusual**　454

rash *adjective*　333

rasp *verb*　**roughen**　356

rate *noun*　**price**　319

　　verb　**measure**　262

ration *verb*　**distribute**　123

rational *adjective*　**sane**　362

rationalize *verb*　**justify**　235

rat on *verb*　**betray**　42

raucous *adjective*　**loud**　253

ravage *verb*　**loot**　253

rave *verb*　333

raw *adjective*　**inexperienced**　217

　　adjective　**wintry**　472

reach *verb*　**come**　74

　　verb　**extend**　148

react *verb*　**answer**　23

reaction *noun*　334

read *verb*　334

ready *adjective*　335

real *adjective*　**actual**　13

realistic *adjective*　**practical**　314

realize *verb*　335

realm *noun*　**country**　90

reason *verb*　**conclude**　81

reasonable *adjective*　**cheap**　61

　　adjective　**moderate**　271

rebel *verb*　336

rebellion *noun*　336

rebellious *adjective*　**defiant**　108

rebound *verb*　**reverse**　352

rebuff *verb*　**refuse**　339

rebuke *verb*　**scold**　366

recalcitrant *adjective*　**defiant**　108

recall *verb*　**remember**　343

recede *verb*　**reverse**　352

receive *verb*　**get**　180

recent *adjective*　**modern**　271

recess *noun*　**rest**　348

reciprocate *verb*　**retaliate**　350

recital *noun*　**concert**　80

reckless *adjective*　**rash**　333

reckon *verb*　**think**　430

reclaim *verb*　**retrieve**　351

recline *verb*　**rest**　349

recluse *noun*　**hermit**　199

reclusive *adjective*　**lonely**　252

recognize *verb* **remember**　343

　　verb　**sense**　372

recollect *verb*　**remember**　343

recommend *verb*　**advise**　16

recommendation *noun*　**suggestion**　416

record *verb*　337

recount *verb*　**tell**　426

recover *verb*　337

recover *verb*　**retrieve**　351

rectify *verb*　**correct**　88

recuperate *verb*　**recover**　337

recurrent *adjective*　**repeated**　345

red *adjective*　338

redeem *verb*　**buy**　54

reduced *adjective*　**cheap**　61

redundant *adjective*　**extra**　148

reel *verb*　**sway**　419

　　verb　**turn**　443

refined *adjective*　**distinguished**　123

reflect on *verb*　**ponder**　310

reform *verb* **correct** 88
refresh *verb* 338
refrigerate *verb* **cool** 86
refuge *noun* 339
refugee *noun* **escapee** 139
refund *verb* **repay** 344
refuse *verb* 339
refuse *noun* **rubbish** 356
regard *noun* **respect** 348
register *verb* **record** 337
regular *adjective* **repeated** 345
regulation *noun* **rule** 357
rehearsal *noun* **practice** 315
reign *verb* **rule** 358
reimburse *verb* **repay** 344
reinforce *verb* **strengthen** 409
reject *verb* **refuse** 339
rejoice *verb* 340
rejuvenate *verb* **refresh** 338
relate *verb* **tell** 426
related *adjective* 340
relations *noun* **family** 152
relatives *noun* **family** 152
relax *verb* **rest** 349
relaxed *adjective* **calm** 56
     adjective **informal** 220
relay *verb* **send** 371
release *noun* **pardon** 296
     verb **free** 172
relevant *adjective* **related** 340
reliable *adjective* 341
relief *noun* **comfort** 75
     noun **help** 197
relieve *verb* **comfort** 75
religion *noun* 341
religious *adjective* 342
relinquish *verb* **sacrifice** 359
relocate *verb* **move** 272
reluctant *adjective* **unwilling** 454
remain *verb* **live** 251
remains *noun* 342
remark *noun* **comment** 76
remarkable *adjective* **astonishing** 30
     adjective **unusual** 454
remedy *verb* **correct** 88
remember *verb* 343

remembrance *noun* **souvenir** 399
remnants *noun* **remains** 342
remorseful *adjective* **sorry** 398
remote *adjective* **distant** 122
remove *verb* 343
rendezvous *noun* **meeting** 263
renew *verb* **refresh** 338
renounce *verb* **refuse** 339
renovate *verb* **repair** 344
renowned *adjective* **famous** 152
rent *verb* **buy** 54
repair *verb* 344
repay *verb* 344
repeal *verb* **cancel** 56
repeated *adjective* 345
repel *verb* 345
repentant *adjective* **sorry** 398
replace *verb* **exchange** 142
replica *noun* **copy** 87
reply *noun* **reaction** 334
     verb **answer** 23
report *noun* 346
report *verb* **betray** 42
     verb **publish** 327
repossess *verb* **retrieve** 351
represent *verb* **describe** 111
repress *verb* **subdue** 412
repressive *adjective* **tyrannical** 444
reprimand *verb* **scold** 366
reproach *verb* **scold** 366
reproduce *verb* **copy** 87
republic *noun* **country** 90
repulse *verb* **repel** 345
repulsive *adjective* **nasty** 276
     adjective **ugly** 445
request *verb* **ask** 28
require *verb* **demand** 110
requisition *noun* **demand** 109
rescue *verb* **free** 172
     verb **save** 363
research *verb* **investigate** 228
resentful *adjective* 346
reserved *adjective* **reticent** 351
reservoir *noun* **lake** 239
reside *verb* 347
residence *noun* **home** 204

residue *noun* **remains** 342

resign *verb* **sacrifice** 359

resilient *adjective* **elastic** 131

resist *verb* 347

resolve *verb* **solve** 397

resonant *adjective* **loud** 253

resourceful *adjective* **shrewd** 381

respect *noun* 348

respect *verb* **worship** 476

respectable *adjective* **decent** 104

respectful *adjective* **polite** 309

resplendent *adjective* **spectacular** 400

respond *verb* **answer** 23

response *noun* **reaction** 334

responsible *adjective* **reliable** 341

rest *noun* 348

rest *verb* 349

rest *verb* **place** 306

restaurant *noun* 349

restless *adjective* **excited** 143

restore *verb* **repair** 344

restrain *verb* **confine** 82

restrained *adjective* **moderate** 271

restrict *verb* **limit** 249

result *noun* 350

résumé *noun* **summary** 417

retail *verb* **sell** 370

retailer *noun* **seller** 371

retain *verb* **keep** 236

retaliate *verb* 350

retard *verb* **hinder** 201

reticent *adjective* 351

retort *verb* **answer** 23

retreat *noun* **refuge** 339

　　　verb **leave** 244

retrieve *verb* 351

return *noun* **profit** 322

　　　verb **answer** 23

reveal *verb* 352

revel in *verb* **rejoice** 340

revere *verb* **worship** 476

reverent *adjective* **religious** 342

reverse *verb* 352

review *verb* **examine** 140

revise *verb* **correct** 88

revive *verb* **refresh** 338

revolt *noun* **rebellion** 336

　　　verb **disgust** 119

　　　verb **rebel** 336

revolting *adjective* **nasty** 276

reward *verb* **repay** 344

rhythm *noun* 353

rhythmical *adjective* **repeated** 345

rib *verb* **tease** 425

ribbon *noun* **prize** 320

rich *adjective* **colourful** 73

　　　adjective **wealthy** 467

riches *noun* **wealth** 467

ridicule *noun* **scorn** 366

　　　verb **tease** 425

ridiculous *adjective* 353

rift *noun* **break** 50

right *adjective* **decent** 104

　　　adjective **fair** 150

　　　adjective **true** 443

rigid *adjective* **hard** 194

　　　adjective **strict** 410

rim *noun* **edge** 130

ring *verb* 354

riot *noun* **commotion** 76

　　　verb **rebel** 336

rip *verb* **tear** 425

rip off *verb* **cheat** 62

risk *verb* **dare** 100

ritual *adjective* **formal** 170

rival *noun* **enemy** 136

roam *verb* **travel** 440

roar *verb* **shout** 380

roast *verb* **toast** 436

rob *verb* **steal** 406

robber *noun* **thief** 429

robust *adjective* **healthy** 196

　　　adjective **strong** 410

rock *noun* **stone** 407

　　　verb **shake** 375

rookie *noun* **student** 411

room *noun* 354

roomy *adjective* **spacious** 399

rot *verb* 355

rotate *verb* **turn** 443

rotten *adjective* **bad** 34

　　　adjective **inedible** 217

Ss

sensible *adjective* 372
sensitive *adjective* **touchy** 438
separate *verb* 373
separate *adjective* **independent** 216
sequel *noun* **result** 350
sequence *noun* **series** 373
serene *adjective* **peaceful** 300
series *noun* 373
serious *adjective* **significant** 385
　　 adjective **solemn** 396
serve *verb* **suit** 416
servile *adjective* **submissive** 412
set *verb* **harden** 194
　　 verb **place** 306
set about *verb* **begin** 38
set an example to *verb* **encourage** 133
setback *noun* **disappointment** 116
set down *verb* **compose** 79
set out *verb* **start** 404
setting *noun* **surroundings** 418
settle *verb* **inhabit** 221
settle a score *verb* **retaliate** 350
severe *adjective* **intense** 226
severity *noun* **violence** 459
sew *verb* 374
shabby *adjective* **mean** 261
　　 adjective **scruffy** 367
shade *verb* **darken** 101
shadow *verb* **follow** 166
shadowy *adjective* 374
shadowy *adjective* **dark** 100
shady *adjective* **dishonest** 119
shaggy *adjective* **rough** 355
shake *verb* 375
shake a leg *verb* **hurry** 208
shambles *noun* **mess** 264
shape *noun* 375
shape *verb* **build** 53
share *noun* 376
share *verb* 376
shark *noun* **crook** 94
sharp *adjective* **shrewd** 381
　　 adjective **tasty** 423
shed *verb* **discard** 118
sheer *adjective* **transparent** 439
shelter *noun* **refuge** 339

sheltered *adjective* **safe** 360
shelve *verb* **defer** 107
shield *noun* **defence** 107
　　 verb **protect** 324
shift *verb* **move** 272
shifty *adjective* **dishonest** 119
shimmer *verb* **sparkle** 400
shine *verb* 377
shine *verb* **polish** 309
　　 verb **succeed** 414
shining *adjective* 377
shinny up *verb* **climb** 67
shiny *adjective* 378
shipshape *adjective* **tidy** 435
shirk *verb* **avoid** 33
shock *verb* 378
shoddy *adjective* **defective** 106
　　 adjective **inferior** 218
shoplifter *noun* **thief** 429
shopper *noun* **buyer** 54
shore *noun* 379
short *adjective* **abrupt** 9
　　 adjective **brief** 50
　　 adjective **insufficient** 225
　　 adjective **small** 392
shortage *noun* **lack** 239
shorten *verb* 379
shout *verb* 380
shove *verb* **push** 329
show *verb* 380
show *noun* **concert** 80
　　 verb **reveal** 352
shower *verb* **rain** 332
show-off *noun* 381
show up *verb* **come** 74
showy *adjective* **gaudy** 179
shrewd *adjective* 381
shriek *verb* 382
shrill *adjective* **high-pitched** 200
　　 adjective **loud** 253
shrink *verb* 382
shrivel *verb* **shrink** 382
shroud *verb* **cover** 92
shudder *verb* **fear** 156
　　 verb **shake** 375
shuffle *verb* **limp** 249

small *adjective* 392
small *adjective* **narrow** 275
small-time *adjective* **insignificant** 224
smart *adjective* **chic** 63
    adjective **clever** 67
smart aleck *noun* **show-off** 381
smear *verb* **coat** 70
    verb **dirty** 115
    verb **slander** 389
smell *noun* 392
smelly *adjective* 393
smile *verb* 393
smirk *verb* **smile** 393
smooth *adjective* 394
smooth *verb* 394
smooth *adjective* **flat** 161
    adjective **fluent** 165
smother *verb* **flood** 163
    verb **suffocate** 415
smudge *verb* **dirty** 115
smug *adjective* **proud** 325
snack *noun* **meal** 260
snack bar *noun* **restaurant** 349
snap *adjective* **sudden** 414
snappy *adjective* **grumpy** 191
snap up *verb* **grab** 186
snare *verb* **catch** 59
snatch *verb* **grab** 186
snicker *verb* **smile** 393
snip *verb* **cut** 98
snobbish *adjective* **pompous** 310
snooping *adjective* **inquisitive** 222
snooty *adjective* **pompous** 310
snooze *verb* **sleep** 389
snowy *adjective* **white** 470
snub *verb* **insult** 225
soak *verb* 395
soar *verb* **fly** 166
sob *verb* **cry** 97
sober *adjective* **solemn** 396
sociable *adjective* **friendly** 173
society *noun* **club** 69
sodden *adjective* **wet** 469
soft *adjective* 395
soft *adjective* **quiet** 330
soften *verb* 396

soggy *adjective* **wet** 469
soil *noun* **earth** 129
    verb **dirty** 115
solace *noun* **comfort** 75
sole *adjective* **single** 388
solemn *adjective* 396
solicitor *noun* **lawyer** 241
solid *adjective* **heavy** 197
    adjective **thick** 428
solidify *verb* **harden** 194
solitary *adjective* **lonely** 252
soloist *noun* **singer** 387
solve *verb* 397
sombre *adjective* **drab** 125
sometime *adjective* **past** 297
song *noun* 397
soothe *verb* **comfort** 75
soprano *adjective* **high-pitched** 200
sorrow *noun* **misery** 268
sorrowful *adjective* **pathetic** 298
sorry *adjective* 398
sort *verb* **arrange** 27
sort out *verb* **simplify** 387
so-so *adjective* **ordinary** 291
sound *adjective* **healthy** 196
    adjective **sane** 362
    verb **pronounce** 323
sour *adjective* 398
souvenir *noun* 399
sovereign *adjective* **independent** 216
spacious *adjective* 399
span *verb* **cross** 95
spare *adjective* **extra** 148
    verb **forgive** 169
sparkle *verb* 400
sparse *adjective* **scant** 364
spasm *noun* **pain** 295
spawn *verb* **produce** 321
speak well of *verb* **praise** 315
specialist *noun* **expert** 147
specific *adjective* **precise** 316
specimen *noun* **example** 141
spectacular *adjective* 400
spectre *noun* **ghost** 181
speed *verb* 401
speedy *adjective* **fast** 153

steel grey *adjective* **grey** 189
steer clear of *verb* **avoid** 33
step *noun* **grade** 186
sterilize *verb* **clean** 66
stern *adjective* **solemn** 396
stew *verb* **boil** 45
    verb **worry** 476
stick *verb* **place** 306
sticker *noun* **label** 238
stick out *verb* **endure** 135
stick to your guns *verb* **persist** 302
stick up for *verb* **befriend** 38
stiff *adjective* **hard** 194
stiffen *verb* **harden** 194
stifle *verb* **limit** 249
    verb **suffocate** 415
still *adjective* 406
stimulate *verb* **refresh** 338
stimulating *adjective* **exciting** 143
stingy *adjective* **thrifty** 433
stinking *adjective* **smelly** 393
stipulate *verb* **demand** 110
stir *verb* **mix** 270
    verb **move** 272
stitch *noun* **pain** 295
    verb **sew** 374
stockpile *verb* **store** 408
stocky *adjective* 407
stoical *adjective* **patient** 298
stone *noun* 407
stop *verb* 408
stop *verb* **end** 134
    verb **prevent** 318
stop by *verb* **visit** 461
store *verb* 408
stout *adjective* **fat** 154
    adjective **stocky** 407
stout-hearted *adjective* **steadfast** 404
stow *verb* **store** 408
straightforward *adjective* **clear** 66
    adjective **frank** 171
straitlaced *adjective* **strict** 410
strand *noun* **thread** 432
strange *adjective* 409
stratagem *noun* **plot** 307
stratum *noun* **layer** 242

stray *verb* **ramble** 332
streak *verb* **speed** 401
stream *verb* **flow** 164
streamline *verb* **simplify** 387
strength *noun* **force** 167
strengthen *verb* 409
stress *verb* **emphasize** 132
stretch *verb* **extend** 148
stretchy *adjective* **elastic** 131
strew *verb* **scatter** 365
strict *adjective* 410
stride *verb* **march** 259
strike *verb* **hit** 202
string *noun* **line** 250
strive for *verb* **seek** 369
stroke *verb* **touch** 437
stroll *verb* **walk** 463
strong *adjective* 410
structure *noun* **shape** 375
struggle *verb* **fight** 159
strut *verb* **march** 259
stubborn *adjective* 411
stubby *adjective* **stocky** 407
stuck-up *adjective* **conceited** 79
student *noun* 411
study *verb* **examine** 140
    verb **read** 334
stumble *verb* **fall** 151
stunned *adjective* **astonished** 29
    adjective **unconscious** 447
stunning *adjective* **beautiful** 37
stupendous *adjective* **astonishing** 30
stupid *adjective* **silly** 385
sturdy *adjective* **hardy** 195
style *noun* **fashion** 153
    noun **method** 265
subdue *verb* 412
submerge *verb* **drop** 127
submission *noun* **offer** 286
submissive *adjective* 412
submit *verb* **give in** 182
subordinate *adjective* 413
subservient *adjective* **submissive** 412
subsidiary *adjective* **subordinate** 413
substandard *adjective* **defective** 106
substantial *adjective* **big** 42

substantiate *verb* **prove** 325

substitute *verb* **exchange** 142

subterfuge *noun* **trickery** 442

subtract *verb* 413

suburb *noun* **city** 64

suburban *adjective* **civic** 65

succeed *verb* 414

success *noun* **achievement** 13

succession *noun* **series** 373

succinct *adjective* **brief** 50

succumb *verb* **give in** 182

sudden *adjective* 414

suffer *verb* **endure** 135

suffice *verb* **suit** 416

sufficient *adjective* 415

suffocate *verb* 415

sugary *adjective* **sweet** 419

suggest *verb* **advise** 16

     verb **hint** 201

suggestion *noun* 416

suit *verb* 416

sullen *adjective* **glum** 184

sultry *adjective* **humid** 207

summarize *verb* **shorten** 379

summary *noun* 417

summit *noun* **top** 437

summons *noun* **order** 291

sum up *verb* **shorten** 379

sunny *adjective* **fine** 160

super *adjective* **great** 188

superb *adjective* **great** 188

superfluous *adjective* **extra** 148

superintendent *noun* **manager** 258

superior *adjective* 417

superior *noun* **boss** 48

supervise *verb* **manage** 258

supervisor *noun* **boss** 48

supple *adjective* **flexible** 163

supplement *verb* **add** 14

support *verb* **help** 198

     verb **steady** 405

supporter *noun* **helper** 198

supportive *adjective* **helpful** 199

suppose *verb* **think** 430

suppress *verb* **prevent** 318

sure *adjective* 418

surface *noun* **outside** 292

surge *verb* **flow** 164

surly *adjective* **glum** 184

surpass *verb* **pass** 297

surplus *noun* **excess** 142

surprised *adjective* **astonished** 29

surrender *verb* **give in** 182

surreptitious *adjective* **secretive** 368

surround *verb* **enclose** 133

surroundings *noun* 418

survey *noun* **inquiry** 222

     verb **inspect** 224

     verb **measure** 262

survive *verb* **continue** 85

     verb **live** 251

susceptible *adjective* **vulnerable** 462

suspect *verb* **think** 430

suspend *verb* **defer** 107

swab *verb* **wipe** 473

swagger *verb* **march** 259

swallow *verb* **drink** 126

swamp *verb* **flood** 163

     verb **soak** 395

swap *verb* **exchange** 142

sway *verb* 419

sway *noun* **influence** 218

sweet *adjective* 419

sweet *adjective* **musical** 273

sweet-talk *verb* **flatter** 162

swell *verb* **protrude** 324

sweltering *adjective* **hot** 205

swift *adjective* **fast** 153

swindle *noun* **trick** 441

     verb **cheat** 62

swindler *noun* **crook** 94

swing *noun* **rhythm** 353

swirl *noun* **coil** 71

     verb **spin** 401

symbol *noun* **sign** 384

symmetrical *adjective* **equal** 138

sympathy *noun* **pity** 305

syndicate *noun* **organization** 292

synonymous *adjective* **similar** 386

synopsis *noun* **summary** 417

syrupy *adjective* **sweet** 419

Tt

tab *noun* **label** 238

tabulate *verb* **list** 251

taciturn *adjective* **reticent** 351

tack *verb* **sew** 374

tackle *verb* **attempt** 32

tack on *verb* **add** 14

tag *noun* **label** 238

    verb **label** 238

    verb **name** 275

tag along *verb* **follow** 166

taint *verb* **spoil** 402

take *verb* 420

take *verb* **choose** 64

take aback *verb* **shock** 378

take a dim view of

    verb **disapprove of** 117

take by surprise *verb* **catch** 59

take exception to

    verb **disapprove of** 117

take for a ride *verb* **deceive** 103

take for granted *verb* **believe** 40

take in *verb* **learn** 243

take it easy *verb* **rest** 349

take notice of *verb* **concentrate** 80

take off *verb* **flee** 162

take revenge *verb* **retaliate** 350

take to your heels *verb* **flee** 162

take with a grain of salt

    verb **doubt** 124

talk *noun* 420

talk *verb* 421

talk *noun* **gossip** 185

talkative *adjective* 421

talk into *verb* **persuade** 303

talk nonsense *verb* **rave** 333

talk out of *verb* **discourage** 118

tall *adjective* 422

tally *verb* **count** 89

tan *adjective* **brown** 52

tangible *adjective* **actual** 13

tangy *adjective* **sour** 398

tap *verb* **hit** 202

tarnished *adjective* **dull** 128

tarry *verb* **dawdle** 102

tart *adjective* **sour** 398

task *noun* 422

taste *verb* **eat** 130

tasteless *adjective* 423

tasteless *adjective* **vulgar** 462

tasty *adjective* 423

taunt *verb* **tease** 425

tawdry *adjective* **gaudy** 179

tawny *adjective* **yellow** 478

tax *verb* **tire** 435

teach *verb* 424

teacher *noun* 424

teammate *noun* **friend** 172

team up *verb* **cooperate** 86

tear *verb* 425

tear *verb* **speed** 401

tease *verb* 425

technique *noun* **method** 265

tedious *adjective* **boring** 47

    adjective **lengthy** 245

teem *verb* **rain** 332

tell *verb* 426

temper *noun* **anger** 20

temperamental *adjective* **fickle** 158

temperate *adjective* **fine** 160

tempo *noun* **rhythm** 353

temporary *adjective* 426

tempting *adjective* **attractive** 33

tenacious *adjective* **persistent** 303

tenacity *noun* **persistence** 302

tender *adjective* **loving** 254

    adjective **soft** 395

    noun **offer** 286

tenderize *verb* **soften** 396

tenderness *noun* **pity** 305

tendril *noun* **thread** 432

term *verb* **name** 275

terminal *adjective* **fatal** 154

terminate *verb* **end** 134

    verb **finish** 161

termination *noun* **end** 134

terracotta *adjective* **orange** 290

terrible *adjective* **horrible** 205

terrific *adjective* **excellent** 141

terrify *verb* **frighten** 173

terrorize *verb* **frighten** 173

Uu

Vv

Ww

write *verb* **compose** 79
writhe *verb* **fidget** 158

Yy

yard *noun* 478
yell *verb* **shout** 380
yellow *adjective* 478

yelp *verb* **shriek** 382
yen *noun* **wish** 474
yield *verb* **give in** 182
    verb **produce** 321
young *adjective* 479
young *noun* **offspring** 287
young man *noun* **male** 257
young woman *noun* **female** 157
youthful *adjective* **young** 479
yummy *adjective* **delicious** 109